A PLACE AMONG GIANTS

22 SEASONS AT DENALI BASECAMP

A Place Among Giants: 22 Seasons at Denali Basecamp is published under Catharsis, a sectionalized division under Di Angelo Publications, Inc.

Catharsis is an imprint of Di Angelo Publications.
Copyright 2024.
All rights reserved.
Printed in the United States of America.

Di Angelo Publications
Los Angeles, California

Library of Congress
A Place Among Giants: 22 Seasons at Denali Basecamp
ISBN: 978-1-962603-06-5
Paperback

Words: Lisa Roderick
Photos: Chandra Llewellyn, Lisa Roderick, Tyler Westhoff, and Mark Westman
Cover Design: Savina Mayeur
Interior Design: Kimberly James
Editors: Willy Rowberry, Matt Samet

Downloadable via www.dapbooks.shop and other e-book retailers.

No part of this publication may be reproduced, distributed, or transmitted in any form or by any means without the prior written permission of the publisher, except in the case of brief quotations embedded in critical reviews and certain other noncommercial uses permitted by copyright law. For permission requests, contact info@diangelopublications.com.

For educational, business, or bulk orders, contact distribution@diangelopublications.com.

1. Biography & Autobiography --- Adventurers & Explorers
2. Sports & Recreation --- Mountaineering
3. Biography & Autobiography --- Personal Memoirs

A PLACE AMONG GIANTS

22 SEASONS AT DENALI BASECAMP

LISA RODERICK

To my brother Paul Roderick, for inspiring me with his immense talent, knowledge, and insights, and for opening up a world of possibilities in my life.

To my husband Mark Westman, for a lifetime of love and adventures, and for always encouraging me to do that one last pitch.

To the Denali glacier pilots, climbers, guides, and rescue rangers, for looking to the Alaskan skies and mountains for adventure, and always being ready to risk it all to save others.

And to Annie Duquette and Frances Randall, for setting the example.

FOREWORD

by Conrad Anker

Thinking back to the summer of 1989, when I was 26 and living life in the mountains, I can't help but remember how those experiences shaped my sense of adventure and responsibility. That season, base camp was like a gateway to incredible opportunities and unforgettable moments.

In the spring of 1989, I had the chance to spend time in the Alaska Range. I teamed up with the late Mugs Stump to climb the Eye Tooth in early April. Although a storm stopped us from reaching the summit, it was still an invaluable experience. After the snow cleared, I worked with photographer Chris Noble and a group of snowboarders in Ruth Gorge, capturing some wild shots of their stunts. Later, I joined Mugs and Paul Fitzgerald for an ascent of Denali, where we collected rock samples for Mugs's brother, Ed Stump, to study the mountain's geological uplift. Once that was done, I spent six weeks working at Denali base camp, getting a firsthand look at the unique rhythm of life in such a remote place.

Cliff Hudson, Jim Okonek, and Doug Geeting were always around, their voices a familiar presence on the radio. Cliff's last flying season was made memorable by his tiny poodle, Skippy, who accompanied him everywhere. Watching Cliff wander through camp with his coffee, telling stories of Alaskan adventures, made me truly appreciate the SE Fork of Kahiltna Glacier and its role in Denali's history.

Central to this narrative are the folks who coordinate the safety of the SE Fork Kahiltna Glacier landing strip. Juggling the needs of the National Park Service, the Federal Aviation Administration, the air services, the climbers, the sightseers, and the dreamers takes a unique type of optimist. The weather rules the glacier, and the environment is filled with hazards. Loud and powerful, the aircraft are what make Alaska Range climbing somewhat less of an absurd approach. But it's tricky landing on a glacier, so pilots rely on precise weather assessments to operate. Between the weather and the expectations of the climbers and sightseers, there is quite a bit of variability, and the base camp manager needs to be able to handle it all.

I first met Lisa during an expedition on Denali in 2011. From the moment she stepped into the role of base camp manager, it was evident that she was not just filling a position, but embodying it. Her calm demeanor shone through as she adapted to the intricate dynamics of climbers, tourists, and the mountain itself. Lisa possessed a rare blend of toughness and warmth, maintaining order amidst chaos while offering a supportive presence that bolstered our spirits.

Denali, with its intimidating maze of ridges, glaciers, and unpredictable weather, is a place of both majestic beauty and formidable danger. The mountain doesn't merely test physical endurance but challenges the very essence of one's character. My own reflections on Denali are filled with awe and respect, and Lisa's narrative captures this duality with profound clarity.

Lisa offers an unvarnished look into her 22 seasons immersed in the Alaskan mountain range. Her account highlights the good, the bad, and the terrifying realities that come with being entrenched in such an environment. It's a testament to her strength and character, showcasing not just the logistical feats of managing base camp, but the emotional and psychological journey intertwined with the role.

In reading "A Place Among Giants," you will not only glimpse the breathtaking beauty and unforgiving reality of Denali but also gain insight into the spirit that keeps the heart of base camp beating. Lisa Roderick's journey is one of resilience, dedication, and unwavering love for these mountains and the community that calls them home. Her story is a reminder that while summits and records may be the face of mountaineering, the soul lies in the untold stories of those who labor quietly and tirelessly to support these endeavors. As Lisa moves on from her role, she leaves behind a legacy defined not just by her ability to manage the chaos of the glacier but by the strength, compassion, and grace she brought to one of the world's most challenging environments. This book is more than a memoir; it is a lasting tribute to the people who, like Lisa, find their place among giants and, in doing so, become giants themselves.

Prologue
June 19, 2000

A furious gust slams the shelter, shaking its sturdy frame and bringing me back to attention. Cups, utensils, food items, and bottles of sunscreen take flight from the makeshift plywood shelves and scatter across the wooden floor. It takes a strong wind to shake the walls of this rugged shelter, which is the same as those used by people working in places like Alaska's North Slope oil fields and the research stations of the Antarctic continent. I set my book on the milk crate that serves as my nightstand, rise from my cot, and head for the door to check the weather. Cold air rushes inside as I open the tent's hinged aluminum door, and I emerge from my heated hovel into a dramatic subarctic mountain landscape.

The white expanse of the Kahiltna Glacier's southeast fork stretches away to my left and right, disappearing into swirling, fast-moving mists. The sun appears but for a moment, casting the strong solar rays of the Alaskan solstice across the icy ramparts of the Alaska Range, before it ducks away again. Small holes open in the clouds, revealing tantalizing glimpses of Mount Hunter's tortured, icy ridges and precipitous granite walls just two miles up-glacier from my camp. In the other direction, bands of clouds frame sections of Mount Foraker's hulking east face, which towers almost 10,000 vertical feet above the Kahiltna Glacier's main fork, four deceptive miles distant. Denali — North America's tallest mountain at 20,310 feet, a magnet for mountain climbers from all over the world, the namesake feature of this national park, and the primary reason for this camp I'm in — lies hidden behind a bank of cloud and mist to the north.

A steady wind streams up the glacier, then all at once its direction changes by more than 90 degrees. A brief squall of wind-driven graupel pellets appears almost out of thin air, stinging my face and spattering a staccato cadence against the tent's vinyl walls. At the mercy of the oscillating winds, they swirl in the air, suspended for a moment, providing the sensation of being inside a popcorn machine.

Twenty minutes ago, an incoming airplane would have had no trouble landing on the glacier. Now, with fog forming over the snowy runway strip, flat light, and gusty tail and crosswinds, I wouldn't dare recommend it. Inconsistency has been the theme of the day. My job, summarized with much simplicity, is to relay to incoming pilots, bringing in their loads of mountain climbers and sightseers, precisely what it is I can see. What they choose to do next is up to them.

Denali Basecamp is a seasonal installation located at 7,200 feet on the southeast fork of the 47-mile-long Kahiltna Glacier in the central Alaska Range. The camp is set deep in the heart of one of the world's most rugged and heavily glaciated mountain environments, with Denali towering in plain sight just six miles to the northeast.

The journey to basecamp begins in the small tourist town of Talkeetna, 65 miles to the southeast, far below in the lowland boreal forests of south-central Alaska, and a 120-mile drive north of Anchorage. From the town's small airport near sea level, it's a 30-to-40-minute flight in either a single-engine Cessna 185 Skywagon or De Havilland Canada DHC-2 Beaver airplane to the glacier landing strip, where the aircraft can land on the snow using retractable hydraulic skis.

Denali was first climbed in 1913 by a group of resourceful Alaskans led by the Archdeacon Hudson Stuck. On this expedition, Walter Harper, a young Alaska native, became the first person to stand on the summit. A series of exploratory and scientific undertakings ensued on Denali in the following decades, most notably a trio of expeditions in 1942, 1947, and 1951, led by the renowned cartographer, surveyor, climber, and researcher H. Bradford Washburn. However, it wasn't until the early 1960s that recreational climbing expeditions began appearing with regularity. Many of these early climbers were inspired by Washburn's iconic aerial photography and his brilliantly crafted topographic map of the Denali area, compiled during the nearly twenty years he spent researching and surveying Denali from land and air. Washburn also published many articles about the Alaska Range in which he used his detailed photography to highlight possibilities for new climbing routes on Denali and other peaks in the range.

In the 1970s, climbing on Denali exploded in popularity, and by the middle of the decade, the annual visitation had swelled to over 500 climbers. In 1976, Cliff Hudson, a legendary local bush pilot who started Hudson Air Service in 1946, recognized the need to have someone stationed full-time at basecamp during the climbing season, to provide real-time weather observations, maintain the glacier airstrip, and keep order in the camp. At the start of that season, Hudson found a willing subject in Frances Randall, and she became Denali's first basecamp manager.

Frances was a concert violinist but also an accomplished mountain climber. In 1964, she became the second woman to reach the summit of Denali. Frances would spend nine seasons operating Denali Basecamp before she passed away from cancer in 1984. She was beloved and respected by the pilots and climbers alike for her dedication to safety, coordinating responses during emergencies on the mountain; precise and attentive weather observations; and the warm friendship that she extended toward everyone who passed through the camp. She earned the nicknames "Guardian of the Glacier" and "Kahiltna Queen," and has a mountain above camp officially named in her honor.

Today, between early May and mid-July of each year, about 1,200 climbers attempt the ascent of Denali. Climbing Denali even by its easiest route — the West Buttress, the route used by more than 90 percent of aspirants — demands specialized experience, and a successful ascent requires that an average team spend about two to three weeks on the mountain. Much of this time is needed for slow acclimatization to the altitude, but it is also due to the area's frigid, sub-arctic climate and a propensity for prolonged and violent storms.

Basecamp is without question the nerve center of human activity on Denali. In addition to being the starting point for the West Buttress, it is also where many other climbers camp while attempting some of the lower-elevation peaks in the area. The six Talkeetna-based air services operating under a concession contract with the National Park Service (NPS) offer both climber transport and flightseeing tours around the Alaska Range. The tours include an option to land on a glacier, and through the course of the busy spring and summer tourist months, basecamp may see hundreds or even thousands of flightseeing tourists touch down. The NPS also maintains a seasonal camp here, which serves as a forward base of operations for search and rescue missions and even includes a temporary fueling site for their high-altitude rescue helicopter. Denali National Park staffs revolving patrols at basecamp as well as longer patrols to the upper elevations of Denali throughout the climbing season, each patrol comprised of a skilled mountaineering ranger and a group of well-vetted volunteers. These rangers and volunteers are experienced climbers and are trained in technical rescue and helicopter operations.

I've been in sole command of Denali Basecamp for three weeks, ever since Annie Duquette, my close friend and the famed manager of basecamp for the past ten years, flew out to Talkeetna for a break and entrusted me with the camp after just three short days of her mentorship. I've been chosen as her replacement. I'm to be the new Denali Basecamp manager after she retires at the end of this 2000 climbing season.

"Basecamp Annie" has established her own impressive legacy during a tenure that has now exceeded that of Frances Randall. Denali's skilled aviators are tasked with flying through a mountain range of almost unfathomable scale and with some of the most volatile weather imaginable. The weather in these mountains often changes at an alarming pace, a brilliantly clear day turning into one whose sky is filled with angry, fast-moving clouds that can rapidly block key passes that the pilots use for ingress into and egress from the interior range. The winds are often amplified by the rugged terrain, and during incoming and outgoing weather systems, there may be tremendous turbulence over ridges and passes. Even on the clearest of days, as a high-pressure system settles in, falling air masses can create deceptive conditions that require the pilots to exert extra vigilance with respect to their flight route and proximity to the terrain.

These talented pilots have developed a deep trust in Annie for her conscientious weather observations and her unfailing dedication to maintaining a glacier runway that can get covered by meters of new snow in a single storm. She's also beloved by the pilots and climbers for her expertise in managing the camp, whether it's keeping impatient homebound climbers at bay, acting as a drill sergeant in expediting people onto their planes or off the runway, or for maternal acts of compassion that might include serving quesadillas and lemonade, nursing minor wounds, or even washing climbers' hair.

I am following in the footsteps of giants, and I have much yet to learn in every aspect of the job, which only amplifies my motivation. *Will I still be here in five years? Ten? Twenty, perhaps?* The question seems absurd after only being on the job for three weeks, during which time I have gotten off with relative ease with respect to the most complex and worrisome task: providing weather observations to the pilots. While there have been occasional challenges, a docile weather pattern has provided a forgiving learning curve. Until now.

Today has been a different animal. The weather has been changing moment to moment, and with a frightening speed that I haven't experienced up to now. I am tasked with constant vigilance while being plagued by ongoing uncertainty. I may, for example, report good weather to the Talkeetna pilots, but that doesn't mean that by the time a pilot arrives, it will still be good. And I've had airplanes circling overhead, above the clouds, in hopes of a clearing that would allow them to land. A clearing most often comes, but only after the pilot has given up and flown halfway back to Talkeetna. It's been like this all day, and it's frustrating for everyone. Very few airplanes have managed to make it to basecamp today, and as the day has worn on, the word has gotten out among the Talkeetna pilots that the area around basecamp is best avoided. Nevertheless, hope springs eternal, and the Talkeetna air services continue calling me hour by hour for weather updates.

Late in the afternoon, the clouds break open and the icy peaks of the Alaska Range reveal themselves once again in their full splendor. Almost on cue, I hear the familiar hum of a Cessna 185 as it rounds the bend of nearby Annie's Ridge — the ridge to the south that is informally named for the person I am replacing. The plane comes into view, already on short final for landing. Pilot Keli Mahoney makes a smooth landing on the glacier and taxis the machine up in front of my tent. She shuts down her engine and climbs out of the plane, brushing her curly light-brown hair aside as she dons a well-worn baseball cap. Following her from the small aircraft are four wide-eyed tourists from Florida enjoying a 90-minute scenic flight around the Alaska Range.

Keli is one of the few female bush pilots in the world, and at age 32 is already a veteran dog musher who has twice run in Alaska's Iditarod; together with her business partner, LeeAnn Wetzel, Keli owns McKinley Air Service, operated under the clever slogan "Two Babes and a Bird." It's one of only four aviation companies in the United States owned and operated by women. Keli has a laid-back demeanor about her, complete with a dry and sometimes sarcastic sense of humor. Like many self-starter Alaskans, her manner understates a remarkable self-confidence and an unflinching can-do attitude.

Keli and I chat for a few minutes as her tourists from Florida throw snowballs, gawk at the mountains, and snap photos. So often, I note that passengers who come to basecamp on these scenic flights are reduced to an almost childlike awe by the grandeur of this landscape.

"Didn't expect to make it over here," Keli says, her placid gaze directed north toward Denali, looming high above multiple layers of dark-gray, serpentine mists. "It looked pretty socked in this way when we left Talkeetna, so I went to the Ruth Glacier. But then I saw it opening up, so I thought I'd come over here.

"I wouldn't wait here too long," I counter, motioning down the glacier, to where fog is creeping low up the Kahiltna Glacier's main fork one mile downhill from camp.

"Better get going, folks," Keli shouts to her passengers, corralling them back into the plane.

With all aboard, Keli's plane roars down the runway, lifts off, and banks around the corner. What was a small finger of fog moments ago has quickly grown into an ominous wall of clouds, ascending with alarming speed up the southeast fork of the Kahiltna toward basecamp. The distant sky changes from a foreboding white to an ominous shade of dark gray, signaling the impending arrival of yet another dynamic squall.

I absorb this sight for a moment, and then duck back inside my tent to turn up my aircraft radio. I feel compelled to keep in contact with Keli until I'm certain that she will make it out of the mountains. Minutes later, I hear another pilot speaking on the radio, but he is so far from basecamp that the transmission is full of static, and I can't understand his words. I am, however, able to hear Keli's reply: "The clouds are blocking the icefall, and I can't make it through. I'm turning around and heading back to basecamp. Lisa, are you up? Is basecamp still open for landing?"

I take one more look outside to be sure. The clock is ticking. "It is, but it won't be for much longer," I reply, speaking into the radio handset.

I wait and watch, hoping she'll get back before this incoming cloud closes us in. A couple of minutes pass before I hear Keli on the radio, once again speaking to the other pilot: "The icefall is completely covered in clouds. Going to basecamp is *not* an option for you." The snow is now falling in thick flakes, the fog is overrunning the glacier, and I can hear Keli's plane for more than a minute before she comes into sight through the murk at the end of the runway. The plane touches down at what seems the last possible moment before everything turns to solid white. Keli and the Floridians climb out into the wild squall. Keli strolls towards me with a casual gait, her hands in her jeans pockets. She shrugs her shoulders and flashes a resigned expression that betrays no apparent frustration. She's cool and calm as always, despite what to me had seemed like a narrow escape.

"What's going on? Who was the pilot you were speaking to?" I ask.

"Don Bowers," she replies. "He was trying to make it in here, but he had to turn around below the icefall and head back to Talkeetna. Then he called again and said that the weather had closed off his exit at the Big Bend of the Kahiltna. He said he saw some light over towards the Lacuna Glacier and was going to head over there to find a way out."

The Big Bend of the Kahiltna is over 30 miles down the glacier from where I am and not far from where the glacier spills out into the lowland plains stretching south for another 100 miles to the waters of Cook Inlet and the North Pacific Ocean. The Lacuna Glacier is west of the Kahiltna — the opposite direction of where Don needs to go.

I clench my jaw and stare down the glacier into the storm. Don, who works for Hudson Air Service, was scheduled to bring in the next NPS basecamp patrol today, led by the mountaineering ranger Cale Shaffer and his two volunteers. Cale was on patrol at basecamp when I first arrived three weeks ago. In my initial days in the camp, he had been a great help to me, and we had become fast friends. I'm guessing that his patrol might be Don's passengers. Cale and I talked on the phone earlier today. I cautioned him that the weather wasn't looking good and I advised him to wait until tomorrow. Until now, I figured he took my recommendation. Don and I, however, have not yet spoken today, and now my thoughts are a mixture of confusion and frustration: *Why the hell didn't Don call me before he decided to launch?*

Don is one of the most cautious pilots I've met. It is unusual for a pilot not to contact the basecamp manager for a weather report before a flight, especially on a day like this, when the weather is so unstable and other pilots have been having difficulties.

An hour passes; Keli and her tourists are huddled in my nine-by-nine-foot tent, hot drinks in hand, sitting on anything that could pass for a chair. Snow pellets crackle against the tent walls as the Floridians stare at me with nervous anticipation.

Keli pokes her head out the door, assesses the weather again, then ducks back in and makes a casual declaration:

"I suspect we may be spending the night here, folks."

"How often has this happened?" a Floridian asks. "This is my first year doing this," I reply, pausing to think as I begin rummaging through a box of food. "I'd have to ask Annie, but for starters, I'll bet you'd be the first Floridians to ever spend the night up here."

The Floridians, to my relief, seem to take it in stride: "Well, I can't say I've ever slept on a glacier before," one of them exclaims. Laughter and nervous excitement cascade through the group, and my apprehension about being an unprepared hostess softens.

Keli heads out to her airplane to place an insulated cover over the engine's cowling, and to retrieve sleeping bags and pads for the Floridians, part of the required survival gear each air service brings for all occupants. In turn, I do my best to play the super-host. I turn on some music, start cooking dinner, and rearrange my tent to make room for the surprise slumber party. I have a very warm sleeping bag, so I set up a small mountaineering tent outside for myself and let the tourists have my space.

I note my approaching evening weather announcement and

use the radio telephone to call the automated weather line, jotting down the Denali weather forecast on a scratch pad. Many years before my arrival at basecamp, a tradition was established wherein the Denali Basecamp manager reads the mountain forecast over the CB radio each night at 8:00 p.m. It's then that every camp on the mountain grows quiet, clusters of climbers visible at their camps on the mountain, standing at full attention and holding their radios skyward with extended antennae.

Setting my notepad aside, I serve my unplanned guests a simple backcountry dinner of pasta with red sauce, bread that I toasted in a frying pan, and water, hoping it will continue to distract them from their tenuous situation. Outside, the snow continues coming down, driven by a relentless up-glacier wind. We're safe and warm in here, but it feels like the day is done.

The radio telephone rings amidst the telling of a humorous story. The laughter in my voice dies out when I hear a concerned female voice on the other end — a young woman who is a newer employee at Hudson, and whose name I can no longer recall.

"Hi, Lisa, this is Hudson Air Service. Have you heard from Don Bowers?"

The room falls silent as my back tenses, my hands turn to ice, and I can feel the blood draining from my face. I check my watch: 7:45 p.m. It's been almost two hours since Don turned around.

"You mean he's not back?" I exclaim.

Keli and I lock eyes.

Don had told Keli that he was detouring west to the Lacuna Glacier, but even with that long detour, he should have been back in Talkeetna at least an hour ago.

"No," comes the reply. "We've been trying to reach him on the aircraft radio, but he's not answering. We were hoping he was weathered in at basecamp."

I fix my gaze on the floor before I lean into the phone's handset and press onward with ideas. "Have you tried the NPS? I think the basecamp patrol was on board. Maybe they called in using the park radio?"

"Yes, the NPS patrol was on the plane," she says, her voice straining with worry. "It's been over an hour and a half since either Don or the rangers called in."

Keli and I relay to her the chain of events that we observed from here, then make a separate call to repeat the same details to Daryl Miller, the South District Ranger for the NPS in Talkeetna. The NPS, in turn, notifies the Rescue Coordination Center (RCC) at Elmendorf Air Force Base, in Anchorage.

Within an hour, the areas of the Alaska Range where Don was last known to be are flooded with search aircraft — a combination of Talkeetna-based air services, NPS, military, and contracted private aircraft looking for Don and the ranger patrol. The distance, along with many ridges and mountains separating me from the search area, leaves me to imagine what is actually happening. I can hear occasional transmissions on the aircraft radio, while the night air over basecamp is filled with the heavy drone of a C-130 military aircraft flying high above the Alaska Range in a circular pattern.

This large aircraft is occupied by the US Air Force 212th Squadron Pararescuemen, also known as the "PJs", based out of Elmendorf. They are flying a high-altitude cover pattern for the benefit of the other search aircraft, warning them of changes in shifting weather and cloud cover which are complicating the search efforts. The 212th, along with other military units from Fort Richardson in Anchorage, or Fort Wainwright in Fairbanks, offer frequent assistance with rescue operations for civilian aircraft or individuals in need of help in remote areas of Alaska where public resources may be inadequate to the task.

Heavy clouds and the fading daylight of the never-quite-dark Alaskan summer solstice suspend the search by midnight, with nothing found and no new clues. I see to it that my tourists are comfortable, getting them situated in their sleeping bags and ensuring that the vented propane heater is turned all the way up. Keli heads out to make up her bunk in the back of her airplane, while I walk outside to my little mountaineering tent, drifted over with newly fallen snow. The clouds open for a moment to reveal a section of hanging ice cliffs and steep rock buttresses poised somewhere in the middle of Mount Foraker's eastern face; I stare at it through a delicate matrix of falling snowflakes while contemplating the gravity of the situation. I struggle to identify if I could have done anything different, consumed as I often am by a protective instinct and an incessant and obsessive worry for the people I love.

I'm supposed to be keeping these pilots safe. Did I do something wrong?

A handful of minor aircraft mishaps involving the Talkeetna air services have occurred through the years, but it has been twenty years since there were any fatalities, a rare occurrence considering the environment and volume of traffic each season. Annie, in her ten seasons here, saw several airplanes get crumpled up in deep snow on the glacier, with minimal or no injuries. I've been here for less than a month, and I may already be facing something she has never experienced.

The wind chills me as snow pellets collect in my hair and the window in the clouds slams shut, leaving me cocooned in a room of sheer white. *How did I get here?* Never in my wildest dreams could I, as a kid growing up in Connecticut, have imagined the arc of my life leading me to climbing cold and dangerous mountains in Alaska, and from there to the responsibilities and crisis I am now facing here in one of the wildest places on earth. Nine years ago, at the age of 23, I left home on a wild impulse in search of spontaneous adventure, a place to call home amongst vibrant people and raw beauty, and of course, love. I have found all of that, and much more, in Alaska.

My emotions spent, I duck inside my tent, zip up the door, and settle into my sleeping bag. I continue to maintain hope that Don has just had to put the plane down, perhaps on a small glacier or a snowy moraine, and is waiting for better weather, but the most recent piece of news is ominous. Rescuers are not picking up an emergency locator transmitter (ELT) signal, which Don would doubtless have activated if he were able. The ELT is also designed to begin signaling in the event of an impact, but some types of incidents, such as a fire or extreme force, may prevent this from happening.

I'm consumed with thoughts of my friends and colleagues in Talkeetna who work for the air services and of the tight-knit group of park service mountaineering rangers. I imagine the intense vigil taking place throughout our community tonight. I keep my handheld aircraft radio with me inside my sleeping bag, the volume turned up, on the improbable chance that I might hear a distress call from Don. Compelled to do something, anything, I transmit every few minutes into the blinding storm.

"Eight-Nine-Fox, this is basecamp calling, do you copy?"

Again and again, I repeat the transmission, each call met only with a cold and agonizing silence.

Chapter One
The Alaska Highway

The sun is sinking deep in the west, its final rays of the day filtering with softness through the thick forest of maple, elm, and pine. Scattered sunbeams break back into the clearing with a golden splash, accentuating the tips of the dry grasses blanketing the field before me. My horse, Bandit, basks with me in the late-summer ambiance, and taps his hoof into the soil. I prod him with a gentle squeeze of my legs, and we continue onward with a relaxed gait, through the field, my eyes ever watchful for the baby deer often found resting in the grass. No destination in mind — it's just me and my beautiful, gentle friend, out in nature in the peaceful northern Connecticut countryside. I want this feeling to last forever.

My bliss is broken by the familiar sound of a distant, clanging bell, ringing from the chimney back home. A chain leads from that bell down into the kitchen, and at this moment, into my father's hands. The bell's message is "Come home now," and is directed at me and my two brothers — Mark, who is two years younger than me, and Paul, who is two years older — wherever we might be around our fifteen-acre farm or the vast woods and fields that border it. With a twinge of disappointment, I am reminded of all the chores and hard work that await me tonight and tomorrow. I take a last look around, draw in a deep breath, and turn Bandit around.

"Alright, Bandit, let's go chase some cars," I shout, as I reach the large field paralleling Quarry Road, a busy two-lane thoroughfare winding through the mixed woodlands and pastures of the small valley lying just north of our family home. I dig in my heels and snap at the reins, and in an instant, we are tearing through the field at a breakneck pace, my ears pinned back and the wind in my hair as Bandit outpaces the nearby traffic. I lose myself in the intoxicating rush of speed and the feeling of pure freedom, and then reign Bandit in as we near my Great Auntie Anne's driveway, which leads past her house and up the steep hill that rolls back onto the Roderick Farm. The farm is a large tract of land consisting of property owned for many decades by Auntie, and later expanded by my father's purchase of an adjacent parcel, which includes the house we now live in.

   I stall my return home by detouring Bandit through the forested trails south of the driveway before emerging into our pasture and passing through the fence that corrals our farm animals. Bandit and I trot past the cornfield and the rows of apple trees along the fence line. We ride past our goats, cows, and sheep, who look up to greet us between mouthfuls of grass. I pass the pigpen and chicken coop before leading Bandit in an arc around the field, to where my parents' prized, one-acre garden sits just outside the fence, between the barn and the tennis court. Rows of onions stretch through the garden, accompanied by lettuce, tomatoes, zucchini, and zinnias.

   I lead Bandit into the barn, dismount, lay a chunk of hay before him, and brush his deep-mahogany coat and long, sweeping black tail. Bandit, a Morgan fifteen hands in height, was a gift from my father when I turned fourteen a year earlier. I cannot imagine a better companion to pass my tumultuous teenage years. I stroke his nose with slow and gentle movements, and our heads touch in silence. "Bandit, you're my best friend," I say in a near-whisper.

"Lisa!"

My moment of zen is broken as I hear my mother calling to me from a distance.

"Coming, Mom," I respond.

I emerge from the barn to see my mom tending to the flowers that line the path connecting the garage to our house. "How was your ride, sweetie?" she asks.

"Great," I reply. "Bandit was really on his game today. What's for dinner?"

My dad is serious about the culinary arts. In particular, he loves classical French cuisine, and he even founded a local gourmet club. It's Sunday, which means tonight's dinner is sure to be a production. All day, I've been imagining what dish he might be preparing. Will it be Beef Bourguignon? Coq Au Vin? Ratatouille, perhaps? Maybe Crepes Suzette for dessert?

"Your father is making one of your favorites tonight, baked stuffed clams," my mom says, leaning in to give me a peck on my cheek.

"Oh, good," I say. "I never got lunch after all of Dad's garden chores earlier. I'm so hungry."

Mom and I walk together toward the house, past our in-ground swimming pool, across the spacious patio and past my dad's prized collection of grills and smokers. My parents often host large dinner parties for friends in the neighborhood in which my father might cook a whole lamb over an open flame, and where the alcohol always flows without restraint.

"There she is," my dad booms, as Mom and I enter the house. Ever the showman, he wears his favorite apron and chef's hat. The dinner table is arranged to perfection with a bouquet of fresh zinnias, and five place settings, the house permeated with a sumptuous aroma.

"What's up, Lisa?" he calls, turning toward me with full hands. "Here. Put this on the table," he instructs, handing me a hot casserole of scalloped potatoes. Mark and Paul appear from down the hall, almost at a run, laughing and pushing each other out of the way in their race for the table. Paul, taller and lankier than Mark, breaks free from Mark's grip on his curly blond hair and arrives first at the table with his usual mischievous facial expression. Mark is stocky, strong, wild, and fearless, and with his mop of shaggy, dirty blond hair, looks uncharacteristically tough for a 13-year-old, especially after having an occasional tooth knocked out playing hockey or football.

"Ah-ah," my dad scolds as everyone takes their seats and the boys' forks are already being picked up. "Grace comes first," he reminds us, as we all join hands. My father's prayers fade into the background as I bow my head and stare at the food on my plate. My dad's "Amen" is followed right away by Paul's more abbreviated prayer: "God's neat, let's eat!" My dad raises a disapproving eyebrow at Paul, as my brothers and I attack our dinner, replenishing the calories we've burned all week between sports, hiking and running around the woods, the endless farm chores, and working for Dad's construction business, which specializes in excavation, foundations, and water and sewer lines. Tonight, I'm just thankful that school is out and not adding to the workload.

My dad expects us to work hard, play hard, and never complain. His mother died when he was an infant, and his father then left him with his sister — my Great Auntie Anne — and never returned. Auntie Anne is essentially a nun in the Catholic church and raised my father under a very strict religious regime. At age 18, he enlisted in the Marine Corps, where he served several peacetime tours in

Okinawa, assigned to a tank unit. Every day, he relentlessly attempts to drill rigid routine, structure, and stoicism into my brothers and me, and whatever he says becomes the law.

"We're playing tennis after dinner," he announces mid-meal. My brothers and I roll our eyes in silent resignation.

Tariffville, Connecticut, is a quiet town in the densely wooded countryside half an hour northwest of Hartford, nestled alongside the Farmington River and the affluent enclaves of Simsbury and Avon. It is a place with four true seasons, and with something appealing about each one. More than any, summer is my favorite, when the weather is warm and school is out, when I can ride my horse through the enchanted forests and peaceful pastures around us, and when my brothers and I swim in the Farmington River for hours. In the winter, we take family trips to Vermont to ski, and we play hockey and ice skate on the pond my dad built in the corner of our property. Of course, all this play is only allowed if we are getting our chores done — and following orders.

"Ten-hut!" my dad announces one Sunday morning as he enters my room. I stand in rigid attention alongside my bed, my hands at my side and chest puffed up, as my father conducts an inspection of my room. He brushes his finger along my desktop, checking for dust, then turns back toward me.

"I better be able to bounce a quarter off this bed," he warns, producing a coin from his pocket. He snaps the quarter onto the taut comforter, and I'm relieved when I see it rebound a few inches into the air.

"Inspection passed," my dad says, grinning for a moment.

"Now, get yourself ready for church, and this afternoon you'll be cleaning out the barn," he orders, as he moves on to inspect my brothers' room.

My father's military service and religious upbringing by Auntie are an ever-present influence passed down upon us. Auntie, in her 80s, still lives in the 1800s-era farm cottage located a few minutes' walk from us, just down the hill from the shop and garage where my father keeps his excavators, bulldozers, dump trucks, and backhoes. Auntie acts as the religious matriarch of the family, frequently lecturing my brothers and me about the teachings of the church, notably during our regular Sunday breakfasts at her house, as she tries to keep us on track to being good Catholics. My brothers and I, like most teenagers, find it stifling. For much of my own life, catechism, for example, has come to represent long hours spent in my Auntie's living room, bored out of my mind, fantasizing about running free in the nearby woods. To me, the teachings of the church make little sense, and all of us are intimidated by Auntie's old-school fire and brimstone. On the other hand, she is also the closest we have to a grandmother, and her home cooking and pies are without question the best food I have ever tasted.

My mother is easily the family's grounding force. She is the nurturing that counters my father's strictness, the seriousness countering my father's flamboyances during our family parties and barbecues, and a surprisingly driven adventurer who might be found racing around the farm on our dirt bikes and dune buggies, being competitive in her bowling league, or traveling with my dad to exotic places like Tahiti. Mom loves Elvis Presley, and the fact that I share the same first and middle names as his daughter — Lisa Marie — who was born exactly four days before me, seems no small coincidence, although I have never been able to confirm. Mom is also a devout Catholic raised by her adoptive father — my Grandpa — who lives just down the street and visits often. Grandpa's wife passed away when my mother was very young. My mom has lived her entire life here in Tariffville, relocating only as far as a nearby community college after high school to take accounting classes.

She is a homemaker by trade, but has put her education to use in managing the finances of the family construction business, serving as a critical foil to my father's often careless spending habits.

I love to think of my mother, with her short, carefully coiffed blonde hair and gentle smile, her facial features closely mirroring Mark's and my own, working cheerfully alongside my father preparing an elaborate meal for guests, sipping wine, and laughing easily and often. And I am filled with love for her thinking of the sack lunches that she hastily puts together for me before school, despite her not being a functional morning person, as well as the hug and kiss with which she sends me away to each school day.

There's plenty of work on the Roderick farm — our dad keeps us busy with nonstop chores, which are just as mandatory as the Sunday mass he and my aunt insist we attend as a family. Our daily duties include feeding and attending to our animals, picking corn and vegetables, and hauling the hay from the field and storing it in the barn for drying. In the spring, we tap the maple trees and use my dad's cooker to make our own maple syrup. My dad keeps honeybees for harvesting honey, while my mom cans the annual bounty of garden vegetables and makes applesauce from the apples on our trees. My brothers and I keep our root cellar stocked with onions and potatoes.

We raise our animals for our meat. I love the animals, and I have to walk a fine line in not getting too attached to them, because one day they'll be in our freezer and then on our plates.

"Is this Bouie or George we're eating?" Paul asks during a family steak dinner. With neither emotion nor irony, Paul is referring to the two cows who had been fixtures in our pasture for the past two years, but were sent away for slaughter last winter. Grandpa, who has joined us for dinner, stops chewing and blanches for a moment. He'd grown fond of Bouie during his frequent visits. Paul's question lays bare the strange circle of life we have with our animals.

My dad also keeps us teenagers busy with the family construction business. On any given summer day, we might find ourselves sweating in New England's hot sun and stifling humidity, digging ditches and laying pipe for water or sewer lines, shoveling gravel, or, if we're lucky, running the machinery. I'm getting better with operating the backhoe and bulldozer, but my brothers seem to have a genuine talent for it. In particular, Mark, only 13, is quite adept, and when not running the machines, he's often out racing in motocross competitions on his powerful dirt bike. My father has a grand vision of his three children taking over the family business as we grow into adulthood. I have my doubts.

It's a chilly autumn day when my brothers enter my room with a flourish. "What's going on?" I ask, as Paul puts his index finger to his pursed lips. Mark speaks in a hushed voice: "Dad's got his yellow notepad out. Let's get out of here while we still can."

The three of us grab a few warm layers and our backpacks. We tiptoe to the kitchen and load them with food. We peek down the hallway and see my dad still sitting at his desk, writing out his list. Paul gives the signal, and without a sound we duck out the kitchen door and run for the woods to escape my father's chores, continuing a tradition that started years earlier as young children.

"Mark, did you get the bologna out of the refrigerator?" Paul asks, breathless, as we run up the hill into the forest, envisioning the campfire we will build, and the bologna cooking up in the pan like bacon. On these crisp, cold autumn and winter days in New England, nothing tastes better.

Our breath shows in the chilly air, the forest floor littered with a thick layer of fallen leaves. The dense stands of trees are barren and ready for winter. My brothers and I sit around our little fire, toasting our homemade sandwiches, listening to the forest.

"Right here. This is what's real," Paul says, running his hand through his curly blond hair and studying the trees overhead, swaying lightly in the breeze. "Not school, not church, not Dad's rules — not any of that stuff." We each lose ourselves in thought. Too soon, the bell in our chimney rings out and interrupts the moment.

"Well, there's Dad already," Mark sighs, his shoulders slumping.

"We'd better get back," I add.

Mark and I, on instinct, train our eyes upon Paul for guidance. He's the oldest among us, and already wise beyond his 16 years. He's intuitive, curious, and carefree, exuding an unpretentious confidence that makes people gravitate toward him, right down to his dating one of the school's most popular cheerleaders.

Paul looks up at us, expressionless for a moment, and studies our faces. The three of us fear invoking the wrath of my father, but for Paul, boundaries are more of a suggestion than a rule. He reads our urgency, and then a mischievous grin crosses his face.

"Dad can wait a little bit," Paul concludes, before reclining back against a log and redirecting his gaze into the trees.

That fall, the start of my ninth-grade school year has me standing in fury in front of Mom and Dad in our kitchen, as they look back at my scowling face with blank, unsympathetic stares. "This isn't fair!" I protest, raising my voice. "Why can't I go to Simsbury High School? That's where all my friends are going."

"Your cousin Lynnie goes to Northwest Catholic," my mother counsels. "She loves it there, and I'm sure you will, too." My father nods in solidarity.

"I want to play sports, and Northwest's athletics program sucks," I continue. "And, I'll have to wear that stupid uniform." I hold back from emphasizing that I also don't want to go to a religious school. Until now, I have been fortunate to attend public school along with my closest friends, most of whom will be attending Simsbury High. I'm just entering high school, and this is not what I want. My only consolation is that Paul has already been at Northwest for a year, and I'll have him to lean on.

Two years later, Mark's prolific athletic skills and a lot of pleading will lead my parents to relent and allow him to attend Simsbury High, where he will have a better chance to excel in football. His good fortune will be of little consolation for me, however, and only feeds my resentment of attending Catholic school and adds to a building sense of rebellion toward my parents.

"Do you want to go the mall with me today, Lisa?" my mother asks one day during my junior year of high school, as I emerge from my room.

"No," I answer, knowing my tone is rude but somehow unable to help myself. For as long as I can remember, I've been terrified that something bad will happen to my parents, my brothers, or anyone and everyone that I love. Still, the wall goes up. I make no eye contact, grab my jacket from the rack, and head out the door.

"Where are you going?" she asks.

"Out," I reply, my abrupt and uncourteous answer making me feel even worse about myself.

Mom is so sweet. Why do I act this way?

A typical night in my junior year sees me sneaking out of the house after my parents retire to their room to read or sleep. They think I'm asleep in bed, but little do they know, my night is just beginning. Hours later, I'll return home from some high-school party. I enter the house through the cellar hatch door, flip on the light, and retrieve the pajamas I have pre-placed here as a disguise. I change into them, climb up the stairs into the kitchen, and tiptoe down the hallway toward my bedroom, alibi in hand.

"Hi, sweetie, what are you doing up?" I look up to see my mother in the living room, sitting in her favorite chair — an old brown La-Z-Boy recliner — a book folded open and resting upon her leg.

"I was just getting some water," I reply, surprised to see Mom up late again, and believing that I've somehow fooled her.

"Okay, well, get some sleep," she answers, before turning her gaze back toward the window and looking out into the night. *She knows.*

Over the next several months, I notice that Mom is staying up late, which is uncharacteristic for her. *She must be having trouble sleeping,* I think. One day, while Mom is off in town, Dad sits with my brothers and me on the patio and addresses us in a more serious tone than usual.

"You guys need to be extra nice to your mom," he says, grasping for words. "She's kind of struggling right now."

I don't know what this means, but I ask no questions. I know that Mom has been trying to lose weight and has been taking a bunch of weird diet pills, but I otherwise haven't noticed anything wrong with her. My ever-present worry for my parents boils up anew, but now that the threat is not abstract, I'm too paralyzed to face it. Maybe if I pretend nothing is wrong, the problem will fix itself. I already have too much to worry about with school, boys, and this constant awkwardness I feel in so many social situations. No one wants to address or talk about this thing called "depression," which seems, to my young mind, to have come over my mother suddenly.

On the morning of May 6, 1985, I awaken to an empty house. Mom and Dad are at work, my brothers are at school, and I've decided to call in sick even though I'm not. I just don't want to go to school today. The phone rings, and I answer. It's the manager at the restaurant where Mom started working last year, for something to do now that my brothers and I aren't home as often.

"Priscilla didn't show up for work. Is everything okay?"

I don't have an answer. In recent months, Mom has started walking the two miles to work because she wanted to lose weight, and at once I am consumed with dread. *Maybe something happened to her on the way there? Hit by a car? Kidnapped?* I strike off running down the street to look for her, asking neighbors along the way if they have seen her. No one has. Panic builds in my chest and I struggle to keep from hyperventilating. I return home to find my father in the kitchen on his lunch break from work.

"Dad, Mom didn't show up for work. No one knows where she is," I say, my eyes welling with tears.

"What do you mean she didn't show up?" he replies, his face turning pale and his eyes widening. My dad paces the room as the hours pass, as phone calls and more visits with our neighbors yield no further news. "Where could she be?" he asks, despair building in his normally stoic voice.

Mark returns home from school. Paul is at baseball practice, and Dad calls the school to ask him to come home. Paul and I set out through the neighborhood to again knock on doors, while Mark heads out toward the pasture. "I'm going to go check the woods — maybe she took a walk and got hurt," Mark says.

It's past five in the evening. Paul, Dad, and I sit in the kitchen in the fading light, waiting, consumed by anxiety. "Maybe I should call the police," Dad says, his tone now almost despondent. Footsteps approach outside, and the door swings open. We sit up in anticipation. Mark steps in and stops in the doorway. He stares at us for a long moment, a shocked expression on his face.

"Mom's dead," Mark says.

Just a few hundred yards from our house, out past the garden, across the brook, and a short distance up the wooded slope, Mark found our mother's lifeless body with a shotgun lying by her side. With no note of explanation, much less any real warning we might have noticed, my mother took her own life.

The next hours are a storm of emotions that I want to banish from memory, pushed away into the darkest corners of my mind. We sit together in the living room in silence, apart from the sound of the ticking clock and the creaks of the house contracting as the evening air cools. An ambulance, police, and the coroner arrive. Question after question ensues, amid the sounds of radio traffic and officers walking into and out of the house, as the flicker of red and blue emergency lights reaches through the window to dance across the walls of our family kitchen. My eyes are red and hollow, my stomach performs somersaults amid waves of nausea, and I am crushed by a suffocating despair.

An unknown number of hours pass. My father, brothers, and I stand close together in front of our home, watching as the ambulance, carrying my mother's body, drives away. My worst childhood fears have been realized. I should have been more concerned. I should have seen the signs. *I should have been more worried. I should have kept her safe.* Mom is gone forever, and nothing will ever be the same.

Dad and I sit together on the patio in the summer sunshine. The air is heavy with humidity, and I swat away mosquitoes. A donkey brays from the pasture, and my mind wanders beyond the field and up into the enchanting forests that sustained me as a child. *There must be something more beyond those woods, beyond Connecticut,* I think.

"Well," Dad says, his voice wistful, "it sure will be nice having Paulie back home for the summer. Everyone back together again."

It has been five years since Mom left us. Dad remarried last year. Paul paid his own way through college and graduated not long ago from the prestigious Embry-Riddle Aeronautical University in Prescott, Arizona, a step toward fulfilling his lifelong goal to become a pilot. Paul's dream of flying was born even before my father bought him a flight lesson at the local airport in Simsbury when he was 10. Before then, Paul often built model airplanes, while Grandpa used to take Paul to the Simsbury airport to watch planes take off and land. And after that first flight lesson, during which they flew over the Roderick Farm and the instructor let Paul do some of the flying, he was hooked. At age 16, Paul constructed an ultralight plane from an amateur kit, but it never got off the ground, a minor relief to the rest of us.

Paul's meteoric trajectory has come as no surprise to those who know him. As for me, I've neither scholastic nor professional achievements to my name. Instead, I've been treading water in a sea of nine-to-five living that has seen my ambitions stifled in favor of mere, rote survival. I'm still waiting for a spark to start the fire.

Six months after Mom passed, my life was a complete mess. When Paul left for college, the absence of his intuitive guidance left another hole in my life. I came to realize that the family construction business was not for me, while Mark poured himself into it with diligence. Between me, Mark, and my father, there was no discussion or processing of Mom's death, much less the manner of it. My father and I suffered in silence, our relationship becoming more and more strained. Early in my senior year, confused and angry, I dropped out of high school and moved in with my then-boyfriend, which only further increased tensions between Dad and me. In time, I found work at a bank in the nearby town of Granby, where I've been working ever since and have worked my way up into customer service and the loan department. Paul has come home every summer, and with each visit I am eager to hear about his schooling and his latest travels to exotic lands.

"Alright. Selamat Siang, everybody."

Paul stands at the patio door, greeting us with a "Good afternoon" in the language of Indonesia, from where he has just returned. His outfit causes us to perform a double take.

"What's that you're wearing? Are you a Buddhist now?" my dad asks, eyebrows raised at Paul's wooden beads, pointed straw hat, and exotic, varicolored tunic.

"Yes, Dad," Paul replies, bringing his hands together in prayer and closing his eyes. "I am one with everything. *Ommm.*"

My dad, who once beamed at the sight of his oldest son serving as an altar boy in the Catholic Church, shakes his head, turns a deep shade of crimson, rises from his chair, and stalks away towards his garden for catharsis. My dad simply cannot imagine, even as a joke, his own children entertaining another faith.

Paul has always operated on a different wavelength, and the further afield he has gone from Connecticut, the more questioning he has become of conventional thought, organized religion, and cultural norms. Even as my father struggles to understand Paul's travels, worldly ideas, and most of all, his increasing distance from the church, he holds obvious pride in Paul's skills and eccentricities. At the bank, I find out that I have won a branch contest for opening the most new accounts in one month. The prize is a trip for two to Cancun, Mexico. I have never left the United States. I am again single and unattached, and none of my girlfriends can go.

"Hey, Paul, do you want to go to Cancun?" I ask.

"Sure. Let's go."

Before I know it, my brother and I are on the sunny beaches of the Yucatan and immersed in Cancun's gaudy tourist scene. It seems exotic to my untrained eye, but after but a few days, Paul is unimpressed.

"Let's take a bus to Belize," Paul says one morning. "This place is a tourist trap."

Mexico isn't wild enough for Paul, so we have to go deeper. Soon, we find ourselves crammed into a rickety bus, along with locals and various poultry, enduring a long, bumpy bus ride down south.

From the bus station in the depths of Belize City, at long past midnight, we hail a taxi to take us to a hotel. A second man sits beside the driver in the front seat. Alarm bells are going off in my head as the taxi driver makes a sudden turn into a dark alley and stops the car with haste. The passenger turns around and brandishes a baseball bat.

"¡Dinero, ahora!" he hisses.

Money. Now.

"No way. I'm not giving you anything," Paul says, staring the man down.

"What are you doing, Paul? Give him the money," I say through clenched teeth.

Paul pitches some bills over the seat.

"Let's go," Paul shouts, pulling me by my arm as he flings open the door.

Clutching our backpacks, we jump from the taxi and run with wild abandon down the alley. Back on the main street, we flag down another taxi — this one with a legitimate driver — which delivers us without further incident to our hotel. The hotel manager bears a look of surprise upon our entry to the lobby.

"You should not be out at night," he says, his brow furrowed with concern. "This is Belize City — *es muy peligrosa*." Very dangerous.

"Gracias," I reply, while Paul chuckles, unfazed.

The next day we take a small plane to one of the islands off the mainland. Long strips of pure white sand abut stunning turquoise waters of a color I've only seen in magazines. We eat fresh fish and snorkel in the reef, and I am stunned by the brilliant palettes of colorful life underwater. Far too soon, I need to start heading home to get back to work. Paul has no such commitments.

"I'm staying," he announces as we re-enter Belize City. "I want to check out Guatemala."

"I have to take the bus back to Mexico alone?" I ask, puzzled.

"You'll be fine. Just keep your eyes on your bag and your hand on your wallet. Just like you would anywhere else."

Paul accompanies me to the bus station and sees me off on the chicken bus for Cancun. Before I duck inside, he calls out a final time.

"Lisa, get out and travel; see the world," he counsels. "Don't settle for the narrow East Coast lifestyle. Don't get stuck there — it's a big and amazing world."

Emboldened by our adventures, I navigate home without incident. Back in Connecticut, the familiarity of the only place I've ever known seems both strange and discomforting. What should be a welcoming feeling is instead replaced by a fear that I'm missing out on life.

Paul's wayward lifestyle and my first real travels have fractured my internal attachments to Connecticut. At the bank, my days are consumed by thoughts of distant horizons and spontaneous adventures that I know I'll never experience here. *Paul had the bravery to just pull up roots and go. Why not me?*

A year has passed since the trip with Paul. I'm now 23 years old. Getting two weeks of vacation each year and saving money in my 401(k) can't possibly be all there is in life. At home, I lay out a map of the United States on my kitchen table. *Where should I go?* I close my eyes, lift my finger, and drop it down on the paper. I open my eyes, and my finger is on Boulder, Colorado. *That's right next to the Rocky Mountains.* That sounds good to me. It's time to cut ties. Over the next few months, I sell my aging horse, break up with the boyfriend I've been with for the past year, quit my job, and move out of my apartment and back home to the farm for the last few weeks of packing and preparing. At last, my Ford Ranger pickup is loaded and ready to go.

I back out of the driveway, turn the wheel, and shift the truck into drive. I glance at my father, standing in front of the house wearing a mixed expression of skepticism and sadness. He couldn't change my mind. I wave and smile. Over the sound of the engine, I hear his shouted parting words:

"You'll be back," he says.

I quickly find an apartment in Boulder, shared with three roommates, including an old friend of Mark's from Connecticut. Boulder is situated on the edge of the prairie of eastern Colorado, in the shadow of the Front Range of the Rockies, and from my apartment I have a nice view of the Flatirons, the iconic, inclined rock formations that loom above the town in the Boulder Mountains.

I find part-time work at a bank, adopt a cat, and enroll in training to work as a travel agent. Soon after, I start working for a travel agency, something that I anticipate will fit well with my newfound wanderlust. In reality, I discover that booking exciting skiing and European vacations for other people — trips that I cannot afford and will not be going on anytime soon — serves only to increase my frustration and FOMO.

On the positive side, Boulder is at the foot of the Rocky Mountains, anchored hard against the Boulder Mountain subrange with their iconic, tipped-up Flatirons formations, and in proximity to plenty of mountain activities that fall within my limited budget. The town's social center is the University of Colorado, but since I'm not a student, I find it challenging to meet people. I seldom date, and money is tight. I use local bulletin boards at places like The North Face store (originally, the country's first Holubar Mountaineering store) to meet partners for snow skiing and other outdoor sports. Through this process, I meet a very nice older man, who takes me rock climbing for the very first time. He teaches me the basics of ropework and proper belaying technique, and then we complete some classic rock climbs in nearby Eldorado Canyon, a tight sandstone canyon with red sandstone buttresses towering 800 feet over South Boulder Creek. I am exhilarated by the combined stimulations of physical movement over steep rock, mental focus, and breathtaking exposure. My roommates and I go on weekend ski trips to places like Winter Park and Copper Mountain. In New England, the skiing was usually on hardpacked, icy slopes, but here in Colorado, it is all about cutting through fresh, deep powder.

Paul, meanwhile, has spent his initial years after graduating from college flying into various places around the country. But a little over a year earlier, in the spring of 1991, he traveled north to Alaska with a plan to climb Denali. Although Paul had little experience with glaciers or high-altitude mountaineering, he arrived in Talkeetna in his classic seat-of-the-pants style: solo, motivated, and looking for a partner. There, he met an eccentric older climber named Ted Gannon, who was on a similar journey, and they teamed up. They made it up to 14,000 feet before being driven off by Denali's notorious weather. Back from the climb, Paul calls me with surprising news.

"I'm staying up here, Lulu," he says, using a nickname he'd given me many years earlier. "This guy in Talkeetna named Jerry Jacques has a bush-flying business and he's going to hire me. I'll be flying hunters and other people into remote lakes and off-grid residences."

"That sounds exciting," I reply. "Are you just staying for the summer?"

"Maybe longer. This place is phenomenal, Lisa. You should come check it out."

Paul does stay longer, and for the past year, he has kept me updated through our frequent calls and letters. He has learned to land small airplanes fitted with large, soft tires suited for rough dirt strips or undeveloped mountain slopes. He has also learned to fly floatplanes and land on and take off from remote lakes. It wasn't long before David Lee, the owner of Talkeetna Air Taxi, one of several air services holding a concession permit with Denali National Park to land climbers and scenic flight passengers on the glaciers of the Alaska Range, took notice of Paul's talents behind the yoke. David hired Paul, trained him to land on glaciers, and taught him the nuances of mountain flying in the extreme environment of the Alaska Range.

Paul has set up shop just outside Talkeetna in a tiny cabin in the woods with no running water, enjoying a simple lifestyle complemented by exciting work. He continues to share his wild stories with me about flying through magnificent landscapes, the friendly locals of Talkeetna, canoeing on the area lakes, and using his plane to access places that would otherwise take weeks of bushwhacking to reach.

"You've got to see this place, Lisa," Paul reminds me again and again.

I can no longer resist. I scrape together my money and fly to Alaska in late summer of 1992. In Anchorage, I am stunned by the sight of jagged, glaciated mountains rising straight out of the ocean. Even as I live in the shadow of the Rockies, I have never seen mountains on this scale — and they are everywhere. Paul gives me the tour as we make the drive north to Talkeetna. "To the right, those are the Chugach Mountains," he says, pointing toward the barrier of black, pyramid-shaped fortresses that rise above a lush green landscape of lower-angled mountain slopes. "That water body on the left is Knik Arm, and it leads out to the Pacific. And that's the Talkeetna Mountains up ahead," he continues. "Great skiing and climbing up there." I struggle to comprehend the scale and beauty of what I'm seeing.

After a few hours, we crest a final overlook above a vast river bar and are greeted by the stunning sight of Denali, standing 65 miles distant and 20,000 vertical feet higher. It's only the high point of a wall of rugged white mountains that fill the horizon. Paul notices me staring in wonder. "The Alaska Range is over 400 miles long. The scale of those peaks you're looking at is pretty hard to believe," he says.

Paul's cabin sits in a quiet boreal forest occupied by robins, woodpeckers, and magpies, the leaves of the dense canopy of poplar trees quaking and twisting in the gentle evening breeze. Late that first night, we sit in the cabin by candlelight as Paul reads aloud from a book of profound quotations and dialogues by the renowned Indian thinker Jiddu Krishnamurti: *"We love to think that someday we shall be better, but in the meantime, we carry on. Progress is* such a comforting word, so reassuring, a word with which we hypnotize ourselves. The thing which IS, cannot become something different," Paul intones, glancing up from the pages to gauge my reaction. "If we're always in a state of 'improving,'" Paul muses, setting the book down, "aren't we really just putting off our transformation to the future?"

"Is it possible for that shift to occur in an instant?" he adds.

I stare off into space. *That's me: Always thinking I'll be better in the future. Always becoming. But never asking, Who am I, right now?*

Talkeetna is set amidst a natural playground, and Paul has all the toys to access the best places. "Let's take my float plane to the Talkeetna Mountains — we'll hike and pick blueberries," Paul announces on my first morning, as we enjoy breakfast in Paul's cabin with our new friend Michelle O'Neil, an accountant who moved here not long ago from the town of Denali Park, two and a half hours north.

The three of us load into Paul's 1947 Aronca Chief on nearby Christiansen Lake, and soon I experience my first ever floatplane takeoff. The plane accelerates, gains lift, and breaks away from the water before lifting high above the deep-green boreal forests that stretch away in all directions, interrupted only by a network of lakes and tarns and swamps. We turn east toward the Talkeetna Mountains, and soon the forest beneath us gives way to bushy slopes of alder, and then tundra grasses speckled by occasional granite boulders. The vastness of the wilderness becomes more apparent the farther into it we fly. Soon, a small lake nestled beneath a rounded mountain comes into view.

"That's Moonshadow Lake," Paul says. "That's our spot." Paul banks the plane into a tight turn, we glide into a soft landing on the lake's placid waters, and then Paul taxis the plane up against the shore.

Compact green bushes and grasses carpet almost everything in view, and the ramparts of the Alaska Range dominate the northwestern horizon across the vast Matanuska-Susitna Valley where Talkeetna lies. As I walk into the fields above the lake, I notice the shrubs I'm walking on are bursting with ripe blueberries. There isn't another soul in sight.

"Alright, time to harvest," Paul exclaims with joy. "It's a little different than Tariffville, huh?" I smile and nod, at a loss for words.

Michelle and I hit it off, peppering each other with questions about our lives in between stuffing our mouths and buckets with berries. Michelle is 27, with a thin, athletic build, a long mane of beautiful dark hair, a generous heart, and a radiant smile that makes me feel as though our souls have met in a prior lifetime. A California native, Michelle followed her own wanderlust north to Alaska two years earlier. "Alaska has a high gravitational field," Michelle explains, in a tone that sounds as cautionary as it does inviting. "Once you're caught in it, it holds onto you forever." Somehow, I already understand what she means.

Hours pass as the three of us fill bucket after bucket with juicy blueberries, pausing only to admire the views and bask in the silence.

"Hmm. It's getting dark," Paul announces, with an air of surprise suggesting it had escaped his notice until now.

"It's easy to forget that it starts getting dark again in August," he muses, absent any urgency. "We better get home."

Paul starts the tiny airplane by hand-propping the propeller, while Michelle and I wait inside. The lake surface is like glass, a condition that makes getting lift for a floatplane more difficult. Wind ripples on the lake allow more air to provide lift beneath the floats, and by contrast, when landing, better vertical depth perception.

Paul's first attempt at taking off is unsuccessful, and he steers the plane back to the shallows.

"Lisa, you need to get out. I'm going to have to take you and Michelle back one at a time," Paul says.

Without a second thought, I jump from the plane's float into waist-deep water and wade back to shore. Paul departs with Michelle, the plane flies out of sight into the growing twilight, and the engine fades away into the most striking silence I've ever known. In it, I can both hear and feel the beating of my heart. Twenty minutes pass. It is almost dark; I am soaking wet and standing alone in the Alaskan wilderness. The deep-orange glow of the late-summer sun lingers behind the Alaska Range looming in the northwest, its ramparts sharply etched against the darkening sky, while the greens of the surrounding tundra fade into blackness. I hear strange animal noises coming from the brush, and mysterious splashing sounds along the shore. I start plotting my survival strategy for the night.

The sound of an approaching airplane puts my plans on hold. Paul lands moments later; he taxis the plane to where I can wade back out and climb in as the engine continues to roar. With no time to spare, he lifts off into the near-darkness of the night sky, broken only by the twinkling of a handful of lights we can soon see out toward Talkeetna.

"How will we land on Christiansen Lake?" I shout over the engine. "It's dark."

"I got Michelle out there in a canoe with flashlights," Paul yells back, smiling in reassurance.

It's too loud to voice my skepticism, but as Paul banks into a landing pattern over the dim outline of a lake in front of us, I see two lights waving in an up-and-down rhythm.

Paul sets the plane down on the black water with little effort, as though it were broad daylight, and I can just see Michelle's face, illuminated by the flashlights, not even fifteen feet to our side as we glide past. I glance back to witness the wake of the plane capsize the canoe, pitching Michelle into the water.

Paul guides the plane to the wooden dock and shuts off the engine. We climb out, and Paul laughs as Michelle swims up, the swamped canoe in tow. "Nice night for a swim," she says, as we help her up onto the dock.

"That was cutting it kinda close, Paul," I scold.

Paul scans what to me looks like a fully dark night sky.

"Aw, we had plenty of time left," he concludes, smiling at his two soaking-wet companions.

In the next few days, I make more friends in Talkeetna, who take me canoeing on some quiet, beautiful lakes near town. I attend dinner parties with casual acquaintances and complete strangers who treat me like an old friend. I feel welcome here like nowhere else. Maybe it's the town's population of only 500 permanent residents, scattered along the fourteen-mile road that dead-ends in the center of town. Paul takes me on a scenic flight around the Alaska Range, up close and personal with Denali. These jagged, ice-draped mountains are stunning when viewed from Talkeetna, but up close, they comprise without question the most spectacular and terrifying landscape I have ever seen. Steep-sided granitic spires draped in colossal hanging glaciers soar thousands of feet above their bases. Wild ridges festooned with enormous cornices frame faces and gullies covered in iron-hard blue ice thousands of years old, while glaciers up to two miles wide flow like immense, frozen rivers from the heights all the way down to the lowland forests, terminating in massive rock moraines from which spring cold and fast rivers flowing toward the distant ocean. Until now, I had no conception that such places existed.

I arrive back in Boulder at summer's end with a new problem: Alaska has sunk its claws into my imagination. Beyond the dramatic landscape, there is also something so alluring about the lifestyle and the Alaskans' hardworking, spontaneous spirit. Life up there is everything that life in Connecticut and Colorado is not. You can be anything you want, free of all the societal judgements and pressure of typical American culture. Boulder has much to offer, but there's something missing, and I have concluded that it is not my final destination in life.

Where shall I go?

My Ford Ranger is filled to the brim, bumping and bouncing along miles of frost-heaved pavement. Dwarf evergreen trees line the roadway, while distant and desolate mountains pierce a blue sky stretching across a massive horizon. I haven't seen another car for over an hour. At last, a small station appears just ahead with signs warning me that I must stop. *I'm here.*

"How long were you in Canada?" asks the US Customs Agent, as his eyes scan the piles of bags and boxes in the backseat and bed of my truck.

"Just long enough to drive through. Four days," I answer, hoping he isn't going to make me pull over for an inspection.

"Purpose of your travel to Alaska?" he continues, raising an eyebrow.

"I'm moving here. I'm starting a new life," I answer, as though this is normal.

The agent responds with a knowing smile,

folds my passport, and hands it back to me. "Well, then. Welcome back to the United States, and welcome to Alaska," he says, and I drive forward from Canada's Yukon Territory into the forty-ninth state.

It's the spring of 1993, and I've spent the past eight months planning my exodus from Colorado. For the past several days, I've been rolling up the Alaska Highway, the anticipation building with each mile. Now, miles upon miles of stunted spruce forests and birch trees unfold before me, the latter still bereft of leaves in the early-spring thaw that is only just commencing in Alaska. Rounded, mysterious, and lonesome mountains rise in every direction, seeming large, until I approach the town of Glennallen. Here, the glacier-cloaked Wrangell Mountains, dominated by 16,000-foot Mount Sanford, appear on the eastern horizon, lording over a vast landscape that somehow feels dwarfed by their ethereal presence.

Hours later, the highway leads me astride the waters of Knik Arm and Cook Inlet, surrounded by mountains, and into Alaska's version of a metropolis: Anchorage.

My new life in Alaska begins with a few short months of work for Paul's friend Sandy, a traveling chiropractor working a regular circuit of Alaska's remote fishing villages. She needs an office assistant to accompany her on her travels. Over the initial months of the summer, I get to experience the unique lifestyles of fishing enclaves like Bristol Bay, or the desolate coastal town of Nome. My days are filled with long hours of work, and the nights are spent in the village bars amongst the hard-partying fisherman. I don't know how Sandy can do this day in and day out, but it's quite an introduction to the blue-collar Alaskan life.

After a few months, I decide to move on from the exhausting itineracy of this work. In the height of the Alaskan summer, I drive to the Kenai Peninsula, south of Anchorage, in search of stable employment and a place to call home. Here, I discover a jaw-dropping landscape of mountains, rivers, and foliage. The waters of Kenai Lake and the Kenai River are a spectacular turquoise, set amidst a range of mountains covered in aspen, birch, cottonwood, and poplar trees. It looks like something out of a storybook. Cooper Landing, on the Kenai River at the outlet of the lake, is also the state's most renowned location for salmon fishing.

I am in love with this land, and in short order, I find a job at the Kenai Princess Lodge, working at their tour desk booking local fishing charters, and boat tours to Kenai Fjords National Park that begin from the town of Seward, an hour down the road. I rent a small cabin nestled in the forest outside the village of Cooper Landing. The cabin has no running water, so I haul in water in jugs and shower at the local RV park. Moose browse and wander about my yard; one morning leaving for work, I find a small black bear sleeping next to my truck. When I return home that evening, the bear is on the roof of my cabin, staring down at me as I go inside. I name him Rufus, and although he seems docile, I ensure that he doesn't get access to food or trash in my yard that might encourage him to become conditioned.

On my days off, I hike on the plentiful trails in the area just minutes from my cabin. My favorite mountain climb is the long, hard scramble up Cecil Rhode Mountain, towering thousands of feet above town, and my favorite trail is the arduous trail to Devil's Pass. The Resurrection Trail also departs both north and south and leads to distant, high passes after long journeys through beautiful, forested valleys. My most frequent hiking companion is LD.

"Come on, LD, let's go for a walk. Good boy, LD," I call out, as I head up the trail off Bean Creek Road.

LD is no human. He's the "Lodge Dog," and is owned by the manager of the lodge where I work. He is a superb hiking partner, helping me to avoid surprise encounters with the plentiful brown and black bears along the trail, a clear and present hazard of hiking in this area. I always feel safe with LD in tow.

Life is at last beginning to make sense. I am in the best shape of my life, and for the first time since leaving Connecticut, I have found a place where I belong. Although I'm still single and have met few men worth mentioning, I am convinced that by following my heart as I have, true love and everything else will find me sooner or later. The specter of my mother's death still resides in my subconscious, however. There is no doubt that my flight from Connecticut and my wanderlust are indelibly related to it. Paul seems wired differently than I do in his ability to face death and loss as an inherent process of life. Amidst this new life of wild adventures in the landscapes of Alaska, I have found perhaps the perfect distraction, but intuitively, I know that running from problems can only leave a person forever haunted. My worst fears being realized — the loss of a loved one — only reinforce those same fears today. Perhaps here in Alaska, I will find stasis.

My first Alaskan winter arrives, and the Princess Lodge is closing down. I find winter work at the Hotel Alyeska in the town of Girdwood, situated beneath Alaska's Alyeska ski resort. Here, the mountains rise straight up out of Turnagain Arm, an ocean inlet that experiences some of the world's most dramatic tidal shifts, as well as infamous bore tides. Glaciers tumble down the mountain slopes and terminate not far from the water. The drive along the arm is dramatic, with a scale so grand it challenges description.

The Hotel Alyeska is an enormous, palacelike structure, built by a Japanese investment company. It has numerous gourmet restaurants, an Olympic-sized swimming pool, a spa, and a workout center. The ski area's aerial tramway station is located at the north end of the hotel, affording easy access to the ski slopes. Best of all,

I am allowed to use all the hotel facilities as well, which makes life feel almost decadent.

I work as the hotel operator answering phones, but my shift doesn't start until 3:00 p.m. My mornings are spent skiing on the mountain, utilizing the free lift pass I get as yet another benefit of employment; I make many new ski buddies in the process.

I live in a cabin twenty miles down the road near Portage Glacier, paying $200 a month for rent. Access to the cabin is by way of a narrow dirt road that crosses under the highway bridge, and passage is not possible during high tides, when the waters of Turnagain Arm flood the road for a few hours. Coming and going on any sort of schedule requires a continuing consultation with the tide tables. The Portage Valley is also one of the windiest and stormiest places imaginable, being the main weakness through the mountains connecting Turnagain Arm with Prince William Sound to the east. Living here feels like living in the wild.

For the next two years, I immerse myself in this cyclical lifestyle of winters in Girdwood and summers in Cooper Landing, alternating my work between the Alyeska Hotel and the Kenai Princess Lodge. In Cooper Landing, I rent the same cabin every summer, and spend all my time outside of work hiking and exploring the mountains, sometimes with friends but more often alone. In Girdwood, I live the ski-bum lifestyle, chasing powder by day and having laughs and drinks in the taverns by night. For the first time in my adult life, everything I am doing has a connection to nature and to real things, while the people in my world have the easygoing manner that comes with doing what they love and being decoupled from the overbearing culture of consumerism and acquisition.

Paul and I live a few hours' drive from one another and visit each other often. My brother always has some wild, spontaneous adventure in mind. During my second winter in Alaska, he phones me up.

"Hey, Lulu, I've been wanting to check out these ice climbs near Portage. We just have to ice-skate across Portage Lake to get there."

Using a patchwork of borrowed and inadequate gear, I soon find myself skating across the lake in -10° temperatures, carrying a huge backpack, thrashing through alders in deep snow, and then following Paul up a near-vertical flow of ice as brittle as fine china. This is only my second time climbing waterfall ice, and for the most part, I have no idea what I'm doing. A swing of my ice tool shatters the thin veneer of ice, and the pick rebounds off the rock just underneath.

"The ice is too thin," I complain.

"Just hook your tools into the little pick holes I left — don't swing, just tap it," Paul instructs.

I'm doing a precarious dance across a horizontal traverse on an off-vertical rock wall just barely covered in fragile ice that looks like Swiss cheese. While leading, Paul encountered poor ice, and had to make this long traverse to reach better ice. He didn't place any protection on the traverse, however, because the ice was too thin to take ice screws. As a result, after I remove his last ice screw, twenty feet of rope stretching sideways separates me from Paul in a drooping arc. If I pop off, I'm going to take a massive pendulum swing. "Watch me, Paul," I mutter, trying not to hyperventilate, my fingers numb from the savage cold.

As I attempt to reposition my feet, I look up and notice a fracture in the ice around my tool placement. A sudden, loud pop rings out, and before I can react, I am flying down and sideways. As though outside of my own body, I notice myself screaming as I anticipate an impact that never comes. The rope stretches as it catches my fall. Then it's over, and I'm looking straight up at Paul, who just a second earlier was well off to my left.

"Nice one, Lulu," Paul exclaims, laughing at my flight as he holds the rope tight. "You okay?"

"No," I reply, breathing to try to calm myself. "I mean, well, yeah — I'm not hurt."

With sharp points on the feet and in the hands, falling while ice climbing is a major faux pas. I am very fortunate that my crampons and tools did not snag on the ice, in which case I might have spent the rest of this winter on crutches, or worse.

Paul gives me a very tight belay as I scratch my way upwards, still unnerved. Soon, I step onto Paul's chopped belay stance and clip into an anchor comprised of three screws half-driven into thin ice, each tied off short to reduce leverage, the whole mess backed up with a single aluminum chock wedged into a crack in the exposed rock just above.

"Good grief," I exclaim. "Is this anchor safe?"

"Sure," Paul answers. "It held your fall, didn't it?" We lock eyes, and a sly smirk washes over Paul's face, a look I know too well. *It means the anchor isn't pretty, but it's adequate.*

Paul laughs at my skepticism. "I figured you'd get a kick out of this anchor," he says. "But look there at the chock — see, it's well wedged, and the rock's good. You could hang a truck on that thing."

On the return across the lake, the frigid temperatures cause the leather of my uninsulated figure skates to crack and separate from the base, forcing me to walk the remaining two miles to the road. It's twilight before we pile into the car, frozen and spent from the day. Such are my adventures with Paul.

My brother's inquisitive nature only strengthens with time, and he continues to meet every risky situation with a playful sense of humor and an indefatigable optimism. To an outsider, these might be mistaken for naïveté or overconfidence. Sometimes I find it annoying when he dismisses my urge to caution. It's hard to tell if he's serious until that smart-alecky grin reveals that he's just trying to see how you'll respond, wants to make you think, and wants to make you laugh at and reevaluate your own emotions. That's my brother — always living in the moment.

The truth is that behind this façade, Paul is a voracious reader, is driven by curiosity, and has a deep well of knowledge about damn near everything. When it comes to all his undertakings — flying, climbing, and his relationships in particular — he's in fact a deeply serious and pragmatic person. Paul never wants to back off without at least taking a look. A go-for-it attitude that is both optimistic and sensible, and a healthy dose of natural skill coupled with a generous attention to intuition thrown in are what have made Paul a rising star in the world of glacier and mountain flying in Alaska.

My third summer in Alaska finds me supplementing my summer job at the Kenai Princess Lodge with work as a rafting guide for a rafting and fishing company on the world-famous Kenai River. It's an easy float trip with only a few small areas of faster water. Each journey down the river sees us passing by throngs of fisherman standing elbow to elbow in its striking light-blue waters, hoping to snag king, sockeye, or silver salmon.

I have visitors from Connecticut. My father, his wife, Barbara, my brother Mark, my 90-year-old Auntie Anne, and Barbara's mother have set aside their disappointment at Paul and I for moving so far away to come to Alaska and see what is such a big deal. They will visit Paul in Talkeetna, but first, they've come to Cooper Landing to see me. My dad is very excited about fishing, and so I book us a charter on the Kenai River. Dad beams with pride upon his return and the family gathers around to survey his catch.

"Barbara, ya gotta see this thirty-seven-pound king salmon I just caught," he crows as he steps up off the boat.

By Alaskan standards, it is just an average king, but to my dad it might as well be the largest fish ever landed. In fact, it gets bigger and bigger every time the story is told, and it's told almost every night of the trip. Of greater importance, I've seen little of my father since leaving home, and this is the happiest I have seen him in many years. The past is finally past.

Six months later, it's a sunny February afternoon and I'm just getting off the slopes of Alyeska and preparing for an evening of work. The dark days of the Alaskan winter are at last beginning to provide nourishing daylight, and I am already thinking ahead to what summer will bring. I get a phone call at work from Paul.

"Hey, Lisa, the deal went through. I am buying Talkeetna Air Taxi," he announces. "I was going to ask if you wanted to move up here and help manage the office for me."

The past three years in the Kenai have been best of my life, but my gut is telling me that this opportunity will lead to something even greater. I'm now 28, and the call of change is too much to resist. I seize on the opportunity to manage an exciting business with my family, and to make Talkeetna my new home.

A week later, I'm back in the Ranger with all my worldly possessions packed inside. I'm driving north again, and for what might be the first time in my life, I am absorbed by a real sense of purpose. As I motor up the Parks Highway, I watch the ramparts of the Alaska Range turn a deep, fiery red in the winter sunlight. In those cold and dangerous apparitions glowing on the horizon, I see harbingers of a promising future. So much of my path I owe to

Paul's example, inspiration, and insight, and perhaps I can now give something back by helping him build up his air service, one that flies tourists and mountain climbers into one of the world's most savage mountain ranges. I think of the mountain flying he does and the palpable risk it carries, also, and I know that, if only for my own sake, I will have to keep an eye on him.

Someone to worry about, someone to keep safe.

Chapter Two
Love and Ambition

I exit my truck and close my eyes. I inhale a long, deep breath. The frigid winter air burns and stings my airways and exhilarates my senses. The sky overhead is subdued and steel gray. Snowflakes flutter downward to gather around my feet. I stretch my legs and take in the view. Barren trees, a copious covering of snow, and silent streets that in summer would be teeming with tourists now empty, seemingly forgotten by the world. Talkeetna looks so different in winter . . .

My boots crunch on the compacted snow and ice as I walk. Large piles of snow pushed by the plows rest in every available space. I walk past Nagley's Store, the town's rustic small grocery and dry-goods supply. Just beyond is the seldom used airstrip that was once the town's primary runway, and which points straight at the historic Fairview Inn, one of Talkeetna's oldest establishments and the town's primary watering hole. Built in the early 1920s with the arrival of the Alaska Railroad, the Fairview is an unassuming two-story building with a white exterior and pitched roof that was placed on the National Register of Historic Places in 1982. I take a quick look inside this local haunt. The old, wooden floor creaks as it should, and is complemented by the smell of beer and popcorn and cigarettes. To the left is a three-sided wooden bar, backed by a giant wall painting of Denali and the Alaska Range. Somber, bearded men in tartan-checked wool shirts hover over their beers, some chatting, others sitting alone with their thoughts. By nightfall, if it's an ordinary night, the Fairview will be filled with people looking to party, and perhaps some local musicians will perform live. The walls are adorned with historic town photos and newspaper clippings. Throughout the bar hang portraits of the area's legendary characters, including famous bush pilots like the late Don Sheldon, who made his mark in the 1950s and 1960s while flying climbers into the Alaska Range and bush residents to their remote cabins. Nearby, a hand-painted wooden sign reads: "Fly an Hour or Walk a Week." For the residents of bush Alaska, where no road access exists, or the mountain climbers with their sights set on Denali, these are the two choices.

I continue my walking tour, taking a back alley to pass the town's snow-covered softball field and the beautiful new Walter Harper Talkeetna Ranger Station, which serves as headquarters for Denali National Park's mountaineering rangers and rescue staff. Back on Main Street, I grab a slice of pizza from the McKinley Deli and stop to admire the town's venerable Roadhouse, where generations of travelers have stayed and enjoyed its home-cooked meals served family-style.

"Hey, Lisa. Welcome to Talkeetna."

The call of a familiar voice causes me to glance to my left, where I see an old red Subaru stopped in the middle of Main Street. In the driver's seat sits Michelle O'Neil, whom I met on my first visit to Talkeetna. I don't recognize her female passenger, but she waves at me with a smile that suggests we must already know one other.

"I heard from Paul that you were moving here," Michelle exclaims, as I approach.

"We're having a painting party at the Roadhouse tonight," she continues, gesturing toward the building. "I just moved back here myself to work there, and Trisha Costello here is the new owner. We're getting it ready for the season. You should come hang out and grab a paint brush."

Trisha leans over from the passenger seat. "Come join us, Lisa," she invites. "There will be lots of great food."

"What time?" I reply. "There's supposed to be a potluck at Talkeetna Air Taxi, but I can be there, too."

I am always impressed by the warm welcome I receive from both friends and strangers every time I visit Talkeetna. Coming here is like coming home. As we chat, I notice a bumper sticker on a nearby car: "Talkeetna: Where the Road Ends, and Life Begins."

Talkeetna is indeed at the end of the road. In cartographic terms, it is situated at the termination of a fourteen-mile spur road that branches off the George Parks Highway connecting Anchorage and Fairbanks, 120 miles north of Anchorage, and is at the meeting point for three large rivers, the Talkeetna, Chulitna, and Susitna. Its isolation has been critical in forming the town's slowed-down pace of life and the relaxed and welcoming attitude of the locals.

I am discovering that many Talkeetna residents are those who, upon passing through on their first visit, decided not to leave. It is a close community comprised of people who found their way here from all over the world and the locals who were born and raised in the area. It is an easygoing mix of eccentrics, artists, loners, dreamers, mountain climbers, entrepreneurs, self-starters, bush pilots, trappers, and people who dislike the anonymity, noise, and chaos of large cities. *My kind of people.*

I need to go get settled, so I bid goodbye to Michelle and Trisha with a plan to meet this evening. I get back in my truck and head for Talkeetna Air Taxi's office, a rustic log cabin situated along the tarmac of the Talkeetna Airport, a quarter mile east of the village.

"You've been here before, so you know where everything is," Paul says, as we walk from the office area past the bathroom and into the hexagonal-shaped living room. The space has a small kitchenette with a countertop and barstools, a wood stove, a couple of sofas, and a large shelf filled with climbing books and magazines. "In early season, we usually let a few climbers crash out down here for a night or so before and after their trip," Paul says, before motioning toward the stairs at the far side of the room. "There's a bed upstairs — the loft is your private quarters. Hopefully the climbers won't bug you."

Now, in February 1996, it's still the off-season, and I am thankful to have a month or so before things get too busy to learn how to manage the office, which includes answering the phone and taking flight reservations as well as balancing Paul's books.

A steady stream of calls comes in from people wanting to book flightseeing tours for their upcoming vacations. I find myself spending a great deal of time explaining the three different tours we offer, including the most popular option, a glacier landing.

The office is also flooded with calls from mountain climbers and backcountry skiers looking to reserve a flight to one of the area's numerous glaciers. The climbing season is April to July. Before that, it's too cold for most, and after July, the glaciers become too soft for landing, crevasses open up, and climbing conditions deteriorate. Most of the climbers I book are bound for Denali, and they reserve their flights to Denali Basecamp on the Kahiltna Glacier, a forty-minute flight from here.

It's the beginning of April when our first two climbers of the season arrive. Through the door walk two young men from the Seattle area named Mark Westman and Joe Puryear. Paul knows them both, as they had flown with him over the past couple seasons, so we have been anticipating their arrival.

"Hi, I'm Mark, and this is Joe," Mark begins, motioning to his strong and wiry partner, who acknowledges me with an impish grin framed by a dark, bushy beard.

"We have a reservation to fly to the Ruth Amphitheater," Mark continues, stealing a furtive glance out the nearby picture window at the ominous clouds that blanket Talkeetna.

"Today, hopefully."

Mark has blond hair, striking Nordic features, and intense green eyes, and I estimate him to be about two hundred pounds of pure muscle. He wears a tan, full-brimmed hat, a matching overcoat, and a serious expression.

It is my turn to speak, and then I realize that I am staring at Mark in silence.

"Um, yes. I remember talking to you on the phone. I'm Lisa Roderick."

Mark raises his eyebrows. "Are you related to Paul?"

"I'm his sister."

Mark studies me for a moment before catching himself. "I think I see a resemblance."

I just stand there smiling before I realize that we are in another awkward silence. I am staring again.

"Well, Paul's out on a scenic flight. But when he gets back, we'll see if he can take you in. You can bring your bags up on the deck."

Mark and Joe thank me and exit through the door, while I recover my composure. *Are all climbers this good looking?*

The two climbers explode an enormous amount of gear and food across the large wooden deck outside, and I watch my first Denali expedition get prepared for battle.

Within the hour, Paul returns from his flight, shuts down his engine, and jumps out.

"Welcome back," Paul cries out, as he walks from the tarmac and greets them each with high-fives and hugs.

Joe smiles and says, "We're psyched to be back."

"Right on," Paul acknowledges. "You're going for the South Buttress again, right?" he adds, asking about a route I'm not familiar with.

"That's the plan," Mark replies. "Starting at the Mountain House. Can you get us in this afternoon?" Mark is referring to a small, historic hexagonal cabin, built by Don Sheldon in the mid-1960s, on a nunatak — spire — overlooking the Ruth Glacier.

Paul shakes his head, looking up at the dark-gray sky overhead. "Nah, I was just at the Mountain House — the weather's getting gnarly in there. I almost flipped the plane over trying to take off. I'm not going back in there today with that wind." He pauses and studies their huge pile of gear.

"This storm looks like a big one — you might want to get comfortable for a couple days," he concludes. "Make yourself at home in the back — you know the drill."

The boys shrug, and then turn back to their organizing. They have over a month and are unhurried.

Mark and Joe settle into the back office, and I am excited to have them as roommates. By this time, Paul's girlfriend, Sue, has arrived from Anchorage for Easter weekend and is hanging out in the office. Sue grew up in Connecticut with Paul and me, and we have been friends for fifteen years. She's now an accountant and is helping teach me how to record sales and track expenses.

"Sue," I whisper, motioning to her and trying not to let Mark and Joe hear me in the next room. She walks over, her brow furrowed with curiosity.

"Check out this gorgeous man," I say, pointing around the corner toward the living room.

We creep over to the doorway and peek around. Mark is sitting on the loft stairs curling a forty-pound dumbbell. He wears a focused expression. Just then, he glances up, and we duck back behind the door, giggling.

As the day wears on, Joe begins showing us card tricks, gloating that he knows the secret to each trick and we don't. Then he produces a game of Yahtzee he has brought for stormy days on the mountain.

"Yahtzee? Are you serious?" I exclaim.

"Oh yeah, and you're playing," he insists. "Sit down over here." My afternoon work will have to wait.

Sue and I take turns trying to get Mark talking, but, though polite, he buries himself in climbing books, listens to music on his headphones, and seems to be brooding, perhaps over his upcoming climb. *He must have a girlfriend*, I think.

"So those guys are trying the South Buttress," I say to Paul, as I help him put the wing covers on the planes in anticipation of the evening's forecasted snow. "What's that route all about?"

Almost every Denali expedition I have booked so far is heading for the standard West Buttress route. A few others are attempting the West Rib, and fewer still, the difficult Cassin Ridge. All these routes begin at Denali Basecamp, on the Kahiltna Glacier, but I haven't seen a single reservation starting their Denali climb from the Ruth Glacier like these guys.

"It's a really long route," Paul explains. "It's rarely climbed. You have to start way down in the Ruth Amphitheater, at the Mountain House, so it has a very long approach."

I know where he's talking about, because I just spent the past two days skiing in the Ruth Amphitheater with Michelle. It's a magnificent place, surrounded by massive, ice-draped granitic peaks like Mount Dan Beard, the Rooster Comb, and my favorite peak, the Mooses Tooth. Denali hovers high over the amphitheater like a presence from another world, and I remember from studying the map that the mountain is in actuality more than ten air miles away. "That's going to be a lot of work," I say.

"Yeah, that'll be a good one, if they pull that off," Paul continues. "Those guys are pretty motivated. They're solid, and have put in some hard days up in the range the last couple of years. They just might get it done."

The first ascent of the South Buttress was made in 1954 by a team led by the NPS park ranger Elton Thayer. They began by approaching the mountains on foot from the small village of Curry, located along the Alaska Railroad north of Talkeetna. Ginny Wood, the wife of team member Morton Wood, was one of the few female mountain pilots of the era and supported the team by airdropping supplies (a tactic later made illegal by the park service) into the Ruth Amphitheater after they had spent over a week walking into the mountains.

The team of four, which also included Les Viereck and George Argus, gained the crest of the five-mile-long South Buttress and toiled for weeks before reaching the summit. The team began their descent down Denali's pioneer climbing route, the Muldrow Glacier, which would make this the first south-to-north traverse of Denali. However, tragedy struck on Karstens Ridge, the steep ridge dropping from the upper mountain into the Muldrow Glacier, when the team suffered a long fall on snow and ice. Thayer was killed in the fall, while Argus suffered a broken hip. Viereck and Wood left Argus in a hastily constructed tent with their food and descended to distant Wonder Lake to initiate a rescue. Argus — by this point AWOL from his military service — would become the first climber evacuated from Denali by helicopter.

Mark related much of this history to me in the office, emphasizing two things that drew him to attempt this route:

"The 1954 team talked about how they worked so well together and became closer friends up there," Mark said. "Joe and I are best friends, and we know we'll be all alone, unlike on the West Buttress. That sort of teamwork and isolation sound like the essence of real mountaineering: just the two of us — and the mountain."

Later that evening, I walk into the kitchenette to make dinner, and there on the couch lies Mark, the supposed hardman climber. On his chest lies Cessna, the tiny white kitten I had adopted several weeks ago. Both are sound asleep. *This is a good sign — I like this guy.*

The following morning is Easter Sunday. It's snowing, and the boys are grounded. Paul, Sue, Mark, Joe and I head to breakfast at a local establishment. Later that afternoon, Mark is stricken by a violent stomach illness.

"It's the ham and cheese omelet," Mark groans, as he vomits repeatedly for an hour. Now, he is pale and unable to stand. Joe and I drag and carry him to my truck, and then drive him to the town physician. The doctor isn't sure what the problem is, although we're all pretty sure it's food poisoning.

"Well, whatever it is, we need to get the nausea under control, so I want to give you a shot of Phenergan," the doctor says to Mark, who struggles to grunt an approval.

The doctor draws a syringe of medication and injects it into

Mark's shoulder.

"It might make him drowsy," he warns, turning toward Joe and me.

As the doctor steps back, Mark's eyes roll back in his head, and he crumples onto the exam table. Joe and I lunge to catch him, saving him from a plunge to the floor.

"Mark? Mark? Oh my God!" the doctor cries, before he bolts out of the room. He returns a moment later, leafing through a medical manual with determination and concern. At this, Joe and I stare at each other in wonder.

"The Phenergan can make you very drowsy," the doctor says, reassessing Mark momentarily.

"I guess so," Joe replies, looking at me askance.

"He'll sleep it off," the doctor concludes. "You can take him home — but let me know if his condition worsens."

Considering that Mark can barely walk, I'm not sure what that might mean, but we make our exit nonetheless.

We carry Mark back to the truck. He is incoherent, unable to open his eyes, and mumbling. We get him situated on the couch back at the office, with a bucket perched beneath his head. Joe, Sue, Paul, and I watch movies until late, while Mark appears to be fast asleep.

The next morning, Mark awakes, looking hungover and haggard. I hear him stirring from my desk in the office and go into the back room to check on him.

"You're alive," I exclaim. "Welcome back."

"What the hell happened?" Mark asks, running his fingers through his hair. "Last thing I remember was getting a shot in that doctor's office."

The weather is sunny, and the mountains are out. Mark wants to fly.

"We had better wait a day to make sure your illness is over," Joe cautions.

Mark agrees, and I am pleased because I want to get to know him better. I accompany him on a walk around the airport as he tries to work the sickness out of his body, and later he sits in the office with me as I answer phones and pace around the room filing paperwork.

"What kind of work do you do?" I ask Mark, starting with the most obvious get-to-know-you question.

"I'm a civil engineer. I've been working for consulting firms in Seattle and Bellevue for the past several years."

"Where did you go to school for that?"

"University of Washington in Seattle. It's a great school — my dad and older brother also went there."

"How did you get the time off for this trip?"

"Well," Mark explains, bursting with pride, "I just quit my job last week, and after this trip, I'm going to work this summer on Mount Rainier as a climbing ranger."

"That's amazing," I reply, knowing that Denali also has climbing rangers and that they do a lot of mountain rescues.

"I'm changing my life," Mark asserts. "I'm 26, and the time to go big is right now."

"And how do you two know each other?" I ask next, as Joe saunters into the room.

"We met three years ago through my roommate. Our ambitions and objectives always seem to line up," Mark answers, before he looks at Joe to see if he has more to add. Joe's contribution is theatrical: "We're taking the climbing world by storm." Mark and

Joe's hands meet in a muscular high-five, and then they hold the pose in a protracted, macho, teeth-gritting moment. While I'm not sure whether to roll my eyes or laugh, I now find myself also curious about Joe.

"So, Joe, what's your story?"

"Oh, I grew up on a winery in Eastern Washington, and I got a degree in math from University of Washington. I've been working at REI in Seattle, but now I'm going to work at Rainier this summer," Joe says, pausing for effect and pointing at Mark, "with *this* guy."

"It's all part of the 'Grand Scheme.'" Mark interjects, using air quotes, a sly grin spreading across his face. "We're going to be famous, and have houses in all the cool climbing spots in the world, with full climbing racks stored in each one. We'll have separate wings in each house for each of us and our future wives."

"You guys are sort of like a married couple already," I joke, as the two of them laugh. *I think they're serious.*

As Mark continues recovering, they ready their monstrous pile of equipment for a flight the next day. I have never been up high on Denali before and can only imagine what it must be like.

I watch Mark and Joe as they load a large dry-bag with a massive amount of food that was repackaged with meticulous care. "You guys must see some amazing sights up there," I say. Almost on cue, Mark and Joe stop what they are doing and jump straight into some sort of character charade.

"Yesss," Joe intones, turning to me with a look of burning intensity, before delivering the punch-line:

"*If only you could see what I've seen with your eyes.*"

"Oh boy," I exclaim, as the reference registers in my memory. They are quoting the classic sci-fi movie *Blade Runner*, and through an unwitting comment, I have triggered a fusillade of movie quotes. This, in turn, gives way to them acting out skits from "The Jerky Boys," a New York duo famous for making juvenile prank calls. In a fitting twist, The Jerky Boys is also the name of Mark and Joe's expedition. For the rest of the day, I listen as they assume the identities of characters such as an obnoxious, job-seeking auto mechanic called "Frank Rizzo," or a confused, needy, elderly New Yorker named "Sol Rosenberg." Mark and Joe decide to play the tapes of the prank calls for me, "so you can better appreciate it," they insist. I'm not so sure it is my kind of humor, but one thing for certain is that Mark and Joe's imitations are even funnier than the real thing. These two are like a synchronized comedy duo.

In the evening, we all watch movies in the back room. Mark cuddles Cessna again, while he now peppers me with questions about my own life.

"I'm impressed that you just packed up and headed west," he says, after I relate the relevant parts of my backstory. "Not many people have the confidence to do something so bold."

The next morning, the sun is out, and the air is crisp and cold. "The Range is booming. Let's load 'er up," Paul says as he walks in into the office, sounding like a coach getting his team spooled up for the big game. Paul is always excited to fly. Mark and Joe stand by their mountain of gear, dressed for the glacier and eager to help Paul load the plane. Soon, my first climbers are off, gone to Denali for a month, and I turn my attention back to my own mountain of office work.

In the mountains, climbers carry a CB radio with which they can talk to Kahiltna Basecamp, NPS rangers, or to pilots flying overhead, who usually monitor the CB mountain frequency. At the office, we have a radio base-station with a tall antenna outside. If climbers high on the mountain have a line of sight to Talkeetna, we can sometimes pick up their transmissions. It's early one afternoon in early May when I hear someone calling on the radio.

"Talkeetna Air Taxi, do you copy?"

I acknowledge, and receive an exuberant reply:

"Hey, it's Mark and Joe. We're on the summit."

It has been almost a month since they left, and we have been getting an avalanche of worried phone calls from Mark's father, Tom. Paul managed to hail them on the radio while flying around the mountain about a week ago, and we were just starting to wonder about them again.

"Awesome," I respond, but before I can add more, I am surprised to hear Annie Duquette, the Denali basecamp manager, break in. It is quite rare for us to be able to hear Annie's transmissions, but this time her voice is quite clear.

"Who's that on the summit?" Annie interjects. "You guys must be the first of the year."

I call Mark's and Joe's families to tell them the good news, and then I get ready to head out to the mountains for my own adventure. That evening, Paul flies me and my friends Thomas Bailly and Kevin Krein up to the Slide Glacier for two days of skiing bracketing an overnight stay. The Slide lies in a hanging valley high above the lower end of the much larger Ruth Glacier. It affords a dramatic view of distant Denali, towering over the spectacular, mile-high granite monoliths of the nearby Great Gorge of the Ruth Glacier, one of the world's top natural wonders.

We spend the evening cutting turns in beautiful spring corn snow on the sunnier aspects, and perfect powder on the shadier northern faces. We have a magical night perched on the ridge with a full view of the ramparts of the Alaska Range as our guardians. The sun arcs low northwest and ducks behind the Alaska Range as the sky turns a spectacular orange hue. I sip hot tea and absorb the scene, smiling in silence as I wonder what I might be doing with my life back in Connecticut.

In the morning, Paul returns to join us for some morning ski runs before we all fly back out together. After a few laps, as we load the plane to head back to Talkeetna, Paul looks up at me with a start.

"Oh, hey. Those Jerky Boys are back," he says. "They just flew out last night. Mark's been asking about you."

"Really?" I respond, trying not to sound too excited, and feeling a sudden rush of urgency to get out, fearing that I might miss them before they depart Alaska. I have been thinking about Mark since he left a full month ago.

Mark and Joe are there to greet us as we unload in Talkeetna. The sun is shining amid an unusual stretch of warm weather for so early in the spring and has triggered the buds on the trees to burst open with greenery over the twenty-four hours I've been gone. The air explodes with life.

"Welcome back, Lisa," Mark and Joe shout. We hug, and I introduce them to my Girdwood ski buddies, who have to take off for Anchorage right away.

The boys have lost noticeable weight, and they set about eating everything in sight. I walk with them to town, where they consume a full Roadhouse standard breakfast of pancakes, eggs, bacon, and scones with butter. In between bites, they relate the details of their 31-day adventure up the South Buttress to the top of Denali, and down the West Buttress to Denali Basecamp.

"It took us so long just to get up on the buttress proper," Mark relates, describing the oppressive weight of their packs and sleds, and days of double- or even triple-carrying sections of the route.

"The buttress itself was awesome," Joe adds. "We were walking along this spine at 15,000 feet for miles, in and above the clouds. It was like we were the last humans left on the planet."

"And getting to visit Thayer Basin was something I'll never forget," Mark continues, referencing a seldom-visited hanging basin at 14,500 feet on the mountain's eastern flank. "It has to be one of the most desolate and remote places in the world!"

Mark and Joe continue a dramatic recounting of how, after summitting on their twenty-eighth day, they managed to drag their gear — which still clocked in at over 110 pounds per person — up and over Denali Pass, the windy saddle at 18,000 feet between the mountain's north and south summits, before wrestling these monstrous loads down the West Buttress in three long days. Their insatiable appetite becomes easier to understand. We are not even 100 yards down the street from the Roadhouse when Joe stops and points.

"Ice cream. I want ice cream," Joe intones, using a robotic voice to emphasize his voracious, primal hunger.

"I'm in," Mark concurs, as they look to me to gauge my interest.

"I'm out. You guys go get it. See you back at the office."

When they return, they fix up a two-quart pot of rice and beans, then head back to Nagley's Store and return with more ice cream, and hamburgers to grill.

"My God, you guys, stop eating," Paul cries with incredulity, as they cook the burgers with a spatula in one hand and a king-sized Snickers bar in the other. I have never seen anyone eat so much food in one day. By evening, Joe is tapped out, but now Mark wants to party.

"Want to head to the Fairview?" he asks with a coy expression. *How could I resist?*

We sit side by side at the bar, talking of the future in dreamy language. We are each in a transformational period of our lives, and anything seems possible. The sharing of these emotions feels magnetic. *Mark and I are on the same wavelength.*

"After I get done working at Rainier in September, I'm traveling somewhere this fall. Maybe Spain," Mark says, a faraway gleam in his eye.

"You and Paul should come climb Rainier this fall, too. I'll take you up," he adds.

"Deal," I answer, without hesitation. In my mind, however, I feel a strange mixture of fear and excitement boiling up as I contemplate what I've just agreed to do. I have never climbed a glaciated mountain in my life, much less a mountain the size of Rainier, which rises to 14,000-plus feet.

The longer Mark and I talk, the more new ideas catch fire. "Maybe we should all travel to Europe together?" Mark muses.

"I'm in," I say, and I tap my glass against his. As we lock eyes for a moment, I see a future of limitless possibility.

The next morning, the shuttle van is all packed with Mark and Joe's gear, ready to transport them to the Anchorage airport. From there, they will fly south to begin their seasonal jobs at Mount Rainier. Mark wraps me in a warm embrace.

"Let's go traveling," I implore. Mark agrees, making clear that our chatter the night before wasn't just the alcohol talking. Joe eyes us with playful suspicion before he, too, gives me a giant bear hug before they get on the shuttle.

"I'm sure going to miss you guys," I say, trying not to get emotional, wondering not without sadness whether all our enthusiastic plans and energy might fade away with distance and the inevitable passage of time.

Over the next two months, Paul and I host and fly some of the world's most renowned mountain climbers: Alex Lowe, Steve Swenson, John Middendorf, Fred Beckey, and Carl Tobin, just to name a few. We stage elaborate barbecue parties on the deck in the evening, and local Talkeetnans join in on the fun. With each passing day, I feel more rooted in this community.

It's a hot July afternoon when I receive a call in the office from an air service up north.

"Paul's airplane was hit by a helicopter," the man on the other end states, and my heart skips a beat. "He's alright, he's still flying, but his tail wheel was chopped off and he's inbound to Talkeetna. FAA has been notified." Soon, I hear sirens and look outside to see fire trucks, an ambulance, and other rescue vehicles racing across the tarmac and positioning alongside the runway in anticipation of Paul's landing, which will be compromised by the missing tail wheel. As I watch, Paul makes a safe landing, but we learn that the helicopter has crashed and the occupants have sustained serious injuries. The rush and subsequent crash of adrenaline I experience are overwhelming, and I spend the remainder of the day unable to focus.

I will soon learn that Paul was flying passengers to a remote lodge on the north side of Denali National Park, when, he related, a helicopter suddenly appeared in his windscreen. He made an instinctive evasive maneuver that resulted in the helicopter passing beneath him, but its rotors impacted his tail wheel. Disaster was averted by mere inches, and I came unnervingly close to reliving my worst nightmares.

Just days later, I'm in the office one afternoon with a group of

Korean women, who are wandering about while waiting for their husbands to return from a scenic flight with one of Paul's pilots. A pilot from another air service contacts our office on the radio.

"One of your planes didn't make the takeoff in the Mountain House," he reports. "The plane is suspended over a crevasse. Paul saw the wreck and is in contact — sounds like everyone is okay, but he says we'll need rescue resources."

I notify the park service and make a couple of calls. I shake my head in disbelief with this, the third incident of the season. Back in March, when I first arrived, one of Paul's planes broke a wheel ski while flying a news crew to cover the Iditarod Sled Dog Race. The plane was stuck in a remote village in western Alaska with no services. I found myself doing something I had never imagined: calling helicopter companies to see if they'd lift our stranded airplane to somewhere it could be repaired. There's more to running an air service than meets the eye.

After the latest incident in the Mountain House, I find myself again doing something unexpected, and that is informing these Korean women, who know virtually no English, as to why their husbands' plane will be so late in returning.

"The plane . . ." I begin, pausing to search for words that they might understand, while using my hand like an airplane. I am horrified at what I hear myself say next.

"Crashed," I state, diving my hand into the table.

"*Crash?*" the women exclaim in unison. "*DEAD?*"

"No, no, no. Everyone is okay," I stress, now trying to reassure them after my poor choice of words. For the next hour, however, the women follow me around the office, seeking further reassurance.

"Dead?" they ask, beginning the process again, until at last their husbands return to Talkeetna. I must learn to choose my words wisely.

More pressing is that the risks which Paul and his pilots face in this line of work have been laid bare for me to see. I want to be part of my brother's operation here, but I don't know if I can take this much anxiety year in and year out. In the wake of these incidents, I reveal my concerns to Paul.

"I don't want to let you down," I tell him one evening, "but after we get through this summer, I might have to do something else next year."

Paul acknowledges with a nod. "That might be better if the stress of this place is too much. We'll talk about it."

As the climbing season trails off in July, Paul wants to do an advertising promotion in the climbing magazines to award one climbing team the "Climb of the Year." None of the star-studded teams of famous climbers we hosted had succeeded on their objectives.

"I think it's got to be Mark and Joe," Paul states. "That South Buttress was cool. We're giving the prize to those Rainier Rangers."

Mark and I have already been exchanging letters. I leave Mark a phone message at Mount Rainier to tell him that they have won our contest. A few days pass before he comes off the mountain and returns my call.

"Are you guys still coming down here to climb in September?" he asks, sounding hopeful. The plans for fall travel and climbing that were hatched between Mark and me over drinks last May during that magical night in the Fairview ended up spreading like wildfire through Paul and the Talkeetna Air Taxi ("TAT") crew by the time Mark and Joe left for Seattle the following day. Mark and I parted ways with loose talk of not only me, but Paul, Pauls' girlfriend, Sue, another TAT pilot (also named Paul), and several other local friends making a group trip to climb Mount Rainier with Mark in the autumn.

"We're working on it," I reply. In fact, at this point, I am the only one who has committed. Everyone else has lost interest.

We continue writing letters, and as September approaches, Mark again asks who is coming. "Just me," I write back. It is becoming impossible to duck the reality that climbing Mount Rainier just might be a date.

I am a nervous wreck. To impress, just before leaving for Seattle, I get a haircut and color done by a local hair stylist. In the middle of the session, the power goes out and the stylist must finish cutting my hair by candlelight. She cuts it too short and leaves the color in too long. My light-brown hair is now an odd shade of red. *This is a disaster.*

Mark greets me at the gate in Seattle with a hug. After a few moments of excited exchange, he makes a polite and neutral observation: "Your hair looks different." We will go to Rainier tomorrow, but tonight we are heading to the bars in Pioneer Square in downtown Seattle, which seems like a good icebreaker. Our fourth tavern of the night is the New Orleans, and by now we are tipsy.

As the evening progresses, our conversation is easy and flowing, and we're riding an electric connection. Mark and I lean in closer to one another to be heard over the music. At some point, I notice that Mark is staring into my eyes with intention, with a look of something like love, and I take that as my cue. Without thinking, I lean in and kiss Mark softly. He kisses me back, and my heart melts away.

Two days later, Mark and I shoulder our packs for the climb from White River Campground to Camp Schurman on Mount Rainier.

"How much elevation gain is it again?" I ask.

"About 5,000 feet to camp," Mark replies.

"That's more than I've ever done in a day," I say. "I'll try to keep up."

Camp Schurman, Mark's summer workstation, is perched in a magnificent location at over 9,500 feet on the eastern slopes of Mount Rainier. A steel hut with a concrete floor stands at the foot of a rocky buttress called Steamboat Prow, around which flow two of the mountain's most massive glaciers, the Emmons on the left, and the Winthrop on the right. Here, I am reunited with Joe, and introduced to his and Mark's longtime friend and now work supervisor, Mike Gauthier.

"I've heard a lot about you," I say to Mike, recalling Mark telling me of their college days together at the University of Washington in Seattle, and that Mike had taken Mark on his first roped climb — right here, on the Emmons Glacier route out of Camp Schurman — in the summer of 1992.

"And I heard you took good care of these guys up in Alaska," Mike replies.

Mike produces a box of wine. "It's our last night up here for the season," he grins. "We're closing this place DOWN." Mark and I have wandered into a spontaneous celebration.

The night's raucous activities result in a later-than-planned start, but at 5:00 a.m., Mark and I set off alone up the Emmons Glacier. The eastern sky is already a deep, breathtaking red with the impending rise of the sun over the Cascade Mountains, creating an otherworldly scene.

Just as we pass 12,000 feet, the aftereffects of the previous night's activities are taking their toll, and I am consumed with nausea. The sun has climbed high into the sky, and the warm temperatures are softening the snow bridges over the enormous crevasses across which we've been tiptoeing all morning.

"We have a ways to go yet, and we should already be descending by now," Mark announces. "We're also the only ones up here today. I think it would be wise to descend."

I can tell from his tone that Mark doesn't want to disappoint me, but as I survey the massive river of chaotic ice upon which we stand, and the mountains stretching away forever beneath us, I feel a deep and quiet sense of satisfaction.

"I'm happy, Mark. Let's go down."

Mark and I head next to the remote wilderness beaches of Olympic National Park, on the Pacific coast. As luck would have it, several days of warm and sunny weather are forecasted for this place that is foggy and rainy most of the time. Mark and I take the ferry across Puget Sound, and then drive late into the evening to reach the Ozette Loop trailhead. Mark prepares our sleeping bags and pads in the back of his pickup truck, and we sit for a while on the tailgate to look at the stars. Mark puts his arms around me. We kiss, long and slow and like we mean it. At this moment, I know something that I have never known before: *I'm falling in love.*

The next day, we hike for miles along the beach, wade the chest-deep Ozette River, and camp alone amongst huge sea stacks, beneath bluffs capped by thick forests of massive cedar and fir trees. We swim in the ocean in 75-degree weather, cook a luxurious dinner, and cap it off with Kahlua. Mark holds me close as the rare clear skies give us a spectacular sunset that fades ever so gradually into a star-filled night sky.

A week later, I am sitting at my desk in Talkeetna, as though awakening from a dream. Mark has taken a temporary job as an engineer for the fall in Seattle, while I will remain up here. It is painful to contemplate a long-distance relationship, but it is even more painful to imagine not trying at all. We commit to the long haul, and over the next three months, we take advantage of cheap airfares between Seattle and Anchorage and trade off flying back and forth.

In October, I bring Mark on one of my favorite hikes in Alaska, to the Juneau Lake cabin near my old home in Cooper Landing. In bitter cold, we walk through a foot of fresh snow for seven miles. Mark, in turn, takes me rock climbing at two of his favorite places in Washington: Index Town Walls, a series of steep granite cliffs about one hour east of Seattle; and Leavenworth, Washington, on the eastern slopes of the Cascade Mountains. In November, we have a Thanksgiving feast together at Talkeetna Air Taxi with Paul, Sue, and some local friends.

As Mark promised the previous spring, there is foreign travel in the works for us. Just before Christmas, Mark leaves his job at the engineering company, and I meet him in Seattle. We have decided on Costa Rica. With just $700 in cash to last us three weeks, we fly to San Jose and set out exploring the country. We ring in 1997 with our only splurge, a nicer hotel on the Caribbean coast, plus a lobster and ceviche dinner. We tent-camp on beaches in stifling humidity, haunted by the spooky calls of howler monkeys in the jungle, audible over the sound of the ocean. We endure horrendous ten-hour bus rides and numerous close calls with crazy drivers on mountain roads. I am stalked by a black panther on a jungle hike, we see jaguar tracks on the beach, and we cross river outlets along the coast said to be home to both sharks and crocodiles. We also see some of the most terrifying insects imaginable, including rainbow-colored spiders with two-inch-diameter bodies, centipedes, and some unidentified flying insect with an opaque body the size of a ping-pong ball whose attack has us spastically flailing our shirts and backpacks inside a cramped, unscreened shelter in a coastal national park. We also see many beautiful tropical birds, and a lot of dingy hotel rooms. We return home, spending our last $20 on the airport departure tax, but we are in fact quite rich — we are madly in love.

That spring of 1997, Mark makes a difficult decision to forego returning to his beloved job at Mount Rainier to move to Talkeetna to be with me. We rent a cabin a quarter mile from the road with no electricity and that requires hauling in water and firewood. It is hard living here in the crushing cold of this spring, and not even Cessna the cat is enjoying it.

After Mark and Joe spend April climbing in the Alaska Range, I'm feeling restless and ready for an adventure of my own. Some good weather is forecasted in a couple of days, and I lounge in the back room of Talkeetna Air Taxi reading *Fifty Classic Climbs of North America* while Mark prepares lunch.

"Hey, sweetie," I say, sitting up with a start. "The West Ridge of the Mooses Tooth looks like a great route. When Michelle and I skied around in there last spring, I was really impressed. We should climb it."

I know little more about it than what I have seen with my own eyes and what's in the book. I also have never climbed anything of this scale. The Mooses Tooth stands at 10,300 feet, and its West Ridge involves five thousand feet of snow and ice climbing.

"Are you ready for something that big?" Mark asks.

"I'm not sure. What do you think?"

"Well, you've climbed steep ice and you've climbed steep snow. The West Ridge has things that you've done before — just a lot of them all at once," Mark says. "But it's still a big mountain, and your experience with crevasse rescue is limited. I'll go with you, but I would feel better if we found a third."

"What about Todd Deis?" I reply, referring to my friend who has been hanging around Talkeetna Air Taxi in between climbs. "He's a good climber."

"Oh yeah, I'd be down with him," Mark says, his eyes lighting up.

It takes but a moment to find Todd outside, repairing his climbing gear on the tarmac.

"Hey, Todd," I shout. "You want to climb the Mooses Tooth with Mark and me? Weather looks good for the next week."

Todd bolts to his feet. "Hell yes!" he says.

Paul sets the three of us down on the Ruth Glacier the following evening, and by the next morning we are cramponing up steep snow through a broken icefall rising above the Ruth Glacier. Mark had touched on a good point back in Talkeetna. Breaking down a big climb is a matter of reducing it to little sections of things I have already done. Right now, we are walking uphill in snow, which I've done before, and what I will face up higher is unimportant in this moment. This approach makes the climb feel less overwhelming.

We bivouac on a level shoulder of the broad ridge about halfway up, and early the next morning, we depart for the summit. After a long climb up the snowy shoulder, we reach a rock buttress that has been looming above us. I have been wondering how we might get around it, but as we pull up and over a small saddle, the route above becomes clear — we'll bypass the buttress to the right, making a 100-foot traverse across a 50-degree rock slab coated with ice and frozen snow. On the far side of the traverse, a steep snow gully shoots up toward the summit ridge. Mark and Todd build a snow anchor, and then Mark leads across the traverse.

"The snow is thin, but it's nice and frozen. It's easy," Mark calls, and I relax. "There's no protection, though, so be careful," he adds, looking ahead to the gully.

I breathe easier, and soon Mark is anchored on the edge of the gully, belaying Todd and I across the slab. I feel free and confident as my crampons bite with a reassuring crunch into the firm snow, while several thousand feet of exposure fall away beneath us. A kick of each foot, a stab of my ice axe, repeat the process. Methodical and meditative.

Todd leads off up the narrow snow and ice gully above, which is lined with granite outcrops that have good cracks for placing protection. Steep, exposed snow and icefields follow, with Mark and Todd leading each pitch while I follow as the apprentice, marveling at the scenery and position. The sun shines unobstructed, and the massive granite peaks of the Ruth Gorge stand like sentinels opposite our location above the gorge's eastern flank.

The final ropelengths to the western summit of the Mooses Tooth are on a snow slope that starts at a lower angle but tilts up to 50-plus degrees. We climb together with protection but without a proper belay, believing it will be easy. Mark is in the lead, and near the top, far above his last protection, he sinks without warning to his waist in the snow, which then collapses. I watch as Mark's feet slide out from under him before he catches himself with his ice tools. It's at this moment I realize that the only protection anchoring us to the mountain is a single, skinny Knifeblade piton.

"Oh shit," Mark exclaims. "This snow is bad. Todd, put in an anchor and get me on belay."

I look down to see Todd digging a pit with urgency, to bury a snow picket. On instinct, I drive the shaft of my ice axe deep into the snow and clip into it.

Mark battles through and soon disappears over onto the west summit, followed a moment later by his joyous call:

"Off belay!"

The final section beneath Mark's belay is on the steepest snow I have ever climbed. Worse, it has the consistency of sugar, which makes every step feel as though it will give out. Now I understand.

Mark's belay location is stunning. The ridge crest just feet from us forms a near knife-edged fin of snow. On the opposite side, the mountain is far steeper than what we climbed, plunging away for thousands of feet at a precipitous angle. Meanwhile, the view across the shadowy north face of the Mooses Tooth reveals a nightmarish landscape of steep snow flutings and hanging glaciers perched above vertical granite cliffs far below. *I'm not in Connecticut anymore.*

"Great job, sweetie," Mark says, putting his arm around me as I sit beside him at his stance. The view is beautiful beyond measure, but I am consumed by fear and the staggering exposure on all sides. I can think of nothing else but how committed we are and the descent we still have awaiting us.

The main summit was never in our plan, and lies another mile to our east along a difficult, undulating, corniced ridge, which would take a strong team another full day to complete. We start down, and the first several rappels go by without incident. It is when we are in the snow-and-ice gully leading down to the slab traverse that the ropes fail to fall after one rappel, having hung up in the rocks above.

"Dammit," Mark exclaims, tying back into the free end of one ropes. "I'll go up and get them."

The sun sets behind the bulk of Denali, and a deep cold settles in as Mark climbs back up the gully. By the time Mark returns, I am chilled in a way I have never felt before: the cold in my core gives rise to a fading sense of focus, that I'm losing control of the situation, and that resistance is futile. Worse, our next step is to reverse the tenuous slab traverse, but now, the thin layer of snow that this morning had allowed easy passage has melted off in the afternoon sun, leaving only bare granite. I notice my breathing speed up as a sensation of raw fear boils up inside. I begin to shiver in uncontrollable fits. Todd looks at me with concern but remains silent as he stacks the rope. Mark notices, too. He places his hand on my shoulder and looks me in the eyes.

"You need to get it together for this, Lisa," he says, in a stern tone I've seldom seen him wield. Mark's words snap me back to attention.

After leading across the traverse, his crampon points balanced on miniscule edges, Mark belays, watching me closely as I climb. I'm belayed at one end by him and from the other by Todd, to minimize the swing if I fall. There are tiny patches of very thin ice, but for the most part, my crampons and ice tools scratch at what seems like holdless rock. My pendulum fall in Portage while ice climbing with Paul enters my mind, and now I am fighting off panic.

"Place the front point of your crampons on that rail to your left. Trust it," Mark says, noticing my distress. I obey the command.

"Now, keep your heels down and your feet still," he directs. "Tap your ice axe into that little patch of ice there. Not too hard. Now seat the pick. Keep it quiet. Trust it and focus."

One move follows another. It is both thrilling and meditative to see the picks of my ice tools seated on the tiny granite edges, and to experience the steel focus of my mind and body working in synchronicity. Mark gradually stops dictating instructions as I find my rhythm and figure out the moves on my own; before I know it, I am stepping down onto the safety of deep snow next to Mark. I have never felt such intensity in my life — this wild swing from feeling out of control to a deep, almost calming focus. Mark puts his arm around me.

"You did it, Lisa. Great job," he says. For the first time in my life, I feel like a mountain climber.

The stress of last season has made me choose not to work for my brother in the spring and summer of 1997. Instead, Mark and I find ourselves working for a local river-rafting company. The hours are long, the pay is low, and our budget has been tight. Frustrated, in early June, Mark makes some calls and lands a month of fill-in work for Rosewater Engineering, a civil-engineering company in Seattle. The lucrative pay makes his decision a no-brainer, but it also leaves us back in a long-distance relationship. Near the end of his term, Mark calls with more news.

"This company is paying me really well, and it's a great place to work. They've extended the offer and say that I can work here as long as I want."

"Okay," I reply, after an awkward pause. "So when will we see each other?"

"That's what I really wanted to talk about," Mark continues. "You said you were interested in going to massage school. I did some research, and Seattle has one of the best schools in the country for it. It's a yearlong program. Move down here with me, we'll bring Cessna, we'll get an apartment, and we'll live and work here for the next year. We'll make some money, and you'll get your license and your very own profession."

It is incredible what the right relationship can bring into one's life. With Mark, I feel like I have a support system that I never realized I needed. Going back to school has never seemed realistic after so many years of living paycheck to paycheck. Now, almost anything seems possible, including moving to Seattle. I contemplate my interest in massage therapy, a field that stands in stark contradiction to the chaos and stresses that have painted my life so far. Perhaps it's the path that I need.

I enroll at Brenneke School of Massage, and Mark and I rent an apartment in the Queen Anne neighborhood, a few blocks from my school and a twenty-minute walk to Mark's office downtown. I attend classes five days a week, and I find a part-time job working in the factory at Feathered Friends, a high-end outdoor clothing and gear company that specializes in down jackets and sleeping bags. Navigating the buses and traffic to work and back to school in this giant city is intimidating, but I am finding my way. Best of all, at the end of each day of classes, Mark is waiting outside to walk with me back to our apartment.

School and work keep me busy, but I am also getting rather swept up in the climbing lifestyle and in Mark's large network of friends, most of whom are dedicated climbers. Mark and I join a climbing gym, and together we climb several beautiful peaks and rock spires in the North Cascades, including Liberty Bell, South Early Winters Spire, and Silver Star Mountain, the latter in a 5,000-vertical-foot day from the car. I am also growing to love rock climbing as an activity by itself, and we spend many weekends cragging in places like Index, Vantage, and Leavenworth. Though I am always the slower member of the team — especially on the trails — Mark always seems content to wait for me. At the same time, I'm growing frustrated because no matter how much I train, be it for climbing or hiking, progress seems to elude me. More specifically, I just feel dogged by inexplicable fatigue on these outings, with inadequate reserves. I also have trouble managing both heat and cold. *Is there something wrong with me? These issues are not my normal.* I don't feel sick, but it's clear that something external is sapping my energy levels. I am only 29, so perhaps it's just operator error? I resolve to dig deeper and to try harder.

Through my relationship with Mark, I am also feeling a thread of kinship with Barbara Washburn, the wife of the famed explorer and cartographer Bradford Washburn. Barbara, who in 1947 became the first woman to climb Denali, acknowledged that one of her primary motivations for climbing was to be with her husband. I do love to climb, but I am not as ambitious about it as Mark, and climbing with him is also a vehicle for maintaining our connection. And, of course, I also want to watch out for him. I cannot shake the feeling that I failed my own mother long ago, and that I am now *compelled* to play the protector for the people whom I care about most.

I graduate from school in August of 1998, newly certified as a Licensed Massage Practitioner. Mark is back working at Mount Rainier again for the summer, after almost a year at Rosewater Engineering.

"Amy" — the owner — "told me I can temp here any time I want, as long they have the workload," Mark said, when he left the company last spring for Rainier. Between this fortuitous arrangement and my plan to start my own private massage-therapy business in Talkeetna, we each now have a solid means to support ourselves as well as flexible schedules to travel and climb when we desire.

It is late winter of 1999. Mark and I are back at work in Seattle after an autumn spent rock climbing in Yosemite and the deserts of California. Joe, Mark, and I are gathered up after work one day to discuss upcoming plans. Another spring climbing season in the Alaska Range is taking shape, and this time, I intend to build upon my experience on the Mooses Tooth by joining the boys for a climb. I've been psyching myself up all winter. I want to challenge myself like never before, and I want to be a stronger partner for Mark both on the mountain and off. And, of course, I am compelled to watch out for him and for Joe.

"I'd like to climb Mount Russell," I say, as we discuss possible objectives.

"Russell looks awesome. I'm down," Joe says, and Mark agrees, saying, "It's a badass mountain. Let's go for it." The three of us high-five.

Several weeks later, the three of us have our gear spread across the floor in the Talkeetna Air Taxi back office. We stuff countless granola bars, oatmeal packets, and various easy-to-cook meals into freezer bags. "I'm psyched to be packing all this food and gear *with* you, instead of *for* you," I remark, studying a photo of the mountain. I had long fixed my gaze on this pyramid-shaped peak, far west of Denali, visible on the skyline as one drives past the overlook on the way into Talkeetna. It sticks up like a shark's fin, beckoning out of the surrounding landscape of wind-battered mountains like a siren.

"You guys will be heroes if you get up Russell," Paul says as he observes our preparations. "That's a good one." Paul's endorsement holds real weight amongst our group. Mark, Joe, and I each want to make him proud.

Only five parties have stood on the summit of remote Mount Russell, and only one woman. At just below 12,000 feet, it's situated in a relative low point of the Alaska Range which, during storms, amplifies the air currents into ferocious wind velocities for its altitude — they're more in line with what one might find on the upper reaches of Denali. We're going to attempt the Northeast Ridge, one of only three routes completed to the summit and the only one that's ever been repeated. It's regarded as the "normal route" — for all of its three total ascents. The only photos we have are in the *American Alpine Journal*. They don't tell a complete story, but the reports from prior ascensionists describe the ridge as a steep, glaciated buttress split by crevasses and blocked by occasional walls of near-vertical ice. Reports of extensive rime ice coating the upper slopes — like that found in Peru's Cordillera Blanca — foretell of the mountain's legendary, moisture-laden winds.

"This," Mark says, turning his gaze toward Joe and me, "should be a *real* adventure."

There is a common refrain in the climbing community: "A good alpinist has a poor memory." As I recall my time on the flanks of the Mooses Tooth, my first alpine climb, what stands out most vividly in my mind are the exhilarating positions, the exposure, and the sense of accomplishment I felt in overcoming my fears. Near forgotten are the raw fears themselves: the cold, the uncertainty, the exhaustion, and the metallic taste of anxiety that boiled up in my throat as I tiptoed across that exposed granite slab in the gloaming.

Being a successful alpinist requires the ability to stow away the fear and anxiety over the possible adverse consequences of a climb, and focus instead on the ambiguous promise of personal glory, and maybe, of some transcendent experience that might await. I wonder if, in climbing, my subconscious self is gravitating toward both the reward and the danger. Growing up on the family farm was marked by constant drama. My father's temper and strict expectations, tending to sick or injured farm animals, our wild neighborhood parties, our family's predilection for risk in both work and play, and even my mother's tragic death are constant reminders that every phase of my life has been flooded with adrenaline. Just look at the Roderick legacy: Paul flies airplanes through glaciated mountains in Alaska. My brother Mark raced in competitive motocross, and my father even once raced cars. Perhaps, then, it is unsurprising that

I have found love with an alpinist, and now have my own stirring ambitions to scale steep glaciated mountains in one of Earth's most hostile environments.

Chapter Three
My Place Among Giants

"How about now, Paul?"

The Alaska satellite imagery on the computer screen shows that a large area of clearing is coming our way.

Paul walks over, leans in, and toggles between the satellite images and the aviation weather maps on the computer. "Eh, it's still shaking out a little, but it'll happen tomorrow," he says. Paul is always right about the weather.

This is our fifth day of waiting to fly into Mount Russell, and Mark, Joe, and I have been spending our days pacing the floor of Talkeetna Air Taxi and checking the weather every hour. It is well below freezing here in Talkeetna, and I am starting to wonder about the wisdom of attempting this mountain in late March. Sometimes, however, motivation overrules wisdom.

That motivation also allows us to brush off the huge, comma-shaped mass of clouds spooling up on the satellite image right behind the promised clearing. If I'm reading the maps right, a large storm is coming in right behind the weather window that we will be using to fly into the mountains tomorrow.

"I've never paid my dues in the Alaska Range," I announce, as we lounge in the back room. At this, Joe stiffens up and looks at me as though I have just cursed the almighty.

"I can't believe you just said that," he says in a hushed tone. "You're poking the bear."

I look to Mark, who just raises his eyebrows. They have seen a side to these mountains that I have not yet experienced, and I sense that I may have just violated a sacred alpine superstition.

Paul is right — again. The following day dawns crystal clear, and soon after we finish loading the plane, we are airborne. I sit mesmerized, as that distant mountain I have for so long admired is growing larger and ever more menacing through the windscreen of the Cessna 185.

Mount Russell is so much more intimidating than I imagined. Steep-sided ridges of perfect symmetry adorned with fantastic towers of rime ice are separated by precipitous faces decorated with enormous hanging glaciers. It looks just as a real mountain should look. My inexperience as a climber is all at once palpable, and as I scan the jagged right-hand skyline of Russell's Northeast Ridge, I cannot imagine any possible way to climb it.

Paul sets the plane down on the deep powder snow of the Yentna Glacier at 8,000 feet. The mountain towers above us, and I step out of the airplane into a deep, biting cold.

"You ready for this, Lulu?" Paul asks. *He senses my apprehension.*

"I guess so," I say, trying to project confidence. Paul knows me better than that.

"The boys will take care of you," he reassures. "I'll come scoop you guys up in six days. Go get it."

As Mark, Joe, and I huddle over our pile of gear, Paul throttles up the engine and accelerates away from us, blasting us with cold powder snow that sparkles in the sunlight. The roar of the airplane's engine gives way to a pitched hum reverberating off the nearby mountain faces, then a clearer buzz as the plane lifts off into the sky. The plane banks to the right, silhouetted against the distant bulk of Mount Foraker, before it disappears behind a low ridge and plunges us into a lonesome and uneasy silence. *I feel very committed.*

"Weather's perfect. We should start climbing now," Joe states matter-of-factly as he applies sunscreen and admires the mountain.

"Agree," Mark concurs. "You good with that plan, Lulu?"

I nod and begin organizing. We load our packs for a three-day ascent. Today, we will start right in, climbing a steep face of snow and ice rising over 1,500 vertical feet above the glacier and which begins just half a mile from where we now stand. The slope leads to a bench on the Northeast Ridge, where we anticipate camping tonight. Tomorrow, we will traverse the level ridge to the main peak, which rises another 2,000 vertical feet at a much steeper angle. To my untrained eye, this section appears almost impossible. Huge crevasses and walls of vertical to overhanging ice appear to block passage in several places. Mark notices me evaluating it with concern.

"We'll find a way around those obstacles. Don't worry," he says, but his voice betrays some uncertainty of his own.

We ski to the face, put on our crampons, and begin ascending a smooth wall of steep, hard snow. My lungs ache in the cold, and as we make steady progress up the 50-degree snow and ice, my calves burn and cramp. *Too late to train more now.* Mark is in the lead, while I am tied into the middle of the rope, and Joe is in the back. Mark places occasional snow pickets and ice screws for protection as the exposure grows beneath us. I kick the frontpoints of my crampons into the hard surface in a methodic rhythm, plant the spike of my ice axe, step up, and repeat the process.

Our ascent proceeds without issue until high on the face, when I hear Joe shouting from below.

"I don't like the looks of this. We've got to move," he exclaims, pointing to the sky.

I have been so focused on my footing, axe placements, and burning calf muscles that I have paid little attention to the weather. In just the past two hours, the morning's beautiful blue skies have turned an ominous white, and the sun now sports a halo. Thick, high cirrus clouds with the classic "mare's tail" hook formations streak over the Alaska Range. All these features are common harbingers of an incoming storm. The satellite image didn't lie.

Almost on cue, the air comes to life with a slight ripple that chills one to the bone in an instant. Soon after, the wind begins to blow with determined force. A lenticular cloud cap forms like a hovering saucer over Mount Russell's summit, spreading rapidly down the flanks of the mountain. Every time I look up, the cloud ceiling has dropped. I place one foot in front of the other, but I can go no faster and my body's core temperature plummets. I now recall with regret the moments that I brushed off Mark's encouragement to train harder while in Seattle this past winter.

In Seattle, Mark was insistent that we climb or hike every weekend, climb in the gym at least twice a week, and do intense cardio sessions or weight training. I had never formally trained for anything as I'd always approached sports recreationally. It was evident that Mark viewed climbing — especially in Alaska — as something far more serious than recreational, and he trained relentlessly, whether he was in the mood for it or not.

During the winter, I trained at a level and frequency that was hard for me — but only when I was in the mood, that mood often tempered by fluctuating energy levels. Underlying this was the persistent lethargy and fatigue that had been dogging me, particularly when it came to cardiovascular activities. Still, I did my best. What I didn't fully realize — until now — was that the goal of all this repetitive training was not only for performance; it was also connected to survival.

"You have to make yourself bulletproof for any situation," Mark warned me repeatedly, but I, ever the optimist, believed I was prepared and that everything would work out.

Now — in the teeth of this growing gale — I understand.

As the angle of the face eases off onto the plateau above, we are met with the full fury of the gale. The sky has met the ground, and we are engulfed in a blizzard. Ice pellets blast against my face amid staggering gusts. *How can the weather change so fast?*

In a defensive move, I don my goggles. They fog up in an instant, and although my face is warmer, now I can't see. Without warning, Joe pulls up alongside me.

"Lisa, are you okay?" he screams over the wind.

"I'm really cold," I reply.

"You have to move — we've got to make it to camp now!" he yells, before bolting ahead toward Mark, a dark shape barely visible through the murk.

I continue my slow march, leaning into the wind, snow, and ice crystals spattering against my face and jacket as I keep my head down and follow the rope connecting me to Mark. The rope stops moving, and a moment later, I look up to see Mark holding out a large down jacket.

"Put this on," he says over the wind's incessant roar. "Joe's going to find us a level spot and start digging in. But you have to move faster. Right now, Lisa — this is serious!"

Mark's face mask and hood are plastered in ice. Through his

goggles, I see fear in his eyes.

For the next several minutes, Mark walks alongside me, encouraging me to move like our lives depend on it. Because, they do. Visibility is less than fifty feet, and at last, ahead through the grim maelstrom, I can make out the dim outline of Joe's figure, shoveling furiously.

Mark, Joe, and I erect the tent in a frantic environment, taking care to anchor it as we work to avoid having it fly away like a kite. I hold the fabric steady as they push the poles through the sleeves, while I pause now and then to pinwheel my arms and dance in place to stay warm. *This is desperate.* The relief of taking shelter in the tent, sipping hot drinks, and savoring the warmth of our sleeping bags is soon supplanted by the harrowing reality that we are bivouacked on a high, exposed ridge in the teeth of a raging Alaskan storm. I have never seen my life change so quickly — *so this is alpinism.*

Until now, my perception of 'survival' was working nine to five, trying to pay the bills, and living on my own at age 17. Here, pinned on the edge of a remote mountain in the Alaska Range, my entire life has been distilled down to my connection with my climbing partners, keeping hydrated and warm, and waiting with no assurance for an opportunity to escape to safety. There is no one who can help us now but ourselves.

The tent slams and shakes and trembles with each furious gust as we consume our hot, freeze-dried meals, rehydrate our enervated bodies with one hot drink after another, and bury ourselves deep inside our sleeping bags for the night. I awaken in the morning to a reassuring stillness. The wind has ceased. Mark stirs, and then peeks outside.

"There's a few clouds around, but it looks pretty good," he reports.

"Great," Joe says. "Let's get the hell out of here while we still can."

We pack up in the frigid temperatures, doing as much as possible inside the tent to delay the inevitable discomfort of exiting into the elements. Now, it's time. Boots and thick gloves pulled on, hats and facemasks in place, we step outside into sunny skies and a light but bone-chilling breeze. The whiteout of the previous afternoon obscured the stunning view that greets us now. Mount Russell stabs into the air a mere half mile down the ridge, its icy obstacles even more menacing up close. To the north and far beneath, a windswept glacier carves a serpentine path between craggy lowland foothills. At its terminus, a frozen river bar winds away into a rolling, infinite, tundra landscape stretching toward a distant horizon. In the opposite direction, the inconceivable mass of 17,400-foot Mount Foraker — Sultana to the native Athabaskan people — stands across the Yentna Glacier, with Denali hulking over its shoulder as a reminder of its dominating height. The twin summits of 14,500-foot Mount Hunter — "Begguya" to the Athabaskans — stand to the right, and to the right of that, a sea of lower-altitude but jagged granite mountains gradually gives way to the vast boreal forests south of the Alaska Range. Somewhere in that far distance lies Talkeetna, and the comforts of home for which I now have a far more acute appreciation. *We must be in one of the wildest places on Earth.*

Our packs loaded, the three of us walk down the slope a few hundred feet until it becomes steep enough that we need to turn face-in and downclimb. It steepens further, and now Mark and Joe rig a snow anchor using aluminum pickets. Mark rappels a full ropelength, places another snow anchor, I rappel to him, and we wait together, attached to the anchor, while Joe retrieves the upper anchor and climbs down to us as Mark belays him. We repeat this process until we've safely crossed a large crevasse at the foot of the slope, arriving back at our cached skis. The sun has been ducking in and out of view behind wispy clouds and vapor throughout our descent, but now it emerges in full, and its faint warmth brings us cheer. Mount Russell knifes skyward in defiance.

A short ski down the glacier brings us back to where Paul left us off only yesterday. We dig through two feet of fresh snow to find the bags of supplies we'd left behind, the cache marked by a tall wand with a flag on top. We erect the tent, get rehydrated, load up on calories, and then begin wondering what to do next. Paul isn't due in to pick us up for another four days, and our only means of communication is a CB radio, which requires a line-of-sight that we don't have, or the hope that a plane monitoring the CB emergency channel 19 might pass overhead.

Mark and Joe stare at the mountain with longing. "Maybe after we regroup for a day or so, if the weather holds, we can try again," Mark muses as Joe nods in approval. I keep my thoughts to myself. *I'm over it.*

We don't have long to ponder our next move. The gentle calm of the noon hour soon gives way to the familiar sight of high clouds streaking in again from the southwest, and along with it, the wind. By nightfall, we are in another full-throated blizzard.

"Your turn to dig, Joe," I say, climbing back inside the tent, my clothes plastered with snow. Joe is already suited up for his shift, and as soon as I'm clear of the door, he climbs outside to continue the endless task of digging out the tent. If we don't stay on top of it, the snow will collapse the tent, burying us.

The blizzard continues for the rest of the day and the two that follow. In between shifts outside digging, we play cards, the boys tell stupid jokes, we listen to music on our headphones, and we play the portable AM/FM radio for news from Anchorage. I have brought a very warm sleeping bag, and I soon discover one of the advantages to being stormbound in a basecamp setting is getting caught up on sleep.

Late on what is now our fourth day in the mountains, the storm begins to clear and the Anchorage news is calling for a day of "partly cloudy" weather.

"I've been thinking," Joe says, looking with intention toward Mark and me. "I bet if we leave behind the bivy gear, we can knock this thing out in one long day." Mark approves, and gives me a gentle bump with his elbow: "What do you think?"

"I'm out, you guys," I say, shaking my head and revealing the doubts that I've been harboring. "That storm up there was scary enough. You guys go send it, and I'll stay here and pack down the runway for us so we'll be ready to go when Paul gets here in a couple days."

"Are you sure?" Mark asks. Mark always asks twice before letting me off the hook. It's sweet, but it's sometimes annoying. I know what I want.

"Yes, sweetie," I reply, taking a deep breath. "I don't think this is a climb for me, and I think I overestimated my abilities."

Mark looks sad for a moment. He sighs, glances at Joe, and says, "Okay then. It's up to us."

Early the next morning under brilliant, clear skies and sunshine, I watch as the boys click into their skis and shoulder their packs.

"Be careful up there, you guys," I caution, slapping them high-fives and trying to project confidence. In my mind, of course, I'm tortured by worry. *What on Earth will I do if they don't come back?*

As Mark and Joe ski away toward Mount Russell, I put on my skis and set to work packing down the snow for a runway, preferring the tedious labor over sitting idle in the striking silence with worry as my only companion. Paul wants his climbers to pack down the runway with skis or snowshoes after snowfalls of six inches or greater. We have had at least three feet of new snow, and without skis, I'm sinking in over my knee. Paul wants the strip to be at least one thousand feet long and about twenty feet wide. My work is cut out for me — just the way I like it.

As I work, I watch the boys dispatch the steep snow face in half the time it took the three of us, then they disappear onto the ridge. Several hours later, and after many passes up and down the glacier, I'm admiring my perfect, well-packed runway when I notice them return into view and begin descending the face. *There's no way they made the summit that fast. Something must have stopped them.*

When Mark and Joe reach their skis at the base of the face, I fire up the stove to have hot drinks ready, and then retrieve more snacks from the food bag. Before long, I hear voices approaching.

"Nice runway, Lisa," Joe exclaims as he skies into camp.

"Thanks," I reply. "It's almost like I found my calling in life. How did it go?"

Joe swings his pack down off his back, and it lands on the snow with a concussive thud.

"We only got halfway down the ridge and the snow kept making big *'whumphfing'* noises," Joe says with a cringing expression. "It was all wind-loaded, way too dangerous. And, you might have been right, Lisa — that upper ridge looked really broken up by seracs. Honestly, I'm not so sure it would go."

Mark skies up a moment later, dumps his pack, and turns toward Joe, raising his hand in expectation. Joe and Mark's hands connect in a high-five with a loud snap, remaining clasped as they stare each other down. *This must be another movie-scene re-enactment.*

I roll my eyes and hand them mugs of steaming-hot tea.

"Alright, you two. You need to get some new material. Let's get out of here tomorrow."

We scan the sky. For the first time, the clear day seems to be holding strong. We all take a few more ski laps on the runway together and then retire to the tent. "Can't wait for those burgers at the Latitude," Mark says.

"Or the McKinley Sundae," Joe adds.

"Rum and cokes at the Fairview," I offer.

In the morning, I awaken to a distressing sound. The tent walls are flapping in the wind. I pull my head out from my thick sleeping bag to assess. Snowflakes hiss against the nylon, and a dull roar emanates from somewhere high above. Mark emerges from his bag. "Oh, no way," he exclaims, rolling up on his side and opening the tent to survey the scene. "It's totally socked in. We're in a full-on storm." Mark ducks his head back inside and then stares at Joe and me, scowling in frustration. I look at my watch. It's 5:00 a.m.

"So much for getting out today," I remark, stating the obvious as I fire up the stove to melt snow for water.

Over the next several hours, the wind increases and batters the tent even harder, snapping it against our faces. The three of us work through breakfast with dejected faces, the radio forecast calling for rain in Anchorage for days ahead. We resign ourselves to a prolonged wait — we've brought enough food and fuel for ten days total, so hopefully we're picked up before then.

Late in the morning, as the tempest continues outside, Joe bolts upright. "Do you hear that?" he asks. We all sit up and listen. Now I hear it: the unmistakable sound of a plane engine. Mark opens the tent door and vestibule; wind-driven snow blasts inside as our three heads poke out into the storm. Far down-glacier, amid broken clouds, a Cessna 185 is just visible, circling through the murk.

"That's Paul, alright," Mark says. "How the hell did he make it in here?"

I turn on the CB radio and I shout as I key the mike:

"Hey, Paul, is that you? What are you doing?"

"Hey there, Lulu. How's the wind down there?" Paul responds.

"Paul, there's no way you can land here, the wind is blowing thirty to forty; snow is blowing everywhere; the visibility is terrible. You should go back."

I flash a glance at Mark and Joe to gauge their approval. We are all desperate to get out, so turning down a potential ride out is hard to swallow. "Yeah, this is way too gnarly, even for Paul," Joe says, as Mark nods in affirmation.

Paul's reply squawks back over the radio: "Yeah, maybe." *Oh my god. He's still thinking of trying it.*

"I mean," Paul continues, "it *is* pretty bumpy up here, and, WHOA!"

An awkward pause follows, as Mark, Joe, and I stare at one another slack-jawed. *What just happened?*

I exhale in relief as Paul resumes talking. "Okay, yeah, that's it. I'm getting rocked. I'm out of here. Sorry, y'all — I'll try again when the weather improves," he says. I believe that I just heard something that I have never before heard in Paul's voice: fear.

It is a sad and lonesome moment as his plane drones away down the valley, replaced by the sound of snow pellets crackling against our tent. Mark, Joe, and I settle back in for a long vigil, one which now will include my worrying about whether Paul made it back to

Talkeetna.

Each day, the Anchorage radio station promises a "partly cloudy" day tomorrow, only to be replaced by "rain likely," which can't be good news for us high up here in the mountains. The temperature plummets at night, and our breath condenses into thick hoar frost on the walls of the tent, only to be shaken off by the wind and onto our sleeping bags and faces. The tent is being drifted over with no respite, requiring us to resume taking digging shifts outside.

At last, three days after Paul came so close to getting us, we emerge from the tent into piercing blue skies and calm conditions. I stand to shake off the stiffness of lying down for most of the past seventy-two hours; Mark shovels nearby in search of our buried duffel bags as I start the stove to melt snow. "Found them," Mark cries out. "There's about four feet of new snow." I glance up, noting a smooth, pristine blanket of snow where my runway once was.

"We have a lot of work to do," I announce, as the three of us click into our skis and grumble.

"I can't believe it's our tenth day," I exclaim hours later, as Mark, Joe, and I stand on the glacier, admiring our new, well-packed runway.

"It feels like a month," Joe replies.

"Paul should be here any time," I say, looking over toward Mount Foraker beaming in the sunshine. Every mountain I can see is plastered white, and vapor forms on the ridgetops above the sun-washed slopes warming beneath them.

"I think I hear a plane," Joe says, raising his head. "For real this time."

Sometimes, the air in the Alaska Range is so still and silent that it induces a phenomenon in which anxious climbers awaiting a pickup will hallucinate airplane sounds. Each of us has fallen victim to this for the past several days, and we have already had several false alarms this morning alone.

I cock my head to listen, and this time, it is no hallucination. The sound of a plane reverberates off the mountains somewhere down the glacier. It must be Paul. Mark and Joe race back toward the tent to begin packing, but after a few minutes, the sound fades away. Then, it's gone.

Hours pass, and the air remains cold and silent. "Why would Paul not come on a day like this?" we each say in revolving bouts of complaining, and indeed it makes no sense. Now, the blue skies are changing to white, and the mare's tail clouds began their familiar and haunting approach. Our freeze-dried dinners are reconstituting with boiling water as the first flakes of snow begin falling and the dreaded wind returns.

A too-familiar process ensues as the evening progresses towards twilight. I pull on every warm layer I have, followed by my hardshell pants and jacket, then my balaclava, the hood of my jacket, and last, my goggles, mitts, and boots. I can hear Joe gasping outside, his shovel blade scraping against the snow, each scoop relieving the pressure on our sad, sagging tent. Joe has made three laps around the tent already, and when he tires, it will be my turn to dig. Soon, Joe piles into the tent, his face caked in snow.

"Jesus Christ," he gasps, ripping his goggles off as he zips the door shut and begins removing his boots while picking large chunks of ice from his bushy black beard. "It's impossible to keep up with it. We just have to keep digging,"

I step out into a ferocious and disorienting whiteout. I take a few steps and realize that if I wander more than a few meters from the tent, I might never find my way back. I begin digging out the tent's vestibule, then continue shoveling around the perimeter, careful to avoid cutting the nylon with the shovel blade. By the time I return to the starting point, the vestibule is as buried as when I started. I take another lap. And another. The tent is just becoming entombed in a deep hole as the glacier surface around us continues to increase in elevation, and the wind wants to fill in that hole with the copious snow falling from the sky. The walls of the hole are becoming so high that I struggle to throw the snow high enough to get it out. *This is futile.*

"Okay, Mark. Your turn," I say as I dive inside and Joe hands me a hot drink. A now battle-ready Mark pulls his goggles over his eyes and disappears into the tempest. The sun has set, and now we are wrapped in darkness.

The constant shaking and trembling of the tent give way to violent gusts that slam the tent's roof and walls down close to our faces. Sometimes it feels as though large men are running toward the tent and throwing their bodies against our fragile shelter.

In the middle of the night, a gust bigger than any we've yet experienced compresses the wall on Mark's side of the tent for a long moment. I watch as Mark battles his way out of his sleeping bag and pushes both hands against the unyielding fabric. It's like an elephant has sat on him. "Help me!" Mark shouts, panic in his voice. Joe and I scramble to reposition ourselves, and soon all three of us sit side by side, pushing with our backs against the windward side of the tent, trying to relieve the strain. Still cocooned in our sleeping bags, we make an aggressive brace, eyeing with apprehension the tent's stressed and stretching seams. The dim light of my headlamp reveals a haunted fear in the eyes of my companions, a strange and comforting affirmation of my own feelings amid this shared traumatic experience. Overhead, an unrelenting, apocalyptic roar crashes down from the sky. The jet stream is pointed straight at us, and we are wide awake in a terrifying, subarctic nightmare.

When daylight returns, the snowfall continues but the violent wind begins to subside to a mere annoyance. Mark leans out into the vestibule. He shakes one of the fuel cans, then digs around in the food bag.

"We have a problem," Mark announces, turning back towards Joe and me. The conversation we have all known was coming is now about to happen.

We planned this trip for six days, but we brought a total of ten days of food to account for contingencies. Today is day twelve. Food and fuel rationing began several days ago, but with supplies now at critical levels, it's time to cut back even further. Breakfast today is one packet of dry oatmeal for each person, and we each get one liter of cold water for the entire day. Late in the morning, Joe produces a single, king-sized Snickers bar from the food bag. Three sets of anxious eyes watch as he cuts it into three pieces, Mark and I supervising to ensure that the portions are perfectly equal.

"Here is your food for today," Joe announces, his tone theatrical. "And here's yours, and here's mine," he continues, as he places each diminutive piece of Snickers into our respective, trembling palms.

"We'll split this single freeze-dried meal between the three of us this evening," Mark adds, holding up a 600-calorie packet of Mountain House Rice with Chicken. "We've only got one more."

As the morning progresses, the only diversions the radio can offer us are overplayed 1970s rock tunes, country music, and a "partly cloudy" Anchorage forecast that keeps getting pushed back by a day. Joe puts his math degree to work by trying to solve the math problem presented as the Sunday puzzle on the radio. Mark and Joe read and re-read aloud the children's trivia printed on our instant-oatmeal packets, and we become learned experts on subjects such as "Dino-Data."

Tired and hungry, we make fewer trips outside to shovel, yielding some ground to the onslaught of drifting snow. On the night of our thirteenth day on this mountain, where we have spent more than twice as long as we intended, the sound of snow pellets crackling against our half-buried tent yet again lulls us to sleep. Our senses are dulled and stifled; hope has become a dangerous proposition.

I awaken to a peculiar sound. The sound of silence. *Are we completely buried?* I open my eyes and peek over the soggy draft collar of my sleeping bag. The sides of the tent are pushed in by all the new snow, and the three of us are now squashed together like sardines in the center of the tent. Every square inch of the tent surface is coated in a thick layer of hoar-frost crystals. The slightest movement knocks them loose, and they drop straight down onto my face to deliver a shocking, cold sensation. The air is more frigid now than it has been since the storm began, which means the clouds must be gone.

"Mark, Joe," I whisper. "Wake up. I think it's cleared off."

Mark stirs, sitting upright, his head brushing against the hoar and leaving a white stripe across his stocking cap. He crawls to the door, unzips it, and reaches outside with a gloved hand to sweep what looks like several feet of fresh, powdery snow off the vestibule. As he burrows through the exit, I spy a ray of sunshine illuminating the arm of his fleece jacket. Mark whoops with joy.

"Splitter," he announces. "We're going home."

"Assuming Paul comes," I say.

Mark pulls on his boots and goes outside. "There's got to be at least another five to six feet of new snow. It is chest deep out here," he says with astonishment.

"Do we even have the energy to stomp a runway?" Joe asks.

"I'm so hungry and weak I can't stand it," Mark replies, crawling back inside. "I bet Paul will be here long before we can do anything useful. Let's just get packed."

In less than an hour, the prominent droning noise we have all been dreaming about reaches our ears from far down the Yentna Glacier. "We're saved," Joe says with a faux dramatic voice, as I fumble for the radio.

"Good morning, Paul."

"There you are," Paul replies. "Hey, where's my runway?"

"Sorry, Paul," I counter. "As you might have guessed, we've had some problems here."

"Alright, well I'll have to lay tracks and make a few passes," he says. "Get yourselves packed up." Paul circles overhead, and then banks for a landing.

The plane touches down and looks like a ship parting the waters as columns of snow spray out to each side. At the far end of the runway, Paul labors to turn the plane around and, without stopping, guns the engine and pushes the plane back down the glacier for a long takeoff run. He repeats this landing-and-takeoff process three times before he pulls up alongside our camp and shuts down.

"What happened in here?" Paul cries, as he steps out of the aircraft and drops past his waist in the snow. "Why didn't you guys pack a runway?" Mark, Joe, and I are almost too tired for words.

"Sorry. We've had very little to eat for the past three days," Mark answers in a sad voice. "There's six feet of new snow, it just cleared up this morning, and we just didn't have the time or energy."

Paul's tone and expression soften as he surveys the scene. "Dang, must have been pretty rowdy in here," he says.

"You have any food, Paul?" Joe interjects, a pleading expression on his face.

"Yeah, hang on a sec." Paul roots around inside the plane for a moment, then tosses a box of Oreos to us. "Sorry, that's all I've got." The three of us tear into the cookies like crazed animals.

"Were you trying to get in when it was nice four days ago?" I ask. "We heard a plane, but then it went away."

"That was me," Paul acknowledges. "I'd almost made it in here, but the wind was blasting me down in the canyon and I was sure it would be worse up this way. It wasn't windy here?"

"Not at all — it was perfect," Mark says. "We heard you, and we were all packed and psyched. Then we got nuked for another four days."

"Ah, shoot," Paul replies, kicking his foot at the snow. "I guess I should have kept on going." Paul scans the deep tracks down the glacier that he just created with his plane. "This takeoff is going to be an interesting one," he muses.

Mark, Joe, and I tear down the tent, finish a haphazard job of packing, and get everything into the plane. Paul pushes the throttle, and the plane slides down the runway slowly. Very slowly. The airplane struggles downhill in the deep snow and toward the broken icefall far below us, and soon I cannot deny the obvious: *We are not gaining speed.* Mark looks over at me and just shakes his head as the brink of the icefall grows closer by the second. With an abrupt motion, Paul pulls back the throttle, and the plane stops cold. My mind races. *What is going on?*

"Sorry, guys," Paul says. "The snow's too deep."

ARE YOU FUCKING KIDDING ME?

Paul can read my mind via my dumbfounded facial expression.

"Lulu, you have to get out of the plane," Paul says, glancing over his shoulder from his pilot's seat. He isn't smiling. "I need you all to push the plane back up the runway."

I take a deep breath, climb out with Mark and Joe, and plunge past my waist in the snow.

The three of us push on the strut of the plane to help get it turned around as Paul throttles the engine. Once aligned with his tracks and now pointing uphill, Paul increases the power as we push against the struts, digging into the soft snow with our feet. Powder blasts our faces accompanied by the acrid smell of aviation fuel, and before long, I'm exhausted and nauseated. I cannot keep up, but Mark and Joe battle on a bit longer as the plane gains uphill speed and then outpaces them. I see Joe drop to his knees, dry-heaving, joined soon after by Mark, who is doubled over and gasping.

Once we recover, Mark and I plod our way uphill while Joe powers ahead of us and to where Paul waits at the top of the runway, by our old camp. I keep my head down, never looking up so I won't know how far I have to go. Then, I hear a peculiar sound, and what I see when I look up is shocking: Paul's airplane is bearing down on us at takeoff speed.

"Move left," Mark implores, as the two of us shuffle out of the way and the plane roars overhead. Now I'm confused. *Where is Joe?* Looking up toward camp a few hundred yards away, I see a pile of gear — but no Joe. I understand, but I can't accept it.

"Did he take Joe? Is he coming back?" I shout to Mark.

"He was too heavy, Lisa," Mark counsels. "He had to leave some gear and take only one person. He'll be back for us."

At our old campsite, Mark begins sorting through the gear Joe and Paul had unloaded in their haste.

"Well, they took the tent," Mark says, slamming a pack down in the snow. With increasing urgency, Mark rifles through another bag, his motions revealing a growing sense of panic.

"What's wrong?" I ask.

"What the fuck?" Mark yells, then turns toward me with a look of exasperation, throwing his hands in the air. "They took the stove, and all the shovels, too."

Mark and I are in the Alaska Range with no shelter, no shovels, and no way to make water. In their haste to depart, they have unintentionally left us without survival gear. I swallow hard and scan the sky, noticing the high clouds again advancing.

"Oh well," Mark says with resignation, as the two of us began walking in a forty-foot-diameter circle in the snow to keep warm.

"We've got the pot, I can dig a snow cave with that," Mark says, talking to himself as he paces. "We have a couple liters of water — let's keep that in our jackets so it doesn't freeze." The sky turns white, and the clouds continue to thicken. Sixty interminable minutes pass, which is a remarkable turnaround, before Paul's plane comes buzzing around the corner and glides in for a landing.

"As we unloaded in Talkeetna, we noticed we took all of your survival gear," Paul acknowledges with a chuckle as he exits the plane. "I refueled and got back in the air as fast as I could."

"Well, thanks for getting us out of here. You always have to make everything as exciting as possible — right, big brother?" I say, as Paul laughs out loud.

"Alright," Paul says. "Get on board. Let's get you two home and get you fed."

As the plane becomes airborne, I can finally exhale. I glance out the window and back toward the now cloud-capped Mount Russell, looking more savage and mysterious than before. Mark sits beside me, his gaze fixed with longing upon the *Infinite Spur* on Mount Foraker, the ridge slashing up the mountain's 9,000foot south face looming out the left window of the airplane.

Mark and Joe have unquenchable ambitions for these mountains and are undaunted by the adversities endemic to mountain climbing in general. After all that we just endured, however, I'm already re-evaluating my ambitions around alpine climbing. I don't ever recall having such a difficult time staying warm while climbing, or even while living through the Alaskan winter, and the same, unexplained fatigue I've been feeling from exertion continues to be a drain on my confidence. These mountains are serious places, requiring a deep well of reserve and resilience, one that I question whether I have. If there's something wrong with my metabolism, or something else, then maybe I should choose more appropriate objectives, like rock climbing, or alpine climbing in less brutal environments — the Sierra, the Cascades, or at least not the Alaska Range in March. Denali remains in my sights, but even in June that mountain can be as tough as what we just experienced, and at a much higher altitude. I will hold on to that dream for now, but I am not so sure that I want to go through an experience like that again. We will see. I press my face into the window to take a last look back: Mount Russell recedes into the distance, resuming its old, familiar place amidst the mosaic of mountains and sky.

Spring gives way to summer. The daylight hours become endless, and the trees and foliage erupt into a spectacular show of greenery and earthy aromas that are a welcome relief from the long, barren Alaskan winter. I settle into a cozy rental cabin in the woods near

Christiansen Lake, three miles outside town. It has no water, but it has electricity, propane for cooking, a wood stove, an outhouse, and a five-minute walk to a good swimming spot at the lake. A deck attached on the side is set amidst a shady forest filled with birdsong.

Mark is working at Mount Rainier for the summer, and it's just me and Cessna the cat. Paul puts me to work in the Talkeetna Air Taxi office, but I also move to launch my massage-therapy practice. I rent a small cabin in downtown Talkeetna, and before long I have established a modest client base from amongst my friends and other locals. The quiet life is good for a time, but beneath the surface I am dogged by a fire for something more.

As the summer passes into autumn, Mark and I are reunited in Yosemite, joined soon after by Paul. We climb long rock routes on the Valley's granite faces until autumn storms chase us out of the mountains. Like vagabonds, we migrate farther south to climb on the quartz monzonite outcrops of Joshua Tree National Park in the Southern California desert, and then yield to the impending winter with a couple of weeks on Kauai. We finish out this annual itinerant cycle with a few months of winter work in Seattle before returning to Talkeetna for the spring. *I may never go back to a conventional life.*

"How many seasons have you been doing this, Annie?" I ask, as I take a seat alongside her on the Talkeetna Air Taxi deck. We're well into the spring of 2000, and the trees are still absent their leaves. Remnant winter snow remains scattered in piles about the edges of the airport and roadways. Everywhere else, mud and large pools of meltwater signal the arrival of the spring breakup season in Alaska. The sun shining in the clear blue sky has but a modest effect upon the persistent chill in the air, a reminder that we are still in the grips of winter.

"This is my tenth," Annie replies. "I never imagined that I would do this for so long."

Annie, now in her late forties, looks at me with kind eyes and an empathetic smile, framed by her long, blonde hair. Our age difference and her caring demeanor make her a figure of deference and respect for me, almost a maternal figure perhaps, a view doubtless shared by many a Denali climber.

Annie manages the Denali Basecamp, where climbers from all over the world begin their attempts on North America's tallest mountain. In the spring of 1991, Annie had been waiting around Talkeetna for her then-boyfriend to return from a climb of Denali. On a whim, one of the air services offered Annie a chance to work managing basecamp while she waited. Annie was working in a New Hampshire dental office at the time, but her free-spirited life had already included playing in an all-female rock band, working as a cocktail waitress in Las Vegas, and many years as a stewardess for Eastern Airlines. Annie accepted the offer on an impulse and spent several weeks at basecamp. By the time she returned home, she had already committed to working the full ten-week season in 1992.

With the upcoming season, Annie will have been doing this job even longer than the legendary Frances Randall, the camp's first basecamp manager, who ran the camp for nine seasons. In the seven-year space between Frances and Annie, a variety of Talkeetna locals and even a few itinerant mountain climbers tended to the camp, but never with any consistency. In 1989, the renowned alpinist and explorer Conrad Anker, then a budding young climber in his twenties, ran the camp for a month. For the most part, however, the Denali Basecamp managers have been nurturing females — the "Kahiltna Queen" and "Basecamp Annie" — working amidst a majority-male climbing demographic, stereotypes be damned.

In her first several seasons, Annie used basecamp as a summer sabbatical from her New Hampshire office job. A few years ago, however, she met and fell in love with Davey Kreutzer, who works for the NPS in Talkeetna managing the helicopter program supporting the Denali mountaineering rangers. She pulled up roots back East, built a house with Davey on a bluff above town, and made Talkeetna her permanent home.

During my first season working at Talkeetna Air Taxi, in 1996, I well remember the whispers and respectful scuttle amongst the locals when she arrived from New Hampshire that April. It meant that the Denali climbing season was officially underway, but the buzz surrounding her presence also carried the suggestion that a celebrity was among us, a notion that the ever-modest Annie resists.

At first, Annie was just a woman I spoke with on the radio telephone every day; she provided us detailed weather updates from the Kahiltna Glacier, advised us of climbers waiting to fly out, and alerted us or the park service about unfolding emergencies on the mountain. We became much closer friends over the years, and one spring I even visited her up at basecamp. I found myself in awe of both the landscape she worked in and of the duties of her job, and even today, I still ask her frequent questions.

"I love it up there, Lisa," Annie says with a wistful expression, as we absorb some precious solar energy on the deck. "But things are changing, and I could really use some help. In fact, I think I'm ready to do something else." What she says next catches me off guard.

"What about you, Lisa?"

"What about me?" I reply, in puzzlement.

"Well, you seem like you'd be a perfect fit. You're young, you like being in the mountains, you're a climber, and you understand mountain weather."

I blink, swallow hard, and struggle for words as Annie presses on.

"I'll be up there all season, but you could come up for a few weeks and I'll train you." Annie leans forward, her eyes riveted upon mine: "What do you think?" *She's serious.*

A rush of adrenaline consumes me as I imagine the possibilities. I would live in the mountains in the heart of the Denali scene. I could go climbing during slow times, at least on the smaller mountains around camp, and have a warm tent to come back to afterward. I would be able to keep my eye on Paul, Mark, Joe, and all the Talkeetna pilots, and help keep them safe. There would be uncertainty, excitement, and responsibility, all the things that motivate me. I imagine myself situated in the company of pilots, climbers, and rangers, while surrounded by Denali, Mount Foraker, and Mount Hunter. *It's a place among giants.*

Before I can form any rational opposition, I hear myself speaking:

"Annie, I'll do it."

Chapter Four
2000-The Learning Curve

The airplane's engine fades into the background, its roar drowned out by a stream of thoughts absorbing my mind. I press my face against the cold window, as though I could merge with the passing landscapes. A sea of serrated black peaks, draped with ice and snow, floats by in rapid succession. I want to study the symmetry of every ridge and battlement, but all too soon each feature recedes from view, replaced by yet another towering monolith. I am forced by this mode of transit into that elusive state of moment-to-moment observation: no leisure to judge or cling to any vision, only enough time to observe and quickly let go. Everywhere in sight, tumbling icefalls convey their shattered cargo to the foot of these peaks. Arterial glaciers extend for miles south toward the distant waters of Cook Inlet. Clouds wisp around the ridges, tearing away from the summits of the Alaska Range, leaving neatly framed views of an impossibly blue sky.

I shift in my cramped seat, shoehorned into the diminutive aircraft along with a pilot, two mountain climbers, and their huge pile of gear. My throat tightens and I grasp the seat in front of me with one hand and the base of my own seat with the other. The plane is aimed toward a V-notch between two mountains looming ahead of us. Precipitous walls flank the final approach, giving the impression that we have only a single chance to make it through. In fact, the name of the pass is "One Shot" — but only because it's the most direct route to Denali Basecamp, and hence the first choice of pilots when the weather is clear.

I notice that the two climbers are also clenching their seats. Unlike them, I've flown this route before, and I know that the pass is much wider than it appears. Nonetheless, I steel myself for the sudden drop that often happens when flying through passes such as this one, where variations in wind and pressure can cause significant turbulence and downdrafts. This time, it never comes, and with plenty of room to spare, we glide straight through the gap and I relax as the vast Kahiltna Glacier spreads out before us.

"We made it through the gauntlet, everybody. Welcome to the mighty Kahiltna," the pilot exclaims cooly, with a vague air of sarcastic pretension that the outcome might somehow have been in doubt.

The two climbers give each other wide-eyed, uneasy smiles as the pilot — my ever-mischievous, ever-confident brother, Paul — flashes a smirk at me over his shoulder, confirming there was never anything close about it.

"Doing alright there, Lulu?" Paul asks, and I reply with a thumbs-up.

Each flight through the Alaska Range is an entirely new experience, a movie I'm seeing for the very first time. Today, it's a necessary distraction from the impending agenda to which this airplane carries me. My destination is Denali Basecamp. I'm not here to climb Denali, however; I'm here to train as the new basecamp manager, fulfilling the agreement I had made with Annie only a few short weeks before. For the next month, the busy camp and airstrip will serve as both my office and my home.

Paul begins pumping a hydraulic handle to lower the skis that will enable us to land on the glacier. I feel butterflies with the steepening descent, accompanied by the knowledge that the visual show is over and the real work is about to begin.

Through my headset comes Annie Duquette's familiar voice, loud and clear.

"Good afternoon, Paul. There's a light down-glacier wind, and the runway is soft. I've got three for you to pick up. See you in a minute."

Paul acknowledges the report, and banks the aircraft into a long, circular arc, giving me a final 360-degree view. The two-mile-wide expanse of the Kahiltna Glacier stretches out below, surrounded by massive, ice-covered mountains of almost unimaginable scale. A tiny, well-worn path follows the glacier's crevassed surface toward the West Buttress of Denali. Paul makes a final left turn to align with the Kahiltna's southeast fork, where streaks in the snow mark the runway. He keys the radio, calling out to other aircraft in the area: "Five-Fox-Kilo, left base, final for basecamp."

The Cessna glides in for a soft touchdown on the runway. Paul brings the plane to a near stop, makes a 180-degree turn, rolls up, and shuts the engine down in front of an incongruous scene of colorful tents perched on the rise above the north side of the runway. It's a splash of vibrant life amidst an otherwise stark and lifeless landscape of ice and stone. Climbers mill about, some fussing with gear, others lounging in the sun; almost all of them stop what they are doing to watch the new arrivals disembark. I feel the rush of entering a cold, snowy environment less than an hour's flight from the earthy greenness of Talkeetna.

Annie approaches to greet us, all at once herding three outgoing climbers onto Paul's plane while barking orders to other waiting groups: "I told you an hour ago to get ready. Your plane will be here in ten minutes, and he's not going to wait for you. Get your stuff packed up and get down here right now," she calls to them.

A pair of bewildered climbers loiter next to their tent and a messy, disorganized campsite, staring in astonishment, as though no one had ever been so direct with them. Annie stops walking at the sight of their inaction.

"I'm not kidding — *right now!*" she shouts, her voice rising, as she breaks character just long enough to flash a smile at us over her shoulder.

Embarrassed, the climbers spring to action like admonished children, dumping out half-finished cups of coffee, tearing down their tent with urgency, and tossing gear into duffel bags.

I turn in a circle to embrace the massive landscape. Down-glacier and to the west, Mount Foraker's east face rises ten thousand vertical feet above the Kahiltna Glacier in a vast sweep of granite and diorite cliffs studded with enormous hanging glaciers. Ice blocks detach from time to time and thunder down its flanks, discharging colossal clouds of ice and snow. To the right is Mount Crosson, a peak of moderate angle named for Joe Crosson, one of Alaska's foremost pioneering aviators — he was the first pilot to land upon a Denali Glacier, in 1932.

To the north stands Mount Frances, a rugged mountain with elegant ridges. Its name will be a constant reminder of the legacy I'll inherit: Frances Randall served as the first basecamp manager, from 1976 to 1984. To its right, Denali's looms above a gap in the ridge extending east from Mount Frances. Though Denali appears close, it's more than six miles away. Denali is framed on the right by an unnamed, 12,200-foot mountain towering over the valley with a pleasing, pointed summit.

Up-glacier stands the appropriately named "Control Tower," a small, pluglike peak that divides the glacier into two branches and keeps a close watch over the basecamp runway. Behind it, a stately spire glimmers at the head of the southeast fork. This peak is often referred to as "Kahiltna Queen," the nickname bestowed upon Frances Randall by the pilots and climbers of her era.

I look to the right and fix my gaze on Mount Hunter, towering 7,000 vertical feet above basecamp. The proximity alone makes Mount Hunter the most impressive peak in view, but from any distance, it is a formidable sight. The mountain's north buttress plunges from its summit plateau in a sweep of near-vertical granite cliffs laced with narrow strips of ashen-gray ice, crisscrossed by horizontal bands of snow. To the right, the mountain's chaotic north face holds some of the largest hanging glaciers imaginable. These seracs have the potential to release thousands of tons of ice down the flanks of the mountain, which then hit the glacier and catapult enormous clouds of pulverized debris across the southeast fork, sometimes billowing up the flanks of the Control Tower, a sight frightening to the newer inhabitants of basecamp.

I glance across the runway at the low ridge barring the view south, the direction from which storms and airplanes usually arrive. Pilots approach the final landing pattern through a small col. These features have become known as Annie's Ridge and Annie's Notch. These two landmarks named for yet another basecamp manager suggest I will have high standards to uphold.

"Lisa, welcome to Denali Basecamp.

Annie's energetic voice brings me back to the present.

"I hope you brought a warm jacket — the nights have been cold," she says, removing her gloves long enough to tuck a wisp of blonde hair inside her stocking cap.

"Take your bags over to the tent — I'll be there shortly. We've got a lot of things to cover."

Annie turns her attention to helping Paul load up the three outgoing climbers, while I drag my duffel bags off the runway and through the soft snow. Paul's voice reverberates from the runway:

"Good luck, Lulu. Annie's got you covered, but let us know if you need anything."

I wave back in acknowledgement. A few moments later, he throttles up the Cessna and accelerates down the runway. The runway pitches down, and its lower part is not visible from camp. I watch from Annie's tent as the plane disappears, and all I can hear is the engine echoing off Annie's Ridge. The sound changes pitch, suggesting that the plane has become airborne, and soon I am relieved to see it climb into view. The airplane becomes a speck against the backdrop of Mount Foraker, and the drone of the engine fades into the silence of the mountains. *I'm committed now.*

Annie's spacious WeatherPort tent is complete with a wooden floor, insulation, and a propane heater. There is a simple cot for sleeping, a table with a white-gas stove, and a small desk with a folding metal chair. A few duffel bags of clothes sit in the corner, and large pots of water rest beneath the table. The desk is stacked with various radios, and a bank of deep-cycle marine batteries is bunched together on the floor beneath it, the whole system connected to solar panels and an array of antennae outside. A small file box marked "on the mountain" holds expedition notecards for teams that are still on Denali, and a separate box marked "off the mountain" holds the cards for expeditions that have already concluded their trips. A plastic cup holds pens, pencils, Sharpies, scissors, and various sticky-note pads.

Annie returns and notices me looking at the electronics.

"Oh good, we can start there," she begins. "That's the radio telephone. Press pound-85 on the phone handset to get the dial tone. Star-85 to hang up. You press the button to talk, release it to listen."

The most technical details of everything else are glossed over in favor of the essentials: the food is here, we get snow for melting there, and the bathroom — a thirty-foot-deep shaft dug in the snow, covered by a wooden structure with a toilet mounted to it — is down that way.

"That's the cache garden up there," Annie says, pointing uphill toward an area fenced off with bamboo wands. "Climbers usually leave some extra food behind for when they return, in case they get stuck and can't fly out." Inside the perimeter, there are dozens of mounds of snow, each marked by avalanche probes or tall, taped-together wands, and with flags or labels containing the owner's expedition name and expected return date. "The rangers are supposed to check it, but I always walk through it every other day or so to make sure there isn't anything melting out. The ravens are looking for food and will tear up anything they see, and they make a huge mess," she continues.

We return to the tent to hide from the sun, and we sit as Annie describes her various daily responsibilities. There's a lot to remember, but the most intimidating parts relate to the weather observations we provide for the pilots throughout the day. This part of the job seems to carry a heavy weight of responsibility.

"How do I know if it's flyable, Annie?" I ask.

"You've spent a lot of time in these mountains, Lisa," Annie says.

My brow furrows, and then Annie looks at me with the kind firmness of a schoolteacher.

"You understand mountain weather. Just describe what you see," she says.

I soon find that I learn the most by just watching Annie work. I pay close attention to her every interaction with pilots on the aircraft radio, and to her phone conversations with the Talkeetna air services, as she relays news that the four climbers who just skied into camp are waiting to fly out or that the down-glacier winds that were blowing at 10 mph this morning have now subsided.

Footsteps approach, and I look up to see a handsome, clean-cut young man wearing a National Park Service ball cap poking his head inside the tent.

"Hey there, you must be Lisa. I'm Cale Shaffer. I'm the mountaineering ranger," he says, stepping into the tent with a boyish smile, extending his hand.

I learn that Cale is 25. Last season, he worked as a backcountry ranger on the north side of the park, and is now in his first season with the Talkeetna-based mountaineering and rescue program.

"I wanted this job more than anything else," he says. His voice brims with pride and excitement.

Most of the mountaineering rangers do a thirty-day mountaineering patrol on the upper mountain each season, but as the "new guy," he's relegated to basecamp patrols, a directive he embraces without complaint.

"Everything we do up here is important," Cale says.

The NPS staffs rangers at basecamp to enforce the park's trash and human-waste regulations, but the rangers also act as a forward presence on the ground for any SAR incidents up on the mountain. At basecamp, the rangers prepare and maintain a landing zone with a fueling site, including a generator and fuel bladder for refueling the helicopter. The rangers are competent mountain climbers trained in emergency medicine, helicopter shorthaul, and high-angle rescue.

"You're filling some big shoes here. I'll be here for a few more days, then I'll be back again later in June," Cale tells me. "In the meantime, if you need help with anything, just let me know." It seems providential to be working alongside someone who is as wide-eyed as I am, navigating the long shadows of the Alaska Range as rookies together.

"This is a great tent," I observe, as Annie and I eat dinner inside with the heat turned up high.

"It is," Annie replies, "but it wasn't until my second season that the WeatherPort company donated it to me. My first year, I was just staying in a mountaineering tent."

"What was that like?" I ask, trying to imagine spending over a month in a cramped tent. The two weeks I spent pinned in the tent on Mount Russell last year were more than I could handle.

"Well," Annie says, "my very first night up here, we had a huge snowstorm, and it got really windy. It snowed about three feet overnight, and my tent collapsed. I'd never slept in a sleeping bag before. I barely got through the night alive. I thought I might freeze to death."

I nod in solidarity. By comparison, my first night here at basecamp is looking pretty tame.

Just before 8:00 p.m., Annie grabs her notepad. "It's time to do the eight o'clock weather," she says, before raising the CB radio handset and keying the microphone.

"Good evening, Denali. This is basecamp with your evening weather report," she announces in a radiant voice.

Annie proceeds to read out a special "Denali Recreational Forecast" she copied down earlier from the National Weather Service's automated weather line. The forecast is issued specifically for various elevations on Denali.

As Annie concludes her report, various climbing teams begin

chatting on the frequency.

"AAI team two, this is AAI team three, are you up?" a male voice says. "We hear ya — let's take this to channel four," comes the reply from a female guide.

"Hey, Basecamp Annie," a man's voice chimes in. "When it said 'chance of snow' tomorrow, is it going to be a lot of snow? When will it clear up?"

"Sorry," Annie replies. "I read it word for word. I wish I had something more to give you."

"We were wondering if we should go for the summit tomorrow?" the man persists.

"That's your decision — I can't make that one for you. Sorry," Annie counters, sounding empathetic, but looking at me and shaking her head.

"These climbers live by the weather report," Annie tells me. "They want certainty, but up here you also have to do your own analysis — sometimes the wind and sky conditions are entirely different than what the forecast promised. Mountain weather is so hard to predict and these forecasts just aren't that accurate."

"Come on, let's go for a walk around camp," she says, rising from her chair.

Strolling through the cache garden, we find a duffel bag starting to melt out. Annie grabs a shovel driven into the snow nearby. "We need to bury this, or the ravens will scatter whatever is in there all over the camp," she notes. "These ravens are incredibly smart. They'll work together in pairs and unzip duffel bags. They make a mess at all the camps up higher on the West Buttress."

After picking up a few stray candy-bar wrappers and an abandoned canister of isobutane gas from an old, vacant campsite,

Annie and I return to the warmth of the tent and prepare to go to sleep. She sets up a second cot for me, and then steps over to the propane heater and, to my dismay, shuts it off.

"No heat tonight?" I ask, feeling timid, and remembering that the forecast Annie read called for lows of around 10 degrees Fahrenheit at 7,000 feet.

"We have to save propane," Annie says, as she climbs into her bag. "You should be plenty warm in that big bag of yours," she adds, looking at my minus-20-degree Feathered Friends bag. She's right, although I'm thinking more about what it will be like getting out of it in the morning.

Hours later, I'm snatched from the depths of sleep by the piercing tone of the radio telephone. Annie and I flail and struggle out of our sleeping bags with haste, if for no other reason than to make the sound stop.

"This is basecamp," Annie answers, a concerned look on her face.

"Hey, Annie, Barry Blanchard here. Sorry for calling at this hour. Carl Tobin and I are at about 11,000 feet on the *Infinite Spur,*" he begins.

I know that the *Infinite Spur*, the route on the south face of Mount Foraker, is one of the longest and most fearsome routes in Alaska. Mark and Joe have talked about trying it. I also know that Barry and Carl are two of the world's most skilled alpinists.

"There's two climbers below us," Barry continues. "They were way off route, and we just witnessed a huge ice avalanche fall into the gully where they were climbing. We heard screams during the slide, but there's been no sign of them since. They aren't responding to our shouts. We're pretty worried, and we thought you should know."

"Okay, thanks, Barry," Annie replies. "I'll alert the park service. Keep us posted if you have any updates. And keep your radio turned on. If the NPS flies over in the morning, they may want to talk with you."

Annie turns to me. "Go wake up Cale and have him come over," she instructs. I run to Cale's tent and awaken him. He scrambles out of his sleeping bag and pulls on his boots; I provide him the details of Barry's call as we hurry back to Annie's tent. There, Cale calls Talkeetna and awakens Daryl Miller, Denali's South District Ranger and the supervisor of Denali's mountaineering and rescue program.

"If Barry is that concerned, then so am I," Daryl tells Cale over the radio, his deep voice calm and professional. "I'll send the LAMA helicopter for an aerial search first thing in the morning. In the meantime, let us know if you hear anything more from Barry. We'll call you when we launch, but it'll probably be around 6:00 a.m." The LAMA is the park's contracted, exclusive-use helicopter that is stationed in Talkeetna from April to July each season. It's an Aerospatiale SA 315B that has been stripped down and modified to operate at Denali's high altitudes.

In the morning, the helicopter search is underway, as pilot Jim Hood and a ranger have flown straight to the scene from Talkeetna. Cale, Annie, and I follow the radio traffic as the helicopter searches the south face of Mount Foraker. After completing the search, the helicopter lands in basecamp, and we all gather to hear the ranger give Talkeetna a report.

"We saw the two climbers' tracks heading toward a large gully at the bottom," the ranger relates to Daryl. "The tracks led straight into a huge pile of fresh avalanche debris. The gully was scoured by the avalanche, and we didn't see anyone up in there. Above and way right, we did see Barry and Carl waving, and we contacted them on the CB radio. They said they still haven't seen any signs of them nor have they gotten any reply to their shouts. There's some clouds obscuring the terrain above the gully."

"Did you see any equipment in the debris?" Daryl asks.

"Negative. It's a massive amount of ice debris, though. There's huge seracs far above the gully, and they feed right into it. If they were in that gully like Barry said, then there's little chance they survived."

'It sounds like they were off-route," Daryl responds. "Okay, well let's see if those clouds break up, and when they do, go fly it again."

The subsequent search finds improved visibility but no sign of the missing climbers. After the helicopter lands again to refuel up-glacier, Cale comes over to break the news to Annie and me.

"They are presumed deceased. The search is suspended," Cale says, casting a somber glance toward Foraker. "Can I trouble you two to go find their cache in the garden and collect it? We need to fly it all out."

Annie and I locate their marker wand, and I begin digging. My shovel soon hits the top of a bag, and we quickly pull out several duffels, a few gallons of white gas, and a box containing some rib-eye steaks and a twelve-pack of beer, along with various personal clothing items that still hold the essence of the owners.

"This seems intrusive," I protest to Annie, as I crouch beside the gear belonging to these two young men, who, we have learned, were only 22 years old.

"I know," Annie replies, her eyes fixed on Mount Hunter and her tone full of doubt. "Somehow this feels premature, packing this all up. What if they're still alive?"

We help Cale load the two climbers' belongings into the helicopter for the flight back to Talkeetna, then stroll back toward our tent. "Lulu," Annie says, stopping now to face me. "I don't want to freak you out, but accidents and death happen up here almost every year."

Annie's voice trails off as she chooses her next words, fixing me with direct eye contact: "I've had planes flip over right here on the runway. We've had the helicopter sling bodies right in here on the end of the shorthaul line. There are some really harsh things to witness and experience up here, but that's just how it is, and it's part of the job. I'm not going to sugarcoat it, but I just want you to be aware of what may happen and what you are getting into."

In the middle of the night, the radio phone again awakens Annie and me from deep slumber.

Now what? I think, as Annie picks up the call.

"Annie, Barry Blanchard here. You're not gonna believe this, but those two guys are okay. They just climbed out of the gully off to our left and are ascending toward us right now. They were hit by the avalanche, but they are unhurt and are continuing their climb."

While Annie continues the call, I run outside and over to Cale's tent.

"Cale," I call. There's no answer. "CALE. Are you in there?" I shout more loudly, grasping his tent and shaking it.

"Hmmph . . . who is that?" a sleepy, muffled voice responds, amid sounds of rustling nylon.

"Cale, it's Lisa," I yell, unable to contain my excitement. "Barry is on the phone — he says the two climbers are alive and uninjured. They're still climbing!"

A hand appears from inside and unzips the tent's vestibule. Inside, Cale is braced on his side, peering up at me from his sleeping bag and wearing a bewildered expression. "Okay . . . thanks . . . I'll call Talkeetna," he mumbles. I walk back toward my tent, somewhat surprised at Cale's lack of emotion.

Annie and I awaken early. While I brew the morning coffee and fire up the propane heater, Annie begins making her 8:00 a.m. calls to each air service in Talkeetna.

"We have clear skies, it's 22 degrees, runway is firm and frozen, with light down-glacier winds. You have five climbers in camp ready for pickup," Annie tells the woman at K2 Aviation.

I answer a knock on the door and am greeted by Cale wearing a radiant smile and holding a mug of steaming coffee.

"Morning, Annie, morning, Lisa," he calls out, as I direct him to come inside.

As Cale sits, he looks over at me with a quizzical smile.

"Yeah, so, Lisa, I had the weirdest dream about you last night," he begins. "You came over to my tent, you woke me up, and told me those guys on Foraker were still alive."

Annie and I freeze, and stare at Cale for a long moment.

"What?" he asks.

"Cale, that wasn't a dream," I exclaim.

Cale's eyes widen, his jaw drops, and his face flushes scarlet. "Oh my god. Hand me the phone — I need to call Daryl." As the phone rings, Cale cracks a slight smile through his embarrassment as Annie and I pat him on the back.

The helicopter returns to Foraker, and this time, four climbers are spotted, standing together and waving. A subsequent radio call from Barry confirms that the two new arrivals are in fact the same two individuals whose deaths were reported on last night's national news broadcasts — and to their families.

"What a pair of awkward phone calls the NPS has to make today," I say to Annie, who just shakes her head at the thought, while I contemplate it further: *How many people ever receive that second phone call, overturning what would have been a lifetime of anguish?*

The following morning, I step outside the tent into a frigid breeze. The sky has turned a curious, transparent white. Snow plumes leap from Mount Hunter's flanks. Long, curling trails of ice crystals dance off Denali's summit ridge. A saucer-shaped cloud hovers motionless.

"Looks like that storm they forecasted is coming in," Annie remarks in an ominous tone.

It seems that the climbers are also aware of the inbound weather, as we are besieged by dozens of teams who have arrived in camp overnight with hopes of getting out before the storm shuts down any chance of flying.

"You MUST get the incoming climbers and their gear off the runway right away," Annie says as we walk out to the runway to greet the day's first wave of airplanes. "Don't let them dally or sit there taking photos. Another plane coming in could hit them or their bags. And have the climbers ready when their plane arrives. Don't EVER make the pilots wait." She interrupts herself for a moment to signal two groups of climbers to follow us out, telling them, "That airplane is for you, and that one's for you guys — come on out," pointing to each aircraft in succession.

As the planes depart, we walk back toward the edge of the runway where dozens of climbers remain, waiting for their turn to fly out, staring at us with anticipation as we walk past. "It'll be about ninety minutes until the next round of planes," she announces. A climber flops back onto his duffel bag and lets out a loud sigh.

"Your morning report on the phone is just the first set of observations," Annie tells me as we enter the tent. "But you need to keep the pilots updated using the radio throughout the day, especially if the weather is anything less than bluebird."

Continues Annie, "They need to know the conditions on the landing strip: is it icy and frozen, or is it soft and slushy? Did we get new snow? How many inches?" As I nod, listen, and jot down notes on a pad of paper, she adds, "What are the winds doing? How many knots is it blowing, and from which direction? Up-glacier, down-glacier, or crosswind? Gusty or steady? If there are clouds in the area, what peaks are visible? Can you estimate the elevation of the cloud ceiling? How far can you see?"

"And," Annie says with a start, "I almost forgot to tell you about packing the runway after storms."

"Oh, I know all about that, Annie," I say. "Remember my Mount Russell experience?"

"Oh, that's right," she replies. "Well, just remember, pack it down after six inches of new snow or more. And don't be shy, Lisa. Get the climbers to help you. Tell them the longer it takes, the longer they'll have to wait. It will motivate them to put on their snowshoes and skis and pitch in."

The sky becomes more overcast as the morning progresses. An orange Cessna 185 zooms through Annie's Notch and passes overhead before banking down toward the Kahiltna. "Hello again, Annie, this is five-five X-ray. Anything different since the last run? Winds have really picked up in the passes just in the past hour. I'm not liking it."

"Fifty five X," Annie replies, "Your winds are still light down-glacier as before, but the clouds have thickened in the past twenty minutes."

"I've noticed," the pilot replies. "Thank you, Annie. I'm going to want a quick turnaround here, so have my folks ready to go. Five-five-X, is left base, final for basecamp."

"See what I mean?" Annie says, turning to me. "There's no one-and-done report; you have to stay on top of the weather and keep the pilots informed."

Before I can answer, a pair of climbers approach the tent's open door. "How many people are before us on the list? Are we going to get out before it snows?" a man asks with a tone of desperation.

"There's eight people in front of you," Annie replies. "TAT is sending two small planes right now, which will take three each, and the Beaver is coming right behind those, so you'll be on that one." The climbers stare at the building clouds and respond with terse gratitude before walking away.

Annie checks the sky, and then faces me.

"This storm sounds bad. The pilots are saying there may be no flying for the next three days. There's an open seat on Hudson's next flight, and I'm going to get on it," she declares.

"What about my training?" I protest. "I thought you were going to stay at least a week with me before going out to town."

"You'll be fine, Lisa. You've got this — you know what to do. I'm a phone call away if you need anything."

An hour later, I watch as Annie climbs into pilot Jay Hudson's airplane, waves, and smiles, and then the plane taxis away, leaving a cloud of snow behind it. As the plane disappears around Annie's Ridge, I turn toward the large crowd of waiting climbers and feel a pit in my stomach. All eyes are on me.

For now, I'm the Denali Basecamp manager.

The next wave of airplanes arrives as the angry clouds overhead continue to sink lower. I brief the climbers as to who is next on the list, while two different pilots call me on the radio wanting to know if the winds are the same and how many climbers they are picking up. Four airplanes land in quick succession. Contrary to my instructions, almost every waiting climber pours onto the runway with their gear, running toward random planes as though it's a free-for-all.

Meanwhile, in the tent, the radio phone is ringing off the hook. "Lisa, where have you been?" a woman from one of the air services scolds when I pick up the phone after a breathless sprint from the runway. "How many climbers do we have left to pick up? And how's the weather holding?"

I hear my name being called from the runway. I end the call and bolt out of the tent to see the pilot Don Bowers striding toward me. "Where are my climbers, Lisa?" he asks, throwing his hands in the air. "Who am I picking up, and why aren't they ready?"

Don is one of Talkeetna's most experienced pilots, and normally one of the most stoic. I find his group and hustle them to the runway. Don tosses their skis into the plane with a clatter. He scratches his gray beard, casting furtive glances at the thickening clouds. Then, he forces a shy smile, as if embarrassed by his haste. "Sorry, I just don't want to get stuck here tonight," he says.

Minutes later, I'm holding an aircraft radio in one hand and the radio telephone in the other as a European climber dressed in loud neon shouts in my face: "LISA. Where is my plane? Why do other groups go first?"

I retreat to my tent and close the door behind me to think. Cale flew out this morning, and the new ranger is sleeping away the day in his tent, oblivious to this pandemonium much less my neophyte's struggles. *I guess I'm on my own,* I think. *What would Annie do?*

I take a few deep breaths, wipe away an errant tear, and exit the tent. The neon-clad climber has been awaiting my emergence. He stomps toward me, raising his index finger. I cut him off, because I am now Basecamp Lisa.

"If you say one more word, your group will be the last one to leave," I declare, planting my feet in the snow.

"Go sit down. I'll tell you when your plane is here. If you climbed Denali, this can't be that difficult for you."

Before he can protest further, his climbing partners grab him by the jacket and frog-march him back to their pile of gear. I hear "Shut up" and "Idiot" among several hushed expletives uttered between them.

I turn to another group: "You three, there. That's your airplane. Go." The climbers look up for but a moment, and then return to fidgeting with their cameras. The pilot looks at us from the runway with an icy glare.

"Really, guys?" I grab two of their heaviest duffels and drag them toward the plane. Surprise and embarrassment ripple across their faces. Thus shamed, they gather their remaining bags and chase me across the runway, stammering out thanks and tepid apologies.

Amidst all this chaos, I smile in recollection with how my tumultuous daily life on the Roderick Farm may have helped lay the groundwork for managing this three-ring circus. Sometimes, you have to shut down your emotions and just get the work done. Another aircraft arrives. I motion to my neon-clad climber, sulking nearby.

"That plane is yours," I say, softening my tone. "That wasn't so bad, right?" I give him a hand-rolled cigarette from my small stash of tobacco. I don't smoke very often, but it's served as an occasional outlet for stress or an accompaniment over a drink ever since my late-teen partying days in Connecticut. Mark has been pressuring me to quit since we met. *Maybe giving it away up here will help me do so once and for all.*

The climber's face lights up, and he puts his hand on my shoulder. Bearing a sheepish smile, he says, "Thank you, Miss Lisa. So sorry for the bad words."

Many climbers returning from their weeks on the mountain seem to have reached their own breaking points, and I'm astonished at their reversion to a primitive or even juvenile level of patience and communicative skill. It's as though they have snapped and cannot be reasoned with in their utter desperation to reach civilization immediately. As the day progresses, I'm learning that when supervising those who have lost all social skills, it helps to be, all at once, assertive, harsh, kind, and ready to lead by example. And if all else fails, to threaten to make them go last.

As the last of my waiting climbers depart for Talkeetna, I estimate that today I have carried over one thousand pounds of gear between camp and the runway, and have engaged in more acts of threat, bribery, and negotiation than in my lifetime so far combined. The learning curve has been steep.

The storm's progress seems to have stalled, and the weather remains flyable into the afternoon, allowing everyone to get in and/or out. Paul flies in with one final group to drop off. Under gloomy skies, he exits the plane; as Paul walks toward me, he slumps in an uncharacteristic manner. He stops and gazes in thought toward Mount Hunter.

"Is something wrong?" I ask. Paul looks down, grimaces, and

kicks the snow. "Seth died," he replies. "He was killed by icefall on Mount Johnson." Paul is stoic and seldom displays emotion, but right now there is a small opening in which I can actually see his pain.

Even as a child, Paul seemingly paid little heed to his emotions, choosing instead to feel and observe in neutrality, as though watching a cloud pass by overhead. When our mother died, he was solemn, but always unwavering. Even as I was uncertain of the damage her death was doing to me, I instinctively knew that Paul was going to be alright. Paul has an innate ability to embrace the *"what is,"* process it, observe it with no judgment or clinging, and then open his hand and let it go free. It's a magnetic trait, and part of what has kept me close to him through the years.

I first met Seth Shaw three years ago, after Mark, Todd Deis, and I descended from our climb of the Mooses Tooth. "We were so psyched for your V-threads on the West Ridge," Seth told us, of the drilled ice anchors we'd left in place, when we met in Talkeetna a day later. He and Scott Simper had just climbed a new route on the mountain's far more difficult north face, and then descended the route we came up. The "Toose's Mooth," they'd called it. Only ten days ago, I sat at a Talkeetna restaurant with Seth, Paul, Mark, and Joe. Seth had described the endless desert cracks and crumbling sandstone towers of his home state. "You should all come to Utah this fall — we'll go climbing in Indian Creek. I got tons of cams you can use," Seth said. Glasses clinked.

Up to now, my adventures in the mountains have been guided by the stuff of romanticized dreams, in which everything always works out the way you plan, and the dangers are abstract and only impact people you don't know. Seth and I weren't close. We hardly knew one another, in fact, but his death nonetheless touches our circle. Suddenly, the hazards seem real.

I look up: a wind-driven snow plume rises from the flanks of Hunter. *Still no word from Mark and Joe.* I have been so overwhelmed with my own work that I've almost forgotten them. Paul knows what I'm thinking. "The boys are okay, Lulu. They bailed off the South Ridge of Hunter. They want to transfer here — I'm going to pick them up right now," he says.

Before long, Mark and Joe climb out of Paul's airplane with their usual theatric flourish, waving and hollering, and toss their duffels onto the glacier. The last remnants of fair weather vanish as Paul flies away. Basecamp shuts down. We're cocooned in the clouds and the softness of a dense, silent snowfall.

For three days, we're shrouded in white. Mark, Joe, and I spend our time shoveling snow and packing the runway. Through breaks in the clouds, I gain a more intimate familiarity with the smaller features of the land: a granite outcrop on Annie's Ridge, an avalanche chute on the south face of Mount Frances. The cacophony of unseen rockfall reveals the mountains' presence, even though they're currently invisible. Between inside jokes and comedy skits, the boys strategize in subdued voices about upcoming ascents. Mark and Joe have climbed with one another on an almost exclusive basis for the past seven years. They are so synchronized that they even have the same gear: white synthetic shirts, matching black bibs, green touring skis.

At last, the forecast predicts four perfect days. I watch Mark and Joe ski toward Mount Foraker's *Sultana Ridge*. The route requires climbing Mount Crosson to reach it, then follows a five-mile corniced and crevassed ridgecrest between Crosson and Foraker, before ascending a long, glaciated slope to Foraker's summit. It's a technically easy route, but it's located on the north-south divide of the Alaska Range and is completely exposed to the wind during storms. I stow away my fears, and I refocus on my pilots' needs. For two days, not a single cloud enters my field of vision. The fine weather allows me ample time to fuss with Annie's equipment.

"Annie, the heater's pilot light keeps going out. What do I do?" I ask one morning, shivering at my desk in 15-degree weather. "You might have to shield the external vent from the wind," she instructs. While we're at it, I ask her about the care and feeding of certain cranky pilots, and we laugh while exchanging our experiences dealing with the various personal dramas that climbers bring to the mountains.

Two days have passed since Mark and Joe left for Foraker. They've been calling on the CB radio from time to time and they've made rapid progress. Just after my 8:00 p.m. weather report, they check in over the radio from their tent bivouac at 14,000 feet on the *Sultana Ridge*.

"We're going for the summit tomorrow morning, Mark reports. "We missed your weather — can you read it again?"

"There's a large low-pressure system moving in from the Aleutians tomorrow afternoon. It calls for four days of snow, with fifty to seventy mile per hour winds above 14,000 feet," I repeat, knowing it's the last thing they want to hear. The *Sultana Ridge* has little technical difficulty but is also very exposed to the wind, with much of the route being on the crest of the Alaska Range.

"Copy that, sweetie. We may leave tonight for the top, try to get up and back and beat this thing. It already looks like the weather is changing from up here. We'll call you tomorrow. Love you."

"Love you, too. Be safe."

I set down the radio receiver, then read and re-read the terrible forecast on my notepad. The silence in my tent is almost unbearable. I peek out the tent door one last time for the night. The sky appears clear and calm, disarming enough to distill any worry as I head off to bed.

In the morning, I am dismayed to emerge into a very changed environment. The storm is upon us. Angry clouds swirl around the peaks, lenticular cloudcaps obscure both Denali and Foraker, and dense fog pours like an incoming bore tide into the valley of the lower Kahiltna Glacier. An energetic wind is gusting up the glacier, driving large snowflakes through camp at a horizontal angle. As the morning progresses, Denali Basecamp is engulfed in a full-blown whiteout and heavy snow begins falling.

I'd thought that living in basecamp would help me to worry less for Mark and Joe, that constant updates would create an illusion of control. If I were in Talkeetna, however, I might be riding my mountain bike, enjoying the birdsong and earthen smells of the boreal forest, unaware of this unfolding drama. Instead, I stand in the wind, my face peppered by snowflakes, looking toward a mountain that I can't even see. *I know too much.*

Midafternoon, I get relief when Mark's voice crackles over the radio, muffled by flapping tent fabric and wind.

"We turned around just below the top at three this morning as the storm started hitting us . . . We got into a cloudcap and had a total whiteout descent . . . We had a hell of an epic finding the tent. We were nearly lost," Mark reports, the strain in his voice evident. "We're getting hammered by the wind here. What's the forecast?"

"Mark, it's gotten worse. It says snow for the next four days. There's a high-wind warning above 14,000 feet — they say winds will be eighty to one hundred mph from the southwest."

"Oh, man," Mark says. A long pause follows. "That's not what we wanted to hear. We are in a bit of a situation here. Our tent has collapsed."

"Can you find shelter? Can you move lower?" I ask, trying not to sound worried.

I know the answer already. They're in one of the windiest places in the range.

"No, we can't move, and we already tried to dig a cave, but the snow is almost bulletproof here and we had to give up digging," Mark replies. "But we're gonna have to go back out and try some more. It's our only option. We'll call you when we can. I love you." There's a snap of static, and then the radio goes silent.

I distract myself with my camp chores, organizing a runway-packing party from the new pile of outgoing climbers who are waiting, not all of them with patience, for the storm to clear so they can get to the Talkeetna pubs. I can only wish that they were my biggest problem.

It is twenty-four agonizing hours later when, at long last, Mark's voice comes over the radio again, at the conclusion of my 8:00 p.m. weather. In the quiet space between, I have been a wreck consumed with worry.

"Lisa, you copy?"

"Yes, where are you?" I blurt.

"It took a lot of work, but we managed to get a snowcave dug yesterday and got inside. We're safe, dry, and warm, but we're getting low on food and fuel."

With the whole mountain listening to the radio for fresh gossip in the wake of the evening weather report, I provide them some unintentional entertainment.

"Why didn't you call me sooner? Last time we spoke you were in trouble, I've been so worried," I cry out.

"Uh . . . I'm sorry, sweetie — we wanted to save our radio batteries for emergencies in case we are pinned down a really long time."

"What about saving your girlfriend from a little worry?" I counter, raising my voice.

An awkward silence follows. Then, an anonymous climber chimes in:

"C'mon, Lisa . . . give him a break."

I laugh to myself and then, in a stern but more empathetic voice, I continue:

"Alright, alright. I'm glad you guys are okay. Be safe and call me when you think you can move down."

"Will do, sweetie. The wind outside our snow cave sounds like a freight train. We're staying put until that changes. Love you."

Two more days pass until the storm spends its energy. In the morning, I am uplifted to step outside to an unobstructed view of Mount Foraker, and even more when Mark calls and says he and Joe are out of their cave and on the move. They arrive fifteen hours later, tired but in good spirits and with a rather harrowing story of their prolonged search for their tent in whiteout conditions on their way down from the summit, their tent blowing down and collapsing on them, and then the hours of desperate chopping into hardpacked snow to build a hail Mary snowcave. As for me, the past five days may have subtracted a year off my life.

Any lingering annoyance I have melts away with their arrival. I cook them a hearty meal to fatten them up, and soon my two strong climbers set about helping me in camp with shoveling, muscle tasks, dragging duffel bags, and expediting unruly climbers toward airplanes, while we spend our evening playing cards and board games. *I love having all this help and company.*

A week later, Mark and Joe are off again. This time, they are headed for the 14,000-Foot Camp on Denali's West Buttress, to acclimatize further, and wait for a period of stable weather during which to attempt the *Cassin Ridge,* one of the routes they've been working toward ever since they met.

I embrace the boys before they click into their skis and shoulder their large backpacks. Mark and Joe drop out of sight at the far end of camp to begin descending Heartbreak Hill, the slope that breaks the hearts of many a returning Denali climber who is too tired to face the final climb back up to basecamp. Watching them depart has me again thinking about climbing Denali. In one way, I am envious of them; in another, not so much. Do I still want to climb Denali? I weigh the joy that I know from climbing against my continuing struggles with low energy, fatigue, and even staying warm right here in camp at only 7,000 feet. *Are the big mountains a reasonable goal for me or am I kidding myself?* I look up toward Denali's seductive summit, six miles distant, and sense my ongoing battle between pleasure and pain, doubt and possibility.

Over the next ten days, the weather is unstable and provides me with a daily array of challenging weather observations. Active weather moves through the range each day, with sudden snow squalls interspersed with disarming periods of calm, sunny weather. Nothing lasts long, and the frequency with which conditions change makes things very difficult both for me and for the pilots.

"How's the weather?" the pilot Doug Geeting asks over the phone from Talkeetna. "I got three to bring in."

Doug is a multi-talented pilot who started flying here in his early twenties, is a twenty-five year veteran of Denali flying, and operates Doug Geeting Aviation as one of the six air services carrying a concession to operate in Denali National Park. Doug is a beloved Talkeetna character who might just be found singing and playing his guitar in one of the town's open-air restaurants after a long day of flying his climbers and scenic flight tours into the Alaska Range. Doug is a folksy character with a boisterous sense of humor. He has a thick build, a boyish cut of wavy, reddish-blonde hair, and a jolly smile, all of which conceal a no-nonsense style, and, at basecamp, a general dislike of waiting around for slow-moving climbers. Doug is straightforward: he likes to take care of business and be on his way, and he does not suffer fools.

"It's been up and down, Doug, but it's been good for the past hour. If you were here, you could land, no problem."

"Okey-dokey. I'm on my way."

Forty minutes later, Doug's voice crackles over the aircraft radio. "Four-Seven Fox, eight thousand five hundred, One Shot for basecamp."

Doug is less than ten minutes away. I step out of the tent and look down-glacier toward Foraker. A tendril of fog that wasn't there five minutes ago is advancing up the Kahiltna at a steady rate. I can see that it's already ascending the southeast fork.

Just as the fog begins crawling over the runway, the drone of Doug's airplane becomes audible. In thirty seconds more, visibility is reduced to less than one hundred feet.

"Lisa, what's going on?" he calls on the radio. "Where'd that fog come from?"

"Sorry, Doug. You were just a minute too late. This might flow back out like the tide — it's been doing that all day."

"Oh, I know how that goes. I'm going to circle here for a few minutes and see if it'll clear," Doug says.

Fifteen minutes later, I'm still in the soup and Doug is still overhead.

"Well, Lisa, I've got just enough fuel to get back to Talkeetna with a cushion. I'll try again later."

A few minutes pass, the fog recedes back down the southeast fork, and I'm basking in the sun. It's a big guessing game, and, recalling Annie's guidance, I remind myself that it's best to just tell the pilots what I see and let them decide what to do with that information.

It's June 19. The solstice is tomorrow, and I have now been at basecamp for over three weeks. The NPS is sending in its final basecamp patrol of the season today. It's going to be led by Cale Shaffer again, along with the volunteer rangers Adam Kolff and Brian Reagan. I am excited to be finishing out my final week at basecamp with Cale before Annie returns to close out the season.

The weather today is the most dynamic I've seen since I've been here, with fast-moving bands of showers, wild clouds, and unpredictable, shifting winds. The atmosphere is chaotic and unstable.

Just after noon, I take an incoming phone call.

"Hey, Lisa, it's Cale Shaffer."

"Hi, Cale. What are you up to?" I ask.

"Well, I've been hanging around the office all day in my Nomex," he begins, referring to the fireproof clothing required by the government for flying on helicopters. "We were supposed to come in with a military helicopter, but they got called away for another mission. Now we're trying to get in with Hudson. I'm psyched to get up there, but I heard the weather isn't good."

"Yeah. It's been bad most of the day, Cale," I answer. "A few planes have made it in, but it's been mostly down all day."

"Do you think it'll get better?"

"Honestly, I don't think so," I offer. "Several pilots have told me it's scary and volatile. They're telling me the passes are open one minute and clouded in the next. And it's very windy also. Everyone has been avoiding the Kahiltna for the past couple hours."

"What should we do?" Cale asks.

"I think you should ditch the Nomex and try again tomorrow, Cale. The pilots don't like it, and I don't either."

"Okay, Lisa, thanks for the update," Cale replies. "I'm really anxious to get up there, so I'll be standing by the rest of the day."

I hope that I was clear enough with Cale. I am beginning to realize that this job is not just about managing a camp; it's also about managing people. In the setting of this hostile environment, I am engaged with a level of responsibility that has real, physical consequences.

I set down the radio-phone receiver and gaze outside at the blackening sky.

I don't think I'll be seeing him.

Chapter Five
June 20, 2000

Don and the rangers are missing. The thought — my very first of the day — tears me away from the warmth and softness of my sleeping bag. My eyes burst open, and I bolt upright to a sitting position. I glance at my watch. It's just after 7:00 a.m., and there's sunlight shimmering on the walls of the tent. I need to find out what's happening with the search and check on the Florida tourists sleeping in the WeatherPort.

I pull on my boots in haste and climb out of the cramped mountaineering tent into a crystal-clear morning — the first in many days — and pace with urgency through the snow toward my WeatherPort. I flip on my handheld aircraft radio as I walk, and in the first instant I am greeted by a barrage of traffic.

"Three Charlie Tango is six thousand three hundred, southbound on the Yentna's west side."

"LAMA copies, we got you in sight. We're gridding to your west, four thousand four hundred; we'll hold back and give you the lead."

Nothing found yet. I am relieved if only for the further delay of what I fear will be bad news.

Inside the WeatherPort, the Floridian tourists, who have just spent the night on a glacier for the first time in their lives, are stirring, and one is putting the kettle on the stove.

"Good morning, everyone," I say, shifting into happy-mountain-host mode. "How was your night?"

"Well, we survived," one of them replies. "In fact, we rather enjoyed it," another says.

"So glad to hear," I reply. "I'll make a French press of coffee, and there's tea if anyone prefers."

After staging cups and coffee accessories, I peek outside to see Keli Mahoney stacking boxes next to her airplane. "I'm going to check in with your pilot," I tell the Floridians. "Help yourself to any food if you're hungry, but the weather is clear, so I imagine a Roadhouse breakfast is in your near future."

I stride out onto the runway. Keli is standing on the boxes, scraping ice off the airplane's wings, her McKinley Air Service baseball cap turned backward. She glances over at me, casual as always, and cracks a wry smile.

"I should have brought my wing covers. Can you give me a hand?" she asks.

"Sure. What are you using for that?"

"Mastercard is accepted here," she says, holding up her credit card. "I'm pretty sure," she continues, producing her wallet from her pocket and removing another card. "They take Visa also." She passes me the card and I join in. *I never imagined anything in a wallet would have value up here.*

"Also, my battery is dead," Keli says. "I'm going to need a new one flown in, and I might ask if one of the other air services can take my folks back to Talkeetna. They've been kept here long enough."

I check in with the air services on the phone. Jay Hudson has, as usual, joined in the aerial search, but this time it's for one of his own pilots and one of his own airplanes. The crisis has every air service at work earlier than normal, with each one looking to help. Talkeetna Air Taxi agrees to bring in a new battery for Keli, and then take her tourists back out while she installs it. Each air service has contributed aircraft to join in with the coordinated search that includes the NPS helicopter, the NPS fixed-wing aircraft, and numerous military resources.

A wave of planes arrives in camp to gather the groups of climbers waiting to fly out, and the Floridians are at long last set free. With the camp now empty and no further chores to be done, I turn my attention back to the ongoing search. *I wonder how Mark and Joe are doing.* I call the rangers at 14,000-Foot Camp — aka 14 Camp — on the West Buttress of Denali. The mountaineering ranger Karen Hilton picks up.

"Have you seen Mark and Joe?" I ask.

"Oh yeah, they're here in the camp somewhere," Karen replies.

"If you happen to be out in camp, could you please tell Mark to call me on the radio?"

"Sure, no problem. In fact, they can use our telephone. I'll go look for them."

I head outside to walk up and down the runway for some exercise, and just to feel busy. I want to switch off the aircraft radio and disconnect from this strain and uncertainty, but I cannot look away while my friends are still missing. The radio traffic continues unabated.

"212th Airborne. ELT not detected. Remaining on the pattern."

That's the US Air Force PJs in the C-130.

"Nine Six Charlie, I'm abeam Chelatna Lake, two thousand two hundred, I'll be northbound up Cripple Creek drainage." *There's Jay*

Hudson.

"LAMA helicopter is three thousand one hundred, will be northbound up Sunflower Creek towards Stern Gulch."

"Three Charlie Tango copies you, LAMA. I'll keep west of Idaho Creek and out of your pattern."

I return from the runway and sit in my lawn chair, staring at Mount Foraker. *Why didn't Don call me before he left Talkeetna?* I just can't let it go.

The phone rings, and I jump up and race inside, wondering if perhaps I've missed something on the radio and there will be news.

"Basecamp," I answer, almost breathless.

"Lisa, it's Mark."

"Oh, I'm so glad to hear from you. Have you heard the news?"

"Yeah," Mark answers. "We saw the C-130 overhead last night and suspected something was wrong. We began hearing rumors in camp a little while ago, and then Karen came over and filled us in. How are you holding up?"

"I'm so worried, Mark. It's Cale Shaffer and his patrol," I reply, my emotions bleeding out.

"I know," Mark acknowledges. 'Hang in there, sweetie. I realize it looks bad, but maybe there's still hope."

"Okay. Well, I just wanted to check in. I'm going to take another walk. I can't sit still."

"Alright," Mark says. "Take some deep breaths, and let's hope they're found soon. Joe and I are sitting here with Karen and Loomis monitoring the radio traffic. Let's talk later. I love you."

"Love you too . . ." I reply. I push star-8-5 on the handset, and the call disconnects. I drop my head to the desk, take that deep breath, stand up, shove in my chair, and head outside again.

I wander through the camp feeling aimless, picking up a few pieces of trash left behind by careless climbers. I check the cache garden, find nothing in need of attention, and then I even look at the marked pee holes to make sure they don't need snow shoveled in them. *This is getting desperate.*

I stare at Denali, and then turn in a slow, moving arc to absorb the mountain panorama. My eyes trace the sheer black-and-tan sheets of granite on Mount Hunter's north buttress, and then follow the ribbons of ice that serpentine through their weaknesses. Spindrift pours down the wall, and a small plume of wind-driven snow spirals off the summit ridge.

There is a dramatic paradox in our relationship to places like these. What I already understood to be true with alpinism now also seems to be so for aviation. The danger and beauty of these mountains are inexorably bonded, and the same attributes which attract so many to these environments are also a source of peril. Wild places such as these possess a unique capacity to humble; they bring one face-to-face with the fragility and transience of life. The mountains have so much to teach, and yet so much capacity to take. The hardest lesson of all, however, is that when the mountains take, they often take big.

At just after 4:00 p.m., I am sitting in my tent with my Alaskan friends Thomas and Mary, who have just returned from a ski trip up Denali. I've been on the phone with the air services and rangers in Talkeetna, and the rangers at the 14,000-Foot Camp. The scene everywhere is the same: everyone sits huddled over their aircraft radios, waiting with anticipation and dread for a development. Now, it comes.

"All search units: We've got positive visual on aircraft wreckage. Stand by for coordinates."

My heart skips a beat, and I sit upright in sharp attention, my eyes riveted on the radio as the location is conveyed by latitude and longitude. Minutes pass until a helicopter reaches the scene, and now we listen, helpless, as the finale of this terrible drama plays out before us, one transmission at a time. The helicopter hovers over the crash site, settling in closer to read out the tail numbers on the downed aircraft.

There, hovering just above a beautiful, lush slope covered in subalpine grasses, perched high above the Yentna Glacier's sprawling river of ice and multihued rock, overlooking a spectacular wilderness of majestic mountains, the searchers aboard the chopper transmit the news that all had feared.

"Tail number is November-One-Five-Eight-Nine-Fox. We have 'confirmation' on all four individuals."

The charred orange-and-white wreckage, scattered for over a mile across the mountain slope, is all that remains of Don's airplane, torn apart in midair by the colossal thunderstorm into which he had flown while trying to escape the mountains the night before.

From my tent to the rangers' tent at 14 Camp, to the ranger station and air-service offices back in Talkeetna, many sets of wide eyes stare at the floor as the radio feedback cuts to silence, and then not a sound can be heard. The Alaska Range also stands in silence — ageless, eternal, and indifferent to the human drama taking place within its walls.

I rise without a word, step outside, and labor several paces from the tent. In a defensive motion, I raise my arms and clasp my hands overhead, still gripping my aircraft radio in one hand. The weight of the world feels crushing, and I struggle to hold it back. I stop and stare at the mountains before easing the radio back to my hip. Tears streak my face and fall onto the snow. I inhale a deep breath of fresh mountain air. *Don Bowers, Cale Shaffer, Adam Kolff, and Brian*

Reagan are gone.

The phone rings, and I return inside. *It's going to be a long night,* I think, as I pick up the receiver to the comforting sound of Mark's voice.

"Lisa. It's me."

"Mark, they're gone," I say. Further words elude me.

"I know. I can't believe it," Mark says, before a long pause as he searches for words. "What can we do to help you?"

"I want you to come down to basecamp. I need you. Will you come down?" My request feels blunt and impulsive, but this is how I feel. Mark replies without hesitation.

"We're packing up and leaving tonight. We'll be there as soon as we can."

In an instant, my heart is lifted by a force, a force that can only be love.

Mark and Joe arrive in the wee hours, having utilized the coldest part of the never-dark Alaskan night to navigate the crevassed lower glacier. In the dim twilight of my tent, I get out of my sleeping bag and greet them each with a long hug.

"I'm so glad you came down," I say to Mark, my head pressed tight against his chest.

Joe stands solemn while Mark hugs me tighter, then moves to embrace me as Mark and I separate.

Amid the dawning of a new day, I'm consumed by a feeling of hollow emptiness. Tragedy seems to bring our world to a standstill, but nothing stops the passage of time. The sun is rising, our colleagues are gone, but we're still here. Another layer of my innocence has been stripped away. Any naiveté I had around the dangers of the mountains has withered. In reality, both in the mountains and out, we are all just a wrong step, a bad decision, or a stroke of bad luck from catastrophe. The notion of universal justice seems suspect. Life simply isn't fair.

We're cheered as our friends Mike Gauthier and David Gottlieb ski into camp from an attempt on Foraker. We gather in my tent over a pot of strong coffee. I met Mike during my first date with Mark on Mount Rainier four years ago. David is another of the Mount Rainier climbing rangers and is one of Mark's closest friends. I've gotten to know them both very well over the past several years, and I even climbed Liberty Bell in the North Cascades with David and Mark a few summers ago.

Mike, David, Joe, and Mark have been working on Mount Rainier together for the past four summers, and they are like brothers. Though none of them really knew Cale, the mountain rescue community is like an extended family, and a death of one hits everyone hard. Here in Alaska, we climbers also hold deep respect for these glacier pilots, whose skill and nerve deliver us to places we might otherwise not go, and who at the end of our expeditions save us from the elements and return us to civilization. Our group's shared history and closeness provide a layer of healing and catharsis, but it is tempered by recent events.

In my mind, I revisit Seth Shaw's death a few short weeks ago. My eyes travel between Mark, Joe, Mike, and David, and a wave of dread washes over me at the thought of a tragedy striking any closer than it already has. David raises his cup in a solemn gesture: "To Don and the rangers." Five cups meet, and we drink in silence.

As the air warms and the sun rises higher, Annie calls. "Lulu, I'm coming back in tomorrow. You don't need to be dealing with this. Whatever you want to do, I'm here for you," she says.

I need to get as far from basecamp and airplanes as possible, I think. *I'm going home to Talkeetna.*

Tomorrow night, Mark and Joe will head for the *Cassin Ridge*. With four days of perfect weather in the forecast, they look upward for catharsis.

Basecamp is bathed in golden light as Annie arrives from Talkeetna the following morning. Not a cloud is in sight, only the mountains towering in every direction. Overhead, above this brilliant black and white and buff landscape of ice and stone, a piercing indigo sky hangs in stark contrast, like a tropical-ocean canopy. Annie steps down from the airplane and gives me a big-hearted embrace, tears welling in her eyes. We help some climbers get loaded up on the outbound aircraft, and then we take refuge from the sun in the WeatherPort. We have an hour before my plane back to Talkeetna arrives, and we spend it telling stories about Don and Cale and trying to process our grief. At last, the aircraft radio crackles to life: "Four Six Echo, final for basecamp."

"That's your ride, Lulu," Annie says, almost in a whisper. "Time to go home."

Mark embraces me on the glacier; Joe bows his head and then stares toward Denali. I squirm into the Cessna, joined by Mike and David. It's comforting to be sitting amongst trusted friends. As I glance through the window once more, Mark and Joe wave back. They look fit and confident, their hands on their hips and feet planted in the snow. My worry for them softens as I draw faith in the strength of their partnership and their humility. The sun accentuates the elegant line of the *Cassin Ridge*. As my plane lifts and passes high above the main fork of the Kahiltna Glacier, I take a last look back toward basecamp. The tiny band of dots grows smaller by the second, receding deeper into the folds and vastness of the Arctic landscape. And then, it's gone.

A month earlier, snow had covered the mountains down to the lowlands. But the warmth and endless daylight of the Alaskan June have transformed the glaciers into barren sheets of gray ice, studded with aquamarine meltwater pools. Enormous piles of rock and dirt and snow lay at the foot of the gullies, and as we drop into the foothills, green flashes across every exposed slope — an explosion of color after weeks in a world of black and white. Farther down, water is everywhere: wild rivers and creeks flowing, tarns and lakes of all sizes dotting the plains and stretching for almost one hundred miles to Cook Inlet and the Pacific Ocean. The plane glides high above the treetops and sets down upon the tarmac at the Talkeetna Airport. I step out into the summer air, into the fragrance of earth, flowers, and cottonwood seeds. It smells like life.

For four days, I relax at home with Cessna the cat, spending much of that time on the porch of my quiet cabin in the forest. I'm bound by no schedule. Sun filters through the trees, casting sinuous shadows across our deck. Poplar leaves quake and twist in the wind. A loon calls from the lake — a plaintive, echoing cry. Cessna rolls on her back in the sun, looking at me with pure and present love.

The boys are back. The aircraft taxis up, and I can see Mark and Joe's broad smiles through the window of the airplane. It is seventy-two degrees. Cottonwood and birch trees sway in the warm breeze, and white, feathery blossoms float through the air. Mark and Joe jump from the airplane and touch pavement for the first time in over forty days. Fresh off a successful ascent of the *Cassin Ridge*, they fall to their knees and kiss the ground in theatrical display of gratitude, then they rise and rush forward to greet me.

The evening finds Mark, Joe, and I standing on the banks of the roiling Susitna River. The sun drops in its long, elliptical summer arc behind Mount Hunter. The endless twilight belies the lateness of the hour. I'm reminded of how life in Alaska is so often a process of striving toward the light. A climber at basecamp asked me if I was the "new Annie." Only now does the answer come freely. Doubt and uncertainty have been replaced by a determined urgency to protect the people I care about, and to do whatever possible to ensure that what happened on June 19 never happens again. As I reflect on the arc of my life, never have I had such certainty. I was meant for this.

I gaze toward the shimmering peaks and back to the restless waters that have journeyed so far from their heights, spellbound by the power of these mountains. I can see my calling amid the ice and stone, among the pilots, rangers, and climbers, the human spirits that infuse an everlasting radiance into the world where I live: I am all in.

Chapter Six
2001-Big Time

"Nine Zero Yankee, departing runway three six, Talkeetna."

A wave of nervous anticipation washes through me: *Here we go.* Paul pushes the throttle forward and spins the plane onto the runway; moments later, we are airborne. A caravan of three different planes carrying me, my nine volunteers, and almost 2,000 pounds of basecamp gear glides over the still-snowy boreal forests and iced-clogged Chulitna River bar, then banks north toward Denali. The Alaska Range grows ever larger in the airplane's windscreen. Paul notices my intensity as I stare at the peaks.

"Excited, Lisa?" he asks. "It's your show now."

I smile and give a thumbs-up, making no mention of the butterflies in my stomach. Favoring optimism and renewal, I push away last season's stress and tragedy as the aircraft carries me into the 2001 season at Denali Basecamp, the first in which I will be in sole command.

The first breath of air as I step out of the airplane feels astonishing and crisp as it rushes inward. *It's well below zero at basecamp.* The snow is deep, powdery, and sparkles like magic in the springtime sun, a far cry from the slushy snowpack it will become in June and July. I take a moment to greet Denali, Hunter, and Foraker, and take note of a handful of climbers bivouacked in camp, but there is little time for delay.

Once I have selected a good site for my tent, my crew and I ferry the gear off the runway to form a convenient pile. I turn on instinct at the sound of Paul's voice, ever the beacon of encouragement.

"We'll be checkin' on ya," he bellows, climbing back into his plane.

"Thanks, Paul. Don't forget about me."

The planes depart, and over the soundtrack of their noisy exit, my volunteers and I commence digging a square hole 14 feet on each side. Here, at 7,200 feet, we're panting and puffing more than we hoped for, but the snowpack is consistent, and we move it with ease using our large snow shovels. Three hours of effort and we've got ourselves a 196-square-foot, 7-foot-deep crater with a flat floor. By late June, the glacier surface will have lost at least that much snow from the long solar days. Annie's words of warning resonate: "If you don't dig the hole deep enough, the tent will end up perched on a pedestal of snow by season's end." I think we've dug the tent's footprint deep enough.

The sky has now turned white, an ominous sign of an approaching storm. "We have to step it up, everyone — the weather is changing," I announce. The last thing I want is my volunteers getting stuck here.

Two hours later, my sturdy tent is constructed. *At least I've got shelter now*, I think, drawing a mouthful of water from my bottle and grabbing a quick snack. With one of my volunteers, I set to work on the tedious process of assembling and connecting the solar panels, batteries, electronics, and antennae, while the remaining helpers shuttle my gear inside the tent.

The radio telephone is connected, and the antenna positioned — pointing at Mount Foraker, off which the analog signal somehow bounces to hit a distant antenna somewhere in the Susitna Valley.

It's a comforting moment when my phone emits a dial tone, and, after some minor antenna adjustments to eliminate static, I punch in Talkeetna Air Taxi's number and am greeted by the office manager and my friend Sandra White's cheery voice.

"Lisa, you sound loud and clear," she cries out, and all at once I feel less alone.

I call the other air services to let them know I am up and running, ready to give basecamp updates and save them the risk of making-weather probe flights into the Alaska Range. It's a far cry from the days of Frances Randall, who had to relay messages to Talkeetna by radioing local aircraft as they passed overhead, talking to them in basecamp or, lacking those options, using her shortwave radio to reach a distant bush resident named "Sunflower," who would then pass her transmissions on to the pilots in Talkeetna.

Soon, my propane heater is fired up, the stove is connected, and the tent is getting warm. I marvel at the fact I am in the wilderness with a durable shelter and a connection to the outside world. I feed my volunteers pizza, sandwiches, and beer for their efforts, and begin putting the final touches on my fortress: lawn chairs, sun umbrella, and even a plastic pink flamingo.

As gray clouds begin scudding into the lower Kahiltna Valley, my volunteers pace back and forth on the snow, watching the sky with intent.

"Do you think the weather will hold?" one asks, his eyes widening.

I will field this question many more times throughout the season. I decide to employ a distraction technique, since I don't have the answer.

"I hope so, but nothing is assured in the Alaska Range — here, have another beer," I reply, pulling a can from the snow.

The weather holds, and the parade of airplanes arrives as

scheduled for 4:00 p.m. pickup. I bid my helpers goodbye, and soon, the last plane to depart is but a speck against Mount Foraker. I am unable to resist a smile as I recall how far I've come. Ten years ago, I was stuck, working at the bank in Connecticut, wearing business suits that were beyond my meager salary, with a future that promised only more of the same. Now, I stand in front of my primitive shelter on Alaska's Kahiltna Glacier as the first incipient snowflakes of an incoming storm begin falling. I'm wrapped in the silence and immensity of the Alaska Range, and filled with a gratifying sense of pride because, for the first time in my life, I have responsibilities with personal meaning, and something I can call my own. Basecamp Lisa is on duty.

My daily routine comes together with ease. I arise at 7:00 a.m., start water for coffee, and check the weather, writing down temperatures and wind speeds, and assessing the snow-surface conditions on the runway. I do a quick sweep of camp to see if anyone is looking to fly out. At 8:00 a.m., I call to each of the air services to convey the morning report, each call following a typical pattern:

"Good morning, Hudson Air Service, this is Jay."

"Hi, Jay. It's Lisa at basecamp."

"Hi, Lisa. What do you have for me?"

"Well, you have three climbers from the 'Denali Dogs' Expedition wanting to fly out, and two from 'French McKinley.' It's currently three degrees Fahrenheit, winds are down-glacier at five to ten miles per hour. The glacier surface is soft and powdery. There are a few clouds over Denali and Foraker, but otherwise visibility is unlimited."

"Okay, thanks, Lisa," Jay says. "We'll be in around ten. We're waiting on a guided team of twelve from Rainier Mountaineering to get ready. Those Denali Dogs just flew in three days ago. What happened?" he asks.

"Oh, one of them said he couldn't stand to be away from his email," I reply, laughing at the absurdity.

Jay Hudson is the son of the famed pioneering bush pilot Cliff Hudson, who began flying climbers, hunters, and trappers into the Alaskan wilderness back in 1946. Jay and his family's small, simple operation has long serviced the climbing community, but prides itself on catering to bush Alaskans. Ever old fashioned, Jay is caught between wanting to keep his business small and the progress of the modern world, which has brought increasing numbers of climbers and sightseeing tourists to Talkeetna.

There is a long history of adversarial competition among the Talkeetna air services that includes a purported incident in which Cliff Hudson and the legendary aviator Don Sheldon engaged in a fist fight inside Nagley's store that reportedly devolved into them throwing tomatoes at one another. Jay has long viewed the expansion of my brother's air service with suspicion, and that suspicion sometimes transfers onto me. At times, I feel like I'm caught in the middle of a feud. "I noticed your brother flew up here the other day when the weather wasn't that great," Jay might say, or he once inquired about why Paul had so much white gas stacked in the company shed, as though I could provide some inside information. Jay also likes to tease me and keep me on my toes. He often asks me to pack the runway when it doesn't need it, telling me that I "need to stay busy." I would prefer to stay out of local politics, but being Paul's sister makes it almost impossible. Still, Jay is always cordial to me, and for me or anyone in need in the Alaska Range, he is often one of the first to lend a hand. He has helped the National Park Service on countless search and rescue missions over the past thirty years.

Most days by 9:00 a.m., I've got planes inbound and things are about to get busy. One morning, Doug Geeting's voice crackles over the radio:

"Four-seven Fox, eight thousand four hundred feet, One Shot Pass, northbound for basecamp. Howdy, Lisa. Make sure my climbers are ready to go."

One Shot Pass is about six to eight minutes flight time from basecamp. The climbers whom Doug is coming to pick up are still not packed up, despite my earlier instructions to be ready.

"CALIFORNIA DREAMERS!!!" I yell, embarrassed at my tone and the awkwardness of screaming out the expedition's name to get their attention.

"Geeting is a few minutes out, and if you're not ready by the time his plane is unloaded, I'm telling him to leave," I continue. I've witnessed Annie use this tactic, and it has the desired effect: the three climbers begin disassembling their camp with fury and determination.

Doug lands and unloads a pair of climbers and their gear. I help him and the outgoing climbers load the plane so we can get Doug back in the air, where he wants to be. As Doug prepares to depart, the climbers he has dropped off stand on the runway taking photos, as another airplane passes overhead, just minutes from landing.

"You guys, take pictures later," I say, shouldering one of their backpacks and grabbing a sled with a duffel bag. "There's a plane landing in a minute, and we need to get everything off this runway."

"Sorry," one of them says, as they both hustle to grab the remaining gear and follow me toward camp.

"Do you have your basecamp card?" I ask. "It's that white notecard you should have gotten from your air service."

"Yes, it's right here," the man replies, pulling it from his pocket.

"Here, come with me," I say, as I take the card from him. "It says you paid for three gallons of white gas — is that right?"

"Yes, that's correct," he says. We approach a sturdy, aluminum-framed red tent that the park service has donated for storing the boxes of white gas the air services stock here in camp. I pass them their fuel cans, and then gesture toward camp.

"That area up there, marked off by wands, is the cache garden for anything you want to leave here," I tell them. "Set up your camp down-glacier from it. The area up-glacier is for me and the rangers, and way up there by that equipment is where the park's rescue helicopter lands, so stay well clear of it.

"Be sure to bury your caches at least three to four feet deep to the top of your items, and mark them with a long wand and the cache tags the park service gave you. If your cache melts out, the ravens will tear your bags apart, eat all your food, and the park service will also give you a ticket for littering."

The climbers nod and smile, having already been warned by the rangers during the mandatory, pre-climb one-hour safety and environmental regulation orientation that each expedition is required to attend at the ranger station.

I point the climbers toward two different common holes that have been staked out for urinating, each marked by a tall orange bicycle flag, and then to a pair of wooden latrines. Each is perched over a thirty-foot hole excavated by the mountaineering rangers and their volunteers at the beginning of the season.

"NOTHING goes in the pee hole except pee. No trash, no poop, no food scraps," I counsel.

I find it especially entertaining trying to convey basecamp bathroom etiquette to climbers who speak little to no English.

"Pee . . . okay. Poop . . . NO okay," I pantomime for a group of twelve Korean climbers one day, as we stand next to the pee hole. I must look ridiculous.

"AHHH," they exclaim as my message is received, before bursting out in semi-embarrassed laughs. I just smile and hope they haven't mixed up the message.

The latrines do have plywood privacy screens, but they sit in a proximity that bursts the boundaries of most people's desired personal space. It makes for an interesting social experiment that requires some adjustments and sometimes a little humor.

"You can't say it ain't beautiful," offers the young man occupying the toilet a mere fifty feet to my right, our incidental eye contact mandating the need for this awkward icebreaker. I do my best to meet the moment:

"It sure is. Best view in town."

The upside is that while using these toilets, one faces west, looking straight toward Mount Foraker's two-mile-high east face. It is an inspiring sight for one's morning constitutional.

Denali-bound climbers most often stay here for one night, and then it might be weeks before I see them again. The camp, however, is populated in early season by climbers who are focused more on steep and technical ascents on the peaks close to basecamp, and are less interested in the plodding and sled-hauling of Denali's West Buttress. Many of the routes are very difficult, and, being at lower elevation, are in safer and more ideal condition during the colder months of April and May.

Among the most challenging and sought after of these objectives is the north buttress of Mount Hunter, a 4,000-foot wall of near-vertical rock and ice that holds many difficult routes of world-class quality. The most prized is the *Moonflower Buttress,* which takes a direct line up the center of the wall and tackles iconic ice features such as the "Twin Runnels," the "Leaning Ramp," and the "Shaft," the latter a 400-foot-tall column of continuous vertical ice. The *Moonflower* is forever associated with the legendary late alpinist Terrance "Mugs" Stump. Although Stump was not the first to attempt the line, nor the first to complete it, he was the first to attempt it in the more visionary fast-and-light style of alpinism evolving in the early 1980s. In 1981, Stump and his partner Paul Aubrey reached a point just short of the top of the buttress in just two days — an astonishing feat for the era — at which point they descended simply because they were satisfied with having climbed through the most difficult terrain, and cared little for reaching the summit.

Each season, there is a gaggle of hopeful suitors that occupies basecamp and who have become known as the "Moonies." These skilled, intense, and single-minded climbers will set up a comfortable camp and allow all of May to wait for an appropriate weather window to make their attempt. Many try, but very few succeed. They spend every spare moment strategizing, plotting, and obsessing over the weather and their intended route.

"Any updates to the forecast, Lisa? You think that storm will hit?" a pair of Colorado climbers asks me for the third time today.

"All I know is what the recorded message from the weather-service line tells me. You should ask Paul the next time he flies in," I parry, knowing full well that Paul will get them out of my hair with his stock answer.

"It's gettin' good. You guys should get on it," Paul tells them when he arrives, just as I predicted.

Paul just might be the most skilled pilot in Talkeetna, and he's also a seasoned climber who knows Alaska Range weather as well as anyone. That knowledge and his willingness to take climbers to more remote, hard-to-reach landing sites have made his business a favorite among the climbing community. Paul just wants his climbers to stop talking and go look.

Basecamp is already filling up with some of the current stars of hardcore alpinism. I am delighted when a plane rolls up in front of my tent and out steps Ian Parnell, a cheerful British climber I met up here last season.

"Cheers, Lisa. We're back for more entertainment," he calls in his delightful English accent, tossing his enormous duffels into the snow. Ian has a shock of curly brown hair and the classic alpinist's build, with thick arms and legs that must provide great power for such endeavors; at the same time, I wonder how he and my own Mark can pull their heavy, muscular frames up vertical faces with such apparent ease. Ian's partner is Kenton Cool, another Briton.

"Right," Kenton exclaims, stepping forward. "Quite pleased to meet you, Lisa," he says in a display of decorum. Then, to my surprise, he leans in and plants a kiss right on my cheek.

Kenton is lanky, with a handsome, chiseled face, a mischievous grin, and a few days' growth of a thin mustache. I like his energy immediately.

"What's your plan?" I ask, hoping they will be anchored here.

"Well," Ian replies with a tinge of superstitious reticence, "I believe we fancy a go on the *Moonflower*. But we're going to take a good look about and see what draws us in. It's Kenton's first holiday in Alaska, and he's pretty keen to get after it."

Kenton, in a moment of comedic hyperbole, grits his teeth and shakes his fist at Mount Hunter.

Soon after, two pleasant young Canadians named Rob Owens and Eamonn Walsh arrive in camp. They are here to attempt Mount Foraker's *Infinite Spur,* the mind-bending 9,000-foot route on the mountain's south face. It somehow provides some reassurance to me that someone else will be on the route well ahead of Mark and Joe, who are due to arrive in a week, the same route on their agenda. The *Infinite Spur* holds a feared reputation in the climbing community for its length, difficulty, and severe commitment.

Rob does most of the talking, while Eamonn, a hulking young man with forearms the size of a normal man's thighs, stands behind Rob in silence, his congenial facial expressions conveying an "aw shucks" demeanor.

"We have a cell phone," Rob says, adding with hesitation, "Do you think we could have your phone number here to call you for weather? We're hoping we can hit Anchorage towers from up there since it looks straight south."

Eamonn stares at Mount Foraker, as Rob conveys to me their itinerary and planned return dates. I watch as they depart for the long ski approach over to Foraker, and I feel a small connection to their adventure. *It must take so much motivation and courage to go to such places.*

Days later, Steve House, one of America's most talented alpinists, arrives from Talkeetna. I met Steve here in basecamp last season when he and his partners made a groundbreaking ascent of Denali's most difficult route, the *Slovak Direct*, climbing it in a superhuman sixty hours nonstop. Steve's partner is the Argentinean Rolando Garibotti, who is renowned for his fitness and famed for his prolific ascents on the granite spires of Southern Patagonia. "Rolo," as he introduces himself, is also one of the more helpful and courteous climbers I have met in my short tenure at basecamp.

"Lisa, is there anything I can help you with? Just let me know," he offers as he hefts his bags and paces off toward camp. I presume he is just being nice, but not long after, Rolo shows himself to be a man of his word. A large group has left their bags on the runway and disappeared into camp to socialize.

"Hey, you guys need to get your bags off the runway," I yell, repeating myself three times as I help a pilot load his plane. The gear's owners are not heeding my calls. As I'm about to lose my temper, I look over to see Rolo already on-scene, carrying three of this group's heavy duffel bags.

"Where should I put these?" he asks, having no apparent trouble with what must be over one hundred pounds of gear.

"Just off the landing strip, so they don't get hit by a plane. Thanks so much, Rolo."

The first patrol of basecamp rangers arrives, bringing in the first-year mountaineering ranger Mik Shain, and his two volunteers — his girlfriend, Heather Sullivan, and his friend Tucker Chenoweth. Mik contains his long brown hair with a loose ponytail and a park-service ball cap. He carries himself with a laid-back and casual manner interrupted on occasion by a goofy, physical sense of humor. Tucker has striking blue eyes, a shock of curly reddish-brown hair, and a soul patch hanging beneath an easygoing smile. He's a ski patroller and classic Colorado ski bum, but he already aspires to work here on Denali. "This is my dream job," he tells me. I'm relieved to have rangers in camp to take over the duties of trash and toilet police, although, since this is my home, too, I view these as shared responsibilities throughout the season.

Accompanying the patrol on their flight in is also Michelle O'Neil, who over the past several years has become one of my closest friends. From social potlucks, to nasty bushwhacking through scary bear country, to extreme blueberry picking, falling into creeks, close encounters with antisocial, armed landowners, and hikes that took three times as long as the map promised, we've been through a lot together.

"Hey, Lisa, how's it going?" she calls across the runway.

"Hey, Michelle — welcome to the party," I respond, and rush out to help with her bags.

Michelle has been recruited as a basecamp volunteer for six weeks. She is the point person for a voluntary study being conducted by the park to determine how much trash an average Denali West Buttress expedition generates. Her main duty will be to weigh each climbing group's trash at the conclusion of their expedition.

"I'll set up my camp near the rangers, so we'll all be close together. This is exciting. It's so beautiful here," she says. Just then, another airplane arrives.

"*We're hee-errre.*"

The call is drawn out, hammy, and almost histrionic. Everyone in camp turns to look. I'd know those voices anywhere, and fix my gaze across the runway to see Mark and Joe piling out of Paul's airplane.

"These knuckleheads are all yours," Paul shouts to me, as he shakes their hands.

The boys stride off the runway as the picture of confidence, duffels over their shoulders and walking toward me with purpose. Mark stops to give me a big hug and kiss.

"I've really missed you," Mark says, turning serious. "I'm so glad to get out of Seattle and away from the engineering desk."

The boys set up an expedition tent close to mine, and then Mark moves his bags into my tent, where he'll stay with me. Mark glances over and smiles as he unpacks.

"We've hit the big time, here, haven't we?" he exclaims, absorbing the almost palatial shelter we now share in the heart of the Alaska Range. The phone rings, and Mark answers.

"Hey, this is Rob and Eamonn up on the *Infinite Spur*."

Mark lights up as he keys the handset to reply.

"Hey, Rob. Lisa told me someone was up there. How's it going?"

"Just reporting in here from the world's worst bivouac," Rob says, sounding crestfallen.

"The weather has been pretty bad for most of the climb," he continues. "We're at a chopped bivy at about 13,500 feet; it's snowing hard, and spindrift is crushing our tent. We're hoping you have a good forecast for us."

Mark glances at my weather notes.

"Forecast is calling for improvement the next couple of days. Low winds, partly cloudy. Hang in there, guys — you got this. Be safe," Mark counsels, before the call ends and he turns toward me with a troubled expression.

"They're really getting their money's worth. I sure hope we have better weather."

Late in the afternoon, I emerge from my tent with an announcement: "Who wants to watch a movie tonight?" I ask, producing my DVD player. Mark, Joe, Ian, and Kenton cease their continuous talking about climbing routes and the weather long enough to raise their hands. "I'm making pizza," I continue, pointing to the propane stove I brought, which also has an oven. Almost every night thereafter, the "evening campfire" alternates between my tent or that of the rangers, and the evenings are filled with hilarious stories, crude jokes, and as much "climber talk" as I can handle. Fortunately, having Michelle there gives me someone to talk to about things other than splitter hand and finger cracks, or which cams you need for the sixth pitch of some route in Yosemite.

As I prepare to read my eight o'clock weather, I think about Frances Randall, Denali's very first basecamp manager. Frances was a concert violinist who played with the Fairbanks Symphony

Orchestra. She was well-remembered for playing her violin over the CB radio for the enjoyment of pilots flying overhead, or for the entertainment of climbers during her evening weather report.

"We need to keep that sort of tradition going." I declare. "What can WE do?"

Mark thinks for a moment, then produces his vast collection of CDs.

"Stand by for the eight o'clock weather," I announce. On cue, Mark then uses a portable speaker to broadcast a musical intro into the radio handset, fading it out after twenty to thirty seconds to tee up my forecast. We decide that the music heralding the forecast each night will be dictated by the current weather and the forecast ahead. Tonight, a happy tune from Mark's collection gives way to me reading a forecast for what promises to be a great summit day tomorrow. But the window won't last. "And now, here's the extended forecast," I say, using a more ominous tone. Over a backdrop of the apocalyptic opening music to the movie *Blade Runner*, by the famed Greek composer Vangelis, I convey the details of a powerful incoming storm that may last for four days.

On subsequent nights, I add in select NBA and baseball scores as well as major news headlines picked up from an FM radio I play during the day for information from the outside world.

"Did the Cubs win last night?" a climber asks one evening.

"Sorry, the Cardinals won, four to two," I reply.

On another evening, rangers Mik and Heather read the entire weather report in heavy New York mob accents that sound like something straight out of *Goodfellas*.

"Yo, Mikey, ya think the weather's gonna be good tomorrow?" Heather asks, painting the accent on thick.

"Yeah, no way. *Fugg-et-about-it,*" Mik says. Before long, a climber somewhere on the mountain breaks in with a scolding tone:

"Is this serious??? We are counting on this forecast to make all our decisions."

Our group holds back laughter as Mik and Heather continue without breaking character:

"Oh, youse betta believe it's serious," Mik retorts. "Serious like a heart attack," Heather adds.

Days later, I produce the author and famed Alaskan alpinist Jonathan Waterman's book *The Quotable Climber* plus a mountain-trivia book, and a new tradition is born: the nightly mountain-trivia question.

"What is the fourth highest mountain in the Alaska Range?" seems to stump everyone, and I catalog the more challenging questions for future repeat usage.

One day, some climbers bring me a twelve-pack of Coors Light. It is a nice gesture, but I don't like beer, so I decide to turn each can into a prize for the first team to chime in with the correct trivia question answer each night. I get their expedition name, write it on their basecamp card, and set the beer aside for them to collect when they return to basecamp. The gambit becomes so popular that any night when I just don't feel like doing the trivia question is met with protests from teams all over the mountain, motivating me to be more consistent.

"No trivia, Lisa?"

Another night, an anonymous climber somewhere on the mountain interrupts my weather broadcast numerous times by hitting the "call" button on their "sports edition" walkie, which in this case emits a howling wolf noise. After the third time, I issue a warning:

"Whoever is doing that, please stop, or this report is going to end early."

I complete but half a sentence more before I'm interrupted by yet another howl.

"Okay, everyone, that's it. You can find and thank the wolf. Have a good night," and I click off my radio.

I go back to reading my book, but Mark soon returns from the ranger's tent with an amusing report on what transpired next.

"People were begging you to come back," he laughs, emphasizing one man's final desperate plea: "Lisa, we're all *REALLY* sorry about the wolf. Please don't go."

The following evening, I begin my report with a pre-emptive warning about interruptions. I never hear the wolf again.

The weather is getting nice as May progresses, and the Moonies and others in camp are getting out climbing. Mark and Joe make a brief attempt on the *Moonflower,* but then return after only one day.

"We didn't train enough — we were way too slow," Mark says as they plod back into camp. Joe shakes his head, adding, "We needed to climb more vertical waterfall ice this winter."

Kenton and Ian head up on the *Moonflower,* while Mik and his volunteers set up the park service's high-powered spotting scope so we can watch them and other teams climbing on the various routes within sight of camp.

Mark and Joe regroup and depart very early one morning for Kahiltna Queen, the 12,380-foot pyramid that dominates the upper end of the southeast fork.

"We have our radio, so we'll check in later," Mark says, as he exits my tent wearing his harness and dressed for the 3:00 a.m. chill. The weather begins sunny, but clouds build throughout the day. By afternoon, the top half of Kahiltna Queen is engulfed in clouds. I try not to worry, but worry is in my DNA. It's late afternoon when I get a radio transmission from Mark.

"We're on the summit," he reports. "It took us a long time to get up here; it's snowing and the visibility is pretty low. It's going to take us quite a while to get down to the base."

I must be distracted, because my interpretation is something quite different:

"We summited and we're at the base of the mountain," is what I hear. Perhaps it's what I want to hear, because then they would be off the mountain and closer to safety. Under the now-mistaken impression that all they have remaining is a thirty-minute ski back to camp, I ask a question without realizing its absurdity:

"Will you be down in time for dinner?"

"Oh. Yeah. Sure," Mark says, and I fail to hear the sarcasm in his voice.

"Cool," I reply. "See you soon."

Seven o'clock comes and goes. I pace the floor between bites of my dinner.

"I'm sure they're fine, Lisa, and they're probably tired," Michelle says, using a tone of reassurance.

Nine o'clock comes, and I'm outside scanning the upper valley with the spotting scope. Mik and the rangers seem unconcerned.

"It's Mark and Joe. They're fine," Mik admonishes.

Steve House, seeing the commotion, walks over and I explain the situation, hoping that America's strongest alpinist will have some words of wisdom.

"I know something has happened to them. We have to go look," I implore.

Steve looks at me with the patience that makes him an effective mountain guide.

"Those guys are solid, Lisa. I'm sure they're fine," he offers.

I try again and again to raise them on the radio, but there is no answer.

I've had enough talk. I click into my skis and, with Michelle scrambling to catch up, I tear out of camp and begin skiing up-glacier in haste and without a plan. I have a radio, but no pack, no climbing harness, no water, and no food. As I ski, the evening sun is still quite warm and I begin removing layers, tossing jackets and hats on the snow behind me without a thought. Michelle, following behind, collects each item and stuffs it into her pack.

Then, I hear something. I stop and cock my head. The sound is unmistakable: panicked screams, coming from somewhere far up-valley. Screams of abject terror. I cannot pinpoint the source, nor can I decipher the shouted words accompanying the terrified shrieks.

In a full-blown panic, I ski up the steep hill aside the Control Tower, the landmark I use for ski laps during down times in the camp, but I climb it faster than ever before. The *Moonflower* towers overhead to our right, while Kahiltna Queen occupies the head of the valley, each mountain glowing in the setting sun.

"Lisa, stop. I have binoculars — let's take a look," Michelle implores, catching her breath as we are reunited atop the hill. She pulls out the binoculars and scans the mountain.

"There they are. I see them," she cries out, passing the glasses to me. Sure enough, there at the foot of the mountain, about two miles distant, are Mark and Joe. They are coiling the rope and packing their packs, their body language casual; it seems highly unlikely that the screaming came from them. I take a long look around at the mountains. *Who could it have been?* It's silent now, and I see no one else on the nearby walls. Whoever it was, wherever it was, the incident must have resolved itself — for better or for worse. I don't even know where else to start looking.

Now, the adrenaline wears off with a crash. *I am so angry I can't speak.* Overwhelmed, embarrassed, and unable to process, I hand the binoculars back to Michelle without a word and ski back toward basecamp.

Mark and Joe return to camp around 11:00 p.m. I'm in no mood to talk, and I greet Mark with an icy silence. Mark, believing himself to be in trouble, grabs his sleeping bag and pad and beats a hasty retreat to Joe's tent. For the remainder of the night, I am consumed by reflection upon my inability to manage my anger in the face of severe stress. I hate making excuses, but somehow, my inquiry always leads me back to my childhood, the example set by my father's volatile temper, and our family's predilection for not talking about problems.

Mark and I sort out the misunderstanding in the morning, and all is forgiven. Soon after, a knock comes on my door. I open it to be greeted by Ian and Kenton, looking sunburnt and tired.

"Greetings, Lisa. Just back from the *Moonflower*. Brilliant route," Ian says with classic British understatement, as though describing a mere stroll in the park.

Ian grins, and then scans the inside of my tent with curiosity.

"You have any sweets?"

I toss him a bag of Skittles, which he annihilates. When I see him eyeballing the bag of pretzels on my desk a moment later, I hand them over without a word, and he goes to work on them as well.

I relay my misadventures of the previous night, and as I reach the part of the story that involves the as-yet-unsolved terrified screaming, the two of them sit up straight as a wave of shame washes over their faces.

"That was me," Kenton admits with an uneasy smile, before offering his explanation.

"We were abseiling the Shaft," Kenton relates, describing the vertical ice runnel that's a landmark feature in the middle of the climb. "It was overhanging, and I got a bit greedy and went to the very end of the rope. We hadn't tied knots in the ends. I was hanging in free space with a handful of skinny cord remaining. Almost lost it."

Ian wears a sheepish grin, while I stare, slack-jawed and horror-stricken. "Sorry for giving you such a fright," Kenton adds.

"Well, your timing couldn't have been worse," I reply, emitting a nervous laugh. "Don't ever do that again."

Rob and Eamonn return a day later having climbed and escaped from the *Infinite Spur*. They've been gone for over a week, and their drooped shoulders and disheveled hair tell of a wild journey. Mark and Joe pepper them with questions about the route, as it is up next on their agenda. They sit riveted as Rob tells their story, while silent Eamonn stands alongside projecting reticence save for the occasional modest grin.

"It was an incredible adventure," Rob concludes, "but I'm not sure I want to go that big again in the mountains any time soon. It felt quite 'out there.'"

A fine, sunny afternoon has Mark, Joe, and the British talking about a night climb of the Control Tower, just up-valley, with the hope that the snow will firm up after the sun sinks to the north.

"I want to go," I announce.

"Me, too," Michelle says.

The last planes of the evening depart from basecamp. Mark, Joe, Michelle, Kenton, Ian, and I set out on skis in the all-night alpenglow. We opt for a steep line on the south face of the peak, a quick, thirty-minute approach from camp. It's not the normal way up the mountain, and it's quite a bit steeper.

I'm roped up with Mark and Joe, while Michelle is with the British. We take a pair of parallel, independent lines up steepening snow, weaving about large rock outcrops, even making a few moves up and over granite steps. The lengthy days of late May have turned the snow to hideous, isothermic mush, and tonight it has just not frozen. We wallow and sink to our chest in places. It feels less like climbing and more like hard labor.

This is supposed to be fun, I think, growing grumpier with every ropelength. Joe belays in a snow hole he excavated at the end of the latest lead, placing himself in a five-foot-deep trench running straight up the slope. Mark stretches the rope to the summit ridge in similar style, before bringing us up off an anchor that is just his 200 pounds braced in the snow. As I plod up to Mark's belay, the improving snow is of no help to my sour mood.

"I'm done. I'm not going any further," I say.

Joe sees my reluctance, shrugs his shoulders, and hurries to catch up to Michelle, Ian, and Kenton, who are already walking down the beautiful ridge toward the high point. Mark sits and remains quiet to allow me a personal moment, and then looks back over at me. "It's maybe ten more minutes of easy walking, Lisa. Look at them go — the snow is good up here," he says.

I observe our friends plodding along a knife edged ridge with the backdrop of a fiery-red sky behind Mount Foraker and Mount Crosson. Suddenly, the fear of missing out is too strong — it makes no sense to have endured all that we have just to forego the route's only enjoyable section.

"Alright. I'm in. Let's keep going," I declare. Discomfort is endemic to alpinism, and the fatigue that keeps slowing me down when climbing adds into that, forcing me to dig deeper and suppress the pain. Some days I feel normal, but others — like today, to an extent — my arms and legs just feel heavy, like dead weight, creating a haze of lethargy that makes it tougher to motivate, not to mention make upward progress. But sublime moments like this — on this exposed tightrope, the *Moonflower* towering across the valley to our left — keep me moving onward. Tipping the scales between fun and not fun may require less suffering for me than it used to, but I'm just grateful I can be here in any capacity.

As I walk, I think about what it means to be a climber. I don't have the wiry, yoga-girl build of many female climbers, or at least, of the models in the gear advertisements. That's fine, but it's distressing how many people Mark and I encounter in our travels who just assume that I'm not a climber. "Oh, you climb, too?" they'll ask. Yes. I do. I look ahead now as we crest a final rise, with nowhere higher to go. Mark and I together take the final steps to rejoin our happy crew on the summit.

"Right then, Lisa. Great job," Kenton cheers, as he notices me approaching. He gives me a hug, and then, to the surprise of everyone except Ian, produces from his pack a striped, stuffed mouse.

"What's this?" I ask.

"This," Kenton explains, his tone turning serious, "is Stripey Mouse. He goes everywhere with me. Every climb."

Ian grins, while Joe is incredulous, saying, "So, a hardman British alpinist brings a stuffed animal with him on routes? Now I've seen it all."

I absorb the panorama, treasuring my first Alaskan midnight summit amid the dusky atmosphere. I look over at Mark. "It was worth the wallow," I acknowledge. Mark smiles, drapes his arm over my shoulder, and casts a faraway gaze across the mountain landscape.

June is soon upon us, and with it, the magnificent weather forecast that Mark and Joe have been waiting for. They begin packing for *the Infinite Spur*. Packing for such a route is an obsessive process and I give them their space. Steve and Rolo are also heading for the same route, which provides me additional reassurance that the boys won't be alone, at least at the beginning of their climb. Steve and Rolo intend to climb in a continuous effort with no bivouacs, while Mark and Joe are planning for more traditional tactics, aiming for a multiday ascent with planned overnights. This will be the most serious objective that Mark and Joe have ever attempted.

"If it goes well, we should be back in seven to nine days. We have at least ten days of fuel," Mark tells me. "We probably won't be able to reach you by radio until we get up high, so I'm not sure how long it will be until you hear from us."

Sporting matching white Capilene tops, black hardshell pants, and pirate-style bandanas, Mark and Joe are ready to leave, and we take pictures in the evening sun to mark the moment. Mark gives me a strong, comforting hug and then gazes into my eyes with intention. "Try not to worry," he says as he touches my cheek with a gentle, loving tap. *He knows me better than that.*

The boys click into their skis, shoulder their packs, and with one final wave to Michelle and me, point themselves toward Mount Foraker. I watch them ski away, my emotions a mixture of pride, admiration, and anxiety. I channel my concern into things that I can control, and that's running basecamp and keeping my pilots well-informed of wind, clouds, and runway conditions.

Two days of beautiful weather follow. *They must be well up onto the route by now.* The following morning, Steve and Rolo return to camp. The fastest of the route's five prior ascents had been seven days. These two climbed it in just twenty-five hours, a superhuman effort.

"We saw Mark and Joe — they camped near us at the base, and we started up the route about an hour before them," Steve tells me.

Rolo adds, "The route is in great condition, Lisa; they should be making good progress."

After a day's rest, Steve and Rolo make an overnight trip to the base of the *Infinite Spur* to retrieve their skis. They return the next morning, bringing back Mark's and Joe's skis in addition to their own.

"We glassed the route and we didn't see them," Rolo tells me. "Safe to assume they're up high and going to make it up and over, so we figured we'd help them out."

"They will be psyched not to have to do that approach again," I answer.

Paul flies in to pick up Steve and Rolo, and I bid them farewell.

"Don't worry, Lisa — those guys should be back soon," Rolo says, and he gives me a big hug and the customary Argentinean kiss on the cheek.

It's Mark and Joe's sixth day on route. *No word yet.* The weather is beautiful today, but the automated weather report is calling for the "biggest storm to hit the mountain in years," with 100 mph winds and 4 days of heavy snowfall. Before my stress level has time to ramp up far, the radio telephone rings.

"Well, howdy there, basecamp — how are ya?" Davey Kreutzer, the park service's helicopter manager, is here with his daily morning-weather check-in, and it couldn't have come at a better time. There could be a blizzard outside, but Davey's animated voice makes any morning feel sunny. His air-operations duties include the development and supervision of Denali's helicopter shorthaul-rescue program. Shorthaul is a technique in which a rescuer is suspended beneath the helicopter on a rope and brought into an incident scene in technical terrain or where it would otherwise be impossible for the helicopter to land nearby. Because of these responsibilities, Davey always has his eyes on the weather, and knows the exact sorts of details that I'm seeking.

I ask Davey about the impending storm. "I see what they're talking about," he says. "I see that storm out in the ocean on the satellite. But the models I'm looking at show it staying down south. It looks like more high pressure for us."

I take a deep breath.

"Don't worry, Lulu. I'll keep watching it for ya," Davey says. "We'll keep Mark and Joe safe."

Davey is more than just a weatherman to me. Davey is married to Annie Duquette, my friend and predecessor at basecamp. Annie's desire to settle down with him in Talkeetna was one of the many reasons I ended up working this job. He's smart, funny, high energy, and has a cheerful and optimistic attitude, traits that always make me feel like someone down in town is looking out for me.

My spirits are further lifted when, just after completing my 8:00 p.m. weather report, Mark's voice is the first one I hear.

"Lisa, this is Mark and Joe. You copy?"

"Great. How's it going, sweetie?"

"Awesome. We're at 14,500 feet, above all the hard climbing. It's so wild here. We should be up and over the summit tomorrow."

"Okay," I say, "but we're getting mixed weather reports. One is talking about a 'catastrophic' storm."

"Huh," Mark responds. "It's been unsettled up here the past couple days, but now it's cleared off. It's absolutely gorgeous here, Lisa. Not a cloud in any direction."

The next day is beautiful. *Davey was right.* In the late afternoon, the boys call in again.

"We did it, Lisa," Mark shouts over the wind, and I can hear Joe howling with delight in the background.

"Great job, you guys," I reply, but I'm compelled to offer a reminder: "Love you — now be careful and get yourselves down safe."

Thirty-six hours later, it's 7:00 a.m. and the sun is just hitting my tent. It's time to get up, but I linger in my warm bag. Michelle comes over, and we get the morning coffee brewing. Now there's another sound approaching. Crunching footsteps growing closer, along with familiar voices. Michelle and I open the door, and there stand Mark and Joe, in the same spot where I bid them a worried farewell eight and a half long days ago. Michelle and I rush forth to them for hugs.

The boys are happy but subdued by exhaustion. Their haggard faces still manage to light up as they recount snippets of their adventure while stripping off their harnesses, unlacing their boots, and sipping fresh coffee from the mugs we press into their tired hands.

"Well, Barry Blanchard was right," Mark states, his eyes widening as Barry's had in emphasis, recounting the legendary Canadian alpinist's assessment of the route from the previous year. "It was . . . INFINITE."

"I can't believe it," Joe mutters to no one in particular, as he stands in the snow staring at Foraker.

"Look, Joe. Our skis are here," Mark says, having just noticed their equipment standing in the snow.

"You can thank House and Rolo — they grabbed them for you," I explain, as they look to Michelle and me in wonder.

"Man, we owe those guys," Joe cries, as he and Mark give each other a big hug in the realization that there is nothing more to be done but relax.

Michelle and I begin cooking a breakfast of eggs and bacon, toast with butter, and as a starter, we pop the champagne I had flown in for the occasion. We make mimosas with fresh-squeezed orange juice. The boys flop down on my cot, taking delicate sips of their drinks. The bacon is just becoming crispy when I glance over to see two sound-asleep alpinists. Michelle and I laugh, but decide they need nourishment before sleep, and we roust them back to life.

"This is the best bacon ever," Joe mumbles through a mouthful of food, as Mark grunts his approval.

I am proud of Mark and Joe, having witnessed firsthand their development as alpinists over the past five years and their progression through an impressive list of climbs, each more difficult than the last. On one hand, my concern for them could be diminished by their continued success, their competence, and their cautious tactics. On the other, I wonder how far they will push it, and if their successes and their entering the realm of world-class climbing objectives should be cause for even greater concern?

The beautiful weather continues, with many of the pilots claiming this to be the finest stretch of June weather they can recall. Mark, Joe, Michelle, and I spend the ensuing days running the camp, having big social dinners with the rangers, and fine-tuning our antics for the evening forecast. One lazy afternoon, Mark and I ski thirty minutes over to a rock buttress at the foot of Mount Frances and climb several nice pitches of steep granite.

Ian and Kenton return from establishing a massive new route on Denali's remote "Fathers and Sons Wall," while other climbers have established difficult first ascents on some of Denali's largest faces. The camp takes on a celebratory atmosphere amid so much contagious success. Within this paradigm, I again find myself thinking about my own climbing. Should I try Denali? Given my position here, it seems foolish not to. Yet, each story that I hear of cold and exhaustion and hunger and all manner of suffering makes me question if it may be best for me to keep my alpinism civilized, especially with my body's unexplained metabolic issues slowing me down. Still, as I spend my days here staring at the giants surrounding me, there's a stirring call from them that just won't go away. Rock climbing and peak bagging in friendlier environs like the Sierra, the Wind River Mountains, and the Cascades are rewarding in every aspect. Why can't that be enough?

We pass the final days of the season in relaxed fashion, under a regime of phenomenal weather. Joe confounds everyone in camp with his mysterious card tricks, and recruits anyone willing into games and contests. One afternoon, I hear a commotion outside my tent and emerge to find a raucous audience cheering for Joe. He is shirtless, clad in sunglasses and a pair of old red long underwear. His greasy hair is pulled into a top knot, and he's performing wild gyrations with a hula hoop. Loud techno music blasts from a speaker. Kenton is quite amused and gives Joe the nickname "Hula Hoopin' Han Solo."

The party days come to an end as Mark, Joe, the British, and most everyone else fly out to Talkeetna and leave Michelle and I to finish out the season. July 1 means the climbing season is almost complete, and I have but a week remaining before I pack up and return to Talkeetna. The day also brings an alarming mountain-weather summary:

"Summer on the mountain is about to come to an end," the forecast begins. "It may be at least three to four weeks before any substantial clearing."

The synopsis on July 2 is even more blunt:

"Summer is over," it begins flatly.

The storm arrives as promised, and, with it, many days of heavy rain, nights of wet, heavy snow, and no flying for almost a week. Departing Denali climbers pile up waiting to fly out, and the days are long and dreary. At long last, I'm greeted by clear skies in camp.

"Today's the day, Lisa," Paul warns when I check in over the phone. "If you want out, you better pack it up. I don't see a break in this for at least another week."

By late afternoon, I find myself exiting the airplane in front of Talkeetna Air Taxi and unloading a mountain of gear. The smell of the earth, the cottonwoods, and the explosion of life that accompanies the Alaskan summer fill me with unmitigated joy. Mark and Joe return from climbing in the Ruth Gorge a week later, and Joe, atypically, lingers around Talkeetna for more than a week before heading home to Washington. I soon discover why.

"So, a friend of mine saw Joe and Michelle in the grocery store down in Wasilla today," Mark says, with a coy expression, as we enjoy dinner on the deck outside our cabin. "He said Joe was looking at Michelle like a puppy dog. Like he was head over heels."

Amid those festive late-June days at basecamp, I had picked up on the chemistry building between them. It all makes perfect sense now as I picture it: two sets of best friends, two couples, and a future filled with promise and adventure.

I look back over this, my first full season, with both relief and gratitude. Everyone made it home safely, the boys attained a long-sought climbing objective, and there was no excessive drama, apart from the misunderstanding amidst the boys' late-night return from Kahiltna Queen. I even got to climb a mountain. The presence of so many high-octane climbers in camp, each taking advantage of the season's outstanding weather to complete world-class alpine objectives, makes me feel like I just witnessed an important moment in Denali and Alaska Range history. Above all, I settled into an easy flow and routine with the job, and I am sure that I will return for some time to come.

I can only hope that every season is like this one. Intuition and experience, however, inform me otherwise — that fickle fate is always lurking in the shadows. I must never become complacent, nor can I ever celebrate too early or too long. For the time being, however, I'm going to savor these feelings of accomplishment until my next shift in managing what just may be the greatest show on Earth.

Chapter Seven
2002-2006
A Cast of Characters

The grandeur of the mountains is at the heart of the appeal of my job managing Denali Basecamp. However, there is a human element to it as well, one that helps render worthwhile all the discomforts and stresses and worries that come with the job's responsibilities. I like to think of the Alaska Range as a theater, and I'm sitting front row at a complex play or character drama, with unpredictable acts ranging from comedy to tragedy. I never know what might happen next, or when I might be pulled from out of the audience and straight into the action. Year after year, I return to manage the stage that is Denali Basecamp, drawn in by the colorful cast of characters.

I have been hearing about the "Funky Monkeys" for several days. During my morning weather call to the office at Talkeetna Air Taxi, Sandra struggles to contain herself while describing their antics of the previous evening.

"These climbers I've been telling you about, they made up a rap song about climbing Denali, and they put on a big show in the office last night. I almost died laughing," she exclaims. "Their expedition name is the 'Funky Monkeys'."

When the Monkeys step off the plane at basecamp, they jump straight into a new rendition of the previous night's rap song. "We made up some new verses for each camp," one of them announces, before they begin their routine, dancing and gyrating while tossing pretend microphones between each singer, all while the pilot, various onlookers, and I all fail to contain our laughter. *Looks like I'm in for the good sort of trouble.*

The Monkeys are in no rush to head up Denali and settle into camp for a few days. Denali National Park's Superintendent, Steve Martin, is also in basecamp, as a guest of the NPS ranger's basecamp patrol.

The Monkeys are grilling up cheeseburgers, drinking beer, and hooting and hollering — I can hear them any time I am outside unloading airplanes.

"Lisa, come over and hang out," they call. "We'll cook you a burger."

"Maybe later. You guys are up to something," I reply, resisting the allure of their laughter and the smell of the burgers. With the park superintendent in my camp, I also want to put on my most professional and serious face, of course.

The Monkeys have no such worries, however, and I watch as they invite him over to their camp for a burger and brew. Perhaps twenty minutes later, I hear a chorus of screams and howls from my tent, 200 yards away. *Something big is happening,* I realize, and, unable to contain my curiosity, I run up to their camp to see what I missed.

Superintendent Martin is on one knee and still trying to regain his composure when I arrive. I learn that after engaging him with disarming small talk, one of the Monkeys asked the superintendent for a minor favor.

"Hey, would you mind grabbing the spices out of that duffel over there" Dwayne had said, spatula in hand, motioning toward a bag resting on a snow shelf. Next to the shelf was the entrance to a spacious snow cave, where they kept their frozen food protected from the sun.

"Sure," the superintendent replied. He unzipped the bag, but instead of spices, he was greeted by a live human head with a deranged face staring up at him.

"I bet he jumped back at least eight feet," Andy says with pride. "Our work is done here."

The Monkeys had carved out a human-sized hiding place beneath the shelf, accessed via the freezer where it would be undetectable to unsuspecting guests. The Monkeys had spent all day pulling this trick on other climbers, but the park's top-ranked officer was doubtless their proudest catch. I'm just pleased that my suspicions of their monkey business kept me from making their list of victims.

Over the years, I have met numerous amputees and climbers with disabilities who went on to climb Denali. No one I've met, however, impressed me more than the two Russian paraplegics who summitted in 2002. Supported by a large group of fellow Russian climbers, the two men sat in sleds connected to climbing ropes. Their team members would move out ahead, secure the far end of the rope to snow anchors, and then each of the paraplegic men would use mechanical ascenders to pull themselves along the ropes, uphill. They repeated this process all the way up Denali, which took them over one month to climb. The team brought over 3,000 feet of rope, and in the more exposed areas above 14,000 feet, the others in the team provided spotting and belays to protect them from falls.

Now, back in basecamp, the Russians are in no hurry to leave. It's a refreshing change from the hurried and anxious attitudes I often encounter from climbers who just cannot wait to get off the mountain. Successfully reaching the summit of Denali with no working legs has motivated the two men and their dedicated friends to hold a multiday celebration.

The Russians have set up a giant tent in camp for socializing and festivities, and it's filled with every type of American junk food you can imagine: Coke, Doritos, Oreos, beef jerky, and more. It's as though they are trying to indulge in every American cliché they know. Only two speak passable English, but somehow, we all seem to understand one another. I have to wait until my workday is done to relent to join their ongoing party. Once I do, entering the Russian tent is like entering a vortex.

"Lisa, you must stay. Please enjoy Russian vodka with us," they implore, as another round of unfamiliar group songs begins. It's fun, but each time I visit, I must invent excuses to leave.

"I'll be back," I say, but I don't always uphold my promise. The last thing I need up here is a hangover.

The feat of climbing Denali as a paraplegic might only be rivaled by the exploits of a peculiar soloist who steps off an airplane one afternoon with aspirations for Denali. Soloing on Alaskan glaciers is a hazardous pursuit due to the exceptional crevasse danger. Some solo climbers attach a ladder or a long pole to their waist with the hope that should they break through a snow bridge spanning one of these insidious slots — which can be 100-plus feet deep — that it would prevent them from falling to their deaths. This man has no such system.

"What's your plan for getting yourself out of a crevasse if you fall in?" I ask.

"I won't fall in," he states, matter-of-factly. "I am a practicing Buddhist, and I will 'hover' over the crevasses."

"Okay, then. Good luck with that," I reply. Some principles of Buddhism make sense to me, but I wasn't aware that embracing them conveys the power to defy gravity. When the man returns several weeks later, having traveled to the summit and back without incident, I must wonder if perhaps he is onto something. It's either hovering, dumb luck, or divine intervention.

Divine intervention or not, I have received gifts from above up here at basecamp. One day, an Alaska National Guard UH-60 Blackhawk carrying US Air Force Pararescuemen circles out of the skies above basecamp while on a mountain-training flight. It sets down upon the snow just up-glacier from the runway. Military helicopters seldom land or operate in this area during their training, to avoid the frequent fixed-wing air traffic, so I'm perplexed.

The helicopter rotors remain spinning as a crew member jumps out with a package in hand and trots across the runway. Meg Perdue, the NPS basecamp ranger, is also stumped, and walks out to meet him halfway. The crewman hands off the package and returns to his ship. The machine lifts and flies away, blasting us with snow. As the cloud settles, Meg walks toward me, staring at the package and shaking her head.

"I can't believe this. It's for you."

She passes me a small, flat box marked "LISA" in large Sharpie marker. I open it to discover a fabulous-looking apple pie. One of Paul's pilots, my friend Matt, is also in the National Guard reserve, and I suspect he may be the source. I look at Meg, who is still stunned. I respond with a casual shrug and say, "From one of my fans, I guess."

For every moment at basecamp where I feel like a celebrity, there's another when I'm starstruck. Such is the case when I encounter a climbing team composed of veteran NASA astronauts led by John Grunsfeld. John has spent more time in space than anyone alive, and now they are in camp after an unsuccessful attempt on Denali, during which, in a twist of irony, two of his teammates became sick from the altitude.

I pepper them with questions about space travel and what it's like living in zero gravity. As their plane arrives to take them home, John and his team give me a beautiful photo of Denali taken from space, and a NASA logo hat autographed with "Lisa, Lunar Basecamp Manager."

"We're going back to the moon, and we could sure use a basecamp manager," John says, laughing and pointing at the sky. "The job is yours if you want it."

"Deal," I reply. "I hope the radio up there will work better there than the one here."

Over the years, numerous documentary and news crews have visited basecamp. The 2003 climbing season, however, is dominated by the presence of a National Geographic film crew with a plan to spend a full two months following the NPS rangers around, both on and off the mountain, looking for drama to capture while profiling the park service's professional rescuers.

The film crew is in basecamp on a bright and sunny day, interviewing various climbers and filming their in-camp antics, when Anchorage's East High School jazz band flies in to give a live concert. Basecamp is crowded with Moonies and other climbers, including Dana Drummond, Bayard Russell, and Freddie Wilkinson, who are part of a wild group of young New Hampshire guides on their first trip to the Alaska Range. They have dug a massive snow cave and constructed a fortified camp to live in for the month of ambitious climbs they have planned. Between climbs, much of their time is spent partying, playing badminton, and golfing with the full set of clubs that topped off their 600 pounds of gear.

The East High jazz band is in fine form, playing an energetic set, while dozens of climbers and rangers form a large circle to watch and tap their feet to the beat. I spy the ever-mischievous Freddie walking through the circle toward me with an expression that indicates he's up to something. If my time in Alaska has taught me anything, it's how to spot troublemakers. I suspect Freddie is aiming to embarrass me in front of the rolling cameras of the National Geographic crew. I make a run for the exit, but it's too late. Freddie grabs my arm and pulls me inside the circle to dance in front of the crowd. Freddie has consumed a few too many drinks, and the result is that Freddie cannot dance very well. The crowd laughs at the spectacle, before some join in and transform the glacier into a dance floor.

I swing Freddie around a couple times before using a moment of separation to bolt out of the circle and past the film crew, laughing and mortified all at once. I fear that the entire incident will someday reach an international television audience.

Later the same day, in a most unusual moment, a Korean camera crew is also in camp, filming a TV soap opera. The scene is set: a young couple is having a romantic moment, staring into one another's eyes. The backdrop is a magnificent glacier, a beautiful mountain . . . and Freddie, skiing from left to right through the frame, his pants around his ankles. The cameraman shouts and gestures in Korean, pointing and laughing, his camera tracking away from the show's stars to follow Freddie's R-rated spectacle. I suspect that this footage will not make the show's final cut.

It's a beautiful day in May 2004 when a compact blonde dressed head to toe in stylish pink mountain attire steps off an airplane from Talkeetna.

"Hi Lisa," she says in a high, almost squeaky voice. "I'm Sue Nott. I've heard all about you — you're the basecamp legend. And this is my climbing partner, Karen McNeill." Karen looks up, flashes a modest smile from beneath her long, dark hair, and waves from inside the airplane, where she is helping the pilot unload gear.

Out of the airplane comes a spectacular pile of duffel bags, backpacks, skis, and more duffel bags. I've never seen two climbers with so much stuff.

"How long are you here for?" I ask, eyeing the growing pile.

"Over a month," Sue replies, growing more animated as she scans the mountains. "We're going to climb the *Cassin*," she adds with resolve, handing me her basecamp card.

"The Glitter Girls," I intone, reading out their expedition name.

"That's us," she says. She produces a shimmering, glitter-covered stocking cap from her pocket and then dons it with a playful grin. "It's all about the style."

"What's in all these bags?" I query.

"Food," Sue says. I raise my eyebrows. Sue looks like she can't weigh more than 100 pounds.

"Don't worry — there's some climbing gear in there, too," Karen adds with a wry smile.

"How many women have climbed the *Cassin?*" I ask, as I reckon the relative rarity of meeting women attempting the more difficult routes up here.

"Not many," Karen replies.

Sue interjects, "And never an all-female team."

"Wow — well, go get it," I reply, impressed as much by their boldness as I am by their rock-star personas.

The Glitter Girls proceed to set up an enormous Mountain Hardwear basecamp tent that looks like a huge orange golf ball. I join in to assist, as it's a multi-person job. "This thing is a palace," I exclaim once it's erected. It's at least fifteen feet in diameter.

"Let's call it "Dome 72,'" Sue announces. "You know, like Studio 54 in New York, but at 7,200 feet on an Alaskan glacier."

Numerous climbers in basecamp come to mingle with the Glitter Girls, who seem to know everyone.

"Sue's a badass big-wall climber, and they're both very strong ice climbers," a guide tells me in a subdued voice, as the girls put the finishing touches on their camp. "Sue lives up in Vail, Colorado, but she's done tons of wall routes in Yosemite and Zion. And Karen lives in Canmore and climbs all those big ice and mixed rigs in the Canadian Rockies."

"Okay, everyone," Sue announces to the crowd. "Party in Dome 72, 6:00 p.m. sharp." Sue turns toward me: "You too, Lisa. No excuses."

That evening, I enter the dome to find a dozen climbers already sitting around the perimeter. In the middle sits Sue, holding court, entertaining the crowd with a story about a storm she once sat out on the peak of Cerro Fitz Roy in Patagonia. A huge bowl is filled with a crisp romaine salad covered with croutons and freshly grated parmesan. Several stoves are roaring away on a spacious central cooking platform. Garlic bread is toasting in a pan, and pasta with sautéed ground beef, mushrooms, and an aromatic red-wine sauce simmers in a large pot.

"Here you go, Lisa — bottoms up," Sue calls as she hands me a martini glass containing a cosmopolitan made with top-shelf liquor, complete with a little pink straw.

"This is my kind of party," I note, taking a seat amongst the piles of foam pads that cover the floor.

I find myself drawn into Dome 72 during most of my downtime in camp, where I find piles of fashion magazines and "Chick-Lit" books, and the girls always eager to collaborate over recipes using the colossal amount of food they have brought. There's no macaroni and cheese, freeze-dried dinners, or top ramen in their bags of basecamp food. Instead, there's fresh veggies, meat, spices, and ingredients that make Dome 72 the ultimate scratch kitchen, with the Alaska Range serving as a refrigerator-freezer.

"Lisa, you need to come over right now," Sue tells me, popping her head into my tent one snowy morning. "It's spa day at Dome 72."

The current storm spells no flying for the day, so I follow her back to her camp intrigued. In short order, the girls and I are doing facials and mud masks, while sipping cosmopolitans through one of the hundreds of colorful straws Sue has packed. Sue, her face caked with mud, rifles through a duffel bag to produce a half dozen clothing items from Mountain Hardwear, her professional gear sponsor.

"Here, Lisa. Take as many as you want."

"To keep?" I ask, puzzled.

"Yes. They're for product testing,"

"Alright, then," I say, admiring the various pink and powder-blue fleece sweaters and wind shells she passes me. "We're going to show those boys. Let's put some color into climbing," I declare as our three martini glasses meet.

The girls set off up Denali a few days later, and basecamp seems empty without them. After a few weeks, I get word from the rangers that Sue and Karen have left 14 Camp on the West Buttress to make their attempt on the *Cassin Ridge*. The rangers tell me that the girls were undeterred by the poor weather and forecast.

"Sue has a reputation for really going for it," Mark explains to me. "She's known for pushing her limits, including climbing in bad weather."

The Cassin is one of the classic moderate technical routes on Denali, but it is also a long and serious endeavor that involves a high level of commitment. From high on the route, there is no easy retreat.

Five days have passed since the girls departed. Before leaving 14 Camp, they talked with ranger Joe Reichert, who has climbed with Sue. Joe indicates they were bringing five days of food.

"I gave them a radio," Joe tells the basecamp ranger during a phone call between camps. "But we haven't heard anything from them, and the weather has been really bad. There's been a lot of new snow, and I'm getting concerned."

A break in the weather on day six has the park's LAMA helicopter en route to 14 Camp for a resupply flight. The rangers decide to have the LAMA fly by the *Cassin* to have a quick look. The girls are spotted camped at 16,000 feet, near the top of the technical climbing but still far from the summit. The weather soon closes back in, and Denali is enveloped in yet another powerful, multiday storm.

Ten days have passed since they departed, and radio silence persists. I'm becoming captured by the wave of concern that has swept up Denali's South District Ranger, Daryl Miller, and his mountaineering rangers, and even my brother Paul, who tends to resist speculation.

"They've been gone too long, and with this weather, the park should start a search," Paul states, after landing in basecamp for the first time in four days.

The LAMA helicopter searches the upper *Cassin Ridge* later that morning. Broken clouds and fog creep around the mountain, but the winds have dropped. After several hover passes find large amounts of fresh snow and no signs of the girls, the helicopter crests the apex of the *Cassin* at 20,120 feet, just 200 feet short of the summit. There, atop the sub-summit known as "Kahiltna Horn," stands a small tent, with Sue and Karen waving from its door.

Days later, the Glitter Girls are back in basecamp.

"It was a great climb — we had quite the adventure," Sue relates upon our reunification in front of Dome 72. I struggle to reconcile her casualness with the finer details that she reveals: climbing in constant high winds and snowfall; Karen collapsing in exhaustion at 18,000 feet after a prolonged bout of trail-breaking in deep snow; and, higher up, triggering an avalanche that carried them a short distance and forced them to use a rope for protection on the final stretches, which do not ordinarily require it. Their near-summit bivouac was a result of being lost and disoriented. Perhaps once or twice in the history of Denali climbing, the first being by the British Himalayan-mountaineering legends Doug Scott and Dougal Haston in 1976, has someone spent the night so near the summit, one of Earth's most unforgiving places.

"Those rangers didn't need to launch that helicopter search," Karen adds, her displeasure palpable. "They were just worried because we were women."

"How come you didn't call on the radio?" I ask in bewilderment.

"Oh, we had the radio Joe gave us. But we forgot the antenna, so the radio didn't work," Karen replies.

Mark has been in basecamp, helping me run the camp between his climbing trips. He's been quietly taking in the conversation.

"I don't know," Mark responds, choosing his words carefully. "To be honest, I think the issue was that you were gone for twice as many days as you had food, the weather was terrible, and you had a radio but never called in. We were all worried."

Sue and Karen gaze into our troubled faces. "Yeah, I get it," Sue concedes. "But we were fine. Nothing was going to happen to us." I stiffen in discomfort with this last remark.

Mark and I exchange an uneasy glance. Ever since my mother's death, I am hypersensitive to warning signs that people I care about are on an unsustainable trajectory. *I view the girls with both admiration and apprehension.*

The connections I make with the climbers I meet, not to mention Mark and his partners, come with the inescapable burden of concern for their safety as they tackle these dangerous mountains. There is a similar dynamic of concern for my pilots, born from the tragedy of my first season, but what also stands out is the maintenance, care, and feeding of so many different working relationships. The results can be amusing.

"Lisa, It's Jay Hudson. You need to get out on the runway with a shovel and fill in those ruts," he says. "K2 and TAT keep landing those huge Otters and Beavers when the snow is soft, and it makes it hard on my little 206."

"Those ruts run the whole upper half of the runway," I protest.

"Well, you gotta get out there and try. And there's some sagging snow bridges over crevasses on the landing side. See if you can fill in the dips."

I turn to Mark, who is spending a few weeks up here with me in camp before heading south for work, and say, "There's no way I'm getting near those crevasses. This is ridiculous."

Mark and I decide to humor Jay by spending over an hour filling in a single, 50-foot section of a 500-foot-long rut that forms a trough 3 feet deep. Then, a K2 Otter lands on the runway and pushes all the snow we shoveled right back out in an instant.

"The hell with this," I exclaim, and when I call Jay to inform him of the utter futility of this endeavor, he is unmoved:

"What else are ya gonna do with your time up there?"

Eric Denkewalter, chief pilot and part owner of Fly Denali aviation, lands in camp and begins unloading a trio of climbers. Fly Denali focuses on scenic flight tours, and they book maybe thirty to forty climbers at most each season. I don't see Eric very often, but every visit is memorable. Eric is a former military pilot with decades of flying experience, and he works on Talkeetna's volunteer fire department. He's one of the most helpful people I have met and has more energy than just about anyone I know. Or maybe, he just drinks a great deal of coffee.

"Howdy, Lisa," he calls, charging with determination across the runway toward my tent. If I didn't know him already, I would assume he is about to report an emergency. It's just Eric, however, and he's got places to go and people to see. "How's it going?" he asks, adjusting his ball cap, which covers his short gray hair, as he strides up.

"Everything good? You need any help with anything? How's your season going?" he rapid-fires. Eric then pauses his interrogation just long enough to relate a funny story about something that happened in Talkeetna. Then, he's on his way again.

"Alright, Lisa, I just wanted to make sure you're doing okay, and if you need anything, just let me know," he says, before stomping off toward his plane.

Two Argentinian climbers snap photos and watch while I help

Mark and the mountaineering ranger John Leonard load Doug Geeting's Otter. Doug finishes tying down the load, hops down from the plane into the snow, glances at the thickening clouds, and then stares at the Argentinians in anticipation. The climbers, oblivious, continue looking around at the mountains and ignore him.

"Okay, guys. All aboard," Doug says, exhaling with an audible sigh. A dark overcast blankets the sky, and the cloud ceiling continues to fall.

"Okay," one of the men acknowledges, and then goes right back to taking photos.

Doug reaches out, grasps the man by the back of his jacket, and shoves him toward the airplane.

"Let's go — no time for dumbness," Doug says, as the man stumbles through the snow toward the plane, looking like a 5-year-old who just got corralled by his dad.

One winter night, over drinks at the West Rib Pub & Grill, I was relating to Doug the difficulties I have with some climbers at basecamp. Doug responded without hesitation: "Lisa, if any of my climbers ever give you a hard time, you let me know. I'll come up there, and I'll rip their fucking ear off."

I love working with Doug.

I try to invoke Doug's spirit whenever I encounter the problem personalities up here. In particular: the impatient, unruly, desperate, and despondent climbers who return to basecamp and for one reason or another — none of which are related to medical or family emergencies — *must* get off the mountain right away. Not an hour from now. Not tomorrow. *Right now.* Even weather delays induce the assumption that I must not be doing my job or that the pilots are just not trying hard enough.

I open my door to swirling snowflakes and less than 100 feet of visibility, the view like the "inside of a ping-pong ball." For better or worse, the view also includes a Polish climber, standing in my doorway for the third time today, asking me the same question as before.

"When will our plane be here, Lisa?" he demands, with greater aggression than the past two times. "You tell them, come right now."

The absurdity is too much for me to bear. "Do you really want to fly through the mountains, in this weather?" I ask, making wild gestures in the direction of invisible mountains cloaked by clouds. I press the issue before he can answer.

"What's so important that you want the pilots to risk their lives to come get you? Do you even know what you're asking?"

The man backs away, shocked, as though no one had ever spoken to him in such direct language. I can tell that he's about to speak again, but I don't need to hear anything else.

"Hold on a second," I say, cutting him off.

I duck back into the tent, emerging a moment later with an unopened bottle of quality Russian vodka, one of the many gifts I've received from past climbers.

"Here. Find a use for this," I command, placing it in his hands. The man's eyes light up, and he stares at me in wonder.

"Oh. Thank you, Lisa. Thank you," he exclaims, walking backward, nodding his head, and smiling, his demeanor transformed.

That night, I hear laughter and music from the Polish tent. In the morning, with the sun shining and planes inbound, the climber and his friends are waving at me and smiling from ear to ear. I have become their hero.

A weary mountain guide pounds on my door at midnight. He's had a bad trip and demands that I call Jay Hudson for a flight out.

"Hudson is closed. I'm not calling him at this hour. You're going to have to wait until morning," I tell him. The Talkeetna air services typically stop flying and close up for the night at 8:00 p.m., and then reopen at 8:00 a.m. The guide slams the door and stalks back to his group. "Wow," Mark mutters. "That was amazing." We settle back into our sleeping bags.

Moments later, the door swings straight open without even a knock. An older man — one of the guide's clients — enters and assumes a menacing stance. This is a man who appears unaccustomed to being told no.

"Call the pilot. I have money. You tell him I'll pay whatever he wants. Call him now," he orders, as though we answer to him.

Before I can even formulate a response, Mark bolts upright and swings his sleeping bag-enshrouded feet onto the floor. Stone-faced, Mark slowly raises a finger and points toward the door.

"Please close the door on your way out. Goodnight," Mark says slowly and deliberately. The man turns and exits without a fight. The following day, as the team is boarding their aircraft, the same client approaches me and extends his hand for a handshake.

"Thank you — I appreciate everything," he says, as though the previous night's events had never occurred, and as I pull my hand back there is something in my palm. It's a $100 bill. This was no bribe, of course; I believe it was a donation for his bad behavior.

Between the desperate after-hours flight requests — typically born of an ego bruised by Denali and/or a desire to reach cold beer in Talkeetna — and the arrival of the following morning's flights, I manage to get some sleep. As the season progresses into June, however, the long, warm days necessitate that climbers travel on the lower glacier at night, when the snow bridges spanning the crevasses are firmer, and the temperatures more comfortable for the exertion required. I do not operate on this schedule, however.

This night schedule creates a class of climbers I refer to as the "4:00 a.m. Crunchers." The snow is soft and slushy during the day but freezes at night. During June and July, many teams arrive back in basecamp from their expedition around 4:00 a.m. Most of these climbers are considerate enough to go set up their camp upon arrival, and then come check in with me at 8:00 a.m.

The 4:00 a.m. Crunchers, however, are those who instead choose to lurk and pace around just outside my tent on the crunchy snow, many of them coughing from their time at high altitude. Their hope, it seems, is to be the first to intercept me to schedule a flight out when I awaken several hours later. Except, they've awakened me already.

"What are you *doing?*" I ask, my head poking out the tent door into the cold, pre-dawn air. This climber has been walking back and forth in front of my tent for the past half hour, and after listening to him repeatedly coughing up phlegm and spitting it into the snow, I can stand this no more.

"I want to check in for a flight to Talkeetna," he replies.

"I'm sleeping," I counter, pointing at the "hours of operation: 8:00 a.m. to 8:00 p.m." scrawled on the outside of my tent. "Go way over there, set up your tent, and come back at eight, please."

This is how "The List" begins. The conflicts around "The List" usually begin building just after 8:00 a.m. when I venture outside to see who wants to fly out, giving my morning callout.

"We got into camp last night twenty minutes before those guys. Why are they going ahead of us?" asks an anxious trio, who wanders over to my tent at 9:00, having slept through morning callout.

"Because they checked in with me at 8:00. I make 'The List' in order of who checks in with me. It's the fairest way to do it," I answer.

The second team overhears the first team attempting to slip in front of them, and the battle begins.

"No way — we were here first."

Now I've got an argument in front of my tent, and my patience is gone.

"Guys, here's the deal," I begin. "All I know is who talked to me first. So that's it. 'The List' stands, as is. Everyone is going to get out today, so go sit down and be nice."

In my off-season job as a massage therapist, yelling at people is not part of my routine. It is times like these when serving lemonade to the tired, thirsty climbers can be useful in bolstering their patience and gratitude, the refreshments a tradition going back to the days of Frances Randall.

Most days, I put the '"The List" on a dry-erase board and prop it up on a lawn chair outside my tent, allowing climbers to consult it for themselves and leave me to my work or to alone time in my tent. Then, as planes land, I emerge, all eyes in camp on me, with the hope that I will be calling their expedition name so they can be on their way toward cheeseburgers and beer. "The List," effective as it is, is not foolproof at preventing confusion, however, especially when language differences and personal eccentricities are involved.

"HO!"

Joe, Mark, and I are sitting in my tent late one evening when we hear a strange call outside. Investigating, we open the door to see a blissful-looking, older Asian man standing one hundred feet away and looking like he comes from a different time. He is wearing camouflage fatigues, a massive external-frame backpack, and aviator sunglasses, while sporting a wild, wispy beard and long, graying hair. He waves at us with a tremendous smile and unexpected exuberance.

"YES," he exclaims, as he unshoulders his pack and dumps it on the snow.

We learn that the man is from Japan and knows almost no English; after an extended game of charades, we determine that he wants to fly out, and by process of elimination, which air service he is using.

It is late in the evening, and the air services are closed for the night. He's also far down on the list. Many climbers have arrived just before him this evening, in the hopes of getting out before a forecasted storm, but the morning brings bad weather that keeps everyone in camp for the next two days.

When the weather clears early morning on the third day, I have over 120 climbers waiting to fly out. It's going to be one of "those days." The planes begin arriving in waves, unloading their incoming passengers, loading up the outgoing passengers, and returning as quickly as they can turn around back in Talkeetna. The runway is milling with people, and it takes everything I've learned here over the years to keep order.

The Japanese man does not understand my instructions, or that he is about number sixty on "The List." With each plane that arrives, regardless of air service, he self-dispatches across the runway with his giant backpack and a huge smile, all the while pointing and yelling "YES," which seems to be his sole word of English.

"NO," I implore, gesturing toward camp. "Go over there and wait. I will tell you when."

I'm unloading yet another plane and shouting for the outgoing team to hurry up: "Alpine Ascents, this is your airplane." As another airplane comes taxiing in, I turn to see my friend walking right in front of the moving aircraft, oblivious to the danger.

"YES," he exclaims again.

My patience dissolves.

"NO! NO!! NO!!!" I scream, shaking my fists and jumping up and down. I'm trying to keep my cool because he is such a nice man, but I'm also worried that he's going to get run over by a plane.

Several waiting climbers have been observing and chuckling at this ongoing spectacle. Now, with my outburst, two of them stage an intervention, approaching the man from each side.

"Hey, dude — let's just go on over here and sit down awhile," one of them counsels in a paternal voice, and the man, still wearing his million-dollar smile, turns and walks with them. "Yes," he repeats. As they escort the Japanese man off the runway, one of the climbers flashes a smile at me over his shoulder, while I mouth "Thank you" in appreciation.

The occasional moments of chaos at basecamp are made much more complicated on days when the weather opens just long enough for one or two planes to get in, then closes and leaves some climbers bewildered as to why their plane isn't coming, too. It's the cruelest twist to raise their hopes, only to crush them a few minutes later.

"Good news — your plane has launched." Then, twenty minutes later: "I'm sorry, it had to turn back due to the weather." And then, twenty minutes later, an airplane from a different air service somehow makes it in and scoops up their passengers, leaving the first group steaming mad and confused. This is what has happened to a Colombian couple on multiple occasions, and they have been growing more and more aggressive and hostile toward me over their past three days of waiting.

"WHY THEY FLY, AND WE DO NOT?" the man shouts in broken English, stepping within inches of my face, his chest puffed up and hands clenched into fists. His body language is menacing; for the first time in memory, I feel threatened at my job.

"Your plane had to turn around because of the weather. I'm sorry, I can't do anything about that," I stammer, flustered. The result is an unrestrained, screaming tirade in Spanish.

At this, John "Loomie" Loomis, the basecamp ranger, appears from nowhere and steps between us, speaking to him in perfect Spanish and using pointed and assertive body language. Whatever he says causes the man to instantly change his attitude and settle down.

"What did you say to him?" I ask him a moment later.

"I told him, 'You're going to calm down, right now, and leave Lisa alone, or we're going to have a real problem,'" John says, raising a single eyebrow.

Loomie is one of my favorite people in the world, and his protector instincts are just one of the many reasons.

Loomie has been working for the Denali rescue program since 1997. He has also been the longtime Commander of Anchorage's 212th Squadron Air Force Pararescue (PJ) unit for many years, and he has served multiple tours of duty in Afghanistan.

Like many military members I have met, Loomie is a straight shooting, no-nonsense sort of guy, and has a macabre sense of humor. His slight build conceals the fact that he is as tough as any man alive. With his grown-out crewcut and a mischievous grin, Loomie is renowned among climbing expeditions for his shock-value, doomsayer climber orientations as part of fulfilling his ranger duties in Talkeetna. These orientations on safety and environmental regulations given by the rangers are a mandatory part of the registration process for every incoming Denali climbing expedition. Loomie's orientation is much heavier-handed than those of his colleagues.

"My god," one climber says upon arrival from Talkeetna. "That ranger in town told us we'd die up here." The other mountaineering rangers have told me of the grim, pale expressions on many a climber's face as they emerge from the briefing room in the ranger station after a "Loomie briefing." Further, Loomie being stationed up at basecamp does not guarantee a reprieve. Here, a team that exhibits any signs of ignorance or inexperience may still end up receiving an impromptu, supplemental Loomie briefing.

"Those guys are clueless — accident waiting to happen," Loomie tells me, with just a hint of sarcasm, about a group that's just arrived. "I told them they should provide their dental records so we can identify them later," he adds, winking, while stuffing a fresh pinch of tobacco behind his lip.

Loomie is both a warrior and a gentle soul, whose blunt demeanor is just part of his way of looking out for people. He's the guy who always has your back. Around camp, he's the most reliable ranger amongst a solid crew, always helping to load planes, pick up litter, clean the toilets, and correct bad behavior. Loomie seems unfazed by the gruesome tasks that come with the rescues and occasional body recoveries that his job demands. His unflappable demeanor under stress borders on the comical, which is good, considering that there always seems to be some sort of poop incident during his basecamp patrols that he gets stuck cleaning up.

"Goddamn it," Loomie exclaims, as he stomps back into the ranger's basecamp kitchen tent after a trip to the helicopter pad a few hundred yards up-glacier. I've just arrived to an invitation to dinner by Loomie and his volunteer. "The sling load that the heli brought down last week was full of shit cans, and they leaked all over the snow." Donning rubber gloves and a hazmat suit, Loomie motions to the pot of pasta and sauce simmering on the stove. "Help yourself. I gotta go clean up this mess. My dinner's fucked now," he says. He smiles and heads off for duty.

The presence of the Talkeetna Mountaineering Rangers helps ease my anxieties when I think of all the things that could go wrong up here, be it a climber with severe injuries, a law-enforcement incident, or an airplane crash. Every great team must have a great leader, and the Talkeetna Mountaineering program is no exception. That leader is Daryl Miller, the park's South District Ranger.

"Lisa, Daryl here. Just checking in with you. How are you doing up there?" Daryl is nearing retirement and hasn't been going on mountain patrols for the past several years, but he remains tuned in with what's going on with his people on the mountain. An evening phone call at basecamp from Daryl is a regular occurrence, even though I'm not a park employee. It's seldom a wordy conversation, but it's a few minutes of his time to let me know that he knows I'm up here, and that he cares. That phone call is just one of many he makes most every evening to his friends and to the rangers he supervises on and off the mountain.

Daryl's vigilance has been an asset for me in many situations, such as in June of 2003, when Mark and our friend Forrest Murphy are climbing the south ridge of Mount Hunter, a difficult route with dangerous, corniced stretches.

"Lisa, I heard Mark is up on the *Happy Cowboys* ridge. Have you heard any updates?" he asks during one of his evening phone calls to me.

"Nothing. The weather here isn't good, and they're out of radio range, so I don't know anything. I wish I did."

"I'm sure they are alright, but we'll be tracking them," he counsels. "Stay positive, keep me posted, and I'll check in tomorrow." Daryl is a steady and reassuring presence for me through every conflict and moment of tension I face in this harsh and unforgiving place.

Daryl has a life story that could fill a book. As a young man, he served as a combat Marine in Vietnam. After his discharge, he embarked on a life of adventure that included traveling with a sideshow featuring boxing chimpanzees, working as a ranch hand in Wyoming, and joining the rodeo as a rodeo clown and bullfighter, a dangerous job that resulted in frequent injuries from violent encounters with angry bulls.

Daryl was introduced to climbing in the late 1970s. He learned to ice climb in Canada, and in 1981, he went on his first Denali expedition. "We spent nine days trapped at High Camp in a vicious storm, and didn't make the summit," he related to me once, talking about the camp at 17,000 feet, also known as 17 Camp. "At that point, I said, 'I'm never coming back here.'"

Daryl would return, however, in 1986, and again in 1989, the latter time as a volunteer ranger on a Denali patrol. In 1991, he was hired as a mountaineering ranger, and began a distinguished career in search and rescue that saw him conducting annual, monthlong patrols to the hostile uppermost flanks of Denali, where he was involved in countless dramatic rescue operations to aid sick or injured climbers.

In 1995, Daryl and the young Talkeetna local Mark Stasik spent over two months completing the first winter circumnavigation of the greater Alaska Range, a feat that has yet to be repeated. Their journey of over 400 miles featured punishing, cold temperatures, falling through river ice at 30 degrees below zero, a perilous tent fire, navigating avalanche-prone slopes, enduring extreme wind and wind chills, and devastating hunger at the end, when their exit took far longer than anticipated.

In 1999, Daryl became Denali's South District Ranger, a job that now has him supervising the entire Talkeetna Ranger Station's mountaineering staff, a crew of rangers that has increased in numbers since the inception of the park's organized rescue program in 1979.

Daryl's once-blond hair has turned gray, but he still has the robust build of a mountain climber and a cheerful, empathetic smile, a hallmark of the steadfast, friendly demeanor that has garnered him such a respected position amongst his peers and in the greater Talkeetna community.

The crop of rangers that Daryl has assembled is seasoned and dedicated, each of them possessing expansive résumés filled with a variety of guiding, mountain climbing, and technical-rescue skills.

Meg Perdue, for example, is a former Alaska Mountaineering School guide, an experienced alpinist, and one of the fittest women I've met. When not on Denali, she might be found running on local trails around Talkeetna or cranking out pull-ups and lifting weights.

Joe Reichert is a veteran climber who has made difficult ascents in the mountains from Alaska to Patagonia. Joe is recognizable for his flowing blond hair, cheerful smile, and a passionate dedication to his job, and has become one of the most senior members of the Denali mountaineering program.

No one on the NPS staff, however, has been here longer than the inimitable Roger Robinson.

"Hello? Hello? Rescue please? Hello?" I hear a faint, plaintive voice with an indeterminate accent outside my tent door early one morning. *"Oh no,"* I think, springing out of my sleeping bag to investigate, concerned that I may have to put my limited medical skills to work. I open the door and see . . . just Roger.

"HA!" Roger laughs as the joke moves to the next stage. "Lisa! Help! WHA! I can't breathe!" he continues, clutching his chest and feigning distress.

"Ah, geez," he then exclaims, struggling to stop cracking himself up before he at last gets down to business: "Hey, I'm making pancakes over here if you're interested."

Roger's basecamp patrol represents my favorite time of every season. No one has funnier mannerisms, knows the area's history better, has such relevant life experience, or can tell a story like Roger can, and no one I know exudes so little ego. Roger wears his sandy brown hair in a trademark bowl cut augmented by a bushy mustache, and carries himself with a near-constant smile that makes him appear perpetually on the verge of telling yet another humorous story. I always learn something new from Roger, not the least of which is his ability to keep in touch with his inner child.

The "Rog," as his teammates sometimes refer to him with affection, started working for the park as a mountaineering ranger in 1980, the second season that the park hired rangers for mountain rescue and patrols. Roger has worked with every mountaineering ranger who has worked for the program to date.

In the mid-1970s, Roger came north from his home state of Oregon, and over a period of several years amassed an impressive series of ascents in the Alaska Range, including Denali's South Buttress in 1975, the second ascent of Mount Huntington's *French Ridge* in 1976, and numerous first ascents of the peaks in the Little Switzerland area. Most climbers, fixated on the taller mountains looming deeper in the range, overlook the parade of lower-elevation peaks that one passes over on the flight into basecamp. But many of these obscure peaks and valleys have been visited by Roger and his friends, including his longtime climbing partner, the beloved local guide Brian Okonek.

Once Roger went to work for the park, he started scaling back his personal mountaineering pursuits and began setting down strong roots in the Talkeetna community. Talkeetna is diverse, but

Roger may just be the archetypal Talkeetna local. He and his wife, Pam, built a log house just outside of town, as well as a remote wilderness cabin thirty miles north of Talkeetna. He has created deep connections within the community, including serving on the town council. Roger can often be seen attending the village's many year-round social events, perhaps playing his hammered dulcimer in the yard during some summer-evening potluck or competing in the "Oosik" Nordic ski race each March.

In recent years, Roger has performed tireless work for the "Sustainable Summits" international initiative in addressing the growing issue of human waste on popular mountains. His efforts and ingenuity resulted in the official launch of the "Clean Mountain Can" (CMC) program on Denali's West Buttress in 2005. Since then, the pit latrines at basecamp and 14,000 feet have been replaced by CMC practices.

The CMC program requires that human waste be contained in sturdy plastic cans with tightly sealing lids, issued to each climbing expedition. The cans are lined with biodegradable bags, which, once full, are deposited into crevasses. We use them here at basecamp as well; when the cans are full, we fly them off the mountain for treatment and cleaning at an industrial facility. The program has helped to make basecamp and the other camps on the West Buttress much cleaner, and the can is also now used by teams climbing and camping in other areas of the Alaska Range.

Roger has just about seen it all on Denali, from the most dramatic search and rescue missions to the most eccentric personalities. Like Daryl, Roger no longer goes on upper-mountain patrols, but he does do the season's first basecamp patrol and supervises the removal of the park's camps from the mountain at the end of each season.

It's mid-July, climbing season is over, and Mark, Roger, and I are all together at Denali Basecamp. We're here to help to load up a pair of US Army CH-47 Chinook helicopters, which are flying the park's massive pile of camp equipment back to Talkeetna.

As we carry load after load into the huge helicopters, Roger, prompted by Mark, recounts all sorts of his past, intriguing adventures, such as the time that instead of flying, he and his climbing team walked forty miles out from Mount Huntington to the Petersville Road at the end of their climbing trip.

"I thought for sure the bears would eat us," he chuckles, as he details the exasperating travel through near-impenetrable brush in the lowlands. "And the mosquitoes . . . whoo," he exclaims, emitting fake shrieks of terror and windmilling his arms around his head cartoonishly.

He also recounts a 1982 NPS backcountry patrol in the remote Kichatna Mountains, where the glacier pilot forgot to pick up Roger and his rangers, forcing them to walk for over thirty miles to a remote wilderness lodge.

"We'd been out of food for days, and there was this porcupine near our camp. We had the porcupine for dinner," he says, animated and laughing like a kid. "Man, it tasted awful."

We break for a snack, and Roger produces his 1960s-era metal lunchbox with *Peanuts* comic strip characters on it.

"Whoa, sweet *Peanuts* lunchbox, Rog," Mark teases.

Roger clutches the lunchbox in a defensive posture. "Oh, hey, hey, don't touch it now," he intones, using a faux-dramatic voice.

"Oh, hey, hey" is an essential Roger-ism, a reaction or a greeting you're bound to receive if you hang around him long enough. It's just Roger, always in search of a playful take on every situation. Having someone around with so much history and perspective makes everything better on Denali, and having someone who bases all of it from humor is the icing on the cake. It's an example I strive to follow.

With the gear packed away, the Chinooks' engines begin the lengthy process of spooling up, the awesome sounds of their intricate transmissions changing gears in rhythm as the helicopters' long fuselages sway in increasing cadence. The Army personnel fire-guarding the turbine engines during the startup process at last seem satisfied that we aren't going to burn, and they step inside the craft.

Against all probability, the oblong machine I'm riding in defies gravity, lifts off the glacier, tilts to the front, and begins gaining forward speed at an astonishing rate. I press my face into the small bubble window and watch the empty stage of basecamp receding behind us.

The curtain falls on yet another Denali climbing season. The events, characters, and storylines from the successive years are beginning to run together in my mind. The end of this season is merely the conclusion of the latest act in a never-ending production, an intermission, while the next set of characters prepares to take the stage. What plot twists might the coming act bring?

Like life itself, it's all an unfolding mystery that I embrace, one little moment at a time.

Chapter Eight
2002-2006
Peril in the Beauty

"Basecamp Lisa, this is Foraker team, do you copy?"

As my 8:00 p.m. weather report concludes, my CB radio crackles back to life with the voice of one of the three brothers whom I have been talking with each of the past several nights at this same time.

"I copy, guys. How's it going over there?"

This trio of Alaskans, ranging in age from 27 to just 15, is attempting Mount Foraker's Southeast Ridge. I have yet to meet the brothers in person, because they were landed about five miles away at a seldom-used airstrip much closer to the start of their route. After their climb, they intend to come to Denali Basecamp, and have arranged for a duffel bag with extra food to be flown in.

"Did our bag get dropped off?" the climber asks, sounding hopeful.

"It's not here yet, but don't worry — I'll make sure the air service has it here by the time you get back," I say, trying to sound reassuring. The last thing they need to worry about is their bag, while they are up in such a serious place.

"Okay, thanks Lisa. We're just above ten thousand feet. The snow is pretty bad up here," he says.

"Alright, well, be careful, and check in with me tomorrow to let me know how you're doing. I'll have the forecast for you, and I'll make sure your bag will be here as well," I offer, before we sign off for the night.

Mark often tells me of the feeling of security he gets from his radio connection to me while high on a route, and I'm sensing that these young men are feeling that, too. With their regular check-ins, I've come to feel a bond with them like that of a protective big sister, and now I am compelled to look out for them as best I can from down here.

The following evening, I hear nothing from the brothers after the evening weather, and they don't respond to my attempts to hail them. Concerned, I walk outside and look over to Mount Foraker. Their climbing route is hidden behind a buttress of the mountain, and I'm left to guess where they might be.

I hope they're okay.

Perhaps they dropped their radio, or their batteries were low. Maybe they just forgot to call. I allow the night and another day to pass, but when the brothers neither call the next evening nor respond to my calls on the radio, I walk to the NPS tent to talk to rangers Mik Shain and Roger Robinson.

"Okay," Mik says, looking toward Foraker. "We'll talk with Daryl and see what he wants to do."

The next morning, I watch as the LAMA helicopter flies off toward Foraker, and I hold yet another tense vigil by the radio. It's been two years since I stared at this same radio filled with anxiety, awaiting an update on Don Bowers, Cale Shaffer, and his volunteers. I am filled with hope that the rangers will spot the brothers climbing along the upper ridge, waving back and wondering what the fuss is all about.

The helicopter returns after a short flight, and I greet Mik as he walks back from the landing pad. He's grim faced and shaking his head.

"They're dead," he states with a bluntness that feels like a punch to the abdomen. "It looks like they triggered an avalanche and were carried far down the face. There was equipment scattered everywhere."

I kick at the snow and struggle to hold back my tears. The young brothers whom I had tasked myself to look after will not be coming home. Mik and Roger discuss the situation over the radio phone with Daryl and Davey back in Talkeetna.

"Daryl," Roger asserts, "I think we should get the hydraulic claw for this."

"I know how dangerous that place is," Daryl says, "so I agree."

The Southeast Ridge begins with a sunbaked snow slope highly prone to avalanches and rockfall, and farther up, traverses beneath an active ice cliff. Many parties have died on this route, including in an incident in 1987 in which two separate teams of two climbers were swept to their deaths by the same avalanche.

"Agree also," Davey concurs. "We can't put a shorthauler in there with all that overhead hazard, and it would take three rotations."

"Okay, Daryl," Roger says, holding the phone's handset close in. "We'll send the LAMA out to Talkeetna to bring in the claw."

The large hydraulic claw is brought in from Talkeetna that afternoon, suspended beneath the helicopter on the longline. The pilot will use the claw to grasp the climbing rope that still connects the three men, and then fly them all together back into basecamp. The rangers here will then place them in body bags and evacuate them by fixed-wing airplane to Talkeetna.

Early in the evening, the LAMA helicopter departs basecamp. A group of tourists on a scenic flight is milling about the runway, and I approach the pilot with a warning: "There's going to be a pretty grim scene here in a few minutes. You might want to corral your people, or otherwise prepare them for this somehow — it might be very upsetting."

Then I realize that this will be a first for me, too. Indeed, nothing I have experienced has prepared me for the horrifying scene that I witness as the brothers are brought into camp and set upon the snow. The flightseeing tourists and climbers have all stopped what they are doing. Some of the tourists cover their mouths with their hands, before looking down and away. The violence of the tragedy laid front and center delivers a chilling blow to the entire camp. How many more times might I have to witness something like this? I must imagine there are a limited number of traumas of this scale that one can withstand before they crack.

Several days later, a flightseeing plane flies over basecamp, and the pilot calls me over the radio.

"Lisa, I have Mrs. Strawn on board. She's the mother of the three brothers lost on Foraker. She'd like to talk with you, if you don't mind?"

"Yes, okay," I agree, already feeling a lump growing in my throat.

"Lisa, I just wanted to check in with you for a moment," she begins, as I watch the plane circling a few miles away in front of Mount Foraker. "I understand you were the last person to talk with my sons, and I heard it was you who alerted the park service to go look for them," she says.

"I just wanted to thank you for looking out for them."

"I'm so sorry for your loss," I answer, proceeding to stammer out more words that just feel hollow. As painful as losing a parent was for me in my teen years, I have to believe that losing a child is even worse. And, to lose multiple children is just unfathomable.

The plane circles a few more times and soon departs. For many days afterward, I feel gutted and emotionally drained. I'm tormented by the complexities of risk and the contradictions inherent to climbing.

Climbing mountains, for me and many others, holds the appeal that it does in part because the outcome — of reaching the summit and returning safely — is not guaranteed. Many climbers go to great lengths to justify risk, insisting that it's not the point of their pursuits but merely a factor that must be accepted. But risk is also tied in an insidious manner to the same uncertainties that give climbing its very appeal.

I have climbed enough to understand that safely navigating a situation with mortal consequences often yields a deeper psychological reward. In climbing, by acting in the presence of palpable danger, I've gained insights and self-knowledge that I believe would be much more difficult to attain through everyday activities.

All these upsides to climbing, however, are rendered hollow and meaningless when face-to-face with the personal wreckage left behind when young people die in the mountains.

Aviation safety also weighs on my mind, and for good reason. Ever since Don Bowers's plane crash, I have been consumed by dreadful thoughts of an aircraft incident occurring right here in basecamp.

Airplane mishaps at basecamp have for the most part been

relegated to planes getting stuck trying to turn around after landing in deep, new snow. This results in some laborious digging to free the plane, and perhaps some extra runway packing, but soon enough the plane is flying away. I am nonetheless tormented by the specter of a worst-case aviation scenario. As a child, my worst fears about something happening to my parents came true, and continue to serve as a subconscious confirmation that my concerns were justified.

How long until lightning strikes again?

A small group of morning planes begins arriving on schedule to pick up climbers. One by one, they touch down, spin around atop the runway, slide up in front of the staging area, and shut down their engines; then, the loading-and-unloading process begins. It's just another day at basecamp. I'm carrying a duffel bag and escorting a group of climbers to their plane, noticing from the corner of my eye a De Havilland Beaver, the final plane in the group, touching down just across the runway.

I glance over on instinct when I hear an unfamiliar pitch to the airplane's engine. What happens next seems to occur in slow motion. The plane stops short of the turnaround loop with sudden and excessive force, and then, to my horror, the tail pitches straight into the air. The propeller strikes the soft snow and the nose augers in, killing the engine. An awkward pause follows, as everyone stares agape at the Beaver tilted at a 70-degree angle in the snow, positioned like a lawn dart.

I break the silence with a shout and begin running straight for the plane, with no idea if the pilot is hurt, and no idea what I will do if he is. The climbers in camp follow in hot pursuit. As I close in, the pilot, to my relief, is already climbing out of the cockpit and down onto the snow, scratching his head in disbelief. He has no passengers.

"Are you okay?" I ask, breathless.

"I bumped my knees a bit, but I think I'm alright," he replies.

"Now what?" I think as I survey the scene and the climbers pace in the snow, staring in wonder.

"We'll need to dig out the nose," the pilot announces. Soon, a group of us are shoveling like crazy to free the propeller and engine cowling, while some climbers use a rope to lasso the airplane's tail. Soon the nose is free, and with a bit of pushing and pulling, the tail thuds back down into the snow.

The pilot makes a brief examination and determines that the propeller appears undamaged, thanks in part to the soft snow it struck. More airplanes are circling overhead, waiting to land, so he starts up the airplane and taxis out of the way, while the climbers and I shovel with reckless abandon to fill in the large hole in the runway left by the airplane's nose.

"What happened?" I ask the pilot when we reconvene.

"I misunderstood a message from one of the pilots here on the ground. I thought he told me the runway was firm and to land on my wheels. So, I didn't lower my skis," he states, shaking his head. "I don't know what I was thinking."

I phone Paul to describe what has happened.

"That's impossible. A Beaver cannot 'lawn-dart,'" Paul protests.

"Well, Paul, I saw it," I counter.

The pilot runs the plane's engine, and while it maintains proper compression, there is always a risk of internal damage from a propeller strike. The air service secures a ferry permit from the FAA for the pilot to fly back to Talkeetna for maintenance. I've had enough drama for one day.

I love it when I get unexpected visits from friends at basecamp, so I'm very excited when a pilot friend who works for my brother lands late one evening. One of his two passengers is also my good friend Sandra White, the Talkeetna Air Taxi office manager. They've been out flying around the mountains just for fun, as the weather has just cleared up and there's beautiful evening light. Their landing here wasn't spontaneous, however. They've brought in a pizza.

We all enjoy some laughs and a few slices, but soon it's past 10:00 p.m. and they need to get home to Talkeetna. I give Sandra a hug, and, with the night's chill setting in, retreat to my sleeping bag.

As I listen to the sound of the plane starting up, a stiff breeze rustles my tent. It's the night's typical down-glacier wind. It's not strong, but it will constitute a tailwind for the plane on its takeoff, which is not ideal, as it can hamper the lift required for flight. I roll up on my side. *Something doesn't feel right.* I get out of my bag and step outside into the cold to watch them take off.

The pilot pushes the throttle, and the Cessna 185 accelerates down the runway. A few hundred feet down, the plane lifts off. I'm about to turn away when I notice the plane bank left, then hard right. In a sudden and surreal flash, the tail rotates skyward as the plane performs a wingtip-to-wingtip cartwheel down the snow, before disappearing beyond the steeper, downsloped pitch of the runway. The engine, whose noise has been reverberating off Annie's Ridge as it always does, falls silent.

Too stunned to speak, I turn toward camp, which is filled with sleeping occupants already bunked in their tents. For a moment, I struggle for the right words, before the words find me:

"PLANE CRASH!" I scream, over and over. No one is stirring, and I don't understand why. In a flash of self-awareness, it occurs to me that I'm just yelling and running in circles. I decide that if I have time to panic, then I have time to do something more productive.

I run back inside my tent to alert Paul to the emergency. There are two NPS patrols in camp with at least ten rangers and volunteers. I'm unaware that they have been getting dressed in a hurry and pulling on their boots inside their tents, until I hear a commotion and look outside to see more than a dozen rangers and other climbers from camp sprinting down the runway.

"Lisa, call Talkeetna for help," a ranger shouts.

"Already did. I'm coming down with you," I say, before turning back to my call with Paul.

"Paul, I gotta go. I'll call you back in fifteen minutes with a report, but get ready to come in — and please call Daryl."

I bolt out the door and hurry down the hill in a full sprint. The wreckage of the plane comes into view as I crest the downslope. The Cessna is lying upside down on the snow. To my shock and relief, I can see that everyone is already out of the plane and on their feet.

"Is anyone hurt?" I call as I approach, trying to catch my breath. Amazingly, apart from some superficial bumps, there are no serious injuries. I take a series of deep breaths and resist the feeling that I might pass out as the adrenaline surge subsides.

I circle the wreckage. The wings are bent but intact, the landing gear and wheel skis are destroyed, and the plane's tail section is crumpled. Of note, the main section of the fuselage is intact and has minimal damage. I shudder, imagining how much worse this would have been had it happened on pavement instead of snow.

The rangers finish their patient assessments, and it looks like everyone is indeed alright. The rangers retrieve a hazmat spill kit from up at the helicopter pad to address the oil leaking from the plane into the snow, and I head back up to my tent to convey the news to Paul and Daryl that there is no urgency for a response from town. The light is dim enough that it's decided everyone will be picked up the next morning.

"It wasn't that violent," Sandra relates, as we all sit in my tent, decompressing. "Everything almost seemed to happen in slow motion." I suspect that the tailwind may have been to blame, but at this point all we have is speculation. What matters is that nobody has been injured.

The cartwheeling effect, dramatic as it appeared, was much friendlier to those inside than what a single blunt-force impact would have delivered. I make everyone comfortable in my tent for the night, but the lingering high from the event yields a night with little sleep.

We all just dodged a bullet.

Annie used to spend the entire ten-week season up here with no breaks. I, too, did that for my first couple of seasons, but in recent years I've started using Mark as a substitute basecamp manager whenever I need a day or two off in Talkeetna. On one such day, Mark is not climbing and agrees to take charge. On the flight out, I am absorbed with thoughts of a hot shower, a restaurant meal, and curling up on the couch to watch a movie with my little Cessna. In addition, I love spending time with Paul and his partner, Whitney's, young daughters, Tatum — born in 2002 — and India — born in 2004. It's all I need to recharge my batteries, and then I'll be back in camp tomorrow, ready for more action.

I can almost taste the food I'm fantasizing about as the airplane touches down in Talkeetna. Without warning, we screech to an abrupt halt, then, in a terrifying moment, the plane rotates forward onto its nose. I see and hear the propeller strike the asphalt, and just as I fear we are going to do a complete forward roll, the process reverses itself and the tail smashes back down again. Everything is quiet. Stunned, I look to the pilot, who is just as surprised as I am.

"The brakes. They got stuck . . ." he says, hushed, as though he is still trying to comprehend what went wrong. I stare ahead through the windscreen at the mangled propeller blades, curled into grotesque shapes. I pat myself down, wondering if, through the rush of adrenaline, anything hurts. Nothing does.

"Are you okay?" I ask the pilot.

"Yes" he replies. "I'm alright. You?" I nod in the affirmative.

Now, there are vehicles and people surrounding us. *I think I was just in a plane crash.* I climb out and stand in shock on the runway. The air-service owners and a couple of pilots ask me some questions, then Jay Hudson appears out of nowhere.

"C'mon, Lisa, you don't need to be here any longer; I'll give you a lift over to your car," he says. "I'm glad you're okay."

Jay whisks me to my car, and then I head over to town for something to eat. At least my appetite remains intact. As I cross the railroad tracks along the road that parallels the Talkeetna airport and approach the stop sign at the junction with the Talkeetna Spur Road, I push the brake pedal to the floor and almost nothing happens.

"Oh, you've got to be kidding me," I yell to no one in particular, as I slam my foot down on the pedal, and then grab the emergency brake to slow the car. Improvising, I drive at a crawl and use the e-brake to get the car without further incident to one of the town's seasonal food carts. Success.

Next, I run into my friend Ted Gannon, wearing his trademark teal sweatpants and his iconic large straw hat to shield the sun from his face, weathered from decades of mountain climbing and outdoor work. Ted, now in his early seventies, lives in Washington, but spends every spring up here helping out around Talkeetna Air Taxi, and talking to anyone who will listen about Eastern philosophy, relationships, and baffling questions about the human ego.

Ted was Paul's Denali climbing partner on his 1991 attempt. He joined the Peace Corps in 1963, and has split his time between Washington and Nepal for more than forty years. Ted takes pride in calling himself an "alien living among humans," in reference to his living in Western culture as a person with an Eastern outlook. Ted has been something of a mentor to Paul, Mark, and me for years. We traveled with Ted to Nepal in the fall of 2000, but we've also spent many a late hour with Ted in Seattle restaurants or walking the city's streets, as he peppers us with deep philosophical questions that we can never seem to answer with sufficient insight. Ted's questions are meant to provoke not a conclusion, but a never-ending discussion.

"Okay, Lisa," Ted begins, getting right into it, enunciating his question in a slow cadence, his eyes narrowing. "Here's the thing: Can we ever be totally free of influence?" Ted steps back with a playful flair, as though he's really hit me with a zinger, and leaves the ball in my court.

I love talking to "Ted the Head" as we call him, but there's no such thing as a short conversation. A proper encounter with Ted requires hours, and his questions need days to consider. Right now, I just want to take a shower.

"Going to have to take a rain check, Ted. I need a shower and a nap. I promise we'll discuss this later," I say. Ted laughs and raises his hands in temporary surrender, as I climb back into my ailing car and limp back home.

My afternoon plans are derailed when my food-cart lunch begins staging a rebellion in my stomach. Not even an hour after getting home, I am vomiting from food poisoning, and the remainder of my mini-vacation is spent in bed. Twenty-four hours later, I find myself in an airplane, sliding to a stop in the snow and looking through the window at my smiling Mark. I never expected to be in accident myself, much less in Talkeetna, but it just goes to show that risk is everywhere. It's a relief to be back to a place where life is simpler, even though the potential for catastrophe lurks around every corner.

May 28, 2003, is one of those "severe clear" days in the mountains, when the sky is a piercing blue and the mountains stand out in every minute detail. A high-pressure system is building in after several days of unsettled weather. I stand on the runway, chatting with Keli Mahoney from McKinley Air Service.

I notice that Keli seems unusually distracted today, but our small talk is otherwise the usual joking back-and-forth about climbers, tourists, the temperament of other pilots, and her typical good-natured teasing of me, which I fire right back in return.

"Okay, well, I need to get going. I have a couple climbers to bring in on my next flight," Keli says, looking toward Denali with detachment. "I'll be back in a couple hours." Keli begins herding her scenic-flight passengers back into the plane, and I head out to reset a runway marker that has fallen over in the snow.

Mark and Joe are here, nearing the end of their climbing trip. They attempted the *Moonflower* a few days ago, but Mark has been sick for over a week with a bad cold, and they are planning to fly out soon. Joe Reichert is the basecamp ranger, and the three of them are helping me out around camp as the air services work to ferry waiting climbers back to Talkeetna.

I'm outside resetting my phone antenna when I hear Talkeetna Air Taxi pilot Richard Olmstead over my handheld aircraft radio, hailing another aircraft. What Richard says next stops me in my tracks:

"Ah, there's a plane down on the glacier in South Hunter Pass," Richard states, his tone ominous. Mark bolts up in his lawn chair, and we cock our heads to listen.

"It looks like a hard impact — no landing tracks," Richard continues. "This doesn't look good. We need to notify the park service or RCC" — the Rescue Coordination Center.

Mark and I lock eyes, and I begin running toward my tent to get to the phone.

"Mark, what time was Paul last in here this morning?" I ask, struggling to maintain my composure. I don't want this to be anyone, of course, but in a selfish impulse I think of my brother first. My heart pounds as I try to remember when he was last here, as it's been a busy morning. I call Talkeetna Air Taxi and learn to my relief that Paul called in just five minutes earlier, and that all their pilots' whereabouts are known.

"Thanks, that's all I needed," I say, choosing not to elaborate on my reason for asking.

I call the remaining air services in succession.

"Are any of your planes overdue?" I ask, but everyone believes they have recent accounting for each of their pilots. Mark, Joe Puryear, and I, along with Joe Reichert and his volunteer, monitor the radio with anxious vigilance in the NPS tent as the park's LAMA helicopter launches from Talkeetna.

"It could be a private pilot, from Wasilla or Anchorage," Mark states, trying to sound reassuring.

The LAMA helicopter arrives on scene. After a few minutes, Davey Kreutzer, the helicopter manager, makes a transmission to Talkeetna.

"We have 'confirmation' on all four occupants," he states with finality. "Stand by for the tail number."

I've been here before.

We hold our breath through an unbearable moment of tension.

"Cessna 185. Tail number, November, seven-zero-one-seven-six."

We glance at one another for a long moment.

"Who is that?" Joe Reichert asks.

"I don't recognize that number," I say, feeling a building sense of relief that it isn't someone I know. The other two Joes exhale, but then Mark stiffens up and looks at me, his face turning ashen.

"That's Keli," Mark says, his voice falling almost to a whisper. Now, in my mind's eye, I can picture the Cessna that was parked here just two short hours ago: the white fuselage, the blue-and-red trim, and the tail number: N70176.

"Oh my god," Joe Reichert says, covering his face with his hands. Joe Puryear slumps down on my cot and drops his head, while Mark puts his arm around me. Inside my head, I'm screaming, but on the outside, I have but silent tears and a blank stare.

"She was just here," I say, as though I'm bargaining with

something unseen.

The recovery effort begins. A fixed-wing landing at the scene isn't possible, so Keli and her passengers will be placed in body bags and a cargo net, and then flown ten minutes by the helicopter to basecamp. Here, they will be reloaded into a fixed-wing aircraft and taken to Talkeetna. Paul volunteers for that duty and arrives in basecamp late in the afternoon. I greet him with a long hug on the runway.

"What a loss. You doing alright, Lisa?" Paul asks. I shake my head.

"I can't believe this. What do you think happened?" I inquire, grasping for a meaning to or reason for this tragedy.

"I'm not sure. The winds in the passes were weird this morning — lots of falling air with this big high pressure," Paul says. "Maybe she caught a downdraft in the pass. It happens, but if you're too low, there's just not enough time to recover."

Paul stares at the mountains, then gives me a somber look. "I don't know if you heard, but Bruce Andrews was on board, with a client."

"I heard," I say, gazing toward Denali in dispassionate numbness, unable to respond with anything more.

Bruce Andrews is beloved in the guiding community and was one of the founders of the Colorado Mountain School. Bruce and I were just chatting in my tent four days ago, as he was preparing to fly out for a break between his back-to-back trips guiding clients up Denali.

I hear the distant drone of the helicopter, and then brace myself at the sight of four orange bags, contained in a cargo net, suspended beneath the helicopter as it swings into view around Annie's Ridge. To the rest of the basecamp residents, who are unaware of the day's events, the package could be anything. I have the unfortunate burden of knowing.

Mark, Joe Puryear, Joe Reichert, Paul, and I watch as the helicopter sets the net down on the snow near Paul's airplane. There is no discussion among us. "Well, let's do this," Joe Puryear finally says with a sigh. We set aside our horror and step forward to help bring them all home. Lifting the four body bags one by one into the small aircraft is a gruesome task that will be imprinted upon me forever.

Paul departs for Talkeetna; Joe Puryear wanders alone up the glacier, Joe Reichert shovels tent platforms in his camp with unusual vigor, and Mark remains alone near the edge of the runway, looking at the mountains. I take a lap around camp to pass the time. My worst fears have been realized yet again. I fear that going forward, every takeoff and landing that I witness, every flight, will be accompanied by a crushing unease and concern. I walk out to rejoin Mark on the runway. Mark drapes his arm around me and continues staring at the mountains before speaking. "I'm worried that I'll never be able to forget that," he says.

I fly out a week later to attend Keli's memorial in Talkeetna. Mark is already waiting for me at home. Hundreds from our traumatized community are in attendance. Emotional eulogies flow, and at the conclusion, five of the Talkeetna pilots — one from each air service — approach the memorial site in a V-shaped pattern overhead. Then, the lead aircraft peels away while the other four planes continue ahead: it's the "missing man formation," honoring the fallen pilot.

As the planes pass over the tearful crowd, I reflect again on how both my social circle and occupation are immersed in a world of extreme risk and dire consequences. Processing repeated exposure to death and injuries, in particular to those we love, is a skill we aren't taught. More often, we're told to be strong and move on.

I worry that in my desire to put these events in my past, I'm just adding another layer of scar tissue to a wound that may never heal. If I'm to continue with what I'm doing, I need to be able to sit with the pain. *I don't ever want to build a wall.*

Search and rescue operations on Denali are complex and risky. What the rangers can accomplish is almost miraculous, given the remoteness and harsh, high-altitude environment. The rangers rely on the park's contract helicopter to extract sick or injured patients high on the mountain, where aggressive medical interventions are neither possible nor practical. Meanwhile, an air-ambulance helicopter from a local company such as Life Flight will often fly to basecamp and stage on the runway for the arrival of the patient, a tactic that allows for the earliest delivery of advanced life support.

Outside the tent, I hear my name being called in the distance as I'm making breakfast one morning. I open the door to see the ranger Meg Perdue striding toward me with purpose.

"A couple of Spanish climbers were pretty badly hurt in a fall above High Camp," she says.

"The LAMA is on its way, and it sounds like we need Life Flight, but they're finishing up another mission, so they'll be delayed getting here. We might need your help with moving the patients," she continues, now scanning the interior of my tent.

"And," Meg continues, "we may need to bring one in here since there's two patients and we don't have room for both of them in our kitchen tent."

"No worries — I'll make space," I acknowledge, already shoving bags under my cots and clearing clutter away. "I'll alert the air services to listen for Life Flight on the air-to-air frequency."

I finish preparing one of my bunks, then head outside to stake a large red bag in the snow above the turnaround on the runway's upper end, to serve as a landing marker for the air ambulance. I hear the LAMA inbound, bringing the patients down from 17,000 feet.

One Spaniard's hands are frozen, but otherwise his injuries are minor and he will fly out by fixed wing. The other man, however, has serious injuries and is in extreme pain. Meg's volunteers and I, along with a couple climbers from camp, help move the man onto the bunk I prepared, placing him in one of the park's sleeping bags. Meg and another medic begin working on him while I attempt to comfort him, but he is in shock and his pain is all that he can think about. The medic suspects a pelvic fracture, which makes his evacuation even more urgent.

I hear Life Flight calling on the aircraft radio, and I hail them:

"Life Flight, this is Kahiltna Basecamp. Your winds are six to eight miles per hour, gusting to seventeen from the northeast. Temperature is twenty degrees Fahrenheit. No known fixed-wing traffic; land on the red marker, at your discretion."

After the helicopter lands and powers down, two medics unload and race into camp. The man in my tent is high priority, and they waste no time in getting an IV line started and administering pain medication and other drugs. A large group of us moves the man to a backboard platter, which we then use to carry him with haste across the runway and toward the helicopter. We get him loaded, and the helicopter departs for the hospital. The manic scene ends with the abruptness that it began, and now it looks like just another day here in basecamp. I go back to fixing my breakfast, fueling up for whatever might come next.

Late evening on June 29, 2004, finds Mark and me drifting off to sleep. The climbing season is nearing its end, and sleeping requires eyeshades due to the endless light of the Alaskan high summer. At this time of the year, Denali never sleeps. Nighttime travel is the norm for teams heading down from 14 Camp or otherwise planning to travel on the lower glacier. This is necessary for finding firmer snow conditions and stronger snow bridges over crevasses, and avoiding the discomfort of the intense summer sun. This season has been so warm, however, that the normal rules have all been turned on their heads. We had rain here at basecamp in early May when it should have been snowing, and there are recent reports from the upper mountain of exceptional crevasse hazard and slushy snow. Most notable and alarming, however, are the reports of water running in places that it never does, and rocks falling from cliffs that are almost always quiet. There can be no doubt that the climate is warming here in Alaska, and it is also impacting climbers' usual tactics and strategies.

Mark and I are jolted awake by frantic shouts for basecamp over the CB radio. *Here we go again.*

"Lisa, are you up on channel one? COME IN PLEASE!" The voice is familiar — and filled with grave urgency. Mark jumps out of his sleeping bag, with me half a second behind, and grabs the handset.

"This is basecamp — go ahead," Mark answers.

"It's Rob Gowler from AMS. A whole rope team in my group just got hit by a massive rockfall at Windy Corner" — an aptly named col at 13,000 feet between the 11,000- and 14,000-foot camps; just above the Corner, the route passes beneath a cliff band of loose, shattered granite.

"We have three with major injuries," Rob continues, breathless, "and we're going to need the helicopter up here right away. I tried calling the rangers at 14, but they aren't answering."

In the background, beyond Rob's fear-stricken voice, we can hear shouts and screams. AMS is the Alaska Mountaineering School, and Rob, a good friend, is one of their senior guides. Rob is always cool and calm, so his tone has me frightened. Mark hands me the radio, and while Rob provides me more details, Mark bolts out the door to alert the rangers sleeping in basecamp.

"We got people that can't move, and we're still getting hit by rockfall. I need to get off the radio now and help with first aid," Rob says.

Mark comes running back into the tent with news. "The rangers at 14 got the word and are preparing to send a team down to Windy Corner on skis right now," he says.

I relay: "Okay, Rob, the rangers know, and help is on the way. Just hang in there and be careful."

I pull Rob's basecamp card, and then I recall that our dear Japanese friend Norio Matsumoto is a client in Rob's group. Norio is a well-known photographer from Japan who spends over a month in the Alaska Range every winter taking photos of the aurora over Denali, while living alone in a snow cave. I'm again faced with the selfish hope that a friend is not among the victims.

Mark and I go to the rangers' tent to listen and offer our help. A ground team at 14 Camp is skiing down to the site, fifteen minutes away, while the LAMA helicopter and more rangers prepare to fly in from Talkeetna. When the rangers get on scene, they radio down with an update.

"Patient one has a suspected spinal injury; patient two, a suspected femur fracture; and patient three is deceased," the ranger relays. "We also have serious overhead hazard from falling rocks."

"Lisa, LifeMed is inbound — can you coordinate with them on the aircraft radio?" Daryl Miller asks me over the radio phone from Talkeetna.

"I can, and it's pretty dusky here so I'm going to go set some markers for ground reference," I say, before I head out the door with my aircraft radio turned all the way up. I secure a red body bag from the ranger cache to the glacier with snow pickets, but we've got two helicopters coming so I also use tropical-punch Kool Aid powder as another marker, dispersing the red crystals all over the snow.

The LAMA reaches the accident scene. The two LifeMed helicopters arrive in basecamp, and I marshal them in, directing them to the markers and giving them environmental conditions.

"Winds are steady at ten mph from the east, temperature is thirty-nine degrees Fahrenheit," I tell them.

No sooner have they touched down than the LAMA arrives in basecamp with the first patient, who is unloaded even as the helicopter remains under full power. The instant the rescuers and patient are out from beneath the rotor disc, the LAMA departs again to retrieve the second patient, to be followed by one final sortie for the deceased.

Camp was silent and asleep just over one hour ago, but it is now a bustling air show. Some climbers have emerged from their tents to watch, while a few offer to help us move the two patients to the LifeMed ships.

The body bag containing the deceased lies alone on the snow near the LAMA helipad as several rangers sort medical gear and repack the helicopter for the return to Talkeetna. I stare at the body bag from a distance, unable to get Norio off my mind.

"Loomie," I say, glancing toward the body bag. "Norio was with this group. Will you please take a look and tell me if that's him?" *I must know.*

Loomie knows Norio also. With no hesitation, Loomie walks to the bag, unzips it, and looks inside. He looks up at me with a solemn face and shakes his head.

"It's not him, Lulu."

I try without success to avert my eyes from the bag. *It's not him, but it's someone.*

The last week of April 2006 marks the beginning of my sixth season running basecamp. I step down from the airplane onto the Kahiltna's cold, powdery snow. My strong crew of volunteers includes Mark and his climbing partner, Eamonn Walsh. I take a deep breath of the frigid mountain air and scan the skyline of familiar mountains that I've been so graced to live amongst. *It's good to be back.*

In recent years, Mark and Joe have drifted apart, and Mark has been climbing with different partners. After they climbed the *Infinite Spur* in 2001, their climbing goals and ambitions began to take different paths. Mark wanted to climb harder routes in Alaska and South America, while Joe had his eye on new routes in the Himalaya. It was also evident to me that they were growing apart as friends. Joe seemed to be steering off on his own path, one that, to Mark's disappointment, didn't include him. Joe and Michelle were married in 2004 and bought a home in Leavenworth, Washington; much to our disappointment, Mark and I now see them far less often than anticipated.

Mark and Eamonn began climbing together a few years back during Mark's trips to Canada to climb waterfall ice, and now they have spent the past two seasons climbing together here in Alaska. They have become very close friends, and Mark raves about Eamonn's skills and boldness on ice and mixed terrain, which have made him a legend in his home range, the Canadian Rockies.

When Mark and I picked up Eamonn at the Anchorage airport in 2005 for their first Alaska expedition together, he was just as I remembered him from basecamp back in 2001: a quiet, burly guy — a "MOG" as Mark terms both himself and Eamonn, i.e., a "Man of Girth." He wore an old-style newsboy cap and carried himself with a polite, modest, and reserved demeanor, something I might expect from a stereotypical Canadian, but not from someone so physically imposing.

I wasn't sure what to think of Eamonn, but when we got back to Talkeetna and the three of us settled into our cramped cabin, everything soon became clear. As Eamonn sat upon our couch, Cessna approached, purring. Enamored, she jumped into his lap and began head-butting his arm for attention. I figured his reaction would tell me a lot about him, and I was right. Eamonn looked at Cessna with an almost anxious expression, as though searching for words, before finding them at last.

"That sure is a cuddly cat," he stated, the last thing I expected to hear from this big mountain man with a reputation for calm in the face of great danger. Eamonn, it turns out, is a giant teddy bear. You could say that I liked Eamonn from the start.

"Lisa. Welcome to basecamp."

I'm jolted from my reverie by a familiar voice. I turn to see a short blonde woman, dressed in pink, looking very much like my favorite basecamp buddy Sue Nott, waving, smiling, and trotting toward me with enthusiasm. Behind her stands the tell, a huge, orange, golf-ball-shaped Mountain Hardwear tent pitched uphill from where I plan to set my own tent.

That's Dome 72. The girls are back.

We meet with a giant hug. "You're back for more," I cry.

"Oh yeah, and we're going big," Sue replies, her excitement uncontained. Up in her camp, I see and recognize John Varco, her boyfriend, and Zoe Hart, who guides for Rainier Mountaineering, waving and cheering in our direction, and I acknowledge them with a fist pump in the air.

"What's the plan?" I ask.

"Well," Sue begins, pointing up-glacier with zeal, "John's going to do some solo climbing, and Zoe and I are going to climb the north buttress of Hunter."

"Which route?"

"*Deprivation*," she states, referring to a route that I've heard Mark speak about and which has a lead known as the "Death Pitch," so named for its difficulty and lack of protection. "Zoe has to guide Denali in ten days, so Karen is flying in right after."

"A Glitter Girls reunion," I cheer. "What then?"

"Foraker. The *Infinite Spur*. First man-less ascent, just like the *Cassin*," she beams, holding up her hand for me to high-five.

"That's awesome," I say, as my hand meets Sue's in midair, even as I remember how haggard Mark, Joe, and everyone else I've welcomed back to basecamp looked upon their return from that monster of a route. Sue and John were here together last year and climbed Foraker's *Talkeetna Ridge*, which is just left of the *Infinite Spur*, so she's familiar with that side of the mountain, as well as the descent. I'm excited to have her energy back in camp for the third straight year, both for her friendship and for her providing a counter to the typical male energy that often pervades the scene up here.

Like Mark and Eamonn, John Varco is also built like a tank, and comes down to help dig the hole for the tent. By midafternoon, my burly crew has got my tent set up in the deepest hole of any year so far. Mark and Eamonn have already completed several hard climbs over in the Ruth Gorge, including a major first ascent, and after they help me set up my camp, they intend to get on the *Moonflower* on Mount Hunter. I am just happy to have my two favorite hungry men to feed. I love to cook, and Eamonn loves to eat. His animated faces and sheer delight and enthusiasm at whatever I prepare for him always make my day.

Mark and Eamonn waste no time the next morning, and ski up the valley with binoculars to scout conditions on *Moonflower*. Sue, Zoe, and I talk by the NPS spotting scope as Mark and Eamonn ski back into camp a short while later.

"How's it looking up there, boys?" Sue inquires.

"Well," Mark begins, "Unfortunately, everything is looking super dry this year. The *Bibler-Klewin's* lower pitches have almost no ice on them. Even *Deprivation* looks like it's out."

"Oh, I'm sure it'll go," Sue scoffs.

"Man, I don't know," Mark says. "I have never seen the wall so bare of ice. The Shaft always has ice, but even that looks discontinuous. I think we're going to try something else."

"You should just go for it anyway," Sue counters. Mark and Eamonn stare back, puzzled.

"It'd be awful slow, maybe aid climbing," Eamonn says, his eyebrows raised.

"Yeah," Mark adds, shaking his head. "The *Moonflower* is

supposed to be a classic ice climb, and that isn't what's there right now. It's not what we came for."

But Sue is insistent.

"Oh, come on, you can do it. *We're* going for it," she teases, glancing at Zoe, who just cracks a wry smile.

The boys throw their hands in the air in defeat and glance back at Mount Hunter as though maybe they need to go have another look. Sue turns to me, smiling, and says, "Dome 72, 3:00 p.m., happy hour."

A day later, Mark, Eamonn, and I watch through the spotting scope as the girls make painstaking progress up the lower sections of *Deprivation*.

"Ugh," Mark grunts, peering into the scope. "Looks like they're aid climbing. It's been at least two hours since they started that pitch. In good conditions, there's easy ice in that part, but through the binoculars yesterday, all I could see was snowy granite slabs."

I look into the scope and watch as heavy spindrift pours down the wall, first over the leader and next the belayer, temporarily shrouding them both from view.

"Well, that doesn't look fun," I conclude.

"Yup, looks miserable," Eamonn concurs, gritting his teeth and shaking his head.

The next morning, we can see Sue and Zoe huddled on a chopped ledge where they spent the previous night. The wall, still in shade, pours with spindrift, which swirls around them to reveal the strong wind that they must be experiencing. Here, in the sun, it's just 8 degrees Fahrenheit, and I shudder to think of how much colder it must be up there in the wind and shade. By noon, the girls are rappelling back to the glacier.

"I can't believe they stuck it out that long," Mark quips, impressed with their tenacity.

When they return, Sue isn't quite as cheerful as usual. She walks over, emits a loud sigh, and then looks me straight in the eye. "I hate bailing," she says, before turning to stare at Mount Hunter, as though already plotting her rematch.

A week later, the girls climb a route up-glacier called the *Mini Moonflower*. The next day, Zoe departs, Karen McNeill arrives, and the second act of the Glitter Girls begins. The next several days feature more Dome 72 parties, numerous Cosmopolitans — with Sue's trademark straws, of course — and the usual nail polish, glitter, fashion magazines, and fine chocolates. I marvel at how they have brought enough food and fuel canisters to stay the entire summer if they wanted, and their tent becomes my second home.

Mark and Eamonn climb a couple of ice routes near basecamp, but with the *Moonflower* not in condition, they decide to fly over to the Coffee Glacier, where they end up climbing a huge new ice and mixed route on the awesome Broken Tooth. Meanwhile, Sue and Karen spend their days acclimatizing, and their evenings making Dome 72 the coolest place in the Alaska Range. Climbers from all over camp come to enjoy the girls' hospitality, and it seems that Sue has made it her mission to feed the entire Kahiltna Basecamp. Some good weather is forecasted, and the ladies declare that it's time to head for Mount Foraker.

"Are you taking a radio?" I ask Sue, as she packs outside her tent.

"Nah, we don't need a radio. Besides, when we didn't call from the *Cassin*, everyone just freaked out," she says. I can tell there is no chance of convincing her. Later, I see Karen alone, and I offer my radio, hoping she will accept it.

"I know, sore subject," I say. "But it's a serious route, Karen, and

I'd feel a lot better if you had some way to communicate with me."

Karen stares at the radio in a moment of contemplation, and then says, "Yeah, you're right, Lisa. We'll take it. Thank you."

"How long do you expect to be up there?" I ask.

"We have fourteen days of food and fuel. We're slow and steady," Karen replies with a broad smile. "That's why our expedition name is 'Turtle Team.'"

"Okay, well please keep in touch when you can."

"We will — don't worry," Karen says, as I walk away thinking about their fourteen-day plan.

Of the seven known ascents of the *Infinite Spur,* six took seven days or longer, the sole exception being Steve House and Rolo Garibotti's groundbreaking, twenty-five-hour ascent in 2001. Everyone else spent at least some of their time caught in storms.

There is no way the weather can hold for that long.

A few hours later, Sue and Karen prepare to leave basecamp for the seven-mile approach to Foraker's south face, home of the *Infinite Spur.* A handful of climbers and I are there to see them off. It's exciting to see these two brave women skiing away toward this colossal objective, one that pushed Mark, Joe, and Eamonn, among many other strong climbers, to their physical and psychological thresholds.

After ten days pass at basecamp, I'm starting to grow concerned that I haven't heard from the girls yet. But Mark reminds me that their radio won't be able to reach basecamp until they are above 14,000 feet. John Varco has flown out, but before he left, he told me he thought they would spend twelve to fifteen days on the route. Various climbers ask me if I've heard from them, as does Daryl Miller in Talkeetna on his evening calls to basecamp. The climbers Will Mayo and Maxime Turgeon, who attempted a new route on Foraker near the *Infinite Spur,* tell me they spoke to and saw the girls starting up their route on May 14 — today is May 23. That contact is the last we know of their progress.

On May 25, what would be Sue and Karen's twelfth day on the route, the wind begins to howl on the upper elevations of Denali, Hunter, and Foraker. For the next six days, the mountains are raked by a furious windstorm the likes of which I had not believed possible. The skies are clear, except for Denali and Mount Foraker, which are capped with dramatic lenticular clouds that spiral and gyrate over and around their lofty summits. Foraker's upper slopes take on a sinister appearance, one made worse by the notion the girls might be trapped in that hellish maelstrom.

"We just had a 100-mile-per-hour gust here," one of the rangers at 14,000 feet reports to the basecamp ranger John Evans over the radio, as the sounds of their flapping tent can be heard in the background. "And Foraker has these crazy clouds circling it that look like *Ghostbusters.* It's pretty scary."

Mark calls from Talkeetna, marveling at the view toward the mountains.

"The lenticular caps on Denali and Foraker look like two giant hands reaching over the Alaska Range," he raves. "I've never seen anything so foreboding. It looks evil."

I keep my CB radio on at all times in the hopes the girls will call, but there is no traffic. Ranger John Evans is in basecamp with me, and we spend undue time with the spotting scope studying their descent route down the *Sultana Ridge* and Mount Crosson, but we see nothing. On May 30, my brother flies over the lower elevations of the *Infinite Spur,* followed by fellow pilot David Lee. There are no signs of the Glitter Girls, and fear for them is mounting.

Paul calls me from Talkeetna the following morning: "I just called Daryl, Lulu. The girls are long overdue, and I have a bad feeling about this. Daryl says they'll launch the heli tomorrow."

The next day, the LAMA helicopter makes several search flights, and while clouds limit the area they can cover, possible tracks are spotted at 14,000 feet on the route. For the second day of the search, the park hires Mark — who with Joe five years ago was the last person to climb the route — to fly on the helicopter and assist in the route search. Mark flies into basecamp, and then he and the ranger Meg Perdue depart in the chopper for the *Infinite Spur.* They return with ominous news.

"We spotted a backpack at the base, in a pile of debris," Mark says through a clenched jaw. Meg uses the radio phone to brief Daryl and the other rangers back in Talkeetna. The pack is at 8,000 feet, and some of its contents, including a sleeping bag, are strewn across the snow.

"There are recent tracks at least as high as 15,000 feet," Mark tells Daryl. "We got an up-close view of the entire route to that altitude, and I feel confident saying that they are not on it."

Meg adds, "It's too dangerous to put someone on the ground to retrieve the pack due to overhead hazard. We'll need to have the hydraulic claw flown in with a fixed wing."

I get a familiar, sinking feeling.

I wait with apprehension as Mark and Meg go up with the helicopter a second time. The LAMA searches the fall line above where the gear was found, hovering its way up an enormous gully, past massive hanging glaciers and the sheer diorite cliffs that spill off the flank of the *Spur.* Mark puzzles together a potential fall scenario, directing pilot Jim Hood to fly a complex maze of rock gullies that might contain more clues. None are discovered.

The third flight of the day uses the hydraulic claw flown in from Talkeetna to retrieve the backpack. At basecamp, the pack's contents are inventoried: a jacket, a wool hat, and a water bottle, all confirmed by descriptions conveyed to John Varco as belonging to Sue. The sleeping bag was also recovered, while some other clothing items presumed to be from the pack were left scattered about in the debris. I recognize each item, including Sue's hat. The upper pouch of the pack also holds one of Sue's trademark straws, and the very same FRS radio that I gave them just before they left.

Over the next four days, the park helicopter continues to fly the route and the summit area, along with an expanded search area covering any possible fall lines and descent options. Fixed-wing aircraft circle the mountain taking high-resolution photos, while rangers and other climbers, hired to assist, study them on the computer for clues. Loomie, who has been analyzing aerial photos in Talkeetna, is convinced that there are faint tracks in the snow above 16,000 feet, almost at the top of the route. Mark, meanwhile, has his own theories.

"At around 11,000 feet," he says, "there's a snow slope that makes a good bivouac site. A pack dropped at that spot *could have* reached the place we found it, although it would have had to take a few lucky bounces. It's also the *only place* on the route where a dropped item could have reached where the pack was found."

John Varco and other climbers who know Sue remark that even a dropped pack containing a sleeping bag and other important gear would little deter Sue from continuing up.

"I suspect," Mark says, as we sit in the tent, tortured by speculation, "that Sue dropped her pack, they continued on, and, lacking some critical survival gear, reached the top of the route just as that wind event hit."

"Could they have survived in a snowcave?" I ask, playing my last card of hope.

"Maybe. But the storm ended almost a week ago," Mark says, pausing for effect. "Where are they?"

In a phone call, Daryl asks Mark if the tracks spotted up high could be from his and Joe's ascent five years earlier.

"No way," Mark replies. "I mean, the wind can do crazy things up there to preserve old tracks from one year to the next, but five years seems way too long."

A week of bad weather follows, and there is no flying possible. By June 11 — twenty-eight days since Will and Max last saw the girls at the foot of the *Spur* — any hope we clung to has evaporated.

"Lisa," Daryl says that night over the radio phone, his voice heavy with disappointment and sadness, "I wanted to tell you myself. We did the math on the fuel they had to melt water with their stove. By our most optimistic estimates, they've been out of fuel, and therefore water, for at least eight to ten days."

I have from the beginning understood the situation, but this analysis brings the cold reality out in the open.

"The probability that they're still alive is very, very low," Daryl continues. "We're going to scale down the search to a limited recovery effort. I'm sorry, Lisa — this is really hard."

John Varco arrives in basecamp to collect the girls' belongings, no small task given their sheer volume of gear and food. In a somber mood, John and I take down Dome 72. It's hard not to feel like we're erasing something by tearing down this camp that was the scene of so much joy and energy. I recall again my very first days in basecamp in late May of 2000, when Annie and I packed up the gear of the "Lads," the climbers believed to have died on the *Infinite Spur* but who later turned up alive. This time, it's my own friends, and this time, they aren't going to miraculously reappear.

I am filled with sadness watching John, stoic as he is, packing up his partner's possessions and holding his composure, trying to imagine myself in that situation were something to happen to Mark. As he readies to fly out, John brings Sue's huge bags of isobutane cartridges and freeze-dried meals over to my tent.

"I'm pretty sure you and Mark can use these. I have more than enough crap to deal with. They're all yours," he says, setting them on the snow. He looks toward Foraker, sighs, and turns back toward the camp to retrieve another load. John's plane arrives to take him to Talkeetna. Mark and I give him a hug, and then he departs, carrying with him the last physical remnants of Sue and Karen's presence.

Sue and Karen's families fly up to camp to pay their respects, and to sprinkle glitter and the girls' favorite chocolates around the camp. Grief stricken and wearing pained smiles, we share stories about their daughters' extraordinary lives in the mountains.

The summer solstice arrives. Just a few short weeks remain of this now-hollow season. I find myself consumed with thoughts of what might have happened to the girls. Death by itself is hard enough to process, but there's scarce possibility for meaningful closure when people simply vanish. That the girls remain on the mountain somehow leaves a door open — to what I can't say, but it's less like they're dead and more that they've just moved on without us. It's easy to speculate on what went wrong, but we'll probably never know, and I'm not sure that I want to know. I prefer to imagine them climbing upward forever, straight into the sun.

The well-known climber and author Gregory Crouch once wrote of risk: "Mountains are not worth dying for, but they are worth risking dying for."

Crouch very accurately summarized a cruel paradox: climbing mountains involves making choices that carry both immeasurable rewards and intolerable consequences. Mark and his friends, and I by proxy, are caught in the middle of this paradox and swept up into something intense. I fear that the risks are cumulative, and that we're hurtling through space on an unstoppable train, our destination either a state of enlightenment or a tragedy of unimaginable proportions.

Through the final days of the season, I catch myself gazing down-glacier toward Mount Foraker, half-expecting to see the girls walking into camp, puzzled, amused, or annoyed at our concern. Sometimes, it's almost like a mirage, and I imagine that, just maybe, I see two approaching figures emerging from the iridescent waves of warm, reflected afternoon sunlight rising from the glacier's surface. It's just a trick of the light, of course, a fata morgana: sparkling snow crystals suspended airborne, the spectrum of colors shimmering across the glacier, and Mount Foraker, forever glittering in the sun.

Chapter Nine
2007-2010
Extreme Alpinism

Mark and I exit Nagley's store in downtown Talkeetna, a bottle of red wine in hand. It's a quiet spring evening, and the seasonal tourists are just starting to filter into town. In a celebratory mood for no particular reason, we load ourselves into my car. Annie Duquette and Davey Kreutzer have just invited us over to dinner, and we're gathering some last-minute supplies to contribute. "We need to stop off at home and grab some salad fixings," I say to Mark, as we drive off down the spur road.

It's the twenty-third day of April 2007, and in just six days I'll be flying into Kahiltna Basecamp to start my eighth season running the camp. Mark is also busy preparing for an ambitious climbing season that will once again begin with him and Eamonn helping me to set up the camp. I'm relishing these last few days of civilized living before I set off to live upon ice for the next two months. We pull into our driveway and roll up in front of the two-story, 1,200-square-foot house that we finished building and moved into just over one year ago. The house is located on the opposite side of the 1.5-acre lot where our original cabin — now a rental unit — still stands.

"Stay here — I'll be right back," I say to Mark. I jog up to the house and duck inside through our kitchen door. I rifle through our cupboards and refrigerator, gathering ingredients. Out of the corner of my eye, I notice the message light blinking on our answering machine. I press play and continue my foraging, but Jed Brown's unsteady voice emanating from it stops me cold. Jed, a friend and climbing partner of Mark's, has been climbing in the Ruth Gorge for the past week with Lara Kellogg. Lara is one of our closest friends, and for many years, has been among Mark's most trusted climbing companions.

As Jed's voice pours through the speaker, my hands turn to ice and I feel lightheaded. I comprehend his words, but I cannot process what I'm hearing. *I need Mark in here.* I rush to the kitchen door and fling it open, flagging my arms and shouting Mark's name so he can hear me over the car's engine.

Mark jumps from the car with a startled look.

"What's wrong?" he asks, his eyes widening.

I don't have the right words.

"Lara died."

Mark slams the car door and bolts into the house.

"Let me hear it," he says, as we step over to the answering machine.

The second time listening to Jed's message is just as traumatic as the first.

"This is Jed, in the Ruth Gorge," he begins. "Lara . . . rappelled off the ends of her ropes . . . and . . . died . . . as we were coming down from Mount Wake. This was about 6:00 p.m. Please tell the park service." Jed is always stoic, but the shock in his stilted voice is unmistakable. I can almost picture my younger brother again, standing in the door of our house after he found my mother in the woods.

Mark draws in a long, deep breath.

"Fuck."

Mark and I collapse into each other's arms.

"We need to call Daryl and Paul, right now," Mark says, gathering his composure. "I don't think anyone can get in there tonight in this weather." The Alaska Range is shrouded in clouds; the foothills are barely visible from town, and a thick overcast covers Talkeetna.

We spend the next several hours pacing our living room. Mark makes a series of agonizing calls to each of our friends in Seattle — where Lara is from, and where we all became friends — to break the news, each call a terrible reliving of the trauma. After we endure a long and sleepless night, Paul calls as dawn breaks over south-central Alaska.

"The Ruth Gorge is open — I'm going to head in with an NPS ranger to bring her back," Paul says. "We've been talking to Jed on the phone; it sounds like he and a Japanese climbing team were able to bring her body back to the landing site with a sled." Mark and I drag ourselves to the car to make our way toward the Talkeetna airport. Few words pass as we drive, while a decade's worth of now-bittersweet memories cascade over me.

Lara was a remarkable woman: tall, blue-eyed, and a striking blonde of Latvian descent, she was a gifted athlete who grew up skateboarding and listening to punk music on the streets of Seattle. In her mid-twenties, she became devoted to snowboarding and climbing, which led her and Mark to meeting more than ten years ago on Mount Rainier. Mark, Joe, and Lara — then known as Lara Bitenieks — were hired by Mike Gauthier as Mount Rainier climbing rangers and spent the summer of 1996 working together on the mountain at Camp Schurman.

That same summer, as Mark and I were writing letters to one another and careening toward our impending relationship, there was also a foundational bonding of this group of budding, hardcore alpinists that would soon come to include exceptional athletes like David Gottlieb and Chad Kellogg. In the years that followed, Lara and Chad fell in love, married in the spring of 2000, settled into professional careers in Seattle, and committed themselves to lives of intense adventures in alpinism and endurance sports.

I came to know Lara over several years, between her occasional climbing trips that passed through basecamp in Alaska, and through the past decade of winters when Mark and I lived in Seattle for his temporary engineering-work assignments. Initially, my drive and ambitions related to climbing — which were modest in comparison to hers — made Lara seem intimidating to me. But Lara made a sincere and persistent effort to wear away at my defenses. Whether our group was on ice-climbing trips in Canada, cragging on the cliffs of Frenchman Coulee in Eastern Washington, or enjoying a nice dinner at their West Seattle home, Lara always treated me as her equal, never pressuring me or judging. She just put in the time to be my friend. As I ponder her death, I think of the trip we took just two short months ago:

"Check it out, Lisa," she said, as Mark and I gathered at Chad and Lara's house, along with Tom Dancs, another of our closest Seattle friends. The five of us were about to cram into their Ford Explorer for a seven-hour drive to go ice climbing for a few days in British Columbia.

"I've got sandwiches made for all of us," she said with pride, opening a Trader Joe's grocery bag. "I also have a whole assortment of snacks for everyone. Water's in that jug. And, Lisa, I brought a pillow for your back — I know how you hate these long road trips."

I seize upon the most treasured memories of our annual winter stays in Seattle: laughter-filled road trips with our friends to the mountains, dinners at the many great restaurants along

West Seattle's California Avenue, and our countless dinners and movie nights at Chad and Lara's house. I smile as I think of Chad, barbecuing and telling jokes with Mark, while Lara chatted me up about a cool clothing shop she'd found, a new recipe, or a neat restaurant she knew about. Mark and Chad, meanwhile, would be in the other room going off about this hard pitch they'd climbed, their latest training regimen, or this crazy mountain route they wanted to try together. I have always loved that while Lara was a fanatical and talented climber on both ice and stone, she couldn't long abide "climber talk," and knowing that I couldn't either, had no problem discussing other topics with me.

Mark and I were married in Girdwood, Alaska, on March 11, 2006, which also happened to be Chad and Lara's anniversary. Mark and I had spent the two months prior living in Chad and Lara's attic to save money on rent while Mark worked at Rosewater Engineering in downtown Seattle. Lara was excited, and didn't hesitate before booking airline tickets for her and Chad to attend our wedding. One evening, not long before my flight home to Alaska, Lara announced a surprise outing for us in Seattle.

"Lisa, I want to take you shopping tomorrow. Let's get you a nice outfit for the wedding dinner," she said.

The next day, she brought me to her favorite boutiques, where we worked through and debated different outfits. I rejected the spiky high-heel shoes she suggested — not my style — but I loved the gorgeous white Cashmere wrap she presented. I had never had someone do anything like this for me before, and she made me feel spoiled. That's who Lara was to me.

My pulse quickens and I feel a paradoxical wave of sadness as I recall Mark and my wedding day, when, under single-digit temperatures, still air, and spectacular blue skies atop the Alyeska ski area tram station, my brother Paul married Mark and me, surrounded by family and friends. Amidst the breathtaking mountain scenery, it was a quick, simple, and informal ceremony followed by a day of skiing, but Lara was the closest thing I had to a matron of honor. And now, she's gone.

Paul's plane taxies up to the hangar at Talkeetna Air Taxi under a somber gray sky. Jed emerges from the plane, his face hollow, and we welcome him into our embrace. Mark and I take a hesitant step or two toward the airplane, with an intention to help with the unloading. Our friend and NPS ranger Mik Shain is also here to assist.

"You don't have to help if you don't want to," he offers.

Mark stops.

"I don't think I can do it," he says, his eyes growing glassy. He steps back, and I step back with him. We did this once before, with Keli Mahoney and Bruce Andrews. This is just too close to home.

We watch in silence as Paul and the rangers unload a bag containing the body of our beloved friend. Clouds obscure the sun, dulling its light and warmth. An appropriate gloom is instead cast across the Talkeetna airfield.

In the following days, we struggle to make sense of the accident. Jed and Lara made it halfway up the 5,000-foot Northeast Ridge of Mount Wake, a fearsome mountain in the Ruth Gorge. The snow was bad, and they made a wise decision to retreat. The day had been otherwise enjoyable. Lara was on rappel, below and out of sight of Jed as she rapped into a gully that hung above a 100-foot step of vertical ice. On the ascent, they had noted that this gully had very little protection. With only one rope, they opted on their descent to fix the rope as a single line, deciding that Lara would rappel, placing whatever protection she could find, make an anchor, and then belay Jed — who was the stronger climber — as he downclimbed to her. A few minutes into Lara's rappel, there was a shout, Jed related, followed by the sound of an impact. Moments later, Jed witnessed Lara tumbling out of the gully and onto the glacier more than 1,000 feet below. They had made a deliberate decision not to knot the end of the rappel rope, a decision which proved to be fatal. Lara, one of the most attentive people we knew, had apparently lost her attention at the worst possible moment, and had slid off the end of the rope while fixated on finding an anchor.

We're left grasping for clues, nonetheless, wondering if there was something we should have noticed, something we should have said, tortured by the thought that we may share some responsibility for the loss of our friend. Over this past winter, there was ambition and a competitive spirit amongst Mark and his group of friends that was stronger than usual, and hard to ignore. Lara was at the epicenter of this seismic energy, but it was also evident that she was putting a great deal of pressure on herself.

"For the past four years," Lara told me one night after dinner, "Chad's been to China, K2, Khan Tengri, and on a bunch of other huge expeditions. I'm 38 years old. I've been staying home working, and putting off the bigger things I want to do. I'm not waiting anymore."

Lara had long been constrained from going on bigger expeditions by her career with the US Forest Service in Seattle, where she worked analyzing fire and forestry data, but outside work she was almost always training, running, going to the climbing gym, or in the mountains doing something wild. She was like a coiled spring, with bigger dreams that could no longer wait.

It seemed like everyone in our circle had big plans for hard and serious alpine climbing for the upcoming spring, and almost every weekend and minute of free time in our group was devoted to training. Joe and Chad were going to China. Mark was planning for an attempt on Mount Hunter with Eamonn, and then for one of the most difficult routes on Denali with Colin Haley, a young but very talented alpinist from Seattle. Lara, meanwhile, had made plans for a trip to Mount Kennedy in southeast Alaska with a large group of climbers, including our close friends Forrest Murphy and Dan Aylward. In time, however, everyone in that group dropped out except Lara — and the young Alaskan climber Jed Brown.

"Lara keeps calling. She seems very anxious about the Alaska trip," Mark told me one day about a month earlier. "She says that she's always been self-conscious about appearing weak, except around Chad and me."

"Well, I can understand that. It's kind of a woman thing. What did you tell her?" I asked.

"Well, first of all I reminded her that Jed is an easygoing guy and he'll go with whatever objective she's into," Mark answered. "I also told her to just go with her intuition, and to choose something that will be enjoyable and a good challenge."

"How did she respond?" I countered.

"I think she's just wary of getting in over her head, and at the same time, putting a lot of pressure on herself to go big for some reason," Mark said. "I mean, I get it. You want to push it, but not too far."

"I brought you something, Lisa," Lara said, when she and Jed arrived in Talkeetna in mid-April and stayed at our house. She handed me a beautiful, colorful coffee mug adorned with a sunflower.

"Mark mentioned that you love sunflowers," she added, shooting a respectful smile in Mark's direction.

The next morning, we accompanied Jed and Lara to Talkeetna Air Taxi to see them off. The sunlight beamed through the window of the log-cabin office, creating a warm atmosphere. We said our goodbyes, and Lara gave me a long hug, which felt both powerful and somehow unsettling. As Mark and I drove away, I mentioned it to him, with hesitation. "Lara gave me this really big hug, like she was never going to see me again," I said. Mark glanced at me, wordless, and then recast his gaze forward again in thought.

"She hugged me pretty hard as well," he said, finally.

Several days have passed since the accident, and a pressing problem remains unresolved. Chad is climbing in a remote part of China with Joe, and now, four days after Lara's death, attempts to reach him have been unsuccessful. In the cruelest twist of fate, Chad will be the last to know.

After much effort by friends and family in Seattle, the outfitter that Chad and Joe are using is at last contacted in a small village in Western China called Rilong. The outfitter dispatches a messenger on horseback to reach Chad and Joe's remote basecamp near the mountain they are attempting. After many hours' ride, the messenger delivers a note stating that Chad needs to come to town and call home, with no further details.

One evening, just a few days before I am supposed to set up basecamp, Mark's phone rings. When Mark picks up and hears Chad's voice, it is obvious from the start that Chad has no idea that Lara has died.

"What's going on?" Chad asks. Mark takes a seat on our basement stairs.

"Chad. What have you heard?" Mark replies cautiously.

"Nothing," Chad answers. "I was told to call home. Talk to me."

"Chad," Mark begins, struggling for words. "Lara died four days ago."

Standing close to Mark with my hand on his shoulder, I can hear Chad's haunting, anguished cries through the phone. Mark paces the house trying to calm and console him, finding out what he needs to get home, and promising to make some more calls for him to Seattle. The call ends; Mark slumps against the living-room wall and buries his head in his hands. Our world is shattered like fine crystal dropped upon a concrete floor.

Mark and I gather Eamonn at the Anchorage airport the following day, and he's arrived to a funeral-like atmosphere in our home. He, too, knew Lara. Her death has left Mark and Eamonn reconsidering their plans, and me reconsidering my obligations.

"The service is in Seattle next week. Should we go?" I say, shocked at hearing myself even ask the question. As I recall the crushing trauma of my own mother's funeral, however, I realize that it's complicated: *Funerals just make me feel worse.*

"I feel so bad, but . . ." Mark stammers, rubbing his forehead as he searches for the right words. He looks up, his face creased with anguish. "I just don't think I can do it. I have to grieve this in my own way."

"I completely understand and am open to anything you guys need to do," Eamonn says in a subdued voice. "Friends and family come first."

I have no one to fill in for me at basecamp. The entire operation is under my sole control, and the air services are dependent on me for the next ten weeks. "I've talked with people in Seattle. Everyone understands," Mark adds, and yet we're still troubled. *Are we rationalizing this decision?* Right or wrong, we reach a weak consensus to flee to the mountains to find solace.

After a day's delay from poor weather, I'm reinstalled at basecamp, with Mark and Eamonn. In an ironic twist, the mountains where Lara lost her life offer catharsis and separation from the online remembrances and news stories that have for the past week locked us all into a cycle of endless pain.

With trauma still numbing our collective senses, Mark and Eamonn decide to waste no time with the present good weather, and they strike off in the morning to attempt the *Moonflower*. The rangers and I observe them through the spotting scope at points where their route is visible. Late in the evening, Mark radios with some disappointing news.

"We're bivied on the first ice band, but I dropped one of my ice tools off the Prow," he says, dejected. The Prow is a huge granite buttress jutting from the wall low on the route, and host to one of the route's most difficult pitches. "We were able to keep going somehow, but we're thinking of descending tomorrow," he adds.

"Call me in the morning and let me know what you're doing," I instruct. "Make good choices. Be careful."

It's out of character for Mark to drop crucial gear, and I'm hoping they'll come down. Mark checks back with me in the morning as promised:

"We just endured a miserable, cold bivouac, and now the weather looks like it's coming in. I don't want to climb the Shaft with one tool. It's overhanging and would be ridiculous. I love you, and I'll see you when we get down," he says.

The boys are back by late afternoon. Soon after that, Paul and much of the Talkeetna Air Taxi office staff arrive in several of their airplanes for a glacier "office party," which will include sled races and a volleyball match, bringing a carnival-like atmosphere to the glacier. Accompanying the crew is our eccentric friend and mentor, Ted Gannon. Ted has flown in for the party, but also to stage an intervention.

"Lara's accident has clouded your focus," he tells Mark, his eyes closed and his hand held up like a mystic. "Dropping a critical piece of equipment shows that you aren't in good relationship to climbing, and are not in the right mindset for engaging in it on a serious level."

"That was one moment," Mark counters. "But what about now?"

"Climbing requires seriousness and energy. You should consider walking away from it altogether," Ted replies.

Mark frowns, while Eamonn twists his face into a puzzled scowl.

"That's like saying a fish should live in the forest," Eamonn says, crossing his huge forearms over his chest.

I've learned much from Ted through the years, but Ted also told Mark and me, on the eve of our wedding, that getting married was "a mistake." I'm not certain that I'm with him on this one, either. Ted departs that evening with the TAT crew but continues to check back in over the next several days. He even tells Paul to hide Mark's mountain boots so he can't climb. Mark and Eamonn think Ted is perhaps a bit crazy, but at the same time, they have utilized this period of unstable weather to hit pause and at least consider what he is saying.

Mark, Eamonn, and I spend the next several days engaging in many long discussions about climbing, partnerships, attention, intuition, and safety. We game out every scenario and possible hazard they could face on *the Moonflower* — and in alpinism more generally.

I will never ask Mark to not climb, but I do ask Mark to contemplate anew the stresses and worry that his repeated engagements with high-end alpinism have inflicted upon me. Mark and I have taken contrasting trajectories with alpine climbing. With each passing year, I choose far less serious and committing objectives in the mountains. My energy levels are hard to predict, and it's intimidating to contemplate these big objectives when you aren't sure if you'll be able to hold up through the whole experience. I have no doubt that I would have kept to the trajectory I intended — to pursue bigger objectives with Mark — were it not for this fatigue and the trouble I have dealing with cold, which is hard enough right here in basecamp. I'll be 40 next year, and I intend to keep doing whatever I can and whatever makes sense for me. I will always love sunny rock climbing at both the crags and in the mountains, even if cold and committing alpinism in the bigger ranges remains beyond my reach.

With Mark, on the other hand, each season brings more difficult and committing objectives, and each one accomplished with mutual friends. There were the *Cassin Ridge* and the *Infinite Spur* with Joe, in 2000 and 2001 respectively. In 2003, Mark and Joe attempted the *Moonflower,* and then Mark and our friend Forrest Murphy from Seattle made a harrowing, five-day traverse of Mount Hunter by way of the mountain's committing and seldom-climbed south ridge, known for its dangerous cornices and wild exposure. Each of these climbs played out while I watched, waited, and worried in basecamp, all while trying to remain engaged with my own duties.

In 2004, Mark and another of our Seattle friends, Dan Aylward, attempted the dangerous north buttress of the Rooster Comb, a climb that ended after Mark was hit so hard in the head by icefall that he almost lost consciousness. Mark and Eamonn's past two spring seasons have seen them picking off several huge, hazardous, and difficult unclimbed lines in the early months, prior to the start of basecamp, sparing me the proximity to the action, but their situations were no less worrisome. Big Eamonn seems indestructible and superhuman, but still, I'm superstitious, and I've convinced myself that my worrying has some effect on keeping Mark and his partners safe, no matter who it may be.

The boys are receptive to my concerns. The three of us open up about their state of mind, their fears, their focus, their attention, and their friendship. They verbalize their trust in one another. Together, we convince ourselves that the voicing of all these concerns and putting everything on the table creates a layer of protection through heightened awareness. We each in our own way understand that climbing is, on the one hand, crazy and pointless, but that, on the other, it also leads to vital life experiences and an intensity of relationships that are hard to replicate in the everyday world.

We also discuss the stress that Lara was under in the weeks and months leading up to her accident. Perhaps, we project, that stress had some metaphysical connection to the moment she lost her attention and situational awareness — something out of character for her — and which subsequently cost Lara her life. I still cannot understand why she wouldn't have decided to knot the end of the single skinny rope on which she was rappelling, especially while on frozen terrain that can ice up the rope. Sometimes, climbers won't knot the rope to avoid the rope hanging up when pulled, but since Jed was planning to downclimb anyway, that was not a risk. Mark, Eamonn, and I talk day and night about such external stressors and distractions, in part because Mark and I feel, having witnessed the stress that Lara was putting upon herself in the lead-up to her climb, that we probably should have had these same discussions with her rather than assuming she'd be fine.

Meanwhile, Mark has rounded up a replacement ice tool, and after daily ski trips up-valley to scope the route, and evenings spent debating Ted's warnings and talking points, Eamonn and he commit to the idea of trying the *Moonflower* again.

Of Ted's proclamations, Eamonn would later write in a trip report for the *Canadian Alpine Journal*:

"It offered many nights and evenings of discussion between Mark, Lisa, and I, but in the end it probably strengthened our resolve to climb the thing. It is quite a strange thing to have someone go out of their way to convince you that what you are about to do is foolish, even if the person is genuinely concerned."

Our open discussions reassure me, but the mountains are still dangerous. If something happens to them, I don't know how I'll be able to live with myself.

The boys depart in the wee hours of May 10, 2007, under clear skies. I follow their progress through the NPS spotting scope. They are moving with rapid efficiency, and arrive at their prior bivouac on the "first ice band" four hours faster than on their first attempt. I watch them hacking at the snow and ice to create a bivy platform, and soon after, Mark hails me on the radio.

"It's going great up here," he reports. "The climbing was awesome, and now we're in the warm sun with a nice, flat, chopped ledge to sleep on."

"The weather looks good tomorrow, but might be changing in the next day or two," I caution them before we sign off. Where they are is just so wild it's hard to imagine, sleeping tied into a thin nylon rope on a narrow ice ledge thousands of feet above the glacier, vertical ice soaring above and below them. To be able to see them through the scope with the detail it provides brings it all closer to home for me. *This is extreme alpinism.*

The next evening, Mark checks in again after my 8:00 p.m. weather broadcast, which is still calling for a front to arrive the following afternoon.

"We're on the third ice band. The Shaft was as incredible as we imagined. It's so steep," Mark reports. "We want to bivouac here, but the weather looks like it's already changing. Any more details?"

I glance outside. There are some vapor tendrils creeping up the Kahiltna at the middle altitudes, and a small lenticular cloud hovers motionless above Foraker. High cirrus clouds streak the sky.

"All I know is what the automated weather line gave me. It's supposed to hit tomorrow afternoon," I reply.

"Well," Mark answers after a pause, "we're not liking the look of it from up here right now. We would have to chop into the ice to bivy here, and this would be a terrible place in a storm."

After another pause, Mark continues. "We're going to just keep on climbing through the night and try to get to the top of the buttress, in case it hits early. At least up there we'll be on more level ground and could dig a snow cave."

Before bedtime, I peek out my tent door one last time to check the weather. The north buttress gleams in the evening sun, which eases my mind, even as ominous clouds seem to have coalesced in the Kahiltna and snow plumes tear away from Foraker's summit.

Deep in the night, I awaken with a feeling of anxiety for Mark and Eamonn, and it's then that I realize that the wind is blowing, and the sound of snowflakes hitting the tent brings me to full attention. I go to the door and look out to a distressing scene. Clouds are everywhere; up-glacier, the bottom of Mount Hunter peeks out, the bulk of it obscured and being raked by strong winds. Spindrift avalanches cascade out of the cloud deck, the wind roaring audibly far above.

The remainder of my night is short on sleep and long with worry for the boys. I've done this so many times, and it never gets easier. At last, Mark calls me at 9:00 a.m., his voice revealing exhaustion and worry.

"We're on top of the buttress, behind the cornice. We've been digging a snow cave for the past three hours. Should have it done in another hour or two. We had one hell of a night getting up here, but for now, we're safe," he says.

"Are you guys okay?" I ask.

"We're okay, all things considered. Eamonn seems to have frostbitten a finger. And I'm not sure about my toes yet. At least we have shelter and can get warmed up and rehydrated."

"What's your plan?" I continue.

"We're going to have to sit tight until the weather breaks. We're kind of worried, though. It's nuking up here, and there's an awful lot of new snow piling up."

"Okay — the weather forecast looks better tomorrow," I tell him. "Get warm and take care of yourselves. I love you."

The following morning, Mark reports that the wind has stopped but it's still whited out, with light snow falling. There's at least three feet of new snow, and none of their options are great. Above them is 1,800 vertical feet of easy walking to the summit on moderate-angled slopes loaded with much new snow and prone to avalanche. To go up and over the summit and down the West Ridge would be longer and easier than rapping *Moonflower*, but very risky.

The avalanche danger makes that option almost unthinkable. On the other hand, rappelling the 4,000 feet of near-vertical terrain they climbed over the past two days has its own set of dangers and problems. In the current conditions, the face will be swept by relentless spindrift avalanches. Making ice anchors for dozens of rappels will also be quite difficult, with snowfall and spindrift pouring down the face, and their ropes could freeze into unwieldy cables.

At just after noon, Mark checks in again, and to his dismay, I've got a changed forecast.

"Now, it says a strong front from the south will arrive tomorrow," I tell him.

There is a long pause before Mark replies.

"Okay. Well, that settles it. We're going to start down right now. It's not good here, but we're going to have to go for it. We're also low on fuel. We'll try to keep in touch, but don't expect to hear from us very often — we've got a ton of rappels and need to keep focused."

Mark next checks in just after my 8:00 p.m. weather.

"Twenty-six rappels done. Just about three more to go," Mark says. "Get the burgers on the grill and chill the beer."

In just another ninety minutes, my two big MOGs are clicking out of their skis in front of my tent. I rush out to them with just what they need: hugs, cold beers, and comfortable snow boots.

"The climbing was so good," Mark begins, "but we paid a steep price for it." Eamonn nods, his eyes widening.

Once we retreat to the rangers' heated tent and the boys hold burgers in hand, they reveal the more terrifying details of their ordeal.

"We spent all night climbing the final icefield in a raging blizzard," Mark relays. "Worst conditions I've ever climbed in. Almost dark, belaying off single ice screws, iron-hard blue ice, numb fingers and toes, eyes frozen shut. We had to make it to the top of the wall to survive."

"Thank god we were able to dig a snow cave up there," Eamonn adds.

"And then, when we got down, the slope at the base was loaded with all the snow cascading off the wall the past several days," Mark continued. "As we rappelled into it, the whole slope settled, and we feared it would slide."

"After all we'd just survived, I thought we might get the chop just minutes from camp," Eamonn emphasizes. "Then we tried to walk down the slope, and we were sinking over our heads. Deepest snow I've ever seen. We ended up rolling down the hill like logs."

"That's a tactic I'd never employed in fifteen years of climbing here," Mark says. "And when I told you to put the burgers on, we were celebrating WAY too soon."

Later that evening, when it's just the two of us, Mark opens up.

"It was grim. I was so mad at myself for getting into that situation, and so soon after what just happened to Lara," he says. "We got lucky, simple as that."

"I'm just glad you're back safe," I say. "But I'm getting tired of worrying about you."

"I know," Mark says.

Mark holds me close as we drift off to sleep.

In late June, Mark is back in basecamp with me and decompressing after a successful ascent of the *Denali Diamond* route on Denali's southwest face with 23-year-old Colin Haley, one of the up-and-coming stars of American alpine climbing. Utilizing the bold, modern style that Mark had learned from watching top alpinists like Steve House and Rolo Garibotti in years past—carrying ultra-light gear, minimal food and fuel, simul-climbing on easier terrain, and leading in blocks — they dispatched the 8,000-foot face in just 45 hours, a significant stylistic achievement on a world-class route that will doubtless make news in the climbing world. The first ascent of this route, in 1983, had been a miserable, 17-day ordeal. Their climb went by so fast that I had little time for concern, while getting regular radio updates from Mark as they charged up the enormous face.

"It was the perfect climb, where everything goes the way you hope when you're planning it at home in the living room," Mark says, with an air of quiet satisfaction.

"Next season, though," he adds with an unexpected twist, "I'm still going to climb, but I think I may dial it back or at least not step it up. The trajectory of always going bigger isn't sustainable."

"I'll believe that when I see it," I reply, smiling but skeptical.

"One of the things that keeps me motivated for these big seasons is knowing that you'll be up here, too," he continues, a faraway gleam in his eye. I nod, but his statement gives me pause. *How long will I be up here? And which of us will reach the breaking point first?*

"Me too, sweetie."

Three years to the date of Lara's death, I find myself engaged with the same old preparations for yet another basecamp season. Somehow, I've remained committed to Denali and all its drama, tragedy, and beauty. I've spent the past several days shopping for food, sorting and inspecting my gear, and staging it out by the tarmac in preparation for setup day. Beyond these familiar rituals, the 2010 climbing season is going to have a very different and exciting dynamic for me. Mark is now a Denali mountaineering ranger.

An unexpected turn of events led to Mark and I sharing an apartment in Seattle with Joe and Michelle over the past winter. Mark's engineering company closed two years ago, and he was left working construction for Chad Kellogg in Seattle. Although Mark enjoyed working with one of his closest friends, it was not the sort of work he dreamed of doing forever. The Denali rangers, meanwhile, have been trying to recruit Mark for years, but Mark's personal goals in Alaska have always come first. The ranger John Leonard took over the program as South District Ranger after Daryl Miller retired in 2008, and this winter, made Mark an offer he couldn't refuse.

"John says he'll give me some time off for the climbs I have planned," Mark says after a phone call with John just before New Year's Day 2010. "They finally talked me into it."

It makes sense that Mark at last has work in the same small town where we live, but I soon discover that the job's duties may result in me seeing him even less than before. The ranger season begins with a six-week block of training, including a medical refresher, weeklong field trips for avalanche safety and technical-rescue rigging, and then proficiency training with the park's shorthaul helicopter. After that, the patrol season begins, and in May, Mark is scheduled to do a twenty-five-day patrol on Denali.

Mark's talk of "dialing it back" with climbing three years ago was, as I anticipated, short-lived. The next year, 2008, he and Eamonn climbed another huge route on Denali called the *Isis Face,* then a new route near basecamp that they named after the breakfasts I had been preparing for them (*Bacon and Eggs*). Last year, 2009, they climbed Mount Huntington, one of Alaska's most challenging and beautiful spires. This season, Mark has even bigger plans.

Eamonn couldn't come to Alaska this season, so Mark has recruited his friend Jesse Huey, a very strong climber from Washington, as a volunteer on his Denali patrol. After the patrol ends, Mark has two weeks off, and he and Jesse will remain on the mountain gunning for a significant climbing objective: the *Slovak Direct* on Denali's 9,000-foot south face, which is possibly the mountain's longest and most difficult route. Mark and Jesse are hopeful about making the route's fifth ascent.

The park service's Denali patrols spend their first two days in basecamp, practicing crevasse rescue, acclimatizing, and getting organized. Mark and his patrol arrive in mid-May, and it is exciting for Mark and me to now be working side by side at basecamp for several days as he conducts official duties, contacts incoming climbers, picks up trash, and tends to the cache garden and pee holes. The dynamic is new and refreshing, after so many years of the way we've been doing this. *We've become stewards of Denali.*

Mark has an uneventful patrol, and while he's at the 14,000-Foot Camp, he's able to use the radio telephone so we can talk every day. On a cold, windy day, their patrol reaches the summit, from where Mark radios me to check in. The fact that he's climbing the mountain for work rather than recreation eases my stress.

He's the rescuer. Maybe nothing can happen to him.

At the end of the patrol, Mark and Jesse remain on the mountain as planned. The two weeks they have allotted to climb are slipping away, and they have come down from 14 Camp to post up here in basecamp. The weather has been poor, and they are growing discouraged that a window will ever materialize. With a major storm inbound, I elect to fly out to Talkeetna for a break and I leave the camp in their hands.

It snows for four full days. When I return, basecamp is flooded with incoming and outgoing climbers. Five planes are parked on the turnaround, and it looks like Grand Central Station. I know this chaos all too well.

"Thank god you're back," Jesse exclaims as I carry my backpack from the plane toward the tent.

"Some of these climbers were so high maintenance," Mark says. "We had 155 people waiting to get out this morning. It's been like herding cats."

Mark's seen this before, but I'm always a bit pleased to watch him get the full taste of what I deal with here on a regular basis. I look around the camp, and I like what I see. I see climbers grouped together by air service. No one seems angry. The boys have a table set up with "The List" on a whiteboard for climbers to view. The camp is clean, the runway is clear, and people are camping where they are supposed to. *I've trained Mark well.*

"It looks like there may be a weather window, and we need to get going today," Mark says.

"Good job, you two," I say, patting Mark on the back. "Now go get packed and get that thing done."

Jesse surveys the scene, shakes his head in disbelief, and says, "I don't know how the hell you do this job, Lisa. Respect."

Mark and Jesse ski out of basecamp in the late morning, after I hug them with wishes of luck and admonitions to stay safe. *I'm getting used to this* — it's a thought that, alongside my superstitions about impending disaster, is worrisome. By the following afternoon, the boys call by radio and are already 2,000 feet up the *Slovak Direct*, settled into one of the few flat bivouac sites on the route's lower two-thirds. They are happy to report that all the boxes are checked: conditions are great, the climbing is magnificent, and they are healthy and happy. The beautiful weather holds over the next several days, allowing me to relax and keep my focus on my duties at basecamp. It's in the afternoon of their fourth day on the route when I get a joyous radio call. They are on top of Denali in bright sunshine with calm wind.

It is at disarming moments like this that I find myself given to reflection. Mark has just climbed one of the continent's longest and most difficult alpine routes, fitting the climb in around his duties as a rescue ranger. A stray thought arises: *Maybe Mark is invincible.* I shudder in an instant at having entertained such an absurd notion. No one is immortal, and Mark would be the last person to believe himself immune to the consequences of risk. In fact, Mark confessed to me that every time he heads into the Alaska Range, he always verbalizes a phrase to himself: "I could die doing this." He seems to think that so bluntly bringing the risk into the open will heighten his awareness and attention, and perhaps, add a shield of immunity. As for me, I have an old, familiar ritual of my own: I feel that if I worry, then it will keep him safe. We are not delusional, however; we simply know that we can never let down our guard in the mountains. Mark and Jesse ski into basecamp the next morning, elated but spent.

Mark sinks into one of my lawn chairs, basking in the morning sunshine. "Not sure if I can ever go bigger," he says. "That might be my Alaska masterpiece."

"It was so 'out there,'" Jesse adds. "There were tears of joy, man."

With no time for a break down in town, Mark is going straight from his monumental climb into his scheduled basecamp patrol, and now I'll have him working in camp with me for the last two weeks of the season. Mark is, in fact, a full day late for work. He is fortunate, however, to have recruited as his volunteer our great friend, the longtime climber and the former NPS Alaska Region Director Ralph Tingey. Ralph has got Mark covered.

"Here you go," Ralph says, emerging from the NPS cook tent

with a fresh French press of gourmet coffee. "Mark, I got the camp chores handled — you go sleep it off whenever you like."

"Well, what's next?" I ask Mark, sensing we've reached a turning point. After a decade of my working on Denali, my husband — having climbed almost everything worthwhile — is now working right alongside me as a rescue ranger. It feels as though we're entering a new era.

Mark smiles and admires the mountains, then turns toward me with a look of contentment.

"Tomorrow," he says.

A few months later, on a late-August morning, Mark and I are on our way through Seattle, lingering over coffee with Joe and Michelle in the same apartment that we all shared last winter. The boys laugh as they recall their running joke from the 1990s — that one day the two of them and their spouses would be living together. What they didn't realize then was that instead of being in some classic mountain town, they would be living in another old apartment in Seattle, just a few miles from the run-down University District apartments they were living in at the time.

Earlier in the summer, Mark and Joe went rock climbing in the North Cascades, having not climbed together in four years. Mark told me that the old magic of their friendship had rekindled, and that they spent the drive home plotting for a future expedition together to China or the Himalaya. As I observe them now, it's clear that the awkwardness that formed between Mark and Joe for the past few years has finally melted away. At long last, we look something like the foursome I long ago envisioned, and the future looks exciting.

In just two weeks, Joe is leaving for a two-month expedition to attempt an unclimbed 7,000-meter mountain in Tibet with our longtime friend David Gottlieb. Mark and I are on our way south to climb in Yosemite and the High Sierra. We have already booked airplane tickets for Thailand in November, and there's discussion about the four of us meeting on the beaches of Ton Sai for some limestone sport climbing, or perhaps some desert sandstone later in the winter.

As we ready to leave the apartment, we drag out the exchange of goodbyes and hugs. Mark pulls back from his hug with Joe. Before they separate, Mark claps his hand on Joe's shoulder, and changing to a serious expression, engages Joe with direct eye contact.

"Be safe over there," Mark counsels.

Joe raises his hand with reassurance. "Don't worry. We've got so much time. We are *assured* of success," he states, waving his hand with an air of confidence. Mark frowns. It's an uncharacteristically casual pronouncement from Joe, who has never been given to premature celebrations, much less declaring victory before a climb has even begun.

The months pass and carry us into autumn, as many pitches of classic Sierra granite pass beneath our calloused hands and feet. Life is good and simple for Mark and me. By October 27, our travels have brought us to Red Rock Canyon near Las Vegas, Nevada, and we're taking refuge in a favorite hotel as a windy autumn storm begins raking the desert.

A ringtone jars me out of a deep sleep. It takes me a moment to come to my senses and recall where I am. I find myself sitting up in bed in a room, the details slowly returning. I see Mark sitting upright beside me, holding his phone. The phone is still ringing, and Mark is staring at it, the screen's glow illuminating his face, now creased with worry.

"It's Michelle" Mark says, his voice rising. "I'm afraid to answer it."

The clock on the nightstand reads 4:58 a.m. *Why would she call at this hour?*

Mark takes a deep breath, and then picks up.

"Michelle, what's going on?"

The "new era" I had sensed is now here, but it's not at all what I expected:

"Joe died."

Chapter Ten
2011-Rescue Season

Ten years gone. It's a great Led Zeppelin song, of course, but this also describes my tenure at basecamp. And that doesn't include the season of 2000, when Annie trained me and I spent just half the season up here. It's April of 2011, and I'm standing in the doorway of my aging tent, set up just today for yet another season, watching the ice crystals sparkle in the frigid air and refract the brilliant sunlight illuminating Mount Hunter. It's a scene so new, and yet so familiar.

Either way, I'm now entering my second decade at basecamp, which means I've been at this job longer than anyone else before me. Annie did ten seasons here, and Frances did nine. It feels like many lifetimes already. My once wide-eyed apprehensions and anxieties about weather and crowd control, along with the novel and recreational feel of being up here, have transitioned to a more sober, businesslike approach to the job. Mark, too, is experiencing the Alaska Range in a different manner, his engagements now rooted more in service to the mountain and its visitors as a rescue ranger than to his personal mountaineering goals. Maybe we are finally growing up, but even now in our forties, I cling ever more tightly to whatever innocence remains. At times, I find I must step outside the familiarity of the process and the setting, and remind myself to look around at the mountains and remain in awe of where I work and its stunning backdrop. I hope to not ever fail to appreciate or take for granted the beauty and uniqueness of this job.

There have been many changes in my time. There are new rangers, new pilots, new climbers and guides, and even new airplanes, as the larger-capacity and more powerful De Havilland turbine Otter aircraft come to replace the Cessna 185s and De Havilland Beavers. And even as the climate in Alaska has warmed, one thing that remains unchanged is that April is still a cold and uncomfortable month in the Alaska Range. Tonight, I retire to my lofted sleeping bag in the clutches of today's sudden jump from near sea level to 7,200 feet, tired by the day's exertion of shoveling and of dragging my heavy equipment through the snow.

After a sound sleep, the season's first morning in camp begins with a call from Paul, conveying tragic news.

"Some climbers camped on the Root Canal got hit by the big serac on the Bear Tooth," Paul says. "It was a couple guided groups, and one of the clients died. The NPS heli is in there right now."

"That's a sketchy place in there," I recall.

"Yeah, I feel bad," Paul replies. "I've always worried about that serac and cautioned people about camping near the landing area, but I'm going to be a lot more heavy-handed about it in the future. There's a safe place to camp just one thousand feet south. I should have been more insistent."

"You can't blame yourself, Paul," I counsel. "Climbers have to make their own judgements."

"I know," Paul says, "but it was preventable."

As Paul and I end the call, I take a deep breath and turn to Michelle, who sits on my cot with a pensive gaze, sipping fresh-brewed coffee. "Sorry. I was hoping that maybe we'd have some time off from these kinds of events," I say.

Michelle smiles and says, "It's a part of life."

Michelle helped me set up basecamp yesterday and will be staying up here with me for the next week. I figured that some time in the mountains among friends would be good catharsis for her after all she's been through. It has now been six months since Joe's death.

Last October, Joe and our friend David Gottlieb were in a remote, desolate part of the Himalaya adjacent to the vast Tibetan Plateau. They had hoped to establish a new route on Labuche Kang, a 7,367-meter peak. At last, after they'd waited out a month of unsettled weather, a window arrived, and they proceeded with their first reconnaissance of their planned route.

They had just gotten started when Joe, climbing unroped on what appeared to be benign terrain, collapsed a hidden cornice on the ridge they were ascending and fell hundreds of feet to his death. David, who was a few minutes behind him on the ridge and had not witnessed the fall, made the horrifying discovery of Joe's footprints leading to a broken edge in the snow, perched above a precipitous drop-off to the glacier far below. David undertook a heroic effort in rappelling down very hazardous terrain to reach Joe, but he found that Joe had died.

After a lengthy bureaucratic process, Joe's body was evacuated to Kathmandu, Nepal. There, in a small ceremony attended by his parents — Gail and Shirley — and Michelle, Joe's remains were cremated in a Buddhist temple. Weeks later, Mark and I met up with Michelle in the California desert, where we climbed and camped and mourned and remembered, hovering each night over a crackling campfire under a million stars in the clear night sky.

In the weeks after Joe's death and in the company of Mark and Michelle, I gave much thought to Joe and the impact he'd had on my life. Joe and I spent an enormous amount of time together, especially during the magical first years of my relationship with Mark. In some ways, Joe was like a brother to me. We climbed ice, we went mixed climbing, we rock-climbed, we hiked, and I was brought into the embrace of the Puryear family with many joyous evenings at the Bonair Winery in Washington's Yakima Valley with Gail and Shirley. Joe and I laughed together, we battled one another like teenagers to compete for Mark's attention, and we suffered together on Mount Russell. I will forever remember him for the energy he put into everything he did, whether it was patiently giving me pointers on ice and mixed climbing in Alaska's Eklutna Canyon many years ago, encouraging me to keep moving as we crested the shoulder of Mount Russell in the blizzard, or just trying to solve a puzzle or brain teaser. Even when I recall the adversarial moments between us, we lived some transformative experiences together that can never be taken away nor replicated.

Michelle is left with processing the unfathomable loss of the love of her life. She is living my absolute worst nightmare, and even as she maintains a stoic composure, I can still see the pain in her eyes. Mark, as well, is still grappling with the loss of a friend — a brother in alpinism — with whom he shared more than fifteen years of intense life experiences in the mountains. I am as sad for them as I am for Joe.

"All the good memories feel hollow now," Mark said to me not long ago. "I feel like the sole proprietor of so many moments, lost in time, that no one else understands or cares about. Joe and I were supposed to get old and reminisce together."

Michelle departs Kahiltna Basecamp, and as my second week up there concludes, Mark flies in for his basecamp patrol. Mark's patrol volunteers are my old ski buddies Thomas Bailly and his wife, Mary, and it feels good to have familiar friends in camp.

"I'm sure glad I didn't have the first 14 patrol," Mark says, as the three of them drag their duffel bags into camp. "We're hearing it's been forty below at High Camp, and the upper mountain is very icy."

For the past several days, basecamp has been experiencing unusually strong winds, with gusts as high as 30 miles per hour. The wind, accompanied by colder than normal temperatures, has also created issues for the pilots. Today the wind has dropped, but it sounds as though the calm will not last.

"Mark, check out this forecast," I say, handing him my notepad as he walks into the tent.

"HIGH WIND WARNING," Mark begins, his eyes widening. "Winds above 17,000 feet from fifty to seventy miles per hour, with gusts over one hundred miles per hour possible. Low temperature minus thirty-five degrees Fahrenheit. Extreme cold warning with wind chills of over one hundred below zero possible."

Mark grimaces and slaps the notepad on my desk, adding, "Well, that sounds like fun."

As the day progresses into evening, the sun drops behind Mount Foraker's *Sultana Ridge* and a deep cold settles into camp. As Mark and I duck back into my tent, I notice long snow plumes streaming off the summit of Denali, a telltale sign of the promised wind event.

I hope nobody went for the summit today.

"Basecamp, 14 Camp."

Loomie's voice transmitting over Mark's handheld park radio jolts me awake. As Mark sits up and grabs the radio, I note that it's 6:00 a.m. *This can't be good.*

"Basecamp, go ahead, Loomie," Mark replies.

"Can you call us on the phone? We have a situation up high."

Mark extricates himself from his sleeping bag and steps over to my phone, while I sink deeper into my own bag and brace myself.

"Hey, Mark," Loomie begins. "We're talking to Pat Ormond from AMS" — Alaska Mountaineering School — "up at High Camp. Dave Staeheli's team took a fall down Pig Hill onto the Football Field at eleven last night on the way down from the summit, and one client broke his leg." Pat is a highly experienced alpine guide at AMS, while Dave Staeheli is one of Denali's most experienced guides, with decades of experience, and who currently works for Mountain Trip. Staeheli made a daring solo winter ascent of the West Rib in 1983. The Football Field is a vast, wind-exposed plateau at 19,600 feet on the West Buttress route, while Pig Hill is a 500-foot snow slope connecting the Football Field to Denali's final summit ridge. The uppermost reaches of Denali are truly hostile terrain, with nowhere to hide from the wind. It is not a place meant for human habitation.

Continues Loomie, "Winds were raging. Dave had to leave the injured client behind in a bivy sack, and then got separated from the other two clients. Dave arrived at 17 Camp at 4:00 a.m., alone, with hypothermia and frostbite."

"Where are the other clients?" Mark asks, his eyes widening.

"Above Denali Pass somewhere, in the wind," Loomie says. "It's not good." Denali Pass is the 18,200-foot saddle separating Denali's main (south) summit from its slightly lower north summit. It's west-to-east orientation and gunsight-like shape create a "venturi meter" effect, wherein the already-ferocious winds that frequently buffet the mountain accelerate through the narrow gap.

I emerge from my sleeping bag, and Mark and I stare at each other in horror.

"Okay. How bad are the winds right now?" Mark asks.

"Nuclear," Loomie emphasizes. "Pat says it's blowing at least fifty miles per hour in High Camp at 17,200, and much higher up in the pass. It started around ten or eleven last night just as Dave's team summited. Pat's group also summited yesterday, but they got up there earlier, and got down just before the wind hit. They're too exhausted to go back up, and the weather's way too gnarly anyway."

"The forecast is for the wind to decrease later today," Mark says. "Looks like we wait."

"John Leonard" — the mountaineering ranger — "has already called RCC, so the PJs are going to go up in the C-130 as soon as they can and assess winds, and also see if they can spot the three clients," Loomie continues. "It's clear, but it's totally nuking. No way can the heli fly in that."

Mark and I step outside into a bitter, clear, and blustery morning. Denali has no lenticular cloud, but a column of blowing snow rips away from the summit, creating a trail of ice crystals easily more than two miles long.

"That looks horrific," Mark says, matter-of-factly. "This situation is as bad as it gets."

I complete my morning check-ins with the air services as Mark comes back from the ranger tent with another update from Loomie.

"One of the clients just made it back to High Camp," Mark says. "He's okay and somehow has no frostbite. But he said the blowing snow was so bad above the pass that he became separated from the other ambulatory climber, and he has no idea where he is."

The winds moderate enough by midday that the US Air Force Pararescuemen are flying a pattern high above the summit area in the C-130. Mark trots out onto the runway as I'm loading an airplane, with astonishing news.

"The PJs spotted the guy with the broken leg. He's alive. He's crawling around on his hands and knees on the Football Field at

19,600."

"No way!" I exclaim, glancing toward the mountain in wonder. "How could he survive a night in winds like that?"

"I don't know, but I was sure we were going to be doing body recoveries. So maybe there's still hope," Mark says, his voice tinged with cautious optimism.

"What about the other missing guy?" I ask.

"They still haven't spotted him. Not sure."

With winds expected to decrease by evening, the talented second-year pilot and Austrian ex-pat Andy Hermansky flies into basecamp with the park's A-Star shorthaul helicopter, bringing along the rangers Chris Erickson and Joe Reichert. They will wait here for the weather to improve.

Andy and the rangers come down to basecamp to discuss the plan. I'm inside my tent when something impacts the wall and knocks my cups and sunscreen bottles to the floor. I step outside; before I can survey the scene, a snowball whizzes past my head. I look up from my defensive posture to see Andy and his smart-alecky smile.

"Well, hello there, Lisa. How are you today?"

"Andy!" I cry in fake outrage. "You behave yourself!"

Andy is fit, handsome, and keeps his hair at military-grade shortness. He has a slight Austrian accent and a flirtatious, teasing manner that always makes me laugh. His lighthearted demeanor belies the fact that he is one of the world's most skilled longline helicopter pilots. I can always count on Andy to lighten up my day.

I head over to the rangers' tent for an update. Joe and Andy are talking about helicopter stuff, while Chris, Mark, Thomas, and Mary banter over cheeseburgers. Chris is in his fourth season at Denali.

Like Mark, he's a handsome, strapping blond with Scandinavian ancestry, and has a similar, goofy sense of humor. I've become good friends with both him and his wife, Amanda.

By 5:00 p.m., the PJs in the C-130 indicate that the winds aloft have dropped below 30 miles per hour, at the upper limit for safe flying. The park helicopter is stripped of its basket and all nonessential equipment to make it as light as possible. Andy launches for a reconnaissance flight over the summit as we all hold an anxious vigil by the radio.

"I see the climber on the Football Field," Andy announces over the radio. "He's moving and waving."

"Unbelievable," Chris intones.

"I see the other climber now," Andy continues, moments later. "He's right in Denali Pass. Looks to be . . . face down in the snow. He is not moving at all. I'm going to hover in closer."

After another long pause, Andy continues:

"Okay. The winds are good enough to do this, and power is adequate. I'm inbound for basecamp, about eight minutes."

"Lisa," Joe Reichert says, "we've had Life Flight on standby, and we're going to send them in here now. Can you go mark a landing zone for them?"

"I'm on it," I say, dashing out of the ranger tent and running a gauntlet of new arrivals asking me to call Talkeetna for flights out. When I return from my mission, I call each air service in succession to warn them of the incoming medical helicopter and of Andy's ongoing flights.

Andy lands in camp soon after. From the runway, I see Mark and the other rangers hooking the longline to the helicopter and attaching the metal Coast Guard rescue basket to the end.

"What's the plan?" I ask, as Mark and Chris walk back into camp from the helipad.

"Andy's going to get the guy on the Football Field, since we know for sure that he's alive," Chris says. "But we don't have the allowable weight for an attendant, so we're hoping this guy will be able to get into the basket by himself."

"What about the other guy?" I ask. Chris's face turns glum.

"Andy hovered close to him, and despite all the rotor wash, the man never moved — just stayed face-down in the snow. It sounds less urgent, if you know what I mean,"

Andy lifts and flies away, the tiny basket dangling 150 feet beneath the ship as it steers toward the mountain.

Soon, Andy transmits that he's on scene, and for the next few moments we're left to picture the operation in our mind's eye. Andy holds a difficult hover in the thin air, placing the basket on the ground next to the man, who after breaking his leg has spent over 18 hours exposed to wind chills surpassing minus 70. The man — as Andy conveys later — sits on the snow, impassive. He remains unaware that a helicopter is hovering just above him and that a basket suspended beneath it — his sole chance at salvation — is right next to him. Andy picks up the basket a few inches, makes a subtle adjustment with his controls, and bumps the basket into the man repeatedly to stir his attention. The man stares at the basket. "Come on . . ." Andy says to himself, as he holds the helicopter steady. "Get in."

Here in basecamp, our group stands rapt in the ranger tent as Andy attempts to perform what would be one of the highest shorthaul extractions in North American history. After many long moments pass, the radio crackles to life.

"I've got him. Three-Alpha-Echo, inbound for basecamp," says

Andy.

Everyone cheers before scrambling outside to receive the patient.

The Life Flight medical helicopter arrives at the same moment and lands on the helispot I have prepared. The paramedic crew comes over to camp to wait alongside us.

Andy hovers into basecamp and, with Chris and Mark directing, sets the basket with the injured man down on the snow just one hundred feet from my tent. Mark and Chris unhook the basket; Andy flies back over to land on the helipad, while Joe jogs in that direction to discuss with him a plan for the man in Denali Pass.

I help Mark, Chris, and the paramedics extract the man from the basket and onto a large foam pad inside a cascade rescue toboggan. The man's nose and cheeks are frostbitten a hideous shade of black, and the rangers remove his gloves to reveal both hands frozen past his wrists and hard as blocks of ice.

The man holds a blank stare as Mark kneels in front of him. "Hey, there. Do you know your name?" Mark asks.

The man focuses on Mark and says, "Jerry."

"Okay, Jerry," Mark continues. "Do you know where you are?"

His reply is emotionless: "No."

Mark and Chris remove Jerry's boot to examine his fractured leg to ensure there is no bleeding. The fracture is closed; however, like his hands, his foot and lower leg are frozen solid.

The Life Flight paramedics complete their initial assessments and start a rapid IV line. "Okay, we're ready, and he needs to go, right now" one says, adding, "His body temperature is 82 degrees." Chris, Mark, a doctor in camp who offers her assistance, and I drag Jerry in the sled over to the helicopter, which zips off for the hospital in Anchorage.

One saved, one to go — I hope we get another miracle.

Joe and Andy have been busy planning with Talkeetna for the next mission.

"Lisa," Joe shouts from the ranger tent. "There's a CH-47 Chinook coming in, ETA forty-five minutes. Better tie things down and let everyone in camp know to do the same."

I scramble to secure loose items to prepare for the Chinook's powerful rotor wash, and warn several climbers camped close to the runway of the large helicopter's impending arrival. Now, I hear the park helicopter spooling up again, and walk back over to the ranger tent to find out what's next.

"The patient at 18,200 is unresponsive, so we need a rescuer on the shorthaul line," Mark tells me. "Kevin Wright is camped at 9,500 feet. He's the lightest ranger on the crew, and with that high altitude, it has to be him."

"But he's not acclimatized," I say.

"He'll only be above 14,000 feet for maybe 15 minutes," Chris adds. "It won't be a factor."

Andy departs, and again we stage a radio vigil to monitor the operation. We follow as Kevin is picked up and transported to the scene. Soon after, we hear Andy's transmission.

"We have the climber. We'll be returning to 9,500 to drop off Kevin, then back to basecamp," Andy reports.

Mark and Chris look at each other stone-faced. "I assume this guy is not alive?" Mark asks.

"Safe to assume," Chris replies.

Moments later, the familiar sound of the A-star helicopter breaks the air, and the machine comes into sight near Mount Frances.

Suspended on the line beneath the helicopter is the unmistakable form of a man, and as Andy maneuvers closer to place him down on the snow, the macabre realization that the man is frozen stiff instills horror in everyone watching.

The rangers unhook the body from the line, Andy sets down on the helipad, and Mark and the rangers place the man inside a red body bag. Moments later, the Chinook careens around Annie's Ridge, the thump of its blades reverberating off the cliffs around us. The giant helicopter alights on the runway, its powerful twin rotor wash blasting us with powdery snow. As the helicopter remains running, Mark and the rangers lift the body bag and carry it over, stopping to speak to the military crew before continuing inside. They emerge a moment later and take cover as the massive ship lifts and flies away, while the climbers occupying basecamp look on with solemn expressions. The rangers depart with Andy for Talkeetna, leaving just Mark, Thomas, Mary, and me standing by. It's a shocking transition back to silence.

"I just talked to Loomie," Mark says as we gather in the ranger tent, where he is preparing hot tea. "Sounds like Dave and the other client can get down on their own."

"That must have been hell up there," I say.

"Indeed," Mark agrees, handing out steaming hot mugs of tea. "And Jerry must be the toughest man in the world."

"Well, here's to Jerry," Thomas says, putting a positive spin on the day. Four cups meet. There has been far too much toasting over tragedy recently. For now, we toast to survival.

Four days later, the rangers camped at 17,200 feet report that a man has been witnessed falling 1,000 feet down the steep and exposed traverse above high camp leading to Denali Pass. This slope, known by the macabre nickname of the "Autobahn," has a lengthy history of fatal falls, most occurring on the descent when climbers are distracted by fatigue.

We follow the drama over the radio as the ranger Matt Hendrickson's patrol brings the body of the 67-year-old climber from Italy back to camp on a sled. The weather is cooperative enough for Andy to fly in and land at High Camp, where the body is loaded inside the helicopter and then flown back to Talkeetna. I'm relieved that we don't have to witness another body in basecamp — this time.

Mark's basecamp patrol comes to an end, Thomas and Mary fly out, and Loomie arrives to take over as the basecamp ranger. Mark, however, has ten days off work and will remain here, with plans to attempt a difficult route on the north buttress of Mount Hunter with his friends Rob Smith and Justin Woods.

Days of unsettled weather pass, and the boys are reluctant to launch. After they make a couple of false starts, Justin decides to head home, while Mark and Rob continue to watch and wait.

At last, the forecast offers something promising, and Mark returns from Rob's tent with a plan. "We're going for it tomorrow, I guess. Gotta start packing," he says, sounding more tentative than decisive. I watch as Mark sits on my floor, sorting gear and staring with uncharacteristic hesitation at certain items.

"Sweetie," he says, all at once looking up at me with a frustrated expression. "I'm not sure I can do this. Something doesn't feel right. The route hasn't shed snow like we'd hoped, and the forecast isn't that great. My gut is saying, 'Don't Go.'"

"Then don't," I counsel. Mark stands up and draws in a deep breath.

"I have to go tell Rob," he says. "I hope he won't be disappointed."

Mark returns awhile later, appearing relieved.

"Rob's cool. He was sort of on the fence also, and respects my decision, but I still hate this," Mark says. "I just . . ." Mark pauses, searching for the right words, and then blurts, "I feel like I have a target on my back."

"Well, you have to go with your intuition," I remind him.

"Always," Mark agrees. "Tomorrow, I think we're just going to go check out something easier and safer up-valley."

The next morning, Rob knocks on my tent door.

"So," Rob says, hesitancy in his voice, "the two Japanese guys camped next to me left three days ago for a day climb on Mount Frances. They still aren't back."

"Yeah, I checked them in down in Talkeetna just before my basecamp patrol," Mark says. "They were planning on eventually trying the *Moonflower* and then the *Cassin.*"

"I know Jiro pretty well — he lives near me in Canmore," Rob continues. "He was very motivated to do the *Moonflower,* and I just don't get why they'd be spending this good weather climbing Mount Frances. I think something bad has happened."

"Let's go talk to Loomie," Mark says.

Loomie and Mark call John Leonard in Talkeetna on the radio phone, and Rob relays his concerns. "The day before they left," Rob says, "it was snowing with strong east winds. They went to the west face, which was getting wind-loaded."

"Alright, and if they're two days overdue, that's enough to justify a search," John says.

Andy and the climbing ranger Mik Shain conduct a reconnaissance flight over Frances, while Loomie, Mark, and I again wait for news at basecamp. The helicopter returns in less than ten minutes and sets down. Mik begins walking the hundred yards from the helipad back to the tents, a sullen look on his face.

"Well," Mik says, "It's very much a recovery mission."

"What happened?" I ask.

"Avalanche from the summit ridge," Mik states, shaking his head. "From their last visible tracks before the fracture line, they went for a 3,000-foot ride — over the ice cliff, through the rocks, and down the gully below. They're in a massive pile of debris all the way out on the glacier."

"Damn," Mark says. "Sounds like a dangerous spot. I presume this is a shorthaul?"

"Oh yeah, it's in the runout zone under the serac, so we wouldn't want to put a ground team in there."

After discussing the plan over the phone with the Talkeetna rangers, Mik, Mark, and Loomie rig the helicopter for the operation. Mik is lifted from basecamp on the end of the line, a shovel attached to his harness, and then Andy flies him around and just out of sight along the west flank of Mount Frances.

On the return ten minutes later, Andy approaches basecamp by flying straight up the runway. Suspended ten feet beneath Mik is the body of one of the climbers, stretched out in a gruesome pose. Andy sets them down, Mik disconnects the body, and then Mik is lifted again to retrieve the second climber.

The horrifying scene is repeated moments later. *This is too difficult to watch.* I don't want to live in denial, but I have a job to do here. Dealing with bodies isn't supposed to be part of it, and yet it still happens. I want to associate this place to the greatest extent possible with positive sights and memories. There are nonetheless some things that just can't be unseen: the three brothers on Foraker, Keli Mahoney's body bag, Lara's body bag, and my own mother as just a few examples that already hold unwanted space in my memory. I'm starting to get hardened to these sights, but even saying that out loud sounds unhealthy. I don't want to get used to trauma. I don't always need to look, lest it give me yet another vision to suppress. Turning away, I notice the other climbers in camp transfixed by the scene. A woman in one campsite covers her mouth in revulsion, while others stand watching, motionless.

Mik walks away from the helipad and down toward the ranger tent, while Mark and Loomie stand over the bodies. Outwardly, Mark handles traumatic situations with strength and stoicism, but I know better. Mark is actually quite sensitive, which makes me fear that he's just stuffing it all down, only to have it manifest later. Loomie, on the other hand, has been doing SAR for many years here, and been deployed in combat situations; outwardly, at least, he seems unbreakable and unfazed.

"Do you need help?" I ask, walking in their direction.

"We got this, Lisa," Mark says, as he and Loomie roll out a pair of red body bags. "In fact, don't come over. It's bad. You don't want to see this."

This is a graphic death, and Mark is right to protect me. I feel twinges of anxiety just imagining what they are looking at. *Just because there's still space to store another traumatic sight, doesn't mean that I need to.*

Mark flies out the following day to prepare for his upcoming Denali patrol, which usually involves two to three days of packing, testing and checking gear, and running orientation for his incoming patrol members. Two nights later, I hear a commotion outside and radio traffic in the direction of the NPS tent. Before I can stir, footsteps approach my tent in a rapid cadence.

"Lisa, it's Loomis. Wake up — we need your help."

"Come in," I call, as I spring from my sleeping bag and begin pulling on warmer clothes. My clock reads 4:30 a.m., and the dim, all-night twilight of late May is just starting to give way to the rising sun, which dispels the gloom in the tent. "What's going on?" I ask, as he steps through the door and I notice his grim expression.

"A guide and three clients fell from Denali Pass around eleven last night," Loomie says. "The guide and one client died in the fall, and the other two are in critical condition in High Camp. Lisa, it was Suzanne Allen."

My back stiffens as I draw in a sharp breath. I know Suzanne from the numerous guided trips she's led in recent years and have chatted with her in my tent on many occasions, including on her way in for this trip just a few weeks earlier.

"Sorry, Lulu," Loomie says, noticing my shocked expression. "Anyway, Andy is inbound from Talkeetna and is going straight to 17,000. We're bringing in two LifeMed helicopters. Can you alert the air taxis, and also go mark a pair of landing spots on the runway?"

"Of course," I reply, putting a kettle on the stove and bundling up against the morning chill outside.

Loomie and I walk together over to the ranger tent. "So what's happening at High Camp right now?" I ask.

"Well, the 212th PJs with Commander Bobby Schnell are up there, along with a Dutch military unit on a joint training exercise," Loomie explains. "They and Kevin Wright's ranger patrol did triage out at the scene. Suzanne and the other client were already dead when they got there. One client had a major head injury, and the other a head laceration and lower-leg fracture. They rushed them back to High Camp with sleds."

"It's a good thing there were so many medics," I say.

"Yep, it's fortunate. They got back to camp, and Bobby used rudimentary tools to do a cricothyrotomy on the head-injury patient right there in the tent."

"Bobby cut open his trachea?" I ask, incredulous.

"Affirmative. He was losing his airway due to brain swelling. Also, it's minus thirty in High Camp right now," Loomie says, raising his eyebrows. "Pretty hardcore."

"All in a day's work for those PJs," I remark. "Has anything like that ever been done on Denali?"

"Don't think so," Loomie says.

I return to my tent to make my calls to Talkeetna. When the two LifeMed helicopters arrive, I marshal them into the landing zones I've marked with red duffel bags. The paramedic teams exit the ships and approach with their jump kits, ready to transfer care.

"Lisa, Andy's inbound with patient number one," Loomie shouts from over at his tent. "Can you help us move the patient from Three Alpha Echo to the LifeMed helicopter?"

"Yep, I'm on it," I reply, grabbing my gloves and hurrying off up-glacier toward the helipad.

"Okay, Andy's going to unload hot so he can take off again right away to get the second patient," he continues, handing me a flight helmet. "Put this on."

The helicopter lands, and Loomie, his volunteer, the LifeMed crew, and I move in toward the chopper, whose rotors are still turning. A PJ is on board attending to the patient, breathing for him using a BVM, or bag-valve-mask device. In this case, the BVM is placed over the stoma that Commander Schnell created to save the man's life. Half a dozen of us grip the backboard and concentrate on walking in the snow. One medic walks at the head of the litter and uses both hands to seal the mask over the man's improvised cricothyrotomy tube, while another medic holds a small oxygen cylinder with one hand and squeezes the bag with the other, delivering oxygen-rich air to the patient. The man is combative, a hallmark sign of a head injury, and has been restrained on the backboard. As we carry him across the runway, Andy lifts and departs for High Camp to retrieve the second patient. It's organized chaos.

I've never been involved in anything quite like this.

Andy returns with the second patient as we stand nearby, ready to receive. This time, we wait for him to shut down the helicopter before approaching. This patient is more stable than the last, but with a mild head injury and lower-leg fracture — occurring in frigid temperatures and at high altitude — some urgency remains. We more slowly transport this climber to the other LifeMed helicopter. The bodies of the two deceased will be recovered in the next few days.

All is quiet again. Loomie, his volunteers, and I relax in the NPS tent and cook up a huge breakfast. "Great work, Lisa. Thanks for the help. More coffee?" Loomie offers, holding out the French press.

As he fills my cup and returns to his usual routine of wry jokes — as though this is just another normal day — I think about how fortunate I am, and the park is, to have someone like Loomie around for stressful incidents like this. What I just experienced seems about as close to "combat medicine" as I can fathom. For him, it surely pales next to his military deployments to Iraq and Afghanistan, combined with fourteen seasons working on Denali as a PJ and ranger — the PJs deploy into combat zones in harsh environments to treat patients, sometimes getting fired upon while doing so. Loomie's unflappable calm in the face of the situations we face here on Denali is a credit to his character and the service and sacrifice he has made for others. "So that others may live" is the Pararescue motto. My own ability to endure and manage individual incidents is steady, but I have begun to wonder about the cumulative effects this sort of stress has on the mind and body. *How much can anyone take?*

Fatalities on guided teams are rare, but this is the third fatality involving a guided team in less than three weeks. Even rarer is the death of a guide, and rarer still, the death of the expedition's lead guide. There have been some years on Denali without a single fatality, but this terrible year is unlike any since I started working here. I am not given to personifying inanimate objects like mountains, but this season, even I might suggest that Denali seems angry — very, very angry.

June is here, and after a four-day delay due to a prolonged storm, my husband at last arrives in basecamp to begin his own Denali patrol. Mark has assembled a fun group of three volunteers. Roy Leggett is an affable firefighter from Colorado who is also a very strong climber and former climbing guide whom Mark has known for years. The married team of Chandra Llewellyn and Corey Rubinfeld lives in Leavenworth, Washington, and has an extensive background with ski patrolling, guiding, and outdoor leadership. Corey is in medical school, while Chandra is a wildlife biologist who studies desert tortoises. They are easygoing, funny, and great company. After a week of packing and waiting together in Talkeetna, the patrol has already formed an obviously tight bond.

"Lisa," Chandra says, brushing her blonde hair aside and motioning me closer to Mark's duffel bag as Corey giggles in the background. "Look what I'm planting in Mark's bag." She reveals a VHS cassette of "8 Minute Abs," lifted from the workout room in the ranger station, and which will be buried deep inside one of Mark's clothing bags. The idea is that he will discover it halfway up Denali. Such pranks are a tradition among the Denali rangers. "Mark told us to watch out for the other rangers in Talkeetna slipping useless items into our duffel bags. We figured he'd never suspect his own volunteers," she adds with a laugh.

"Mark's gonna love that," I counter.

The next day, the four of them practice setting snow anchors and doing mock-ups for hauling systems and crevasse rescue. I join them for a bit and try to refresh my skills, before they head up over the hill to continue their drills in some larger slots just north of basecamp, while I must stay anchored here to receive incoming climbers. It's hot and sunny, and word from the upper mountain is that a lot of climbers are going for the summit today.

Denali patrols allot two full days in camp before heading up the mountain, but because of their lengthy fly-in delay, Mark's patrol is now four days behind schedule. I am disappointed that they'll be leaving tomorrow. Chris Erickson is on basecamp duty with one volunteer, and our group has a big dinner planned, to be enjoyed in the evening sun in our lawn chairs. Everything changes when the ranger Tucker Chenoweth radios in from high on Denali.

"I'm on the Football Field with a patient," Tucker reports. "Possible HACE [high-altitude cerebral edema]. Non-ambulatory," he states, his voice stoic and controlled. The Football Field, at 19,600 feet, is an austere no-man's land. Mark describes it, and the whole of Denali's upper elevations, as "a place humans aren't supposed to be for very long."

Tucker and I first met in 2001, when he was Mik Shain's basecamp volunteer. In 2006, he made good on his ambition to become a

Denali ranger, and is now in his sixth season. Today, Tucker is on a summit patrol from High Camp with his volunteers. Lucky for the patient, today's weather is perfect. Being anchored to a patient at this altitude, however, is every ranger's worst nightmare. Taking care of oneself is hard enough up there, as evidenced by the recent incident involving Dave Staeheli, one of Denali's most experienced guides, who could do little to help his injured client and came close to losing his own life.

"Weather's good, winds are light. Let's get the helicopter going," Tucker continues, and the gears start turning. Mark, Chris, 14 Camp, and Talkeetna game out the details; before long, Andy is again inbound in helicopter Three-Alpha-Echo. He drops helicopter manager Joe Reichert at basecamp, and after a reconnaissance mission, a plan is developed. They will extract the climber using a "screamer suit," a three-point harness that can be swiftly secured in the field. The suit is put on the patient like a jacket and then clipped into the shorthaul line, after which the patient and rescuer are carried to safety. Because of the high altitude and weight limitations of the helicopter, this patient will not fly with a ranger on the line as is customary, but instead will be flown alone down to the 14,000-Foot Camp, where the rangers will de-rig the line from the helicopter, load the patient inside the chopper, and fly him down to basecamp. From there, LifeMed will fly him to the hospital.

In basecamp, an older Serbian man is camped nearby. He's been pestering me for days with requests for odd items to be flown in from Talkeetna — including a comb, despite his very short hair. The man approaches Mark and Chris at the NPS tent as they prepare for the helicopter mission.

"My boy, he is going to the summit today, and something is wrong," he asserts in broken English, displaying a handheld radio. "This radio not working right, cannot understand."

Chris hails Tucker on the radio: "Do we have an ID on the patient, and what's his status?"

"His partners are here, and they are from Serbia. Don't have a name yet," Tucker replies. "His partners said the patient was vomiting in camp last night. It's definitely altitude illness."

"I tell them, 'Today is the day for the summit,'" the old man continues in an insistent tone. "What is the problem?"

We learn that the man is the "team leader" and has been radioing commands to his much younger teammates from basecamp throughout their expedition.

"Your friend, he is not well. He is very sick," Chris explains.

"Okay, I tell him come down now," the man replies. Mark and Chris cast wary glances at one another.

"No, you're not understanding us," Mark says. "He cannot walk — he is almost unconscious. He will be coming down in the helicopter."

"No, no, no," the man protests. "He is strong boy. I talk with him this morning; he is okay. Is no problem."

"I'm sorry, but he is not well and is going to be rescued," Mark says. Undaunted, the man makes a pained expression. He steps outside and continues his futile attempts to raise his team on the radio, but the Football Field is notorious for having poor line of sight for FRS radio communications.

"Chris! Chris!" the man shouts, again entering the tent a short while later and pointing at his radio. "This no work. Piece of shit. Kid's toy. Talkie-walkie," he rambles, raising his voice in frustration. Mark and Chris struggle to keep a straight face as they escort the man outside. "Sir, everything is going to be okay, and we have this handled," Chris tells him in a paternal tone. "Please be patient."

Andy is preparing to depart from Basecamp to the scene when Tucker calls again from the Football Field.

"Um, you're not going to believe this, but we now have a second patient. A Japanese climber just walked up and collapsed on the snow right next to me," Tucker says.

"Andy, hang on, we have a change in plan," Mark calls out, bringing Andy back into the tent to hear it.

"So, let's shorthaul the Serbian down to 14, put the screamer back on the line, and then just have Andy turn right around and get this guy, too," Tucker instructs. "Weather is good for it, so let's get it done. I'm going to send most of my volunteers down to High Camp now — it's getting cold, and there's nothing more for them to do up here anyway."

Andy departs, and we follow the radio traffic as Andy performs back to back shorthaul evolutions from 19,600 feet, twice duplicating the impressive high altitude extraction he performed just a few short weeks ago during the rescue of Dave Staeheli's client. Just before the second patient is hooked up on the Football Field, Tucker transmits more shocking news.

"Ah, another party just reported a possible third patient down below me somewhere, between here and Denali Pass. I'm going to head down and investigate after we send this guy," he reports, his voice strained by fatigue. Mark, Chris, his volunteer Skander Spies, and I look at each other in wonder.

"Man, Tucker's been up there for hours; that's got to be stressful — and exhausting," Chris observes. I look at my watch. It's almost 10:00 p.m. The mountaintops are lit by a fiery red glow, and I shudder to imagine the cold.

Two LifeMed helicopters land in basecamp on the markers I have once again set out, just before Andy arrives from 14 Camp with the Serbian and Japanese climbers on board. Both men are unsteady, but are now conscious and oriented. Swift recovery from cerebral edema from a rapid descent to a lower altitude is a common occurrence with this malady, but follow-up care is always advised. The Serbian climber is brought into the ranger tent, while the Japanese man is led into my tent, each of them placed on oxygen. Both men are soon fully alert.

Tucker radios again: "I'm on scene at 18,700 feet with a Japanese climber. Looks like HACE, and this patient is unresponsive. Come on back up."

Andy launches for one last mission. Even with the long days of June, it's grown dim and dusky, and the timing and weather are rolling in everyone's favor tonight. Ground evacuations from this high on the mountain are almost always impossible, as it strains the physical limits of even the fittest climbers. Denali's shorthaul helicopter is yielding dividends.

Meanwhile, the Serbian climber and his expedition leader, along with the Japanese climber, are each refusing further care, against the advice of the park's medical director. The Japanese man has a friend in camp with an extra sleeping bag and tent, but the Serbian team is short provisioned.

"We stay here tonight. Can you give us sleeping bag and tent for him?" the older man asks Chris, while gesturing toward our former patient.

"Do you understand that if we give you gear, we are rescuing you for a second time, and you will again be considered a patient?" Chris explains.

"Okay," the man replies, rethinking his request. "I will share my bag with him tonight. We fly to Talkeetna tomorrow."

Andy is inbound with patient number three. "This patient is in pretty bad shape," Andy reports. "You're going to want LifeMed to stick around."

As Andy lands, Mark, Skander, and I approach to help unload, followed by three LifeMed paramedics carrying a stretcher. The young Japanese man is moaning and semi-conscious. As we carry him across the runway toward the medical helicopter, he begins regaining lucidity. He opens his eyes, scans the area, and expresses his shock as he realizes where he is. "OH," he exclaims. "BASECAMP! BASECAMP!" This change of scenery from his last conscious memories must be quite a surprise.

Tucker soon relays that he and his team are safe at 17 Camp. "Nice work up there," Chris conveys.

"Thanks," Tucker acknowledges. "Three saves, no losses. We'll take it."

Mark's patrol departs the next morning for the West Buttress. The weather is overcast, and the clouds are thickening. Less than an hour later, Mark radios Chris.

"We have picked up a patient here on the Kahiltna with an acute cardiac issue," he reports. "This is urgent. We are requesting a LifeMed helicopter, if it can get here."

Another one. When will it end?

The weather is deteriorating, and Chris and his basecamp volunteers ready themselves to ski down to meet Mark et al. if a ground evacuation back to basecamp becomes necessary, while Loomie, down in Talkeetna, coordinates the helicopter dispatch and gathers GPS coordinates from Mark.

"We don't have long here," Mark tells Loomie over the radio. "The weather is dropping fast."

The cloud ceiling continues to lower as the helicopter arrives.

The LifeMed pilot is well-acquainted with basecamp after all the recent incidents, but Mark's patrol is out in the middle of the Kahiltna Glacier several miles away, and the pilot is having trouble spotting him in the thickening mist.

Paul, who happens to be here dropping off climbers, makes radio contact with the circling helicopter as he readies to take off from basecamp. "I know where they are — follow me," he tells the pilot. Once airborne, Paul directs the helicopter to the scene.

Chris, Skander, and I follow the extraction over the radio. "We've got packs and have stained the snow with red drink mix," Mark tells the helicopter pilot. "It's a slight slope up to your twelve o'clock, but rotor clearance should be okay."

"Copy. Light is very flat, but I think we can do it," the pilot replies.

Moments later, Mark again comes over the park radio: "Basecamp, Westman. LifeMed is off the ground with the patient and enroute to Mat-Su Regional Medical Center in Palmer. Thanks for all your help."

Less than twenty minutes later, it's snowing and whited out, and it's not flyable again until the following day. Another last-minute save.

The weeks while Mark's patrol is on the mountain pass in haste, but with a subdued level of drama. While Mark is still down at 11,000 feet, a man dies of cardiac arrest at 14 Camp. Once up high, Mark's patrol deals with the usual array of frostbite cases, minor medical issues, and altitude-illness patients, but nothing on the scale of what we experienced in prior weeks. I'm grateful for the reprieve, which has also given me time to reflect with pride on the work we are all doing up here, and how this season has presented such an extraordinary series of challenging events.

By mid-June, warm weather combined with a light winter snowpack has turned the lower Kahiltna into a mess. Climbers returning from the mountain complain of how bad the glacier conditions are, describing sloppy snow and scary crevasse crossings spanned by weak, paper-thin snow bridges. Numerous teams are taking crevasse falls, and I remind climbers during my evening weather broadcasts to travel the lower glacier during the coldest hours of the night — between 1:00 and 6:00 a.m., below the 10,000-foot level. Not everyone listens. It's in the hottest part of the afternoon one day when a strange transmission comes over the FRS radio.

A man is shouting the words "Bloody head" over FRS channel one. The NPS basecamp volunteer and I look at each other, puzzled. Before I can respond, the ranger Coley Gentzel up at 14 Camp answers the radio and begins trying to decipher what is going on, but the man's English is limited — and he sounds quite young — and so it takes a significant amount of time to figure out what has happened.

In time, it's learned that the leader, who is the sole adult amongst a team of Taiwanese high school students, has taken a significant crevasse fall. The remaining team of teenagers seems uncertain as to how to extract him. In addition, the young man on the radio continues shouting "bloody head," leaving the rangers debating the possible injuries and if a helicopter response may be necessary. The lower glacier is so hazardous at this time of day due to the soft snow and crevasse danger that a daytime ground response is ruled out.

Coley's patrol at 14 Camp persists in their communication. They are able, with difficulty, to talk the kids through a refresher on crevasse rescue. It seems that the kids do have some knowledge, but with their leader out of the picture, they just need a little more encouragement. The leader is hauled to the surface uninjured, apart from a small cut on his "bloody head."

That crisis averted, now it is my turn to deal with them. "Lisa, we come down to basecamp now," the leader announces.

"No, you should stay where you are until late tonight when it gets cold and the snow freezes. The snow bridges are too dangerous right now," I instruct. Hours later, after my 8:00 p.m. weather, the team calls out to me: "Lisa, can we leave now?"

"No," I say. "You must wait until the snow surface is hard and frozen."

Not an hour later, another call comes: "Lisa. We leave now?" they repeat. I fire right back. "NO! Wait until 2:00 a.m. Snow must be frozen solid." I am not comfortable telling people how to climb, but the last thing we need is another incident. When I awaken the next morning, the youth are safe in camp, hopefully wiser, and eager for a flight to Talkeetna. This season cannot end soon enough.

Mark's entire patrol reaches the summit together on a beautiful day and are then pinned in High Camp for several days in a powerful storm. We talk on the FRS radio a few times each day, and it is nice being able to remain connected. They return at last to basecamp one morning, going on and on about how awful the lower-glacier conditions are and feeling thankful to have avoided crevasse falls. They fly out to Talkeetna, and I'm excited to be joining Mark in less than a week after this tragic season comes to a close.

The mountain, however, is not yet done exacting its toll. Later that same day, the NPS helicopter is flying around the upper mountain, searching for an Austrian climber overdue from a summit attempt. It's hard to imagine there's room for yet another tragedy on Denali in the 2011 season, but the unfortunate missing climber is found deceased at the base of the enormous west face, which towers above the 14 Camp. He fell thousands of feet.

In my final days of the season, I am treated to the additional complication of having to again shift air operations to a different airstrip about a mile up-glacier. The air services started using this alternate strip in late season a few years ago, after a very warm summer and a low snowpack left the normal airstrip bumpy, rutted, and riddled with open crevasses. It's happening again now. Climate change continues to hit Alaska hard, and it seems we are now seeing the effects in real time as the glaciers recede and become ever more broken from one year to the next. The climbing season on Denali now ends almost a month earlier than it did during Frances Randall's tenure, and I suspect it could move back even more in the coming years.

When operations shift to the upper airstrip, moving my whole camp and my 900-pound tent a mile uphill is not possible. As such, my workday is complicated by an up-glacier commute each morning, when the air taxis prefer to do their climber pickups and drop-offs to take advantage of firmer snow conditions. At least this commute lacks the honking horns and traffic of cities, replaced instead by occasional ice avalanches, the call of a raven looking for scraps, and the wind. With each ski to the upper strip, I must bring my handheld aircraft radio, my FRS radio, and my satellite phone, as well as food and water in case I am up there longer than expected. If the weather is bad, I ask climbing-team leaders to keep their radios turned on while I'm down in camp so that I may alert them to an impending break in the weather. On the fine-weather days, the air taxis will scoop up all their waiting climbers by late morning, and then they're done with climbers and glacier landings for the day. They then shift their focus to scenic flights, while I retreat down to camp for the remainder of the day. Climbers only arrive back in camp from the mountain at night during this time of the season, so this leaves me with long days alone in basecamp — and little to do but read my books or watch DVD movies.

I suspect many people would welcome the thought of ample time alone in the mountains. But it's times like these, as the season winds down, when I begin to question what I am doing up here and whether it is worth it. As grand as the scenery may be, the truth is that sitting in utter silence day over day, cycling between stifling heat and chilling cold, can be almost maddening. I like my quiet time, but the novelty of this location has tempered plenty after so many years, and after almost two months on the glacier each season, it is no longer enough to satiate my need for companionship and the sensory stimuli of trees, color, water, and the smell of the earth — not to mention the freedom to venture beyond the 100-yard radius of my anchor point, so as to avoid any lurking crevasses. This time of year, with its quietude, contributes, paradoxically, to a feeling of being utterly trapped in one of the most beautiful places on the planet. I think beauty and experiences have infinitely more value when shared.

After ten weeks on the job, the thought that July in Talkeetna is taking place without me always fills me with the fear of missing out. Never has that feeling been greater than at the end of this nightmare season, which has drawn comparisons to the 1992 season, during which eleven climbers died on Denali, leaving Annie and the Denali rangers scarred and traumatized. The endless solitude, broken only by the buzz of overhead scenic flights, has given way to a feeling of having been left behind in the wilderness, the world having moved on without me. The ghosts of the nine climbers who lost their lives in the Alaska Range this year are at present my sole remaining companions. I need to go home.

Chapter Eleven
2012
Occupational Hazards

A single year at age 24 is a much larger percentage of your lifetime so far than at age 44, where I am now, in 2012. It's a study in relativity. A year used to seem like a long time. Now, as another season begins and yet another crew of eager volunteers finishes digging the same huge hole for my tent, I reflect on how it seems like only yesterday that I was packing up my camp in the hot July sun of the previous summer.

In the brief space between, Mark and I attended Joe's celebration of life in Washington in late July, climbed desert towers in Utah in October, and explored the jungles of Indonesia and went scuba diving in the Celebes Sea near the equator in November. Finally, came the bitter winter days at home in Talkeetna, sleeping in late and ski touring on the area's many groomed tracks and trails. Our circle of life seems to close and begin again right here in basecamp every spring, and the years pass with an ever-increasing swiftness.

There are changes in store for the 2012 season. The one that will impact me most is that John Leonard, the park's South District Ranger, is trying to reduce the park's footprint and impact at basecamp. The rangers will not begin staffing basecamp with patrols until mid-May, and they'll also be removing their presence in the third week of June. This cuts off two weeks on either end, leaving me alone in camp for a greater amount of time as the sole first responder — hence shouldering greater responsibility. Because of this, I took a weeklong Wilderness First Responder course this past spring to obtain some emergency medical training.

It has been very cold up high — normal for early May — and numerous teams are already returning from the mountain with frostbite. In past seasons, I've witnessed rangers bandaging up the frostbitten fingers and toes of returning climbers, but I have never had to deal with treating cold injuries on my own. I am therefore relieved that the season's first basecamp ranger patrol is already here when the season's first team to summit Denali skis back into basecamp. A climber hobbles up to the NPS tent as we sit in the sun outside.

"I was wondering if I could get someone to look at my feet," the man asks. "We had a really cold summit day, and they've been hurting ever since."

The rangers and I bring him into the tent. The climber removes his boots to reveal ten blackened toes, most sporting fluid-filled blisters. It is grotesque and is the worst frostbite I have ever seen. We apply dry gauze spacers between his toes to protect them, and then instruct him to wear down booties and to stay out of his tight plastic boots.

"Don't break the blisters, walk as little as possible, and get to the hospital as soon as you get out," I tell him. "There is an excellent frostbite treatment center in Anchorage. Don't delay — early treatment is critical."

Quiet days in camp sometimes put me on edge, as it never stays dull here for long. True to form, one evening, I'm chatting with Denali guide Vern Tejas, an icon on Denali who in February and March 1988 made the peak's first winter solo, using a customized extension ladder as his "safeguard" against unforeseen crevasse falls, staying in touch with the world via a transistor radio amongst weeks of extreme cold, snow, wind, and darkness. Vern has been guiding on Denali for over thirty years. Just then, an incoming pilot calls to me on the aircraft radio.

"Hey, Lisa," he calls. "There's a brown bear just a few hundred yards below the end of the runway. Looks like he's heading your direction."

My gaze shifts from my radio to the pots of aromatic food cooking in the nearby kitchen tent belonging to Vern's team. Next, I scan the entire camp and take note of the fact that almost *everyone* seems to be busy preparing dinner. I look at Vern, who grins back at me with mischief in his eyes.

"Well, this is a new and different problem," I say, as Vern nods. The bear is obviously lost, as the lowlands — and her normal food supply — are thirty-five miles down-glacier. She must be quite hungry, also, and has no doubt picked up the scents emanating from basecamp.

Word spreads around camp, and everyone is on guard. As I assist the reporting pilot with unloading his plane, my eyes dart down-glacier in anticipation of what might become the most unique occupational hazard I have yet encountered. The pilot departs, and then moments later radios an update: "Okay, Lisa, the bear saw my plane coming and now she's tearing down the glacier away from you at full speed. Looks like you might be off the hook."

A hungry bear marauding through basecamp might have made for a better story, but everyone agrees that the bear's frightened flight and no-show are for the best.

"Morning, Lisa, I brought coffee and Costco muffins," says the basecamp ranger Dave Weber, who stands smiling in my doorway, French press in one hand and just-thawed bakery goods in the other. I hold out my cup with gratitude, the aroma of the fresh-brewed java beckoning.

Dave has a bushy beard and the lanky build of a distance runner. He's soft-spoken, calm, and kind, all of which make him a solid mountaineering ranger — and made him a natural at his prior job guiding on Denali, which is how we first met. Dave joined the park service as a mountaineering ranger in 2010, the same year as Mark. He has become my newest best friend, and I always appreciate his professionalism on the mountain as well as his generous friendship.

"When do you head home to Salt Lake City?" I ask, knowing that his manic schedule working double duty for the park service in Alaska and as a Life Flight paramedic in Utah just might kill an ordinary man.

Replies Dave, "The same night I fly out from this patrol. I have back-to-back twenty-four hour shifts for Life Flight and then I fly out to visit Katie" — Katie Russell, his fiancée, who is back east doing her residency as a pediatric surgeon — "in Pennsylvania for a couple days. Then it's straight back here to get ready for Denali."

Mark and his Denali-patrol volunteers fly overhead on final approach for basecamp as Dave regales me about the fun he and Mark had on a recent climbing patrol in the Ruth, where they climbed two different peaks.

"Here comes that hubby of yours," Dave exclaims, as the plane banks in line for landing. "So psyched to get to hang out with you both up here."

Mark hugs Dave and me as he exits the plane. "Buddy," Dave intones. "Welcome. Great to see ya." The comradery among the current crop of rangers might be the best I have seen to date. The party is short lived, however, as not even an hour after Mark's patrol arrives, we get a call from Tucker Chenoweth at 14 Camp.

"We just got a report that a German climber fell from the top of the fixed lines, off the north side of the ridge and down towards the Peters Glacier," Tucker says. "He fell out of sight and he's not visible."

"Have you called Leonard?" Mark asks.

"Yeah, I just got off the phone with him — he wants you to call him. Andy is coming in and is going to grab Weber from basecamp for a recon flight," says Tucker.

Andy arrives within the hour and keeps the helicopter running. Dave jumps aboard and they depart, while Mark and I settle in to follow the action by radio. Dave soon issues an ominous transmission:

"We've spotted him," Dave says. "He's not moving. Looks like we can toe-in the heli next to him."

Some long moments pass before the next transmission, this one from Andy:

"Basecamp, Three Alpha Echo. We have the patient on board. Patient is deceased. We're inbound for basecamp, eight minutes out."

"What a way to start my patrol," Mark says, his faced contorted in a grim expression. "I hope this year isn't another 2011."

Alternating currents of joy and sadness, triumph and tragedy, and life and death continue to be a stark theme here at basecamp. One moment, I'm helping evacuate people with critical injuries, advising a pilot circling overhead about a swirling, shifting fog layer over the runway, or, as I am right now, watching Dave and Mark place a deceased climber in a body bag. The next, I might be sitting amongst friends on a sun-washed evening as we laugh our way through a robust wilderness dinner, as we do just a few days later.

A team of strong Korean climbers has been in camp for the past month. They've made a rapid ascent of the *Moonflower*, while a couple of them also went up Denali. They have paid regular visits to my tent and have been delightful company. Now, the leader tells me, they are ready to fly out tomorrow, but he has one final request:

"We would like to make a traditional Korean dinner for you tonight," he announces with pride, as the others smile and nod in agreement.

We invite them to use the NPS tent for cooking, and they prepare a dinner I will not soon forget. There is hot kimchee, cold kimchee, and marinated crispy fried pork with glass noodles, plus two or three types of fried rice with pork and vegetables. It's one of the best meals I've ever eaten on a glacier. I'm impressed to see these climbers sticking to such a delicious and healthy diet compared to the freeze-dried travesties to which so many climbing expeditions surrender.

Just three days after the German fatality, the current again shifts to sadness. A Finnish skier attempting to ski the West Rib from the summit plateau has died after falling 2,000 feet and then plunging over 100 feet into a large crevasse. I listen in to the park radio and follow the recovery effort led by Tucker Chenoweth, all while filled with an acute sense of numbness that feels ever so inappropriate.

I'm already noticing myself employing distractions to stave off the memories and comparisons to last season, using my morning calls to the air services to catch up on events in the outside world. I dream about warm, sunny days in July and August, when Mark and I will be paddleboarding on Christiansen Lake, riding our mountain bikes on the Talkeetna trails, and relaxing in our yard, enveloped by the peaceful sounds of the forest. *When I put it that way, it sounds like I just don't want to be up here right now.*

Bittersweet memories from my first weeks at basecamp a dozen years earlier return to the fore as I learn that the National Park Service will be naming its new Emergency Services and Fire Management facility the Shaffer Building, in honor of the ranger Cale Shaffer, who died in the terrible plane crash back in 2000 that killed him, his volunteer rangers Brian Reagan and Adam Kolff, and the pilot Don Bowers. It also gives me pause.

The risks that Mark faces in his personal climbing have always been obvious to me, but here in his third season working for the park, my usual worries have been subdued. The plane crash that Cale and the others died in *should* serve as a constant reminder of the variable risks that Mark and the Denali mountaineering rangers — and anyone flying into the range, really — encounter. Perhaps I have needed relief from the stress of his personal climbs to the extent that I've deluded myself into believing that professional rescuers are more insulated from risk. To be sure, there is a strong culture of safety among the Denali rangers, shaped by the deaths of two volunteer rangers in the 1990s — one in a climbing fall, the other after being caught in a storm above 14 Camp and succumbing to hypothermia — and by Cale's accident. Nonetheless, the mountains still hold inherent risks, and those risks are often amplified by seemingly innocuous decisions, minor errors in judgment, or by one of the hardest aspects to control: being in the wrong place at the wrong time.

Mark has been on his Denali patrol for over three weeks and has spent much of his time anchored at 14 Camp, unable to go any higher due to persistent poor weather. At last, an improved forecast lures him and one of his most experienced volunteers, Chris Olson, to move up to 17 Camp, at 17,200 feet.

"We'll see how it goes, sweetie," Mark says over the phone as he prepares to leave from 14 Camp. "The rest of my patrol is staying behind. They don't trust the forecast."

The forecast is, in fact, dead wrong, as the upper mountain is hit that afternoon by a strong front from the northwest with 60-mile-per-hour winds. I cringe as Mark later relates to me over the radio of their having to set up camp in raging winds, which has me recalling that terrible day on Mount Russell so many years ago. The storm stays on them for the next 36 hours, and at its height, Mark calls me on the radio, filled with regret.

"It's completely hostile up here," he tells me. "We're no good to anyone in these conditions. We shouldn't have come up."

A morning later, Mark calls again:

"It's twenty-five below zero," he states. "Way below normal temperatures. But it's clear and calm."

He reports that there is a guided team in camp, led by a veteran Denali guide, waiting out the poor weather at High Camp for an extraordinary eleven days.

"After all this time and bad weather, I thought for sure they'd be heading *down*," Mark says. "But they say they're heading up, to assess the snow-loading on the Autobahn. Which sounds like a weird thing for a guided group to be doing."

A few hours later, another report from Mark:

"The guided group is at Denali Pass and continuing up. Chris and I are going to follow them," Mark says. "There's no other climbers here besides us, and if they experience any issues, we might be in a better position to assist," he adds.

"Okay," I reply. "Be careful and keep me posted."

I'm having dinner in the ranger tent with Kevin Wright when I hear Mark check in with Chris Erickson at 14 Camp on the park radio.

"It's really cold up here," he reports. "The wind has been light but looks like it's starting to pick up, and there's some vapor over the summit just above us. I can't reach Lisa on the FRS — can you get me an updated forecast?"

"Mostly clear tonight, winds twenty miles per hour." Chris replies. "Not showing anything bad."

I look outside. There are a few wisps of cloud above Denali's summit but nothing concerning, and I get busy again as another wave of airplanes arrive. At least an hour passes. I've been so engrossed with camp tasks that I haven't thought to look toward Denali. When I do, I cannot believe the changed scene.

The peak's upper 2,000 feet are engulfed by one of the scariest-looking wind clouds I have ever seen. On the downwind side, the cloud tears and streams away in a ragged wall of vapor that must extend out from the summit for at least ten miles. I see my friend Colby Coombs, a veteran Alaska Range climber and owner of Alaska Mountaineering School, busy packing his sled and preparing to depart up-glacier with his clients.

"Colby," I plead. "Mark's up near the summit in the wind, and I'm so worried."

Colby gives me a look of reassurance and says, "It's Mark Westman, Lisa. He's fine." He then takes a casual glance toward Denali, but then does an immediate double-take as his eyes grow larger. Turning back to me, Colby straightens up and tries again to reassure me, saying, "Um, don't worry, Lisa, I'm sure he's coming down."

How can I not worry?

I am more scared for Mark than I have been in a very long time. In a panic, I call Chris at 14 Camp to ask when they last heard from Mark.

"He asked for the weather around seven," Chris says. I check my watch: 8:30 p.m.

I pace around camp trying to occupy my mind, but I'm only getting more panicked. Half an hour later, I go to the ranger tent and again phone Chris at 14 Camp. Chris attempts a familiar tactic: "It's Mark Westman, Lisa. He'll be alright." His voice, however, betrays his concern, and after the call ends, I hear Chris trying without success to raise Mark on the radio.

I return to my tent alone, and the minutes turn to hours while I resist the urge to hyperventilate and cry. I need something to do, and I find a temporary solution by reading a celebrity gossip magazine that a climber had brought me for entertainment. It buys me fifteen minutes of relief, but soon I'm back to my vigil. It's almost 11:00 p.m., and Denali remains shrouded in cloud.

As I wait, I recall how I'd urged Mark to take this job so that we could work on the mountain together. After all that he's survived, will this be how "it" happens? My worst fears as a child were manifested by my mother's suicide; here, in the silence of my tent, I'm flooded with a cascade of similar thoughts. *No. I can't go there.*

The phone rings, and I bolt across the tent to answer. "Lisa, it's Chris. Mark just radioed from the Autobahn. They're okay and they're almost down. Bit of an epic. He'll call you on the FRS when he gets to camp."

Soon, Mark is calling my name over the FRS radio, his voice nearly eclipsed by static. "What's going on? Are you safe?" — I hammer him with multiple questions as fast as I can think.

"We're back in High Camp; we're real cold, but we're okay," he explains, his voice heavy with fear and exhaustion. "A lenticular cloud formed out of nowhere and dropped on us, right on the summit ridge. Winds went from fifteen to sixty in a matter of seconds. Getting down was a total nightmare."

"Why didn't you call me sooner? Or 14 Camp?" I continue, trying to understand.

"If I had taken my mitts off to work the radio, I would have frozen my fingers," Mark explains. "Once we got onto the Autobahn, we were out of the wind, and I was able to let 14 know we were okay. The FRS radio can't hit basecamp from the Autobahn or the Football Field."

"I was so worried," I say, my voice trailing off.

"I know, and so were we. I'm sorry, Lisa. We were in survival mode. It was out of control."

I'm so wound up that no sleep is possible. The following afternoon, Mark phones from 14 Camp.

"All three guides and all four clients from that guide group have frostbite," Mark reports. "They didn't turn around when we did; they just kept on going to the summit, into the storm. I can't believe they thought that was a good idea."

"How bad is their frostbite?" I ask.

"Pretty bad," Mark says. "I suspect at least one of the clients is going to lose his fingers, and another client froze the entire side of her face. One guide's fingers and another's feet also look not so good. Chris's volunteers and my team doctor are bandaging them all up in the medical tent right now."

"What about you and Chris Olson?" I ask.

"We've both got some blisters on our cheeks and the tips of our noses, but I think it's just superficial. I look like I got punched in the face."

Mark has been climbing in the Alaska Range for nineteen seasons, and here, as a rescue ranger, is the first time he's ever been frostbitten.

"We should never have gone up to 17 Camp," Mark laments. "And we shouldn't have gone *above* 17 Camp, either. And, having made those two mistakes, we should have turned around at the Football Field when it was obvious the weather was changing, instead of trying to dash for the summit. It was too cold and there was too much new snow and the forecasts were bunk."

"What was your thought process?" I ask, wondering why he would make decisions so out of character.

"I think I put some unnecessary pressure on myself as a ranger," Mark answers. He sounds solemn and reflective. "And I really wanted to get Chris to the top, if I'm being honest. It was all just bad judgment on my part. I messed up, and I own it."

Later in the afternoon, I'm inside my tent hiding from the sun, trying to decompress. I fear that this latest episode has subtracted yet another year from my life. I have chosen to do this job year in and year out, but then, I am always free to choose something else. I must own my decisions. So right now, I just wait with eager anticipation for the arrival of Mark's patrol sometime late tonight.

There's a soft knock on the door, which I open to reveal an elderly Japanese gentleman. He looks utterly exhausted, and wears an expression of urgency as he asks to come inside. I can tell by the metallic smell coming off him that he must be very dehydrated, and I hand him a liter of lemonade, noticing also that his fingertips appear frostbitten.

"Hot tea. Please?" he asks gently, pointing at the kettle on my stove.

"Yes. Please sit here," I say, motioning to my desk chair. As I heat up the water, the man stares at his feet in silence. I pass him his tea, and then he begins speaking in his limited English.

"My friends," he begins. "Lost."

"Lost?" I ask, puzzled.

"My friends . . . missing," he says, struggling to find the right word.

"Where did you last see them?" I ask, thinking that maybe they just became separated on the way down.

The man looks up at me in sadness. "Avalanche," he states, making a sweeping motion with his hand. "Four friend. Lost."

I almost drop my cup in shock. "Please, stay here — hold on one minute," I exclaim, and bolt out of the tent to find Kevin Wright, the basecamp ranger. I return with Kevin and his volunteer, and we continue trying to gather more information, but it becomes apparent that we will need an interpreter. We call John Leonard at the Talkeetna Ranger Station to report the accident, and John connects us within minutes to a Japanese interpreter.

We come to learn that the man is 69 years old. He was descending with four others yesterday afternoon. They were atop Motorcycle Hill at 12,000 feet when they triggered a large slab avalanche. The five Japanese were carried several hundred feet down the slope before plunging into a deep crevasse. Tons of sliding snow entered with them. The man sitting in my tent was the last of the five to fall in, dropping 25 feet to stop atop the mass of snow and ice that now plugged the crevasse beneath him. Unfortunately, his four teammates were all buried in that same debris, the rope between the man and the next climber severed by a block of ice.

The man describes his prolonged and futile effort to dig for his teammates in the dense, compacted snow, and how he then managed to scale a 25-foot wall of vertical and overhanging snow while wearing his large backpack. He spent the remainder of yesterday and most of today descending the lower glacier to basecamp, stopping to sleep at the camp at 7,800 feet. Although he passed numerous climbers on his way down, he reported the accident to no one, perhaps owing to the psychological shock and his apparent certainty that there was nothing anyone could do to save his friends.

It has now been more than twenty-four hours since the avalanche. Snow-burial victims seldom survive more than twenty to thirty minutes. As the park service mobilizes to respond with the hopes of a save, the unspoken presumption is that this will be a recovery.

Mark's patrol is descending from 14 Camp and conducts a hasty search in the debris field. They find nothing, and arrive back in basecamp at 5:00 a.m. I get out of my sleeping bag and greet them with hot drinks and hugs. Mark flops down on my cot.

"I'm spent," Mark says, looking defeated in a way I've never seen him. I've seen him sport a thousand-yard stare after difficult climbs, but at those times he had a spark in his eye ignited by having had a transcendent adventure. Here and now, however, there's a dullness in his eyes which speaks to an ordeal of fear and pain, and his slumped shoulders signal his exhaustion.

Just two hours later, Andy arrives in the helicopter. Mark, Chris Olson, and Kevin have been directed to fly back to the accident site and spend the day searching the crevasses and the debris field for evidence. Mark and Chris are not happy.

"We haven't slept in almost four days," Mark grumbles, repacking his pack. "And we have frostbite. Meanwhile, there's three rangers sitting in the office today."

Mark, Chris. and Kevin are flown back to 11,000 feet and spend hours walking the debris and checking crevasses. The park helicopter begins shuttling in search dogs and more personnel. The rescuers soon locate the crevasse where the team is entombed. They noted the surviving man's tracks emerging from it, and, peering inside, see a severed climbing rope disappearing into a massive pile of snow and ice blocks plugging the fissure.

Mark and the rangers are flown back to basecamp in the afternoon. "They couldn't have survived," Mark tells me. "They're so deeply buried, and I don't think they'll ever be able to get them out. It's tons of compacted debris, and there's also unstable ice blocks hanging overhead in the crevasse."

Mark flies out, and the search continues with fresh personnel for another two days. With the chances of survival near zero and unreasonable overhead hazard inside the crevasse, the park is forced to call a halt to the recovery operation. The four Japanese climbers — two female, two male — will remain on the mountain forever.

Several days later, family members of the lost climbers fly to basecamp to look at Denali and to pay their final respects. This part of these accidents is often the most difficult for me. To hear of an unseen accident is one thing, but to directly experience the grief of the people left behind makes it more real. I just try to listen and empathize, as there is little else I can do.

The husband of one of the lost women is here. Through an interpreter, he asks me to tell his wife that he misses her, and to say goodbye for him. I'm taken aback, and I struggle to suppress the lump in my throat. The man is composed, but his grief and emptiness at losing the love of his life are unmistakable. I've seen this many times before up here. I see it still in Michelle Puryear and Chad Kellogg. The grief may fade over time, but it's forever. The man looks toward Denali for a long final moment, and then turns to me, forcing a polite, gentle smile. "Thank you," he says, before walking back to his plane with the others.

Some quiet days pass, and that is just what I need. An interesting piece of trivia is relayed to me from Talkeetna — that, this season, Denali has seen its 20,000th pair of boots to stand on its summit since the first pair, worn by the Alaska native Walter Harper, touched it in 1913.

I'm often interested in certain climbers' fanatical fixation on summits. As a climber myself, I recognize that the summit is an obvious goal, but, for me, the point of climbing has always been more the process and the action; the summit is merely a single point amidst a longer story. I have met many parties here in basecamp who did not reach the summit but appeared to have had a much more enjoyable trip than some "successful" groups who arrived in camp sullen, grouchy, and, in some cases, no longer speaking to each other. A key part of the process is sharing the joy that the climb provides. I view the most successful climbers as those who have the best relationships with their partners.

I'm having dinner with the rangers as an inbound plane touches down. I'm a bit puzzled, as I was under the impression that the air services had no further flights planned for the evening. I head outside to see who it could be. It's Paul, and I'm happy to see that his passenger is Mead Treadwell.

Mead is a longtime Alaskan and pilot and has been friends with Paul for years. He flies to Talkeetna on occasion to visit Paul, and I got to know him from my early days working at Talkeetna Air Taxi.

Over the years, he's also been a regular visitor to basecamp, always bringing champagne. Two years ago, he became Alaska's lieutenant governor, and I'm surprised to see him taking time from his busy schedule to show up here again, champagne bottle in hand as always. We sit in our lawn chairs in the evening sun, sipping the champagne — Paul abstaining, of course — and toast to the many good things life has provided.

It's yet another hot summer down here on the lower glacier, not what anyone from outside might expect of classic Alaska. Rocks cascade down the nearby mountains with increasing frequency, and the recession of the glaciers just since I took over for Annie is apparent. By late June, the runway is in such poor shape that I decide it's time to break down my big tent and fly out everything but the essentials while the planes can still land. The park's helicopter will be removing the NPS camp later in July, but that option isn't available to me. The military and their Chinooks, which have taken my gear out along with the NPS camp in previous seasons, are deployed overseas right now. By the time I fly out next week, it may not be possible for an airplane to land at basecamp, and hauling all the heavy pieces and parts a mile up-glacier to the upper airstrip by myself is not an option. This leaves me only with what I can carry by myself to the upper airstrip on the day of my departure. The park service rangers are no longer staffing basecamp, but have left their sturdy cook tent for the incoming and outgoing upper-mountain patrols as they pass through the camp. John Leonard tells me that I, too, can use it for cooking, sleeping, and sheltering.

I'm all alone for almost a full week. It's that time of year again. The weather is crap, no one can fly in, and the few climbers remaining are all up high, waiting for the weather to break for their shot at the summit. I've read the same books and magazines multiple times, and I try to keep to a checklist of chores just to keep from dying of boredom. Some would give anything to be alone in the mountains, but it takes living it for real to find out what you are made of, and whether it is worthwhile. I have come to realize over many seasons that I am not doing this job for the solitude.

I step outside the park tent to fix the radio antennae, which are mounted to wooden two-by-fours and are starting to lean over at steep angles. This time of the year the snow is always soft, and I must check the antennae daily if I don't want to find them fallen over in the snow, losing phone reception in the process.

I replant the antennae, and on my way back to the tent, my leg plunges without warning deep into the snow. My foot waving around in free air yields the realization that I have slotted my leg into a crevasse. I freeze in terror, unsure of how large this previously hidden fissure might be. I extract my dangling foot, then with extreme caution, lean over to peek back into the hole. I recoil at the sight of a black, bottomless cavern expanding underfoot.

Shaken, I make my way back to the rangers' tent, happy to not be trapped in an icy tomb of the sort that's killed numerous climbers. All I can think about now is that had I fallen into this cavern — and who knows how far that fall might have been — there was no one else here in camp. Even if I survived the plummet, help might not have come for days, or longer. I am the only person who knows this crevasse is here. Another occupational hazard catalogued.

A blonde Russian woman flies into camp. She informs me that her boyfriend and another man, both Russians whom I recall flying in here a couple of weeks ago, are on the mountain and should be returning soon. She had intended to climb with them but hadn't registered with the NPS in time, within the sixty day pre-registration timeframe. She sets up her tent and begins chatting up incoming climbers and bumming food off outgoing climbers. I call John Leonard in Talkeetna to ask about her.

"She's been instructed not to climb higher than 10,000 feet

because she does not have a Denali permit," John tells me. "Keep an eye on her — I'm not sure she intends to comply."

The final expedition flying in for the season is a group of Danish climbers, and the Russian woman begins talking with them about accompanying them as far as Camp 1 at 7,800 feet, where she hopes to camp and meet up with her boyfriend on his way down.

The Danish are an odd team. They intend to climb the West Buttress, go over the mountain, descend the Muldrow Glacier on Denali's north side, and walk out to Wonder Lake. It's a rugged journey that will require twenty-five miles of hiking across the tundra in big-game country while crossing two major rivers after exiting the Muldrow. The rangers are leaving the mountain soon, and by the time this team is up high, they will almost certainly be the only climbers left on the mountain.

"Do you have an aircraft radio or a satellite phone?" I ask one of the Danes. "You're going to be all alone up there soon, and passing airplanes will be your only hope of reaching anyone in an emergency."

"We do not need a radio or a phone," the man replies with a dismissive gesture. "You should not concern yourself with this."

"Okay," I say. "Well, also, I heard that you might be taking that Russian woman with you? She does not have a Denali permit, and the rangers don't want her to go higher than 10,000 feet."

"She is going with us just to Camp 1, so it's no problem."

"Can you please take this FRS radio?" I insist. "If something goes wrong, you're on your own."

The man relents and takes the radio; that evening, the Danes depart for 7,800-Foot Camp. Two mornings later, I'm packed up early and preparing for my own flight out. I can already taste the comforts of home, about which I've dreamed all summer. Several climbing teams have rolled in overnight, including the two Russians whom the woman was awaiting. One man — who gives his name, which I recall as the same moniker the woman used to describe her boyfriend — seems very experienced and quite full of himself. His partner seems like a complete novice, and needs assistance with his gear and just about everything else — he appears quite out of his element. I am now certain this is an illegal-guiding arrangement.

"Where is your girlfriend?" I ask.

The man looks at me, confused, and says, "She is here, in camp, waiting for me."

As I feared would happen, he was not expecting her to be at 7,800 feet and walked right past her camp overnight.

"She's waiting for you back up at Camp 1," I cry. "You're going to have to go back up there and get her."

"No. I want to fly out today," he says, not a shred of concern apparent. We argue for long minutes, but I get nowhere. He is not going back for her. *What an asshole.* The man notices the other climbers heading toward the upper airstrip. He and his partner shoulder their packs and continue up-glacier, while I am left dumbfounded at his indifference.

An hour later, he calls me on the FRS radio.

"LISA! LISA! LISA!" he shouts. "Where is my airplane?"

The weather is bad in Talkeetna, and planes cannot make it here. My own departure is on hold as well, but I decide to employ a bluff.

"I'm not calling your plane until you go back to get your girlfriend at Camp 1," I tell him.

"I'm not going back. She is not my girlfriend," he replies.

It is after this transmission that a female voice, with a Russian accent, joins the conversation.

"WHAT DO YOU MEAN I'M NOT YOUR GIRLFRIEND?" she shouts. That's when the fight starts.

For the next thirty minutes, the two of them stage a furious argument over the radio for all of us to hear. "You had better come and get me," she demands, while he remains steadfast in his refusal. Insults fly, while the man repeats himself: "You are getting me into trouble." A possible illegal guide, I imagine that he's not happy about the attention this is bringing upon him, with the rangers listening in.

At some point, Chris Erickson, who is at 14 Camp, calls me on the phone.

"Are you listening to this?" he cries, laughter from his patrol volunteers audible in the background of the ranger's tent.

"This is pure comedy," I reply, laughing so hard it hurts.

Before long, ranger Coley Gentzel, who is descending to basecamp from 14 Camp, gets wind of what's going on. Through a convoluted, three-way conversation, Coley agrees that his patrol will pick up the Russian woman when he passes through Camp 1 later this evening.

With that part of the crisis averted, the Russian resumes calling me about his flight. "LISA! LISA! LISA!" he screams, his voice rising with each repetition. "Where is my airplane?" I explain to him that the weather is not good in Talkeetna, and he'll have to wait. Here, there's just a few clouds floating around, so he does not believe me. "LISA! LISA! LISA!" he continues. After many more minutes of this nonsense, I slowly twist my radio dial to the "off" position, and life is good again.

I turn the radio back on about every twenty minutes or so. Each time, he's still there, pleading "LISA! LISA! LISA!" It's unbelievable.

After an hour, I issue a calculated response: "Listen. One more word out of you and I'll make sure you don't get off this glacier until next week." At this, the man falls silent.

In the evening, the weather breaks and the airplanes are on their way to basecamp. "Get ready — one of the two planes coming in is yours," I tell the man over the radio, as I begin skiing up the glacier with my big backpack and a duffel bag lashed to a sled. Real food, a nice bed, and green grass await me in Talkeetna. I'm on a mission.

As I reach the runway, two planes land. One is for the Russians and another team; the other is for a third team and for me. I look down-glacier, and my heart stops. It's the dreaded Kahiltna fog, snaking around the corner at the bottom of the southeast fork and heading our way like a serpent. Moments later, with the planes loaded and ready to depart, the tongue of fog overruns the upper strip. I get back out of the plane, and the pilot and I stand on the snow and chat while we wait for the fog to retreat. I notice, from the other airplane, an icy stare directed at me from the world's worst boyfriend, his fury steaming up the plane's window.

As the fog dissipates, I relay to the pilot the tale of the Russian and his abandoned companion, and we laugh together, as the man's glaring continues unabated. I shake my head in disbelief that he thinks the delay is my fault, and not that of the fog. At last, the fog recedes. Soon, we're airborne, and I no longer need concern myself with this man or his drama.

I'm watching the scenery out my window morph from ice-plastered sentinels of rock and plummeting glaciers, to deep-green foothills and rivers filled bank to bank with the summer snowmelt rushing toward the Pacific Ocean. I see myself in that water, freed from the grip of the inhospitable high places, tumbling down toward friendlier lands, teeming with life and earthy greenness and other beings with whom I can interact.

Thus returned to the land of the living, I have a sound sleep in my bed with Mark — and Cessna the cat, of course. I stop by the ranger station the following day to check in with John Leonard, and I see Coley's patrol, just flown off the mountain, unpacking in the garage bay.

"Hey, Lisa . . ." Coley says, his expression suggesting he's got an interesting story to tell. "We had an entertaining evening with that Russian woman we picked up at 7,800-Foot Camp. She's going to stop by later to show us the emails proving that her ex was illegally guiding. She is a woman scorned who is now on the warpath."

"Well," I say, "the boyfriend was quite a piece of work, as I'm sure you heard on the radio."

"Yep. Oh, and when we got into camp late last night, I threw my sleeping bag and pad down inside your old tent platform to catch a few Zs. I must have been tired, because this morning when I rolled over, it turns out there was a gaping crevasse about a foot from my head, and I was staring straight down into a black hole. It was quite a way to start the day," Coley exclaims, shaking his head in disbelief.

"I had a close encounter of my own, over by the ranger's tent," I respond. "The camp was so sketchy."

"Well, I just figured you'd be psyched to know, it was even worse than you thought," Coley says with sarcasm. We each clench our teeth with thoughts of what could have befallen either of us. The crevasse Coley encountered was well concealed when I took down my tent last week, and I must have stepped on the thinning snow bridge dozens of times in my final days there before I moved to the NPS tent. I was alone for most of those final weeks. After Coley's story, I vow to never again be by myself up there in late season. I will find a helper and work in pairs, if necessary. As I return to my car, Roger Robinson flags me down.

"Hey, Lisa," he calls to me, trotting outside. "That Russian guy you told me about on the phone yesterday came in here a little while ago. Oh geez, was he ever mad. He said he wanted to speak to 'Lisa's boss.'" Roger and I find this part the most amusing, since I don't even work for the NPS.

"What was his problem?" I ask, half-knowing the answer already.

"He said you forced him to wait at basecamp," Roger says, rolling his eyes.

"The fog made him wait," I counter.

"Oh, I know. And then he says, 'I want to file a complaint about Lisa.'"

"What did you tell him?"

Roger raises his eyebrows and pantomimes his faux-serious response:

"I told him, 'OH, hey, hey . . . we'll get right on that.'"

Roger laughs again, pats me on the shoulder, and then turns back toward his office with a "Welcome home, Lisa."

Weeks pass. It's late July and the season is far enough in the rearview mirror that I've moved on to my summer life with Mark and Cessna. Mark calls me one day from the ranger station with some season-ending news that's both surprising and somehow not. The Danish team that had pooh-poohed my advice to bring a radio has been struck by an avalanche above High Camp, and several of the climbers have injuries. They are the last group left on the mountain, and summoned assistance only by using the radio I convinced them to bring.

The rangers rescue them with the helicopter, despite no longer being acclimated after weeks of being off the mountain, but they have to use supplemental oxygen during the extraction flight from 17,200 feet. The excitement persists right to the bitter end.

Only now, with everyone in my Denali family off the mountain and safe, has the season truly ended, and at last I have space to breathe — until next season, of course, when the hamster wheel of chaos, triumph, and tragedy will start up all over again.

Chapter Twelve
2017-Higher Ground

The clock on the wall ticks away the minutes, its sharp, staccato cadence the sole noise in the room. Mark is anxious, tapping his foot on the wooden floor, as I read the anatomy charts on the wall and scan the counter, looking at all the various diagnostic equipment. I grasp Mark's hand and give it a squeeze. "It's going to be good, Mark. We got this," I say, wondering if my voice betrays my worry. The tension is shattered as the door swings open.

"Hello, your CT scan looks good," Dr. Yordy says before he's halfway into the room. His face is cheerful, and he waves his hand in reassurance. I've coached him to tell us the scan results before proceeding with small talk.

Mark and I release audible breaths and break into matching smiles of relief, and I seize Mark's arm with enthusiasm.

"Well, sweetie. It looks like we're going up Denali," I say.

I am registered as a park-service volunteer for the upcoming, 2017 season and will be joining Mark's Denali patrol in late May. It's a dream hatched four years ago, in July of 2013, after I accompanied Mark and numerous other Denali rangers on an exciting backcountry patrol. After being flown in the park helicopter to the lower Muldrow Glacier, we walked more than thirty miles out to the park road at Wonder Lake. Our mission was picking up trash and historic expedition artifacts along the bare ice of the lower Muldrow Glacier, the mountain's pioneer climbing route. I experienced the stunning beauty of this side of the mountain for the very first time, and I endured ferocious mosquitos, witnessed a charging grizzly, observed a multitude of other wildlife including fox, caribou, and moose, and braved a dangerous crossing of the flooding McKinley River. Most of all, I enjoyed a classic Alaskan wilderness challenge with great friends, all while having a sense of being a part of something important.

From the first day that Mark joined the mountaineering staff, I have mused about going on a real Denali patrol, at least as far as 14 Camp, but the overlap with my job at basecamp and the intimidation I felt in the face of the cold, wind, altitude, and heavy packs has always given me pause. No longer. The Muldrow experience reawakened my thirst for an alpine adventure that I hadn't felt for some time, and tapped into my interest in climbing Denali, which dates back to the first time I saw it, in 1993. As we drove the eighty-eight-mile park road from Wonder Lake back toward Denali Park at the conclusion of our Muldrow adventure, I turned toward Mark.

"I think," I began, measuring my words, "that I'm ready for that Denali patrol."

The next two years, however, Mark was assigned the season's first patrol. This is the coldest and most difficult, requiring days of laborious construction to set up the camp at 14,000 feet amid raw, bitter-cold temperatures. Mark wanted to set me up for success, so I waited until last year, 2016, when he was assigned a June patrol slot. In June, it would be much warmer, and we'd be arriving in 14 to a fully established camp.

For the patrol, Mark even recruited the legendary former Denali ranger, alpinist, and renowned author Jonathan Waterman, one of our very own heroes. For my part, I managed to secure my friend Julie Hentrich to run basecamp for the time I would be away. Everything was in place. Life, however, is full of unpleasant surprises.

One year ago, just two weeks before I was to set up basecamp for the 2016 season, Mark and I received devastating news. A series of blood tests in the spring followed by a CT scan revealed the reason for Mark not feeling well over the previous winter: he had an eleven-centimeter mass on his left adrenal gland. Soon after the discovery, Mark underwent a very serious surgery in Seattle.

Through the months-long series of doctor visits, tests, scans, and even the surgery, I remained in denial, trying to convince myself that it was nothing serious. I maintained that delusion right up until the moment that Mark's surgeon called him with the pathology report. The diagnosis was adrenal cortical carcinoma, an extremely rare and aggressive cancer. To say that I was shattered is a gross understatement.

A long recovery, six weeks of radiation therapy, and an agonizing decision followed in which Mark refused a suggested chemotherapy for which the only surety was sickness and permanent side effects. I spent much of May in Seattle with Mark for his surgery, while Julie and my friend Sandra White managed Kahiltna Basecamp. Mark returned to Alaska in June and resumed light-duty work in the ranger station while ill from his daily radiation treatments, and I went back up to run basecamp with his encouragement. Meanwhile, our close friend Clint Helander rallied the climbing community to buy photos from Mark's mountain-photography website. The effort helped offset our massive medical bills and lost wages, and left us ever appreciative of the connections we have made through the mountain world.

We have spent the past year emerging from the blackness

of this period into a time of living with greater immediacy and purpose, aided by Mark's continued good fortune with his cancer not returning. Getting this far has involved a constant struggle with anxiety, insomnia, and living each day on the cusp of my worst fears coming true. Mark has experienced some dark moments of his own, but overall, his attitude has been remarkable. He is driven by optimism and a refusal to be deterred, which has been a point of light for me throughout this journey. In July, Mark performed a shorthaul rescue for an injured woman in the park. By August, he was working a detail assignment on a wildland-fire helitack crew at Mount Rainier National Park. And by autumn, Mark was rock climbing again and scaling large faces in Yosemite with his friend Ben Erdmann, and desert towers in Utah with me. In September, we brought home a two-month-old puppy, a white golden retriever we named Harper.

"I love her so much," Mark said, as he cradled the tiny, adorable puppy in his arms, joy in his eyes for the first time in ages. In that moment, I reflected on the additional traumas that have tarnished our recent years. In early 2014, we received the news that Chad Kellogg had been killed by rockfall in Patagonia. There is a photo on our refrigerator, taken at our wedding in 2006 atop the Alyeska ski area. The story it once told has become bittersweet. Mark and I are surrounded by our Seattle climbing friends. Three of them — Lara, Joe, and now Chad — are gone.

"I don't even know how to react to news like this anymore," Mark said after hearing the news of Chad's death. "I don't even feel sad. I don't feel *anything*."

When Cessna the cat passed away later that year, at age 18, it was like the light went out in our life for a time. After the repression of so many emotions, it took the loss of our cat to break us both down. It's hard not to suspect a connection between stress and Mark's subsequent illness. The reflexive numbness he described must be the result of a multiyear pattern of suppressing one's emotions and instinctive reactions to risk and trauma. As first responders in rescue, we must maintain emotional detachment to function, and in climbing, we have to set aside our mortal fears to climb, and sometimes just to survive. Mark has made an entire life out of this, and has had the additional burden of losing many of his closest friends. I sense a growing risk of a similar affliction in myself. I fear that adding a new layer of armor with each incident will end with my own inability to feel sadness, joy, or anything at all. I want to retain the ability to feel. I have decided that Harper is here to save us both.

Fired by optimism, Mark and I have spent all winter planning for our Denali patrol, building his team of volunteers, and giving the middle finger to his medical situation. We have been striving to return life to some sense of normalcy all while living amongst grave and immediate uncertainties. Every three months, Mark gets a CT scan; so far, each has been clear. We plan our lives in three-month increments.

What that means today, as we leave the doctor's office, is that the Denali patrol is on track. I've been training all winter, and now, I double down on my efforts, going skate skiing, towing a heavy sled around Christiansen Lake and the forested trails in the biting cold of the March north wind, and doing everything and anything to ready myself for the harshness that awaits me. I even go waterfall ice climbing in Hunter Creek for a day with Mark to brush up my skills and my confidence in crampons, something this warm-weather rock climber doesn't use very often anymore.

Three years ago, I visited a doctor and discovered at last why exercise has become so much more difficult for me, why I have struggled to keep my weight down, why my legs have for so long

LISA RODERICK

felt so heavy when hiking, and why I have had problems dealing with both cold and hot temperatures. I was diagnosed with hypothyroidism, which was very likely affecting me for many years. I now take synthetic thyroid hormone and must watch my diet. Some days are better than others. It is frustrating and it feels like my body has let me down, but it also feels good to have an answer and a plan for addressing my condition going forward.

I work the first month of the basecamp season, while Mark checks in Denali expeditions in Talkeetna and spends quality time with Harper. I love Harper so much that being away from home and up on the glacier is now that much harder. In camp, I dedicate myself to skiing up and down the ski hill a mile up-glacier every day to make myself as bulletproof as I can. Julie Hentrich will again be my substitute basecamp manager, and when she arrives, we spend a short time reviewing procedures before I fly off to start prepping with the crew.

The combination of my thyroid issue and just wanting to keep the challenge manageable has made me decide that going to the summit is not a priority; I will focus instead on getting to 14 Camp and spending time there, perhaps going higher if the weather allows. I also feel a strong enough sense of duty to my job that I don't want to be gone from basecamp any longer than three weeks. Because the patrol is almost four weeks long, Tucker has given me two options for exiting a week or two early.

"About ten days after you'll get to 14, Dave Weber's patrol will be descending, and you could ski down with them," Tucker says. "Or, in all likelihood, we'll have a helicopter resupply at 14, and if we do that, you can probably just fly off with Andy."

For our patrol, Mark has assembled a strong group. Sam Luthy is a climbing ranger from Mount Rainier. Pat Gault is a PJ with the 212th in Anchorage and was on Mark's patrol two years ago. Gabe Webster is a close friend whom we've climbed with on many occasions in the Utah desert, and with Pat is the second paramedic in our group. Finally, Adam Burns is a friendly Canadian who works on the search and rescue team in Squamish, British Columbia.

We spend our first morning in the gravel driveway outside the garage bay of the ranger station, setting up tents to check for damage, testing the camp stoves, and dividing up team gear. The afternoon is spent in the NPS food room, situated in a back alley between Main Street and the busy tracks of the Alaska Railroad that pass through the town. The food room has a dazzling array of processed snacks, preservative-laced dried fruit, bulk oats, white rice, and everyone's favorite: freeze-dried meals. There's some good stuff too, of course, but I don't think I could survive on this menu for an entire month. By the time we've assembled eight days of meals for six people, we are laden with a collection of rather large bags. Mark and I have augmented our menu with personal food as part of the healthier diets we have undertaken in response to our illnesses. It will be enough food for us to reach 14 Camp, where there is a massive food cache already in place, delivered by helicopter at the beginning of the season, and which gets resupplied from time to time along with oxygen, medical supplies, and other sundries.

On our second packing day, we meet Andy on the helipad at the airport for a helicopter-safety orientation, which begins with Andy teasingly referring to me as "Ranger Lisa." The park's helicopter is a red and silver A-Star AS350 B3e, a workhorse helicopter for transporting passengers and doing longline work. This one has a higher-horsepower engine and special modifications for flying at extreme altitudes. The volunteers need to know how to work the doors and seatbelts, how to secure a litter into the ship, and where the emergency locator transmitter (ELT) and fuel-shutoff switches are in the event of a crash. There's also a list of general protocols to know while working under moving rotors, chief among them never raising anything overhead and never walking toward the rear of the helicopter and the tail rotor.

"Mark will direct you as to where to position yourself when I land at 14 Camp," Andy instructs. "But when you're under the rotors, always slow down, take your time, and keep your eyes on me."

Next, we meet in the ranger station with Tucker Chenoweth. Tucker has just taken over as the South District Ranger after John Leonard's departure last year. The South District Ranger gives each patrol a short talk about professional expectations and responsibilities.

Tucker has come a long way from the young volunteer he was in my first full season at basecamp. Once the consummate ski and climbing bum, he's now a father, and although it's still easy to draw out his wry sense of humor and sentimentalities, he is also serious about his new responsibilities. "Remember," he instructs us, "you're wearing the NPS emblem, you are public servants, and you're a representative of this program. Always be safe, always be professional. No one gets hurt, no one gets frostbite. As Daryl Miller always said, 'Their emergency is not your emergency.'"

We spend the remainder of the day putting the finishing touches on our packs and sleds, gathering fuel, bamboo wands for marking caches, and doing last-minute personal errands. The next day is our day to fly in, but the weather is poor and we're grounded.

I decide to take Harper for a rainy hike at X-Y Lakes, our favorite local trail. Harper knows this trail well and, as an almost year-old puppy, is always spooled up for this hike and its all-intriguing smells, birds, squirrels, and swimming holes. At some point, however, I lose her. She runs far off into the woods after a scent and doesn't return. I run down the trail in the rich boreal forest of poplar and spruce, calling out in vain before phoning Mark in a panic.

"Mark, we have a SAR!" I cry, utilizing the acronym for "search and rescue."

"We'll be right there," Mark replies. Ten minutes later, Mark calls. "We've got her," he announces. "We're just a hundred yards from the trailhead."

I race back down the trail and reunite with Mark and our crew, who are all taking turns throwing a stick for Harper. "Harper's homing instinct brought her right back here," Mark says.

"Thank god — I was so worried," I exhale.

"Okay," Pat says, using his best military voice. "Time for the after-action review and incident debrief."

"Oh," Sam begins, a wry smile on his face. "I think this went pretty well. We had a well-planned search grid."

"Agree," Adam continues, turning to Harper, who wags her tail with vigor and nudges a stick in his direction. "But next time, young lady, you need to remember to keep your hiking partners in sight." *This team's off to a good start.*

We remain grounded in the rain for a second day. We're behind schedule, so we spend a few hours in the NPS garage bay rigging hauling systems for crevasse rescue and mocking up rescue scenarios. Mark walks us through the myriad possible issues and visitor encounters we might face.

"At basecamp and on the way to 14, the most likely rescue response for us is a crevasse fall. I have, however, seen altitude illness and a knee injury at 11,000 feet, and a heart attack at 8,000 feet. 14 Camp is where the biggest drama most often happens," Mark explains. "So, hopefully, we'll be able to ease into it."

Our moment is here. We load the plane under a sunny morning sky. I feel butterflies in my stomach of the sort I have not felt for some time. The airplane carries us across the deep-green lowland forests. The silty Chulitna River beneath us churns and rushes along, bankfull in the height of springtime runoff. Ahead, the skyline of the Alaska Range looms large as ever. My intention to go higher than I ever have in these mountains makes them appear more ominous, a familiar feeling that dates back to my earliest climbing trips in the range. Mark grabs my hand and points toward Denali over the hum of the airplane's turbine engine.

For the first time since the days of Annie, I arrive in basecamp as a "civilian," with no business to attend to around the planes or the runway. I am also pleased that because we are behind schedule, Mark wants to forego the typical day or two in basecamp, and instead hitch up the sleds and depart for Camp 1 right now. It's the end of May, and in normal temperatures, a night schedule would be more appropriate for the lower glacier, but the recent storm has left colder weather in its wake.

The first section out of camp is down Heartbreak Hill to the main Kahiltna. I've been down this many times, but never with the combination of Randonnée skis, a large pack, and a heavy sled. There is no crevasse danger here, and we do this unroped. Skiing with a sled is difficult enough; doing it roped up is even harder. At the base of the hill, we rope up in two teams of three. I'm in the middle of the rope between Mark, in the lead, and Adam, in the back. My pack is about twenty-five pounds, while my sled is about forty-five pounds. A normal expedition would have much more weight, but the rangers pre-placing most of the food and fuel for the patrol at 14 Camp makes our loads quite a bit lighter.

The first few kicks of the skis and pulling on the sled feel a bit awkward, but we soon fall into a nice rhythm, and Mark sets a consistent pace that I can manage. It feels great to be on our way. No more thinking about it — we're doing it.

We make good time up the glacier, passing between Mount Frances and Mount Crosson, before gaining a view into the east fork of the Kahiltna that is new to me. Much of Denali's lower flanks are hidden from view in basecamp, but out here on the Kahiltna's main branch, the mountain's full 13,000-vertical-foot relief is revealed.

"The scale is overwhelming," I say to Mark, as we stop for our hourly water and snack break.

"It is," Mark agrees. "And just wait. All these large mountains around us will look kind of small from up at 14."

In a few short hours, we draw up our sleds at the foot of a slope looming ahead known as Ski Hill, stopping at the site of Camp 1, at 7,800 feet, and selecting a vacated camp spot that needs minor improving — though much less digging than if we started from scratch in the fresh snow.

"There are many deep crevasses in this area," Mark announces. "Let's probe the area before we gather and mark the safe zone with wands. After that, nobody goes outside the wand perimeter without a rope."

We find no slots with the avalanche probes, wand the perimeter, set up the tents, and get comfortable. As we prepare dinner, I admire the Kahiltna Glacier stretching away for miles to the south, the grandness of Mount Hunter towering over Mount Frances, and Denali, of course, looming two vertical miles above the foreboding, narrow canyon of the Kahiltna's nearby northeast fork.

The morning brings sunshine and brilliant blue skies. We pack up with haste, trying to beat the heat for the lengthy climb up Ski

Hill. Some patrols try to make a big move all the way to 11,000 feet, but others break the climb up into two days. I'm hoping we'll do the latter.

Ski Hill is long and tedious, and dragging the sled up it is laborious. Yesterday's temperatures were manageable, but now, just halfway up, the heat is oppressive and I'm down to a tank top, illustrating one of the paradoxes of climbing in Alaska in June.

"We should have done this part at night," Mark admits, as we stop for a water break, apply sunscreen, and don loose-fitting bandanas beneath our caps to better shield us from the sun.

We top the main hill at last, and following this are a couple of shorter rises in the glacier separated by long plateaus. Just about a mile ahead of us is Kahiltna Pass, a gap situated at 10,000 feet on the crest of the Alaska Range. During storms, this area is notorious for high winds and immense snowfalls, as evidenced by the near absence of exposed rock along the slopes bordering the glacier.

The heat becomes too much, and at the intermediate camp at 9,600 feet used by many expeditions, I issue a request to make camp. "I'm good with that," Gabe says.

Everyone is sweating out their hats and shirts, and nods their approval. "It's too hot," Sam agrees. "Let's make camp."

"Daryl Miller used to call this place 'The land of the ghost wands,'" Mark says. "It can be almost impossible to navigate through here during storms."

The next morning is chilly, but I am up and motivated, working to get the stove started for hot water and breakfast. I want to beat the heat. Mark and the boys are moving more slowly than I'd like, and I am pacing back and forth in the snow, already harnessed up and ready to move while the others finish with their bathroom visits and last-minute packing. At ten o'clock, we're on the move.

The route climbs at a gentle pitch toward Kahiltna Pass, but just before reaching it, turns hard to the right and begins a steady, steepening climb. As I feared, the final, steep slope into the camp at 11,000 feet is accomplished in stifling heat, made worse by the reflection of the sun off the icy walls that hem in our narrowing valley. Heat sensitivity is a hallmark issue with low thyroid, and I spend the final twenty minutes reaching camp while dealing with an energy crash. Soon it's over, the packs are off, and we're getting our camp dug in.

11,000-Foot Camp is a busy little tent city, filled with teams acclimatizing for several nights before moving up to 14 Camp. I am relieved that we plan for three nights here, and that we have just one more big day ahead of us to reach 14 Camp. We dig up a cache of food and fuel left behind by a previous ranger patrol, hoping perhaps that their food selection was better, and we get a nice camp pitched.

Between tasks, I take some moments to set my gaze down-glacier. Mounts Foraker and Crosson rise above a glaciated foreground ridge blanketed in ice and snow. In fact, in every direction, there is almost no visible rock. The exception is uphill, where the golden granite wall of Denali's West Buttress towers thousands of feet overhead. It is exciting to put imagery to these places I've heard about for so long, and to see these mountains from a different vantage.

"It snows a lot in this camp," Mark says, noticing me admiring the area's heavy glaciation. "This is probably the largest deposition zone on the route."

The weather remains sunny, and we spend our rest day being rangers, walking the camp to talk to climbers, ensuring they are using the CMC for human waste, and just checking in to make sure people are well. We also check cache tags, which list expedition names and fly-out dates, to look for caches that have been abandoned by descending teams. Teams that abandon caches are mailed a citation for littering.

I hear my name being called — "Lisa, great to see you up here" — and I look over to see several of my mountain-guide friends waving at me in solidarity.

"Psyched to be getting the new perspective," I reply.

This camp keeps sun from midmorning until very late evening, creating ideal conditions for "hot tent naps" as Mark calls them, but the doors need to be kept wide open to let a breeze pass through. As we relax, climbers above us are laboring up Motorcycle Hill, a steep, imposing slope that starts right out of this camp. Many of the climbers are dragging sleds and making painstaking progress, a sight that has me worried.

"Do you think I can make it up that?" I ask Mark. "Maybe I should head back to basecamp."

"No way," Mark says. "We won't even have sleds. You can do this, Lisa — it's no problem."

Although Mark's confidence in me is emboldening, I strike a deal with him: I feel pretty good at this altitude so far, and I decide that I'm going to sit out tomorrow's acclimatization hike to the cache site at 13,500 feet. The terrain ahead feels daunting, and I only want to do it one time. The crew heads out the next morning, and once the sun hits our camp, I spend the day talking with climbers and friends and playing 11 Camp ranger. When my teammates return in the afternoon, I have hot drinks and food ready.

Our final night at 11,000 feet passes, and we awaken early. The sun doesn't hit here until 10:00 a.m., and the interior of the tent is still coated in hoar frost as we begin packing to leave. All we need to bring is our personal clothes, sleeping bags, climbing gear, shovels, and a first-aid kit. Everything else we need is at 14 Camp, and we cache our heavy camp gear here for the return.

"It's going to be so nice not to have that damned sled anymore," I exclaim, picking up my backpack with ease.

I have been worried about Motorcycle Hill for our entire time at 11 Camp, but once underway, I am forced to admit that my worry was for nothing. We ascend it in less than an hour, and find ourselves resting at the base of the next hill just beyond, the shorter but steeper Squirrel Hill.

"That was a piece of cake," I say to Mark, as he brings in the rope between us for our first water break.

"You did great, and I knew you would," Mark replies.

I take in the dramatic and changed view. 11 Camp looks like dots in the snow far beneath us, and beyond, we can now see over Kahiltna Pass and far off into the tundra north of the Alaska Range, where thousands of little lakes and tarns speckle the deep-green landscape, in stark contrast to our world of ice and stone. Our climb has brought us even with the divide to our north, which now reveals a precipitous drop of several thousand feet into the Peters Glacier on the north side of the mountain. Directly across the chasm of the Peters stands an enormous face known as the "Fathers and Sons Wall," stretching from the Peters Glacier far below to the wind-scoured heights of the Northwest Buttress thousands of feet overhead, its jet-black rock ramparts stretching away toward Denali's distant north summit. The scale is beyond comprehension.

"That's a 7,000-vertical-foot wall you're looking at," Mark says.

"This is an incredible perspective. It finally feels like we're getting up high," I remark.

The snow we're standing on slopes down to our left, funneling into narrowing, windswept troughs of hard blue ice that pass between rock outcrops studding an oblique ridge, a popular rest area known as the Lunch Rocks.

"Right over there is where that accident with the French climber happened in 2010," Mark notes, gesturing to a strip of blue ice that stretches within a few meters of the exposed rest spot. "The guy unhitched his sled, and it started sliding; he dove on it and rode it right over the cliff. Beyond that drop-off is a 200-foot vertical rock face and then a 2,500-foot ice slope."

"I remember that one," I say, turning toward the other volunteers as they scan the scene with trepidation. "The rangers in the helicopter spotted him in a deep crevasse, and they lowered Kevin Wright in there on the shorthaul line, but it was too dangerous to do the recovery."

We begin the traversing climb up Squirrel Hill. The triangular face of the West Buttress looms overhead, its beautiful granite buttresses separated by precipitous gullies of iron-hard blue ice. We ascend a slope of steep, hard snow alongside a cleaver of granite before the icy slope rolls over onto a long, level plateau called the Polo Field.

"It's often very windy here, and if it's bad here, its way worse up at Windy Corner," Mark says, pointing towards a low saddle right of the West Buttress. "It's a good thing we have such a nice day."

"What kind of winds are we talking here during a storm?" Adam asks.

"It can be calm at 14 Camp, and blowing eighty to one hundred at the corner," Pat explains. "It's like a funnel."

The Polo Field is the start of a long, gradual climb. A slight breeze ripples as we approach, and for the first time on the trip, I feel cold. The final slope to Windy Corner is tedious but brings us to a beautiful perch from which Foraker and Hunter are again visible. Before us, an enormous glacier coming from 14 Camp terminates in a massive ice cliff. The wind is slack, and we turn left to begin rounding the corner of the buttress, traversing between the shattered cliffs of the West Buttress overhead and the broken glacier beneath us.

"This is where Rob Gowler's team with Norio Matsumoto got hit by rockfall in 2004 and one of Rob's clients was killed. Let's not stop until we're past this area," Mark cautions, picking up the pace. Mark's comment has me recalling the agonizing wait I went through that night, wondering if our friend Norio had been the victim.

We navigate around a series of crevasses spanned by flimsy snow bridges punched through by boot holes, providing unnerving glimpses into the black depths. Soon, we are able to move out onto the glacier and away from the overhead hazards, and we reach the cache site at 13,500 feet, where clusters of wands and probes mark buried treasure, including some items Mark and the crew brought up here yesterday, which we dig up to take with us. Many teams acclimatize by making the climb to here from 11,000 feet, caching food and fuel, and returning to camp for the night, employing the tried-and-true "climb high, sleep low" strategy.

Thick clouds and fog have formed over the glacier in the afternoon heat. Up to now I have felt great, but as I stand up at the conclusion of our nutrition break, I notice the effects of the altitude with the beginnings of a headache. *I should have done the acclimatization carry with the crew yesterday. I made a mistake.* We begin plodding up a long, tedious slope leading toward a crevassed step in the glacier. My pace slows to single steps separated by long, deep breaths.

I put my head down and press on, but with each step I feel sicker and lower in energy. Following a theme in the Alaska Range, every landmark is farther away than it appears. We make a long, leftward traverse around a gigantic crevasse, then follow a direct line up into a huge, flat basin. Mark is in the lead, the rope between us as taut as a guitar string.

"How much farther?" I ask, my head pounding and my body feeling the inadequate oxygen.

"Almost there, Lulu," Mark calls.

We crest one final small hill, and through the fog I see people, and then tents. *I'm here.* The rangers' compound is beyond the uphill side of 14 Camp, and to get there we have a long, slow march past dozens of colorful tents surrounded by snow-block walls and housing hundreds of climbers. As we leg out the final paces, I am washed over with emotions. I shed some tears thinking of all it has taken for me to get here after eighteen years of working on Denali. Even feeling sick, there is nowhere that I would rather be right now.

Ranger Dan Corn and his volunteers come out to welcome our patrol into camp. Mark, Pat, Gabe, Adam, and Sam pat me on the back as I swing my pack off my shoulder and onto the snow. My friend Dr. Jenn Dow, the park service's medical director, is up here on patrol also, and comes forth to give me a big hug. "It's about time," Jenn cheers. I am almost too tired to respond.

As I relax inside the huge communications tent outfitted with a propane heater, a desk, and several cots with pads, Dan and his volunteers press warm drinks into our hands, along with plates of hot, crispy egg rolls. "Thanks for the warm welcome," I exclaim, as my patrol mates grunt with approval, their mouths filled with hot food.

Unfortunately, I'm starting to feel worse. I am cold and I have a terrible headache. Mark has set up a sleeping tent for us and helps me settle in. "Here's ibuprofen and Tylenol," he says, handing me several pills. As I climb into my sleeping bag, Mark hands me a hot water bottle, saying, "Put this in the bag with you — it'll help."

I burrow inside my bag and shut my eyes, but can't really fall asleep. Mark returns later to check on me. "Very sick," I mumble, with little strength for more words.

"Be right back," Mark says, returning a moment later with Jenn.

"Tell me what's going on, Lisa," Jenn says as she crawls inside the tent.

"It's like the worst hangover I've ever had," I groan.

Jenn checks my pulse, oxygen saturation, and blood pressure. "Nothing that I wouldn't expect from someone who just arrived here, but your headache and nausea worry me, so I'm going to give you Dexamethasone, Nifedipine, and Diamox as a precaution, and Zofran for your nausea," Jenn says.

The altitude-sickness and anti-nausea drugs take effect, and I fall into a deep sleep. I awaken some time later, feeling much better. I sit up in the tent, look at my watch, and realize I've been in here for a few hours. I hear laughing from the kitchen tent and decide to go investigate. I exit the tent to a stunning landscape, one that was concealed upon our arrival by the fog. The rocky spine of the West Buttress traces an arc high overhead, connecting into the vast, 6,000-foot wall of Denali's main summit mass. Turning around, I see Hunter's pointed summit poking above the huge plateau upon which we are situated. So many years I've looked up at Mount Hunter, and now its summit is dead even from my vantage. Foraker's bulk dominates the southwestern horizon. The view is simply staggering.

Inside the spacious canvas cook tent, Mark's and Dan's patrols mingle over the preparing of a large dinner, and I sit to join them. After dinner, Dan's patrol is leaving for basecamp, and then we'll be in sole command.

"Lisa," Dan asks with a pleasant smile, "Are you feeling better? We got salmon burgers, rice, and veggie stir-fry here if you're hungry."

"Thanks, Dan. I'm so much better, but I think I'll just have some of that rice to keep my stomach settled," I reply, and then add, "Jenn, thank you — the meds helped a lot."

Jenn grins and says, "Just happy to help." Jenn has been on many patrols over the years, and has been a tremendous asset to the rangers in their treatment of sick and injured climbers.

I have a miserable night's sleep. It is ten below zero, and even with a minus-30 sleeping bag, I just cannot warm up. Down below, it was heat sensitivity; up here, it's cold. Intolerance for both is part of my thyroid issue and a normal part of my life now. Late in the night, Mark rolls over and says, "Sweetie, you should go sleep on the cot in the comms tent and crank up the heat. You'll sleep way better." I accept that option with enthusiasm, and the remainder of the night is more restful.

First thing in the morning, we learn through a call to Talkeetna that late last night, an unroped climber fell sixty feet into a narrow crevasse near Camp 1. The climber is alive but wedged as tight as a cork. The NPS helicopter has brought in several rangers from Talkeetna to assist guides who were already on scene, and Dan's descending patrol also has arrived on scene.

"Will our patrol have to respond?" I ask Mark.

"No, we can't leave this camp unattended and we need upper-mountain coverage. The Talkeetna rangers and guides got this one," he says.

I take a seat at the communications-tent desk, feeling sleepy but otherwise well again. With strong coffee in hand, I monitor the radio and answer the telephone, which works through a boosted, fixed wireless signal. Mark and the crew begin referring to me as the "14 Camp Manager," and though I like the ring of it, I'm pretty sure I will stick to the lower altitudes for my work.

"We'll rest here for at least two days, but I'm hoping we'll then have a chance to go up the fixed lines," Mark says, talking about the fixed ropes climbers attach jumars — rope ascenders — to as they climb a steep, icy headwall above. "The weather isn't looking that great for the next week, so we'll see."

I walk around the camp admiring the views of all the places I've so far only heard about and envisioned in my mind's eye. Above, I observe a long line of climbers, looking like ants, following the snow slopes up to the headwall of hard blue ice. Above, a string of climbers spaced at close intervals reveals the location of the fixed lines, which run the height of the 600-foot headwall to the crest of the West Buttress. *The view up there must be magnificent,* I think, wondering if I'll have a chance to see it.

The rangers' cook tent is an impressive shelter. It's a big-top-like tent with sturdy poles and a walk-in vestibule. Inside, they have a two-burner propane stove situated beneath a customized range hood with an exhaust fan. The tent's outside perimeter is surrounded by plastic bins filled with all sorts of food, including hamburgers, salmon burgers, bacon, pancakes, bagels, cheese, salsa, chips, and almost anything you can imagine that Costco sells.

There's also a medical tent with a propane heater and space to accommodate two patients, along with an extensive stock of medical supplies, including oxygen cylinders. It's not an ER, but it has served to keep many patients alive long enough to be flown off the mountain.

The communications tent is where the patrol hangs out when

they're not outside. It's spacious, and there's a good assortment of leftover reading material and crossword puzzles. Another nice patrol perk is that we were each allowed to have twenty pounds of items that we wouldn't need lower down flown in. Our bags were waiting for us when we arrived. I packed my winter-insulated "Muck" brand boots, which feel decadent after a week in ski-touring boots.

After a good, greasy breakfast, Mark corrals us to visit "Edge of the World," reached by skiing twenty minutes to the edge of the plateau to the south. Mark promises a breathtaking drop-off and an inspiring view down into the Kahiltna Glacier's northeast fork. We make it just a few minutes out of camp before the fog, which tends to form by midmorning on warm, sunny days, begins to scud in over us, shortly thereafter enclosing us in a misty whiteout. The view is the point, so we retreat with a plan to try again later.

For most of the day we're in "the white room," the sun appearing as a faint disc through the clouds, if it appears at all. We relax in the communications tent as a steady stream of climbers stops by to ask questions, mostly about the weather, while Jenn does some quick medical consults.

The park's camp is not a walk-in clinic, a point the rangers try hard to drive home. Threats to life, limb, or eyesight are the types of issues they will treat, but climbers come over with all matter of minor complaints.

"We'll consult with anyone, but if we take them on as a patient, their permit is revoked and they are going down," Jenn explains. "We just don't have the resources or the bandwidth to fix things like a simple blister."

Dramatic updates continue from 7,800-Foot Camp, where the man remains trapped in the crevasse. The park helicopter has brought in more rangers, along with a generator, a chainsaw, a pneumatic chisel, and a blowtorch, while several more guides and independent climbers have joined in on the effort.

"The patient is alive but hypothermic and unconscious," Chris Erickson reports over the radio. "We're doing everything we can."

At 3:00 p.m., Chris calls again: "The patient has been freed and is being hauled to the surface," he says. "The military helicopter is inbound, and he'll be transported to the hospital in Fairbanks." The heroic confined-space extrication had taken fifteen hours of claustrophobic, dangerous work by the rangers, guides, and climbers.

Tucker calls in the evening. "We're going to have Andy fly up tomorrow with a load of food and propane. He's going to fly Jenn Dow off and whatever gear and trash needs to go, but there should be room in the helicopter for you, Lisa, if you want to go, too," he says. "Looking at the weather, it's probably your only chance to fly off; otherwise, you should plan to descend with Weber's patrol when he comes down from 17,000 Camp."

"Okay, thanks Tucker. I need to chat with Mark — I'll let you know."

Mark and I check the forecast: increasing winds, 30 to 50 miles per hour, and increasing chances of snow for the next five to seven days, which is the amount of time I have remaining.

"That's not good," Mark says. "I want you to have a chance to go up, though. Let's check it again in the morning."

After dinner, we relax in the comms tent, telling jokes, sipping hot cocoa and tea, and playing cards. I listen to Julie reading the 8:00 p.m. weather over the FRS, and I smile as she thrills the mountain with the nightly trivia question. After eighteen years of anchoring the lower elevations, listening from here feels almost surreal.

The night is again restless, and now I suspect that the altitude is just making it hard for me to sleep. I arise early, step over to the cook tent to make coffee, and then migrate back to the comms tent to sit by the heater and read.

Mark comes in, pours coffee from the French press, and calls the National Weather Service to get the Denali forecast. Good weather today, but as before, deteriorating this evening and throughout the week.

"Well," Mark says, looking crestfallen. "Doesn't look like we're going up anytime soon. I'm still hoping you'll stay, but it's up to you."

"It's hard," I say, thinking out loud. "To be honest, I'm kind of worried about skiing down with Dave's crew. They're all really good skiers — but I'm just average, and I don't know if I'll be able to keep up. I'd feel better if you were along."

"Dave will have your back — he'll stay with you," Mark counters.

"I know he will," I say, "but I'm also not sleeping, and I'm worried about all the crevasse falls we've been hearing about on the lower glacier. A couple of the rangers who chopped that guy out had two close calls on their way back to basecamp. I really do want to stay, but if there's little to no chance of going any higher, it seems like maybe it would be best to fly out with Jenn."

Mark's sad face tugs at my heart. "Are you sure? We can make it fun up here," he counters. I take a moment.

"I feel like this trip is already a success," I conclude. "I wanted to go to 14 and I did. I'm wary of getting in over my head, and the pull of three or four days back down in the green with Harper is strong."

"Good point," Mark says, wrapping his arms around me. "You did amazing, sweetie. I'm so glad we got to come up here together. A well-earned rest with Harper awaits you."

Jenn and I are packed and ready. Tucker calls to tell us that

Andy has launched and to be ready, as the weather — the clouds are already building and starting to fill in the basin — might make this a quick load-and-go. Jenn, Mark, and I kneel upon the heli pad waiting to hear the distant thump of the helicopter's rotor blades, while the fog keeps moving in and out. With the oscillation of the clouds, my thoughts alternate between a restaurant dinner and a walk along the lake with Harper, versus Costco Orange Chicken and being entombed in my sleeping bag inside a frozen tent.

With my decision made, I feel a curious impatience building inside as the weather toys with my emotions. If the feeling is familiar, it's because I have seen this in thousands of other climbers over the years in basecamp. After spending weeks draining the reservoir of patience, when the exit is in sight, the heart wants what the heart wants.

The clouds part, and I hear the familiar sound of the A-Star as the red helicopter swings into view. Jenn and I crouch by the outgoing gear pile as Mark kneels on the head of the pad as a guide, and Andy lands within inches of him. Mark and Andy give each other a jovial army salute, then Mark rises and opens the helicopter's right-side door. Remembering the instruction to slow down while working beneath moving rotors, we deliberately unload the food and propane Andy has brought in, and then load the outgoing trash and our personal bags. Jenn and I climb into our seats, buckle our seatbelts, and are ready to go. Before closing the door, Mark leans in for a kiss, our flight helmets bang together, and Andy laughs and makes kissy faces.

Mark shuts the slider door and kneels in front of the helicopter. We lift off the pad, and I watch the camp and my waving Mark receding. The helicopter passes the brink of the glacier holding 14 Camp, and all at once there is over 5,000 vertical feet of air beneath us as we pass over the northeast fork. The southwest face of Denali, all 8,000 feet of it, soars in a mighty sweep to the left. Now I see the 7,800 Camp off to the right, far below, and the glacier that had seemed so innocuous a week ago now seamed by huge, open slots. Mount Frances passes by out the left window, and everything is happening too quickly. The helicopter swings in over basecamp and sets down upon the helipad. A week's uphill toil has been reversed in five short minutes.

The helicopter has several sorties to do between here and 7,800 feet, where there is still a pile of tools and equipment left over from yesterday's crevasse rescue. Jenn and I have time to visit with Julie and catch up on the week's news from her side of the mountain.

Hours later, I'm sitting on the shores of Christiansen Lake, listening to the birds in the forest and throwing rocks into the water for Harper to snorkel and retrieve. Just getting to 14,000 feet on Denali, after everything I've been through, is something I am very proud to have accomplished. In another life, I would have liked to have gone higher. The savage cold at even that altitude and the scale of that mountain have given me a renewed respect for what the climbers endure. Even with a warm sleeping bag and the park's heated communications tent, I found it difficult to live up there even for a few days.

While I still feel the buzz of achievement and adrenaline, I also think about the disappointment I have that my body has betrayed me. It could not live up to my personal climbing ambitions, but I've spent much of the past fifteen years trying my hardest anyway, all the while baffled about why I don't respond to exercise the way others do. All the days of my legs and arms feeling like 100-pound weights were attached to them, all the hikes and climbs on which I felt too hot or too cold regardless of the temperature, and all the days of unexplained lethargy now have an answer — though it still seems like an injustice.

It's hard on my ego, also. Back in the 1990s, people assumed I didn't climb because I was a woman. Now, with many more women climbing, I still experience that judgment, but it's mainly because I don't have a ripped, lanky climber physique. My climbing résumé includes the Mooses Tooth, of course, but also a dozen desert towers in Utah and a long list of multi-pitch routes up to the relatively advanced grade of 5.10 in Yosemite Valley, Tuolumne Meadows, and the High Sierra. I've climbed in Tahoe, the Needles, Red Rock, Zion, Indian Creek, City of Rocks, the Wind River Mountains, the Tetons, Cochise Stronghold, the Canadian Rockies, Squamish, Index, the North Cascades, and Joshua Tree National Park (where I've done 100-plus routes), among other places. Outside of the United States, I've rock climbed in Greece, New Zealand, Argentina, and Thailand. I don't lead very often, and my technical skills are modest, but the point is that for more than twenty years, I have spent three to six months of every year *being a climber*. I climb because I enjoy it and to spend quality time with Mark. My experiences with climbing have taken me to some spectacular places, produced lifelong friendships, and have helped mold me into a stronger person.

As I drive back into town to grab dinner with friends, Denali makes a brief appearance through a veil of clouds. Now I understand what Mark has been saying for so many years. Even without reaching the summit, the mountain will never look quite the same, and I'll always feel different. I smile and drive onward, Harper by my side.

Two days later, I'm back at basecamp, recharged and refreshed. Mark and his patrol, meanwhile, have just moved to High Camp, a full week after I flew off from 14 Camp.

"You didn't miss anything," Mark assures me over the FRS radio. "The winds have been bad, and we couldn't get to the ridge until today. Also, Weber said the ski conditions on their descent were terrible. You made the right call, although you missed some good card games and processed food."

A couple mornings later, the basecamp ranger Chris Erickson comes over as I'm up preparing breakfast and readying for my 8:00 a.m. check-in calls with the air services.

"Well, not sure if you overheard, but last night Mark got the call no ranger ever wants to get," he says.

"What happened?" I exclaim, and Chris notices my tension.

"Mark's okay, and he's going to call you later," he says. "But he and his team and five AMS guides spent all night bringing a sick climber down from the Autobahn in a raging storm. The man died just ten minutes from camp."

"Oh my gosh!" I exclaim. "Mark and everyone are alright, though?"

"Yeah, Mark said the weather was brutal. Getting anyone off the Autobahn in any weather is a big deal," Chris replies. "He was worried about his team getting frostbite, but they're all okay. They're sleeping now."

Mark calls me later. "Be glad you weren't with us for this one," he says. "It was grim. Forty-mile-per-hour winds, near-zero visibility, and about twenty below. Going up into the storm might have been the hardest decision I have ever had to make. I was so worried about anyone on my team getting frostbite or injured."

A ground rescue for anyone above High Camp is a serious proposition, and the Autobahn is part of the reason why. Mark has described it to me previously and does so again as we chat.

"The Autobahn gets more exposed the higher you go," Mark relates of the mile-long, steeply traversing slope. "We weren't even sure how far up the Autobahn the patient was, but I sent Pat and Sam — our strongest people — up ahead to gather information. The climber wasn't very far up, fortunately. Up higher, it would have required a technical lowering operation, and I don't think we could have done that without people getting frostbite. From where he was, we were able to lower him sixty meters, then just drag him down the last part of the traverse into the bowl with all the muscle we had. Unfortunately, he was in advanced cerebral edema and late-stage hypothermia. It was too late to save him."

The next day, the weather is calm and clear, and Andy flies to 17 Camp for the longline body recovery. Mark radios just after. "There's some fog and clouds forming, but there's no wind. Pat, Sam, and I are going to try for the summit today," he announces.

After all that Mark has endured with his health over the past year, he has said little about his ambitions to go back to the top of Denali, a mountain he's climbed many times already, and by many of its hardest routes. But knowing Mark, I am sure that in his most private thoughts he views reaching the summit as the ultimate symbolic victory over his dicey trials of the past year. Summit or not, Mark has already made an incredible comeback.

Mark's call on the FRS radio catches me at 9:00 p.m., just as I'm readying to climb into my bunk.

"Lisa," he says, his voice joyful but slurred by fatigue and cold. "We made it. We're on top."

"Congratulations," I say. "I'm proud of you."

"We broke trail the whole way," Mark continues. "We're all alone. It's the coldest and hardest summit day I've had, but this one means everything. I wish you were here."

"Me, too. Be careful on the way down," I caution.

"We will. Don't worry. I love you so much."

"I love you too," I respond, trying not to get emotional.

As the air goes quiet, I'm taken to reflection. Between my own engagement with climbing, my eighteen years managing Kahiltna Basecamp, my husband's extreme alpinism and dangerous job, my brother Paul's mountain flying, and a lengthy list of friends who have died young, my life and social circle have been defined by danger and exposure to risk.

Risking nothing is said to be the greatest risk of all, but are these risks we take worth it? As I examine the arc of my life, all that is certain is that I would not trade my community nor my life experiences away to avoid exposure to the vulnerabilities I've created through my life's choices. Perhaps I equate worry to a measure of my love for others, and through that delusion, have brought many of these peripheral stresses upon myself. I have spent my entire life worrying about something happening to the people I love, not recognizing that something uncontrollable — life itself — is always happening to each of us already.

I now recognize worry for what it almost always is: a form of control over things that simply cannot be controlled. Worry is not love. Tonight, as Mark and his companions descend from the top of our continent, awash in a transcendent subarctic summer evening, I burrow inside my sleeping bag feeling a strange sense of unburdening. Beyond the summit, beyond the mountain, beyond the confines of basecamp, what lies ahead of us has been, and always will be, unyielding: vast possibilities, no guarantees, and the inevitability of our shared impermanence.

Chapter Thirteen
The Beginning of the End

My paddleboard slices through the black and still waters of Christiansen Lake, a symmetrical ripple pattern trailing behind me as the lone imperfection in the glasslike surface. As I push my paddle gently through the lake, the drips and drops and the mellow swirling of the water break the stillness. Across the long span of water and far to the north, Denali's ghostly white rampart rises high above the lake's distant edge, standing in sharp contrast to the lush canopy of deep--green poplar and birch trees lining the shoreline. Puffy cumulus clouds float past, concealing the sun for brief moments, as they build their way toward the Talkeetna Mountains to the east. A faint breeze disrupts the lake's placid surface and cools my skin. The haunting, plaintive call of a loon emanates from an unseen bay.

It's the summer solstice in Alaska. In an ordinary year, I would be alone on the Kahiltna Glacier, awaiting the early-morning arrivals of Talkeetna-bound climbers, and anchored in camp by rainy weather or the fear of falling into a crevasse. Instead, I am basking in the warm sun, seeming to walk upon the surface of this lake just a five-minute walk from my house. Fifty feet away, Mark lies prone on his paddleboard, having found his own peaceful stasis. Harper the golden retriever has found hers as well, sitting at full attention on the front of Mark's boat, watching and waiting for the possible surfacing of a loon or a grebe.

"I could get used to this, Mark," I say, steering in his direction.

"Oh, I bet you could," he says, remaining motionless on his back, sunglasses shading his eyes. "I'm pretty sure *I* could. What were we thinking all these years?"

"It's too bad it's not always this nice in the summer, but when it is, it's enough to make you rethink your priorities," I add.

The spring and summer of 2020 have brought drastic life changes for everyone. Not even here in the sparsely populated subarctic regions could we escape the Covid-19 pandemic. In March, as the virus swept through Talkeetna, Denali National Park closed its ranger stations. This meant that no Denali or Foraker permits could be issued for the season, nor could the rangers administer the mandatory in-person briefings to incoming expeditions. The Denali climbing season was cancelled. The rest of the Alaska Range has remained open for visitation, but the Talkeetna air services, and almost every other business in town, have also shut down their operations. The sole access to the mountains now is by private pilot, or by walking for a week. With major travel restrictions in place, no one is coming anyway, and our normally tourist-filled town is enveloped in quietude.

For the first time since 1999, I have been home for the entirety of May and June, which often have the best weather of the year. The sting of losing all my income from my basecamp job, massage therapy, and the slideshow presentations about my job at basecamp that I started doing at the Mount McKinley Princess Lodge — a forty-five-minute drive north of Talkeetna — has been mitigated by the government's pandemic loans for small businesses, with the added bonus of getting to enjoy bucolic scenes like the one out paddleboarding today or to spend hours tending to the flower gardens around our yard, planting vegetables in the raised beds that

Mark built for me, or throwing the Frisbee on the lawn for Harper while sunning myself in my favorite chair, a cold drink in hand.

This stands in contrast to how I felt two months ago, amidst the cold reality that my season was cancelled when I should have been flying in for my usual late-April setup day. *What am I supposed to do now?* I wondered.

It took browsing through Denali National Park's *Denali Dispatches*, a blog maintained by the Talkeetna Ranger Station's mountaineering staff, to adjust my perspective on the sorts of things I might be "missing" at basecamp. The blog keeps the public up to date on climbing conditions, weather, rescues, and ranger patrol activity. An entry from early May of 2018, only two years ago, resurrected mixed memories:

"Lisa Roderick, flight coordinator for TAT and K2, is now comfortably settled into her spring/summer home on the southeast fork of the Kahiltna Glacier, also known as Basecamp. After a 6-day weather delay flying in, she got walloped shortly after arrival (May 5–6) by the strongest windstorm she has endured in her 19 years on the glacier. She clocked winds at 48 mph at 7,200 feet, a personal best. Between blowing and falling snow, the storm total was ~2 feet, coupled with temperatures in the single digits."

One of the features of climate change is not just warmer weather, but storms of greater and more prolonged severity, and we have been seeing that here. That six-day delay in setting up camp was the longest I have endured, and was part of a nine-day stretch during which the air services were unable to fly, among the longest any pilot could recall. In those nine days, climbers in the mountains reported new snowfall depths of twelve to fifteen *feet*. By the time the weather pattern changed later in May, many parts of the Alaska Range had received more than twenty feet of new snow. Many inbound climbing expeditions never departed Talkeetna. The upside, for me, was that the deep snowfalls and cloudy days in May created the best late-season glacier conditions I had seen in many years.

This spring, my being forced by the pandemic to slow down, stay home, and experience life from a different perspective has brought forth with renewed urgency my long-simmering thoughts of change. Last season, 2019, was my twentieth season running basecamp. I am 52 years old. At this age, it feels like there is still time to do something new and creative. However, being closer to 70 than 30, I can also feel the clock of life ticking. A persistent question is reinforced by the memories and events of recent years: *What more remains for me to accomplish or contribute at basecamp?*

In June of 2018, Mark was in camp for his basecamp patrol when Tucker Chenoweth flew in for the afternoon. Tucker had work to do up at the fuel site by the helipad, but I soon learned that he had another mission.

"Hey, Lisa," Tucker said, approaching me near the runway. *Tucker has a sentimental look on his face — why?* "We've got something for ya." It was then that I noticed Mark, his volunteer Amanda, and some other climbers and guides I knew gathering around as well.

"Oh no. What's going on?" I asked, my face flushing.

Tucker produced the 2018 Denali Pro Pin and placed it into my hand.

"Take a look."

The pin featured an embossed, artistic rendering of Peak 12,200, the large mountain that stands above basecamp and anchors the lower end of Denali's South Buttress. In the upper left corner, in elegant cursive script, it read: *Lisa's Peak. Peak 12,200'*.

I stared at it in wonder, then looked back at Tucker, Mark, and everyone else's smiling faces.

"You got your own mountain, Lisa, and it's well-deserved," Tucker said, enveloping me in a big hug, as Mark and the others followed suit.

Clutching my pin, I scanned the mountain perimeter around basecamp in a clockwise arc: Annie's Ridge, Foraker, Mount Frances, Denali, Lisa's Peak, Kahiltna Queen, Hunter. A lump formed in my throat and my eyes became misty. *My name now actually has a place among giants.*

An entry in the park service's *Denali Dispatches* blog offers more context:

"In addition to recognizing climbers, the actual pin itself features a different mountain or route each year. This year, the featured peak is Peak 12,200, which is the first major high point on the South Buttress of Denali. Peak 12,200, however is more significant than just a bump on a ridge. For some time now, Peak 12,200 has been referred to as Lisa's Peak, which is one of many unofficial names of points surrounding Kahiltna Basecamp. Lisa's Peak is named for Lisa Roderick, who has been the Basecamp manager for almost 20 years, and is a fixture on the Kahiltna during the climbing season. Mount Frances, the 10,450' peak just to the north of Basecamp, is named for Frances Randall, who was the first Basecamp manager. Annie's Ridge is a dramatic ridgeline directly south of Basecamp that runs parallel to the landing strip, and was named for Annie Duquette, the Basecamp manager who preceded Lisa. The view north from Basecamp is that of Denali, perfectly framed between

Mt. Frances on the left and Lisa's Peak on the right. In addition to honoring Lisa, the 2018 Pro Pin recognizes an unofficial name that climbers have been using for years, but does not show up on maps or official records."

The Denali Pro Pin is part of a program known as the Mislow-Swanson Denali Pro Award. It is named for Andrew Swanson and John Mislow, two climbers who assisted the park with a rescue in 2000, and then several years later lost their lives in a fall on Denali's West Rib.

The program is best summarized by the description on the NPS webpage:

"The program honors members of the Denali climbing community who exhibit the highest standards in the sport for safety, self-sufficiency, Leave No Trace ethics, and assisting fellow mountaineers. Throughout each climbing season, Denali mountaineering rangers recognize climbers with a Denali Pro lapel pin for exemplary expedition behavior, such as protecting the mountain environment, assisting fellow climbers, and using good judgment to limit or eliminate injury.

At the end of each season, mountaineering rangers collectively select a Mislow-Swanson Denali Pro Award winner from the pin recipients. The name of the annual winner, or winners in the event a team is selected, is added to the award plaque on display near the front desk of the Walter Harper Talkeetna Ranger Station."

Several years before, I had found myself standing with equal surprise in the Talkeetna Ranger Station while being presented with the 2015 Mislow-Swanson Denali Pro Award by my friend, the ranger Joey McBrayer, while Mark and Tucker smiled with pride nearby.

"This," Joey said, "is something that's way overdue, Lisa. It's the least we can do to show our thanks."

My brother Paul had won the award in 2003 for his crucial assistance in the rescue of two injured climbers. My award was given not for a singular event but for my many years of service on the mountain. The NPS webpage issued the following statement:

"For the majority of climbers on Denali, the expedition begins and ends with Lisa Roderick. Lisa has gone well beyond her duties as flight coordinator for the Kahiltna Basecamp. She is the familiar voice on the radio, the steward of the Kahiltna, and sometimes the first to respond to emergencies. The Walter Harper Talkeetna Ranger Station staff would like to recognize Lisa Roderick as the 2015 Mislow-Swanson Denali Pro Award recipient.

For fifteen years, Lisa has been a fixture at basecamp. Maintaining a safe runway, coordinating flights on and off the glacier, and calling in weather reports to pilots have without a doubt made travel to and from the mountains safer. But perhaps she is best known for her willingness and good attitude toward helping climbers. Due to her dedication to keep tabs on climbers through her radio, Lisa has been the first alerted to accidents or any communications of parties needing help. Her influence on these visitors is far reaching and helps contribute to a positive and safe mountaineering ethic that is shared by all. In the 15 years at basecamp, Lisa has gone the extra mile keeping it clean. With the positive rapport that Lisa has with visitors, she has been able to instill those same values."

The Denali mountaineering rangers greatly value her contributions and would like to recognize her efforts with the 2015 Mislow-Swanson Denali Pro Award. Although it is a small token of our appreciation relative to the tremendous job she does, her name will have a place among the best."

What pulls at me more than any awards, however, is the steady departure of the old guard of pilots, climbers, and rangers. The irreplaceable Roger Robinson, for example, retired at the end of the 2019 season, after forty years working for Denali. Perhaps the most impactful departure, however, is that of my own Mark, who also made 2019 his final season with Denali. Later, this summer of 2020 when the forests begin burning across the United States, he will work as an on-demand wildland firefighter, something for which he has spent the past five years building experience and qualifications in his goal to become a fire helicopter manager.

"I think I'm finally over it, sweetie," Mark told me last year in resignation, as he and his weary Denali patrol arrived back in basecamp after almost four weeks on the mountain. "I'm not learning anything new anymore, and there's no opportunity to advance. This job is also making me hate and dread going to the mountains."

"Well, believe me, I understand," I said.

A month later, Mark phoned me from Seattle minutes after his father, Tom, passed away at age 84 from cancer. "My dad really cared for you," Mark said, "and he also emphasized his admiration at the way you and I have lived by following our passions. We need to keep doing that."

That sentiment carries much more weight than words alone can convey. In late 2017, just months after Mark and I had completed our Denali patrol, we'd stood in shock as Mark's endocrinologist, Dr. Nolan, scowled in disapproval as he read the report from Mark's latest CT scan.

"The lung nodule found in the September scan three months ago has grown from 7 millimeters to 10 millimeters," he read aloud, dropping the report on the table and turning toward Mark and me with intention. "That kind of growth suggests metastasis. I'd recommend you have this removed with surgery if possible. Don't mess around with chemo — just get it out." Mark and I stared back, our future once again lifted into the whirling blades of fate.

With help from Dave Weber and Katie Russell, we found a quality thoracic surgeon in Utah. Two days after Christmas of 2017, Mark lay recovering in a hospital bed, a small piece of his cancerous left lung removed. The finding was metastatic adrenal cancer. Mark was now again without evidence of cancer, but he was also considered stage 4 and at higher risk for further recurrence. Dave, Katie, and our dear friends Tom and Bridget Dancs again rallied to our side.

"Once a recurrence of ACC occurs," Mark said, pausing for effect as he read aloud from a peer-reviewed study from the National Institutes of Health on adrenocortical carcinoma, "*Virtually all patients die within five years.*"

Mark lowered his phone and set it on the table. "We'll see about that," he said. "I'm not a statistic."

Although Mark tried to remain stoic, it was clear that this recurrence had rattled him more than the discovery of the original tumor in 2016, and in the months that followed, Mark struggled with anxiety and depression. Our roles were now reversed. It was my turn to offer quiet support, as Mark needed me to be strong. Our experience had taught us that both of us cannot be down at the same time, and someone always had to step up. We were also coming to grips with the reality that none of us are getting out alive, and that worrying over the inevitable was a waste of the time that remains.

In the two and a half years since that surgery, Mark has again climbed high on Denali, spent two summers digging fireline on wildland fire hand crews, attained his senior wildland-firefighter qualification, and continued pursuing rock and ice climbing. He is stronger than ever, and his cancer has not returned.

LISA RODERICK

In early July 2020, the decline in Covid-related panic leads Mark and me to travel to Washington, where we attempt Mount Olympus in Olympic National Park. A twenty-mile approach carries us through the lush Hoh River valley rainforest. Massive Douglas firs and cedars hundreds of years old and hundreds of feet tall soar skyward, adorned in thick curtains of moss and dampness that shield us from this hot summer day. Ferns and delicate plants carpet the understory, birds chirp and sing cheerful tunes, and the faint, distant sound of the rushing Hoh River filters through the dense organic biome. The mysterious forests give way to lush subalpine meadows filled with colorful wildflowers. These lead us to loose scree slopes, glacial moraines, and then to the glacial ice and snow of the immense Blue Glacier. I grow tired and I want to leave enough energy for the return to our high camp, so we turn back a little short of the summit of Olympus, divert off the glacier to tag Panic Peak, and take a long break on a rock perch overlooking the Hoh Valley. I am just grateful I can make it to places like this — and to have the chance to do so this summer season, away from the vortex of Kahiltna Basecamp.

Days later, Mark and I walk the coast on Cape Alava, the same stretch of beach where we fell in love twenty-four years ago. Wind-worn cedars stand high on the cliffs overhead, braced against the elements. Barnacle-covered rock outcrops sit exposed in the low tide, as the seabirds flock and scream. Craggy sea stacks rise offshore, battered by the ceaseless force of the ocean.

"I don't know how much longer I can keep doing basecamp," I say as we stroll along. "You made your move, and now, with this taste of spring and summer outside of that bubble, I'm seeing the light, too." Mark has never encouraged me to leave basecamp in the past, but now he grabs my hand in support.

I've seen the light for years, but it is hard to unwind from the insidious coils of habit and identity and nostalgia. Mark even feels attached on my behalf: "I know it's got to end someday, but it makes me sad to even think of you not being up there anymore," he says. Later, Mark and I part ways as I fly back to Alaska, while Mark joins the Mount Rainier helicopter crew to fight the building fires now rampaging through the western United States. The summer progresses into the fall and winter with an ever-present thought that has plagued me for years: *I need to find my replacement.*

Ever since Mark joined the mountaineering rangers ten years ago and could no longer fill in at basecamp to give me breaks out in Talkeetna, I've been hiring seasonal helpers. For several seasons, Daryl Miller and his wife, Judy, relieved me over long weekends. It was a great fit, as Judy is a former pilot and Daryl just loved staying connected to the climbers, guides, and rangers on Denali. My friend Sandra White, now married to Loomie, also filled in on numerous occasions. In more recent seasons, however, I've recruited helpers with an eye toward their potential as the next basecamp manager. The Michigan native Allison Groenleer worked with me for much of the 2013, 2014, and 2018 seasons. She did great at the job and was always enthusiastic; we became close friends, but her distance from home and her career prevented her from being "the one." Similar issues stood in the way for my friends Sarah McConkie from Utah and Julie Hentrich from Washington, who also filled in over numerous seasons. It's only a ten-week job, but it requires full commitment, and it has been a difficult sell for those living far from the area. I have come to realize that maybe the next basecamp manager might best be found locally. Or maybe I just need to stop trying to find the next Annie, the next Frances, or the next Lisa, and find someone who just wants to do it right now.

In the winter of 2021, I run into my friend Chip Faurot at the Talkeetna post office. Chip is a local general contractor who built our house. He was a longtime guide for Alaska Denali Guiding in the 1980s and 1990s and has intimate knowledge of Denali and its climbing culture.

"What's happening, Chip?" I ask as he exits his pickup truck, its roof rack stacked with lumber.

"Oh," he says, in his casual way, "I've got a remote job I'm gettin' ready for out on Illinois Creek. Fly-out job, off the grid. It'll keep me busy for a few weeks."

"How's Gabby doing?" I ask, referring to his 22-year-old daughter. Back in the summer of 2005, when she was 6, Gabby would play in our yard with her dog, Coco, throwing "fairy dust" around our driveway as Chip and his crew framed our house. Chip beams with pride as he relates Gabby's latest adventures with school, climbing, and skiing. As he speaks, I am struck by an impulsive thought.

"Do you think Gabby would be interested in running basecamp?" I ask.

Chip furrows his brow and then replies, "Maybe?" his eyes wandering to the sky for a moment.

"She loves the mountains," I continue, thinking out loud. "She's young, she climbs, she's unattached, and she's smart." *I sound just like Annie talking to me, twenty-one years ago.*

"You looking to leave?" Chip asks, his eyes growing wider.

"I'm thinking about it," I say.

"Well, you've had an epic run. Longer than anyone by far."

"Yeah, but I care a lot about the job and everything I worked for up there. I don't want to pass it to just anyone. A lot of my past helpers didn't work out because they lived far away and had lives and careers elsewhere. I've been thinking a local person might be the best fit."

"Sure, give her a call," Chip says, tapping out a text message. "Here's her number. She might be keen."

"If she is, I'll train her this coming season and see how it goes. You never know how anyone will react until they get thrown into the Denali meat grinder," I say with a laugh.

"You got that right," Chip agrees, with a sly, knowing grin. "The Alaska Range is a great test of one's mettle — and a perfect test of character."

It's just a few short months later when I exit Paul's plane and step down onto the snow of the Kahiltna Glacier. I take a deep breath, that old familiar, clean, cold air biting at my lungs as I watch the vapors creeping around the upper reaches of Mount Hunter. Small wisps of cloud stream from Denali, in sharp contrast to the bright-blue sky. The mountains all around wear a fresh, deep coat of pristine winter snow. For a moment, everything feels new again.

"Where do you want your tent, Lisa?" Mark calls, standing beside a sled-load of gear he has just dragged across the runway toward camp.

Absorbed in the landscape, I have almost forgotten why I'm here. It's setup day, and my volunteers and I have hours of hard work ahead.

"About fifty more feet uphill," I reply. I turn toward Gabby, who is helping Chip stack boxes in a sled next to the plane, as the pilot passes my camp gear out the door to them and the rest of the volunteers. She looks up and gives a cheery thumbs-up, her expression that of a child on Christmas morning.

"I find it good to put the tent close to the runway, so you don't have to walk too far each time you go out — but not right on the edge, or it'll be too noisy," I tell Gabby, gesturing. "I've always put it just down-glacier from the rangers' camp there, and just a little below where we'll put the cache garden. That walls off our camp from the climbers and gives us some personal space."

Gabby beams as we begin pulling our sleds toward the growing pile of gear. "I'm so excited you asked me to do this, Lisa. I'm really looking forward to learning from you," she says.

For the first time, I have informed my assistant from the very start that they are being trained as my eventual replacement. I intend for Gabby's learning curve and training experience to be more thorough and measured than mine was twenty-one years ago, when I spent my first day digging up the caches of presumed-deceased climbers, and my third day all alone with over one hundred anxious outbound climbers as a blizzard crashed into the Alaska Range.

Gabby will spend the next four days with me, getting a comprehensive rundown on everything she might face. After, she will fly out to attend a first-aid course, while I will continue with the first two-week shift. In a strange twist, I am also hoping we may have some inclement weather during these first few days, which would provide an opportunity for her to learn what I think is the most important part of the job: the nuances of weather observation. There is a big difference between seeing borderline, marginal flying conditions and describing them in a way that's useful to the pilots.

A combination of the endless free time I enjoyed at home last year in the absence of the climbing season and a desire to get Gabby immersed in running basecamp, has me relinquishing a significant amount of work time to her. I will work six weeks at basecamp, while Gabby will work four. It should be ample time for her, and me, to determine if this job is a good fit.

The 2021 Denali season is on, but Covid-19 precautions are still in place. There is concern about Covid spreading amongst climbers in the higher camps, and about the possibility of having to fly Covid patients off in the helicopter or via fixed-wing aircraft. The air services are mandating that all passengers wear masks, and I'm asking that climbers stay away from my tent.

The mountaineering staff in Talkeetna has experienced significant turnover in the past several years and need helicopter managers. Mark has Alaska climbing plans in June, and a new job with Mount Rainier's helicopter program beginning in July, but he has agreed to fill in as helicopter manager at Denali for the month of May.

"I have to admit," Mark says, as we put the finishing touches on my tent, "I'm pretty excited to run SAR and project operations from Talkeetna and to not be on a Denali patrol. This should be more enjoyable."

"Yeah," I counter. "But I'm bummed you don't have a basecamp patrol. I'll miss having you up here. I'm just glad I got you for setup. It's been awhile."

I think often of the people I already miss, and those I'll be missing soon. Dave Weber and the helicopter pilot Andy Hermansky — who both started here in 2010, the same year as Mark — have each announced that this will be their final season on Denali. Dave and Andy are my best buddies up here.

"Everyone is leaving," I say. "It makes me sad."

"I know," Mark concurs. "It's been hard for me too, watching the crew go their separate ways. And it gets tougher to make new friends as we get older."

"And, it takes a long time to make *old* friends," I add. Mark nods in approval, his eyes studying the granite buttresses of Denali's south face.

"Seems like yesterday that Joe and I were up there climbing the *Cassin Ridge,* while you had just flown out to Talkeetna after Don's plane crash," Mark says. "A lot of memories and history live here."

Mark and the volunteers depart for Talkeetna, leaving Gabby and me to our training. The closing days of April offer a peaceful respite before the first waves of Denali climbers arrive in early May. I have ample free time to impart to Gabby the critical duties of the job, the nuances of the electronics and the sometimes-finicky heater, and how to get the camp organized the way I prefer.

"We have to put more markers down the center of the runway," I say, noting that there are only two, placed by Paul about a week ago.

"Are those the plastic climber sleds you're using for markers?" Gabby asks, grabbing a shovel.

"Yes," I reply, "you bury them upright, about halfway in. When it gets warmer, you need to check them every so often, as they'll melt out."

We install the markers, then walk out through the camp area and use tall wands to mark two spots for pee holes, shoveling down to create a privacy screen for the ladies. "Next, we have to wand a perimeter for the cache garden," I continue. "It's always uphill of my tent, but we don't put it too close or in June we'll be listening to people digging up their caches at three in the morning."

"No more radio telephone," I tell Gabby, as I produce an InReach satellite communicator. "The phone company just stopped supporting the old antenna network, so it won't work anymore. We have to convey all messages including weather observations to Talkeetna each morning with this. If you pair it to your phone, at least the typing will be faster."

"I've used the InReach before — it's easy," Gabby says.

"Oh good. And we also have a satellite phone now," I say, pointing to it on the table. "But the sat coverage up here in Alaska is bad, and it's rare to keep a call going for more than a minute or two."

Gabby flies out a few days later, imprinted with the information I've passed on to her. She is intelligent and intuitive, which gives me confidence in her ability to read weather conditions and convey the right information to the pilots. She's also even-tempered, a useful asset for the impatient personalities she is destined to encounter. I'm relaxed as I watch her plane lift off over the Kahiltna and bank left around Annie's Ridge.

I have a good feeling about her.

Throughout my initial weeks at basecamp, the typical Denali drama unfolds. High winds rake the upper mountain for weeks, preventing most climbers from ascending beyond 14 Camp. On many days, I exit my tent in the morning to an apocalyptic mountain scene: streamers of wind-driven snow launching from Denali's ridgelines, or a saucer-like cloudcap sinking down upon the mountain's vast upper elevations.

Early one morning, Mark texts me on the InReach from Talkeetna. "**Heading into the West Fork of the Ruth with Andy. Two climbers hit by icefall. One fatality.**"

The limitations of the InReach with its 160-character limit, and the attendant impracticality of imparting more details, make moments like these the most frustrating. *I miss my radio phone.*

An afternoon message from Mark provides an update: "**Rescued one climber with head injury. Weather prevented recovery of deceased. Will do shorthaul early AM tomorrow before cloud** buildup."

The next day, Mark texts another report: "**Andy, Dave, and I got recovery done. I was on the line, Dave spotted in the heli. Climber was in massive ice debris, big serac overhead. Sketchy.**"

My "comfort zone" of worrying for Mark has always revolved around radio and telephone communications. Text messages, I've decided, are even more stressful. Context and tone are difficult to discern.

The following morning, Gabby flies in, and we overlap for an hour to review procedures. "I feel confident with everything up here, Lisa. Go relax and have fun with Mark and Harper," she says.

"Okay, good luck and let me know if you need anything," I reply, reassured, as my ride, a Talkeetna Air Taxi Otter, arrives with a perfect landing.

My two-week break flashes by. I savor the days of trail walks with Mark and Harper, planting my garden starts, and getting spring cleaning accomplished, but before I know it, I am landing upon the Kahiltna for another round of tent life.

Joe Reichert is the basecamp ranger, and — to my delight — his volunteers are my friends Katie and Ben Weaver, who were on Mark's 2015 Denali patrol, and also Steve Mock, who has worked for years with Denali Rescue Volunteers, a nonprofit that supports the Denali volunteer-mountaineering-ranger program.

"Hi, Lisa," Katie shouts, jogging out to greet me.

"Back for more?" I reply, as the others trail behind her. "Joe," I cry out, as I notice him walking over. "You just had double hip surgery. No shoveling for you."

Joe laughs it off with a casual wave and says, "I'm almost healed. No way am I going to miss out on my mountain time."

Chris Erickson hails us on the radio from 14 Camp in the afternoon.

"We have two climbers in camp with pretty bad frostbite," he begins. "They camped on the 16K ridge a few hundred feet below High Camp last night in the wind; their tent was destroyed, and they lost most of their gear. Just a heads-up: we're going to have Andy fly in and bring them to basecamp, and they can fly out from there."

A few hours pass before Andy arrives in camp from 14, sets down, and unloads the two frostbitten climbers. Joe and his volunteers escort them into camp, as Andy pops over to my tent.

"Well, hello Lisa," he says. "Your husband and I have been busy saving people, as I'm sure you've heard."

"You know you're the only pilot I want him flying with, Andy," I say.

"Aww, well, don't worry — I'll take good care of him and keep him out of trouble," Andy says. He produces his phone and says, "Hey, check this out. This is video I took flying over the Muldrow last week."

I watch the footage with stunned astonishment. The smooth glacier I remember walking upon during our cleanup patrol in 2013 is now torn asunder. The video reveals a nightmarish, chaotic mass of thrusted, jumbled ice blocks, with more crevasses than I can count. Walls of ice towering 200 to 300 feet tall guard access to the glacier from McGonagall Pass, the point from which we stepped right off the ice and scrambled up loose moraines.

A few months ago, the Muldrow Glacier began surging, a phenomenon that last occurred on the Muldrow in 1957. The glacier has continued to surge throughout the season, drawing interest and study from park scientists, who have calculated that the Muldrow's ice has been moving at up to sixty feet per day, or almost one hundred times its normal flow rate.

"I'm glad I got to walk on it before that happened," I say.

Andy raises his eyebrows and shakes his head. "It *is* unbelievable. It might be a generation before anyone can climb that route again," he says.

Two days later, Andy is back in camp. He's been flying park-service scientist and friend Mike Loso around various parts of the Kahiltna today. Mike is taking glacier measurements and servicing the telemetry stations the park has installed at 10,000 feet near Kahiltna Pass and at 14 Camp. Mike is working on the basecamp site just atop the hill to the north.

It's a sunny, lazy afternoon, and a welcome break from the prolonged stretch of stormy weather we've been enduring for much of the month. The quiet is shattered by the mountain guide Sam Hennessey calling out to the rangers at 14 Camp over the FRS radio.

"This is Sam at 17 Camp. We just witnessed a climber fall from Denali Pass down the Autobahn. He went the whole distance, over 1,000 feet. We can see him lying at the bottom, and he's not moving."

Joe bolts outside and calls to Andy, napping in a nearby lawn chair: "Andy, we have a SAR on the upper mountain."

Andy jumps to his feet and joins in on the briefing. Because we lack phone service in basecamp, the plan is relayed from Talkeetna through 14 Camp, which has a boosted cell-signal telephone, and down to us at basecamp by radio.

"Westman is IC in Talkeetna, Tucker is aviation ops," Chris says from 14 Camp, designating Mark as the incident commander and putting Tucker in charge of flight logistics. "Mark says launch Andy and have him pick me up here. We're hoping we can toe-in next to the patient." Andy departs within minutes. The rest of us follow the action by radio as Andy flies to 14 Camp, picks up Chris Erickson, and departs for the scene at 17,000 feet. Some long moments later, Chris radios with an update.

"We have the patient on board. Multiple-systems trauma, head injury, probable chest-wall injuries, and airway compromise. Patient is combative. We are going to fly him straight to Talkeetna. We're requesting LifeMed helicopter for transfer at Talkeetna Airport."

Joe looks at his watch and says, "Amazing. Twenty-seven minutes from the fall to being in the helicopter. That never happens."

"Hopefully he makes it," Ben adds.

The following day, we receive an update from Talkeetna. "The patient made it to the hospital," Joe says. "He's critical but he's alive. That's one of the better saves I can remember." This is Joe's twenty-eighth season working on Denali.

There have been many saves up here and many adverse outcomes. At varying levels, each event is an exposure to trauma, as are the idle moments of worry in which I've all too often found myself engaged. I ponder again and again the cumulative effect of the stresses I've been subjected to here at basecamp. I have gravitated toward arenas of hazard for most of my life, consuming myself with obsessive concern for others, keeping people safe, and contributing what I can. At some point, I may need to think about saving myself.

The sands of the narrow Homer Spit, on the Kenai Peninsula, stretch into the distance as Mark, Harper, and I walk along the beach. The days following the summer solstice have yielded endless warm weather and deep-blue skies. Ahead of us, beyond the choppy waters of Kachemak Bay, the craggy, snow-covered peaks of the southern peninsula rise far above the temperate rain forests where the mountains meet the sea. Tumbling glaciers reveal themselves in high, hanging valleys that lead up toward mysterious, unseen sources. Cook Inlet sprawls to our right, and beyond, the white, glaciated masses of Mount Redoubt and Iliamna Volcano rise over two vertical miles above the water, shimmering through the atmosphere. Harper alternates between scanning the ocean for signs of life, retrieving pieces of driftwood, and insisting we throw the Frisbee. A mature bald eagle rests upon the sand and glares at us with suspicion. A steady breeze off the inlet tousles my hair. As Mark and Harper sprint down the beach, water, mountains, sand, and snow fill my view in every direction. I am surrounded by everything I love.

Gabby is at basecamp for her final shift, while Mark and I are taking advantage of this stretch of good weather to get out of Talkeetna. In a few days, we'll fly back into basecamp, help Gabby tear everything down, and fly it all out. Gabby has been a quick study, giving me the confidence to let go and to better enjoy my life while on my breaks. The worry is just not worth it. Not anymore.

It's appropriate that we end up breaking down camp on Independence Day. Mark, Gabby, and I pack up the tent, toss random items into mystery boxes, and move all the pieces toward the waiting aircraft with haste.

"Keep it moving," Mark encourages, as we ferry load after load and help the pilot secure it inside. "It's nice here, but those clouds in the lowlands are heading our way."

Much of the pure-white snow that blanketed the surrounding peaks at season's opening is now stained by dirt and dust from rockfalls. The bases of most gullies are filled with enormous piles of avalanche debris. Snowfields on Mount Frances are now scree fields, while snow chutes on Annie's Ridge have been replaced by streaks of black ice, the remnants of broken-off cornices heaped at the foot of the wall. Everything looks worn out and used up. Denali towers above these heat-scarred lowlands, insulated by its lofty elevation from the above-freezing temperatures down here, and looking even whiter than it did in April. The seasons have turned again, and now it's time for us to leave.

"What do you think, Gabby?" I ask. "Next year?"

Gabby grins.

"Definitely," she answers. "The long stretches were kind of tough, but it was fun, and I learned a lot. I'm totally psyched for next season."

"Great," I say. "We'll do this all again next April."

We — I guess I'm in, too.

We're all buckled in. The airplane's turbine engine spools up, the pilot pushes the throttle, and the powerful Otter bumps along the rutted snow before lifting with ease off the glacier. The pilot banks into a 180-degree turn and flies past the massive, dark wall of Hunter's north buttress. We glide out over the drainage of the tumbling Tokositna Glacier, as the savage granitic pyramid of Mount Huntington soars to our left.

Ahead, an advancing layer of dense, low clouds fills the lower elevations of the Alaska Range and the Susitna Valley as far as the eye can see. The summits of eight granite monoliths astride the Ruth Glacier pierce this cloud deck, rising defiantly into the sunlight from the damp, unseen depths, offering striking contrasts amid a sea of otherwise featureless white.

As I contemplate the future, I feel a bit like those mountains outside my window: struggling to keep my head above the incoming tide of change, hardened and scarred by the forces of erosion, suspended between worlds of illumination and obscurity.

The disquieting drama of Denali is my addiction. Like many people in my life, I draw a sense of purpose, identity, and strength from the intensity of the harsh environment and through exposure to risk, loss, and danger. As with any form of dependence, however, the rewards often come at a steep cost. Just as a climber cannot forever remain on the summit, I know that sometime soon I will have to come down from the mountain to find serenity in the valley.

I can envision a day when I lift my eyes toward the mountains, fulfilled and content with the knowledge of what lies above, decoupled from this intoxicating compulsion that keeps me in a constant state of vigilance.

All I have to do is let go and walk away.

Chapter Fourteen
Letting Go

Heat waves shimmer across the glacier as I lounge in a chair beneath my sun umbrella, my feet resting on a milk crate. A bang rings out like a rifle shot. I look up from my book to witness a large cornice free-falling from the crest of Annie's Ridge. It breaks into pieces as it impacts sharp granite outcrops on its way down the face. The mass of pulverized snow becomes a river of debris that pours past overhangs and cascades down gullies of black- and blue-streaked ice before coming to rest in a pile upon the glacier. The sun beats down with unrelenting fury, reflecting off the snow and heating the air. Behind me, loud booms like cannon fire signal yet another rockfall strafing the south face of Mount Frances. The sounds of running water reverberate from indeterminate sources around me. A pair of ravens circles the camp in search of food scraps, squawking at one another as they zero in on an abandoned campsite. There is not a breath of wind.

Twenty-two. The number repeats itself in my mind. The year 2022 is my twenty-second season on the mountain. By my own estimates, I have spent more than 1,100 days, or over three years of my life, living on the Kahiltna Glacier.

"I can't believe you've been doing this for so long," a climber said to me this morning, his facial expression revealing both surprise and confusion. The astonishment in his voice gave me pause. Is it so unusual for someone to work at the same place for so many years? My father drove tanks as a Marine, then spent his entire working life running heavy equipment. Aren't we supposed to find something we like, do it well, and do it for a long duration?

It's already mid-June, the season over halfway completed. This spring has had endless sunshine and high pressure, which made my recent two-week break in Talkeetna a delightful experience of long, sunny days, trail hikes with Harper, paddling on the lake, and wondering what has for so long compelled me to abandon those sorts of joys each spring to stay immersed in winter, up here in the alpine.

I have a full schedule of well-paying slideshow presentations at the Mount McKinley Princess Wilderness Lodge during my off time and for the remainder of the summer after the climbing season. Utilizing my photos and digging deeply into Mark's massive Alaska Range collection, I show the lodge's guests what it's like living on a glacier for over two months a year, and the intricacies of my unique job. I share photos of the more amusing situations and interesting characters — such as the Russian paraplegic team, the high school jazz-band parties, and the Funky Monkeys. I also describe what the rangers do on the mountain and touch on the tragedies and mishaps. I talk at length about Alaska's notorious weather and the difficulties it presents for the rangers, climbers, pilots, and me. At the conclusion, I play a six-minute movie that Mark created consisting of a montage of spectacular still images and video from some of his many Alaskan ascents. The audience absolutely loves it, and my show gets many positive reviews from the lodge's guests. This feedback has me scheming about renting a space closer to home as well, to give the show to guests of other Alaska tourist groups.

There is a certain beauty in the fact that when I finish talking to a fascinated audience about planes and climbers and CMCs, I can go sleep in my own bed and not have to deal with the 4:00 a.m. Crunchers, the cold, "The List," or pacifying someone's fury about why the planes aren't flying in a blizzard to take them home. It's an ironic twist that, even as I scale back my actual time spent working at basecamp, I am spending increasing amounts of time sharing the adventures of this job with affable and curious tourists enjoying their Alaskan vacations.

This season, I put Gabby in charge of gathering her own volunteers and directing basecamp setup back in April. Gabby needed to attend her college graduation just four days after setup, so I flew in with her crew, helped construct the camp, and took the first two-week shift. I have also given Gabby six of the ten weeks of the season. Small steps toward the exit, but I continue hanging on.

"You'll know when it's time to leave." Annie's advice from many years ago still resonates, and now, I'm paying even closer attention. Last fall, while on a two-month rock-climbing trip with Mark in Moab, Utah, I had to go to the hospital one night for severe abdominal pain, a significant escalation of the more moderate pain I'd been occasionally having for the past year. By the following morning, I was in emergency surgery having my infected gall bladder removed.

As if that weren't enough, just a few months ago, I was given a diagnosis of Hashimoto's Disease, an autoimmune condition. My immune system is now attacking and destroying my long-malfunctioning thyroid gland, making me wonder if I've had this disease for far longer. When I was diagnosed with hypothyroidism almost ten years ago, I had hoped that the diagnosis and medication would lead to improvement of fatigue and my ability to regulate temperature. There's been some relief, but getting the medication dosage correct has proven elusive at times and will remain an ongoing process. Now, this new diagnosis takes things to the next level, adding in an array of even more medications along with heavy dietary restrictions, and makes me question if living on a remote glacier is the best place for me, anymore. Mark and I have been navigating the age range in life when the unexpected whims of genetics and cellular-level maladies start sorting us all out. It's frustrating, but it is what it is. We're alive, we're still chasing the things we love, and for that we cannot be anything other than grateful.

Mark has taken a new job this summer as a climbing ranger at Rocky Mountain National Park in Estes Park, Colorado. I haven't seen him since he saw Gabby and me off at the airport as we flew in to set up basecamp, but he's coming home for a visit in late June just after this, my final two-week shift of the season, comes to an end.

Mark loves his new job and it's a welcome shift on a professional level, but we're also back to a long-distance relationship. Mark's absence from Alaska makes being at basecamp feel even more isolated, and, as I think again of my many friends who have departed Denali in recent years, even more pointless. Even the views of the Alaska Range lose their luster when favored companions are not there to share them.

I can't take this heat any longer. I rise from my camp chair and retreat to the shaded vestibule of my new tent. This "Arctic Oven" is the same as the tents now used by the rangers both here and at 14 Camp. Gone are the pair of unwieldy, 150-pound pieces of wood flooring and the 100 pounds of poles that supported the tent I used since 2014, which in turn replaced the 900-pound monstrosity I had inherited from Annie. In their place, I have a two-layer nylon tent supported by much lighter aluminum poles, and a floor of ultralight foam and thin plywood sheeting. Gabby's father, Chip, designed and cut each piece of flooring to be easy to carry and to fit inside the airplanes. The lighter setup opens up the possibility of relocating my entire camp to the upper strip in the later weeks of these ever-warming seasons. This year is again one of them.

The walls of the deep hole we dug back in April have now melted away, and the tent floor is buckling with the uneven decline in the snow surface. Sagging crevasses seam the runway, and the snow is sloppy and increasingly difficult for the planes to navigate. A text message comes in from Paul on the inReach: "**Upper airstrip only from now on. Starting first thing tomorrow morning.**" It's June 10, the earliest I can recall this switchover happening.

"There's almost a month left in the season," Paul says as we meet at the upper airstrip the next morning. "You should just move your whole camp up here, so you don't have to ski up every day."

"Okay, but I'll need some people to come in and help me," I reply.

"Just put your gear in a pile," Paul replies. "Tomorrow or the day after, I can just taxi the Otter back and forth between the camps with your gear."

"Gotta love those Otters," I say, motioning toward the red, white, and blue turbine aircraft nearby.

"They're so powerful," Paul says with pride. "We can do way more with them than we ever could with the 185s or the Beavers."

Two days later, Paul has a change in plans.

"The crevasses down there are opening up," he says, pointing down-glacier as we stand at the upper airstrip. "Sorry, but I don't want to take a plane down there. You'll have to ski everything up here."

"I don't know if can do that by myself," I protest. "It'll take me a week, and I'm afraid I'll hurt my back."

"Just get a sled and start making carries," Paul says.

I spend the rest of the day packing up camp, with a plan to begin the big move tomorrow. By evening, I have bags and boxes sorted and ready. Three Polish climbers approach my tent as the sun sets behind Foraker.

"We want to fly out right now," one man says in a sharp tone.

"Sorry," I say. "The air services stopped flying this afternoon. The weather is bad down in Talkeetna, and they can't make it in here. You'll have to set up your tent for the night."

"What do you mean? Weather is good here," the man counters, pointing at the blue skies overhead with visible annoyance.

"I know, but the lower elevations of the mountains are clouded in, and the planes cannot get through," I explain. "They'll try again in the morning."

The man turns to his teammates, shaking his head and speaking in Polish, while pointing at me in derision. The two others glare at me in silence.

"Go to the upper airstrip and set up your tent. I will come talk to you in the morning with an update," I instruct, pointing up-glacier and suppressing my growing anger. The man huffs as the others let out melodramatic groans of displeasure, before hefting their packs and continuing up the glacier.

Early the following morning, I make a quick trip to the upper airstrip with a light load of gear and to give the climbers who have arrived overnight a weather and flight update.

"Sorry, everyone," I begin, "but the weather is still bad in Talkeetna, and it's all clouded in through the lower elevations. The planes are on hold, and the pilots say the weather might not break today. I'll let you know if and when they are able to fly." I gesture at the blue skies and bright sunshine, shrugging my shoulders at the odd contrast in the weather. A loud, angry male voice booms from behind me.

"WHAT TIME WILL THE WEATHER CLEAR?!"

I spin around to see the leader of the Polish team I encountered last night facing me with an aggressive stance.

"I have no idea," I reply. "The pilots will make that decision. I've told them it's good up here, and that's all I can do."

The man mutters something in Polish, gestures at the sky, and stomps back over to his friends. I turn and head downhill to get my camp-relocation project underway. *I'm so sick of this shit. How many hundreds of times have I had to deal with irate, entitled climbers?*

Awhile later, I kick my left ski behind me, while driving my right ski forward with a steady push from my ski poles. The tether from my backpack snaps tight against the loaded sled for an instant before the sled breaks free and slides ahead in obedience. Kick right, drive forward left, push off the poles, repeat. I draw from my memories of those days on the West Buttress patrol to find the sweet spot that maintains constant tension on the sled tether without letting it tug or bounce against the waist belt of my pack. *You've done this before — just keep laboring away.*

The well-packed trail in the snow brings me over the final rise in the glacier and into the level staging area adjacent the top end of the upper airstrip. This is my fifth load of the day. I feel like Sisyphus, pushing that boulder up the same hill forever only to have it roll back down. Sweat drizzles into my eyes as the hot sun beats down, and my leg muscles twitch with the first hints of fatigue and dehydration. I haul up beside a growing pile of my camp gear, slam my pack down on the snow, and then flop down upon it. I reach for my water bottle as I take in the scene across camp.

A collection of half-pitched tents is scattered about, thrown up for some hasty shade by several dozen climbers awaiting their rides to civilization. It's still socked in and raining in the lower elevations, and the planes are still grounded in Talkeetna. The more optimistic among the climbers have resisted setting up their tents and instead lie prone on top of their duffel bags, shading their faces with bandanas and ball caps. Several familiar guides observe me with curiosity.

"Do you need some help, Lisa?" one asks, rising from his pile of gear, as others nearby begin stirring in anticipation of having something to do besides stare at the sky.

"If you're offering," I reply. "I'm moving my whole camp up here by myself."

"Come on, everyone," the guide commands, drafting all his assistants, some clients, and a few other nearby guides. "Let's help Lisa out."

Three round trips a piece and about three hours later, almost all my camp has been relocated, apart from a few minor items. I mix up two large pitchers of cold lemonade for my crew.

"Thanks so much, you guys," I say. "I'll get the rest — you all go relax."

As I return awhile later with yet another load, I look up to see the Polish man stomping toward me in a take-no-prisoners manner indicating that argument number three is about to begin.

"Lisa, why are you not telling us what is going on?" he scolds.

"Because there's nothing to tell you at the moment. The situation is unchanged."

"Yes, but you don't tell us ANYTHING," the man retorts, raising his voice.

"Because there's nothing to tell you — there's no news."

The other climbers in camp look up and take notice of our shouts.

"You should tell us more," the man yells back.

"TELL YOU WHAT?! That nothing has changed, and the planes aren't coming?" I argue, gesturing in exasperation at the empty skies overhead.

"YES!" he barks.

"So, I'm supposed to track you down you every hour and tell you the planes aren't coming?"

"Yes."

"Did you notice that I'm really busy today?"

He and his companions nod.

"Well, maybe if you helped out, like a lot of the other climbers here have been doing, I would have more time available to tell you that nothing is happening," I say. My sarcasm having boiled over, I turn my back and ski away toward the lower camp to retrieve the final load of the day. When I return an hour later, the man is again lying in wait.

"WHY AREN'T YOU TELLING US WHAT IS GOING ON?" he screams.

I throw my pack down in the snow and erupt in fury.

"I told you last night, AND this morning, that when the planes are flying, I WILL LET YOU KNOW!!!" I shout, almost shocked at the sound of my own unhinged voice.

"Here's an update for you," I continue with increasing animation. "If you say another word to me, YOU THREE are going to the BOTTOM of the list. YOU'LL GO LAST."

The three climbers stare at me, mouths agape, frozen stiff. I grab my pack, swing it up over my shoulder with a wild flair, and stomp away to my pile of gear to finish setting up my tent. I'm well aware that all the climbers in camp are watching.

I complete my tent set-up, and then take a moment inside to sit and decompress. I'm embarrassed. I've had it out with climbers here in camp many times before, but this time, something is different. *I lost my composure. What's happening to me?*

Approaching footsteps and a friendly, familiar male voice calling my name break me out of my trance.

I look up to see the lead Alaska Mountaineering School guide who had helped me earlier standing at my tent door. Behind him are one of his assistants along with two guides from a different group. They each smile and pat me on the back as they enter.

"Don't let those jerks wreck your day, Lisa," the guide says in an empathetic voice. "We brought you some cookies," he adds, holding out a bag and grinning.

I smile back in appreciation as I accept the offering. "Thanks, you guys," I say, my voice subdued. "After twenty-two years, I thought I knew how to handle those types. I've had worse people, but maybe I've just been doing this for too long."

More climbers from other groups rotate through to visit as I prepare my dinner. "So sorry, Lisa," one woman consoles. "You don't deserve to be spoken to like that. No one does."

Later, I sit alone in my camp chair, sipping hot tea and watching the sun arc westward. A wispy lenticular cloud caps Mount Foraker, while fog and low clouds have rolled up from the lower glacier and now scud in over the southeast fork, obscuring the sun. I am exhausted from disassembling my entire camp, hauling load after load up the glacier, having these repeated and stupid arguments with the Polish, and then rebuilding my camp. A disturbing thought crosses my mind: *Maybe the others were just being nice to me so I'll call in the airplanes.*

The thought gives me pause. *Am I really that jaded?*

I rise from my chair as though struck by an epiphany, pacing around on the snow in front of my tent like a mad scientist who has just discovered a secret formula. I just entertained the thought that climbers were being nice only because they wanted something from me.

I have never been this cynical. What is wrong with me?

I hear Annie's voice again: *You'll know when it's time.*

I turn in a circle, tracking the horizon of each mountain and ridgeline, my eyes filling with tears of joy and sadness. And now, I know.

That's it. I'm done.

"Gabby," I say aloud to no one, my eyes fixed in soft focus across the glacier. "It's all yours."

After years of deliberations and doubts and clinging and sentimentality, the decision became a choiceless act, as though made by someone else on my behalf. Thus accomplished, the sensation of being trapped up here alone has transformed into one of liberation. There's no going back.

I poke my head outside the tent. The fog is ebbing back down-glacier, and the sun is out again. Almost on cue, the InReach beeps with an incoming text. "**Mountains opening up. How is your weather?**"

"**Some fog down-glacier but all good here currently. Come on in,**" I type in reply. I still dislike the impersonality and labor of these text messages. Nothing has been the same without my old radio phone. *Another reason to leave, as if I needed one.*

An hour later, the hum of a turbine engine breaks the silence as the first of a half dozen airplanes from K2 and Talkeetna Air Taxi banks around the distant end of Annie's Ridge for short final to basecamp. I trade stories and laughs with the guides who helped me move camp as the first airplane rolls to a stop in front of the crowd. Aglow with my newfound lightness of being, I turn toward the three Polish climbers who have unwittingly helped initiate the end of my tenure at basecamp, and then I reverse my earlier threat.

"This first plane is yours."

The climbers rise to their feet, eyebrows raised in puzzled surprise.

"Go on. They're waiting," I prod, nodding my head and grinning.

The three gather their equipment and, with no more words, trudge away toward the plane. I've accomplished the impossible in managing to make myself appear benevolent while also succeeding in no longer having them glare at me. Sometimes, I've learned, you just have to let things go.

Several days later, my friend Courtney Shaffer smiles in wonder as we sit side-by-side on the glacier, taking a short break while making yet another gear carry between camps.

"Lisa, this is so amazing. You have the most incredible job," she says.

Courtney has flown up from Talkeetna to stay in basecamp for a night, and made a gracious offer to ski down-glacier with me to help bring up the few remaining pieces of lightweight foam flooring material.

"There's certainly no job on the planet like this one," I acknowledge.

Courtney nods, her eyes transfixed on Denali looming between

Mount Frances and Lisa's Peak. I have told Mark, but I have otherwise made no mention to Courtney or anyone else of my impending retirement. It will remain this way for awhile, at least until I'm off the mountain and the season is over. Maybe I'm just making sure it wasn't an impulsive decision, or maybe I'm leaving the door cracked open. Letting go of Denali just isn't that easy.

Courtney is Talkeetna Air Taxi's office manager as well as my Talkeetna companion for hikes, walks, doggy playdates, and potluck dinners. She arrived in Talkeetna several years ago and was enraptured in an instant by the lifestyle and beauty of Alaska, just as I had been when I first discovered it almost thirty years ago. She is good company in these moments of monumental change, helping me to remember old perspectives from another time and place.

The evening finds Courtney and me preparing dinner with our ranger pals Tucker Chenoweth and Brandon Latham, who have just flown into basecamp. Tuck and Brandon are on an "old friends" reunion patrol for the park, and tomorrow they'll head off up the West Buttress for just a few days before they must both get back to the administrative responsibilities of their respective jobs.

Tucker has been a friend to Mark and me for almost twenty years and, like his predecessors John Leonard and Daryl Miller, has become proficient in his job as Denali's South District Ranger. Between us, Tucker and I have seen almost everything up here, and because of it, we always understand each other. Brandon was a Denali mountaineering ranger from 2008 to 2014, and now works in Yosemite. He's one of the many faces of Denali that remind me of another lifetime here in this very same place. As the evening deepens, our stories from decades of Denali experience pour out as quickly as the wine and cocktails in which we're indulging.

"Remember that guy who left his twelve-year-old kid unattended in basecamp while he went off to climb the mountain for a couple weeks?" Tucker exclaims.

"Oh yeah," I reply. "This kid was wandering around near the crevasses every day, and I asked him what he was doing. They had to track down the father up at 14, and he got a real earful from Roger and Daryl when he got out."

"Or what about that Saudi prince a few years ago who had three private guides?" I continue. "When he wanted to fly out, there was a long line, and he offered my brother ten thousand dollars to jump the line."

"Did he take it?" Brandon asks in disbelief.

"Nope," I say. "Paul isn't moved by money. He'd prefer to see people like that have to wait like everyone else."

"Weren't there some climbers who hid an FRS radio deep in the pee hole in basecamp?" Tucker says, his eyes lighting up in remembrance.

"Oh yeah, that was classic," I concur, turning to Courtney to elaborate. "They would sit in their camp with a second radio and wait for some unsuspecting climber to use the pee hole. Then they'd transmit things like, 'HELP! Get me out of here.' And the climber would jump back ten feet."

As Courtney, Brandon, and I laugh, Tucker adds, "I also remember them saying to some of the male climbers, 'Wow, is that all you've got?'"

"Do you remember the hungover tourists who came up here on a scenic, and one went to propose to his girlfriend and dropped the engagement ring in the snow, and then they couldn't find it?" I recall.

"I don't remember that one," Brandon says, "but sounds about right."

"Oh," Tucker exclaims, sitting and holding up his index finger. "Don't forget about 'Luggage Lynn.'"

"Who's that?" Courtney asks, intrigued.

"This woman who wasn't a climber came up here with a pink wheeled suitcase, trying to follow or stalk some guide who was on the West Buttress," I explain. "She dragged her suitcase up the glacier all by herself, but the guide didn't want anything to do with her."

"Yeah, and she also didn't have a permit," Brandon adds. "Tuck saw her at 9,500 and told her to go down. The next day, she showed up at 11 Camp and wanted to come snuggle in Tucker's tent for the night."

Tucker covers his eyes in embarrassment. "Yeah. Good times. I ordered her off the mountain, and when she got back to Talkeetna, Coley wrote her a bunch of tickets. She had issues."

"Oh my god," Courtney exclaims, trying to contain her laughter. "So many characters."

"Too many," I offer. "I also remember these entrepreneurial girls in camp trading use of their solar charger for food. Or the Japanese climbers I saw putting a bag salad into a pot of boiling water. Or, Tuck, do you remember telling me about that Italian guy who was drinking out of his CMC?"

"Oh god, yes." Tucker says, shaking his head. "That was at 11 Camp. Something was lost in translation during the Talkeetna briefing."

"You must get a lot of gifts," Courtney says. "Climbers at TAT are always asking us what they should bring you."

"I do," I answer. "Over the years, I've gotten alcohol, fruit, vegetables, candies, fine chocolates. I even got French perfume."

"Well, of course — you're a celebrity, Lisa," Tucker says.

"Maybe," I say. "But sometimes there's an ulterior motive. I've had a bunch of different climbers come back to find a long waiting list to fly out, and then the sweet talk begins." I pantomime the archetypal example: "Lisa, remember I brought you those fine French truffles on the way in (*wink, wink*)? Any chance I can go on the next plane?"

The laughter and conversation wind down as the wine induces heavy eyelids, and thoughts of warm sleeping bags begin to beckon. The evening light casts a sublime golden hue across the glacier, and the four of us fall silent for a few moments of reflection. Then Tucker straightens up from his chair and flashes a smile that tells me he's about to get sentimental. "I tell ya, I appreciate every minute I get in these mountains," he says, raising his cup toward our group. "Especially, with good friends."

My companions depart camp the following day, leaving me to a string of days in solitary confinement. A week passes, these late-season days running together in a blur of repetition that I recognize all too well. I put an X on the calendar with every midnight sunset hard on the heels of those long afternoons marked by silence, save for the occasional visit of a scenic flight, the calls of the ravens, the rush of snow avalanches, or a volley of stones ricocheting down some nearby mountain face. I have much time to reflect, and I am consumed by alternating waves of joy and nostalgia. It is so hard to let go of the identification, the memories, and the moments of excitement and action Denali has provided. But the mountain also subjects me to so much isolation, along with the physical stresses on my aging body and the emotional traumas and tragedies and deprivations and much too much time away from the people I love. This existence is not sustainable anymore. It's been a wild ride, but it is time to get off and move on.

> "You cannot stay on the summit forever; you have to come down again. So why bother in the first place? Just this: What is above knows what is below, but what is below does not know what is above. One climbs, one sees. One descends, one sees no longer, but one has seen."
> —René Daumal

My calendar shows Gabby flying in tomorrow morning. It's my final night on the glacier. I feel a spring in my step as I stride around the camp, straightening up the solar panels and antennae and picking up bits of trash left near the runway by departing groups. A gentle breeze blows down-glacier, and I notice plumes of snow curling away from the summit pyramid of Mount Hunter and all along Denali's brooding crest. Perhaps there's a storm coming?

As I duck inside my tent to prepare my last basecamp dinner, the breeze grows into a steady and purposeful wind that flaps and ripples the tent. I hear a few loose items blowing around outside, which sends me back out to secure them. I take notice of the minimal number of anchors I placed to secure my tent when I moved it up here last week. *It'll be fine. The winds are seldom over 20 here.*

I'm ready for bed, dreaming of the comforts of home that await me the next day. The wind continues to snap at the tent, so I stuff in my earplugs, pull on some eyeshades, and nestle into my sleeping bag. I've just crossed the threshold of consciousness when a loud crash and a sense of something dynamic happening jolt me awake.

I bolt upright, disoriented as I fight my way out of my sleeping bag. I rip off the eyeshades to see my desk lying upside down across the tent from where it was. All my radios and other items that were once stacked upon it are strewn about the floor. Where the desk once stood, the tent floor is billowing like a balloon while its windward wall is flattening down and trembling under the force of the gale. The tent poles in each corner are bouncing off the ground and doing their best to resist. My failure to anchor this otherwise sturdy tent has turned it into a giant sail.

"What the hell?" I shout, still getting my bearings.

I struggle to remove my foam earplugs, and when I succeed, I hear the roar of the wind outside. I leap to my feet to assess where to begin tamping down the chaos. The tent vestibule has broken free of its snow stakes and is flapping so hard that I fear it will be torn to pieces. Boxes of gear I have stacked inside are being knocked around by the snapping fabric, and if anything gets outside, it could very well blow away. I spring to secure the vestibule, fighting to hold down loose items with each foot while clasping the fabric tight and anchoring it with a snow picket. In similar fashion, I secure the other side of the door, all the while feeling like I am trapped inside a washing machine on spin cycle.

I not only neglected to place sufficient tent anchors last week; I also left some of the foam-and-wood flooring stacked outside, feeling it not worth the trouble to fully rebuild the floor with just a few weeks left in the season. Fearing it has blown away, I slip outside to find the flooring still hanging on, the foam pieces piled underneath the much heavier plywood. I rush to drive in more snow pickets at each of the tent's corners and guylines, and bring two pieces of plywood inside the tent and place them on the still-billowing floor. I push the heavier items toward the windward side to secure it and prevent it from ballooning up again. I reset my desk and electronics before flopping down in my desk chair, catching my breath, and wondering what to do next.

Now, high overhead, I hear what sounds like a jet plane being ripped from the sky and falling straight down on top of me. *Is that a plane about to crash?* I bolt up and look outside. There are indeed no aircraft, just a crystal-clear, twilight sky being torn asunder by the wind. Mark has described the phenomenon of such wind sounds heard high on Denali, but I never imagined it could happen down here, much less experienced it before.

A moment later, the wind stops with as little warning as it began. The air is silent, as though none of this ever happened. The strangest fifteen-minute wind event I have ever experienced is over. In a moment of pretend, I imagine that Denali is displeased with my decision to retire.

"*How dare you?*" I can hear it shouting, in the only language Denali speaks — that dreaded wind that can kill with a kiss.

I step back outside into the strange stillness of the night air, in need of more time to burn off the coursing flood of adrenaline. The summer solstice passed just four days ago. Mount Hunter's north face burns fiery red as the unseen sun still hangs somewhere beneath the rugged skyline of Denali but above the even more distant arctic horizon to my north. I draw several long, deep breaths, taking in all I can of the scene. I add a few more snow anchors to the tent, shovel snow on the flaps, and double-check that everything outside is secure. I take a final pensive glance around me before I zip up the vestibule and crawl back into my sleeping bag.

Minutes later, as the first traces of sleep begin to overtake me again, a calamitous roar like artillery fire thrusts me forth once more into full consciousness. I sit upright in near panic, recognizing the unmistakable sound of a massive rockfall coming from the nearby Control Tower. In the normal basecamp location, there would be no risk, but this camp is much closer, and I've never thought to assess the overhead risks. I am now, however. It sounds as though it is directly overhead, and for the moment, I am certain that the rocks are going to crash down on my tent and bury me forever under tons of debris.

There's nowhere to run, so I duck inside my sleeping bag, accept my fate, and brace for impact. Trembling in the darkness of my bag,

I feel a sense of relief begin to build as the sound dissipates and the crushing blow I have anticipated never comes. The roar transitions to a rumble, a gravelly trickle, and then silence.

"I'll come back to visit," I call out to the mountains, bargaining with the inanimate and uncaring as I re-emerge from my bag. "I promise."

The wall of the tent flutters in a momentary wisp of wind. I fall into a deep and sound sleep.

I awaken in near blackness. It takes a moment to come around to my sense of place, which is burrowed deep inside my warm, cozy sleeping bag. I can sense that I've been sleeping for a long time. It must be morning. I force my way out of the bag and am greeted by the bright interior of my sunlit tent. The ever-reliable morning down-glacier breeze rustles the tent walls, while filtered sunbeams shimmer through the room in cadence with the gentle movements of the fabric.

Today is the day. I arise and put on a kettle. One last morning weather report for the air services, one final head count of climbers to fly out, one final cup of Kaladi coffee, enjoyed to the backdrop of this magnificent mountain view. Will I ever start a workday like this again?

I pack my bags amidst a flood of bittersweet memories. Memories of little things that made me laugh, cry, and scratch my head; the games, the pranks, the contests, the movie nights, the trivia questions, and all the many things that could only happen here. Most of all, I think of the humans with whom I shared each and every adventure, tragedy, trial, and moment of doubt. The company I enjoyed for every mountain climb, glacier ski tour, sunset dinner, morning coffee, or just a cold drink and conversation under the umbrella. The deep comradery that develops from living amongst and engaging with cold and dangerous mountains, and which is so difficult to replicate elsewhere.

I stand on the snow, basking in the morning sunshine, surveying Mount Foraker's illuminated east face. I study the little details of the distant and familiar wall, taking note of how the large-scale architecture of the icefalls and seracs has remained so consistent through the decades, even as the cast of characters on Denali has not. As I sip from my steaming mug of coffee, I reminisce about past Denali rangers. Daryl Miller's unceasing kindness and oversight let me know that a trusted friend always had my back while I was on the mountain. Davey Kreutzer's cheerful demeanor could change my worst day into the greatest. John "Loomie" Loomis never failed to come to my rescue in stressful situations, and was always prepared to make me laugh with his cutting wit. Roger Robinson's institutional well of knowledge and singular sense of humor provided one of the greatest treasures of working on Denali for me — one I may not have fully appreciated until he retired.

I can still visit Daryl in Anchorage, meet Annie and Dave for a Talkeetna dinner, bump into Loomie at the hardware store at the Talkeetna "Y," and make the five-minute walk between our house and Roger and Pam's near Christiansen Lake. But there may never be anything quite as magical as those days when we all lived and worked together in Denali's looming shadow, watching and waiting at our posts in anticipation of helping someone in need.

I will have to travel to see the other rangers who made their mark upon my life. Dave Weber now works at Grand Teton National Park. The autumn rock-climbing road trips I take with Mark might now pass through there or Park City, Utah, which he and Katie call home. Port Angeles, Washington, is where we can find Chris Erickson, along with his wife and my close friend Amanda, who moved there when Chris took a new position at Olympic National Park last year after fourteen years of working on Denali. Joey McBrayer and his

LISA RODERICK

wife, the former mountaineering ranger and Denali guide Melis Coady, departed Talkeetna in 2018 for new work in Yosemite, but they have just moved back and again live less than a mile from us. Denali lost a giant last year with the departure of Andy Hermansky, one of the world's most skilled high-altitude longline pilots, but at least I can still give Andy a hard time here in Talkeetna at one of the local breakfast trucks downtown.

There are some who I can only visit in my memories. John Evans, the kind Welshman who worked for Denali during my first ten years, fell from a sea cliff near his home in Wales not long after his final season. And, of course, Cale Shaffer will forever be the handsome and enthusiastic 24-year-old ranger I met on my wide-eyed first day in basecamp. Cale's tragic death changed park-service aviation policies, and it galvanized my own commitment to this job and to helping mitigate the dangers the glacier pilots face every day.

I take another sip of coffee and sigh as the down-glacier breeze, warm and summerlike, tousles my hair. I pull my trusty handheld aircraft radio from my jacket pocket and stare at it with melancholy. My mind shuffles through the many dozens of pilots I've talked to over the years with this same device, almost always carrying it around in my chest harness or clipped to my belt.

Legendary glacier pilots like Doug Geeting, Tony Martin, and Jim Okonek, who were flying in the Alaska Range since Paul and I were running around in the woods of Connecticut, are now retired. Jay Hudson passed away from cancer in 2009. Many others, including Paul's longtime chief pilot, Richard Olmstead, have moved on to fly elsewhere after numerous years on Denali.

I hold back emotions as I think of Keli Mahoney and Don Bowers, and the horrific aftermaths of their deaths in my first years at basecamp. I remember my old friend Zach Babat, one of Paul's former pilots, who died in a midair collision in 2016 while flying in western Alaska. And there was Jeff Babcock, a former K2 Aviation pilot of seven years, who lost his life in a plane crash in Canada in 2019.

I wasn't close with many of the pilots outside of work, but I have had a special connection with most of them while up here on the mountain, and I have always viewed their safety as my primary responsibility. On more than one occasion, I helped talk a pilot down through ragged clouds, thick fog, or squirrely, shifting winds, and into a safe landing on the glacier. Many more times than that, I radioed incoming planes advising them to turn back due to a rapid deterioration of conditions at basecamp. There are so many moments to recall, from the frantic tossing of gear into the hands of a worried pilot while shouting at climbers to hurry up and get to the plane, as the cloud ceiling drops and the pilot has mere minutes to get off the ground; to standing on the snow while a plane sits powered up, waiting to tell him over the radio when the gusting winds have dropped so he can attempt to take off. We have all been through so much together.

My brother Paul, and his old mountain-flying mentor, David Lee of Sheldon Air Service, are about the last two Talkeetna glacier pilots from the 1980s and 1990s still working here. With tireless optimism, forward thinking, and smart business acumen, Paul has built Talkeetna Air Taxi into a respected, major air service with a large and modernized fleet of aircraft. He's one of the Alaska Range's most celebrated pilots, and among climbers, he's long been known as THE guy to fly with for getting into remote places. His daughters — my beloved nieces Tatum and India — were born during my first few seasons at basecamp. They are now attending college in Colorado and Washington, respectively. Paul and his wife, Whitney, have made idle talk of moving on someday, but for now Paul remains ever devoted to flying his customers into and around Denali.

"Hot water's ready."

Two hundred feet away, a guided team of twelve laughs with joy as the guides prepare their clients a final mountain breakfast and hot drinks in celebration of their recent successful summit trip. I feel a pang of envy watching them, wondering as I have many times before if maybe I should have made a try for Denali's summit when I was younger and healthier. The guides on Denali work very hard in this arduous and cruel environment to keep their clients safe and healthy, exhibit an impressive level of patience, and, if the weather permits, get their clients to the top of North America. I imagine it's one of the world's toughest jobs.

It feels overwhelming trying to recall the multiple generations of guides who have passed through basecamp while I've been in charge. For years, I would see many of the same guides return, until the time came when I realized that I was seeing more new faces than familiar ones. I have forgotten more of them than I remember, but almost all the guides were friendly and quick to help whenever I found myself in need of an extra set of hands, or just eager to come to my tent for some conversation.

I smile remembering the legacy guides like Vern Tejas, Colby Coombs, and Dave Hahn, who have been fixtures on the mountain for decades, long preceding my time and now persisting beyond it. I think of old guide friends and Denali regulars from my early years, like Matt Szundy, Seth Hobby, and Tim Connelly, and the many others who grew to represent an extended family. The Alaska Mountaineering School guide Rob Gowler would surprise me with a cheeseburger without fail every time he flew in from Talkeetna to guide another expedition.

I turn to look once more at Mount Hunter's precipitous north buttress, its sheets of vertical granite soaring skyward and laced with strips of azure and gray ice. Year upon year, I've lived in the shadow of one of the greatest alpine challenges in the world, witnessing skilled alpinists from around the globe, including my own Mark, hurling themselves at it with fire and determination.

The generation of hardcore alpinists who were tearing up the Alaska Range in my initial seasons at basecamp were then in their twenties, thirties, and forties. Today, these same climbers are in their forties, fifties, and sixties, and while some of them still climb, very few are lighting their hair on fire in the mountains like they once did. A new, bolder, and even more skilled generation of alpinists is now rewriting the old rules and adjusting perceptions of what is possible in the big mountains.

Mark and Eamonn are still close, and still climb together on occasion. Eamonn is now a father, however, and the pair's ambitions and risk tolerance have moderated with age. Gone are the proving years, Mark insists, the huge risks and willingness to suffer replaced by the pursuit of pure fun. Mark and Eamonn are true survivors, but sadly, the same cannot be said for many others in our little community.

Denali shimmers above the glacier and the shoulder of Lisa's Peak. Memories of personal loss rush through my mind now in a cruel torrent, reminding me how the mountains often take far more than they give.

I recall Joe Puryear's inimitable sense of humor, mischievous tricks and puzzles and card games, and the endless days we were stuck in the tent on Mount Russell. Most of all, I remember the inseparable bond he shared with Mark for so many of those years that coincided with my own blossoming relationship with Mark, and later, the love Joe shared with Michelle. I push away the pain for a smile as I remember Lara Kellogg's radiant face, engaging positivity, and devoted friendship. I do the same in recalling Chad

Kellogg's unbreakable spirit and intense drive for excellence that overlay a kind and caring soul.

My eyes settle again upon Mount Foraker, where Sue Nott and Karen McNeill remain at rest somewhere on the immense, spreading massif. I will never forget the Glitter Girls' raw energy, overwhelming basecamp with their Dome 72 parties, the generous and inclusive companionship they provided, and their attitude that no goal was too large or impossible.

I notice the NPS fuel site and helicopter pad down-glacier near the old basecamp, and I can almost hear the LAMA, the A-Star, the Chinook, and the Life Flight helicopters droning above the morning breeze, recalling that insidious phenomenon in which the yearning for human contact in the mountains evokes imagined sounds of overhead aircraft. It is hard not to associate the sounds of helicopters with the many adrenaline-fueled moments of tension I experienced amid the rescues of sick or injured climbers, the searches for missing climbers, or worse, the body recoveries that came through basecamp.

I position a solitary camp chair so it faces up-glacier toward the sun, sit, and then close my eyes. More than anyone, I miss having Mark up here. He recognized when it was time to walk away from Denali, and I have reached that time myself. We are excited to write the next chapter of our lives together.

I am not, in fact, leaving because of last week's fight with those impatient climbers. I'm leaving because the exodus and attrition of the people with whom I've spent the most important part of my life have eroded too much of the joy and wonder that made all the discomforts up here worthwhile. There is nothing better than having old friends, because they are decades in the making. There will always be new people behind the yoke, behind the badge, and on the rope. But the departed are *my* people. In the absence of their companionship, the Alaska Range has become an ever more lonesome and hostile place.

I remember a striking and appropriate passage from *Wind, Sand and Stars*, written by the famed French aviator Antoine de St. Exupéry:

"*Old friends cannot be created out of hand. Nothing can match the treasure of common memories, of trials endured together, of quarrels and reconciliations and generous emotions. It is idle, having planted an acorn in the morning, to expect that afternoon to sit in the shade of the oak.*"

The silky whirr of a turbine engine breaks the silence as a red, white, and blue Otter appears from behind Annie's Ridge. *There's Paul and Gabby. That's my ride.* The plane makes a long, wide turn out over the main Kahiltna Glacier and swings back around into alignment for its final approach. The plane lands, spins around atop the runway, and shuts down.

"Hey, Lisa," Gabby shouts, as she climbs down from the co-pilot's seat and jumps onto the snow.

"Just a few groups to fly out here," I say as I approach. "That group of three is first, then the Alpine Ascents team, but the list and other notes I've been making are on the desk inside the tent."

"Okay, cool," Gabby acknowledges. "There are two more planes coming in right behind us, and that should get everyone cleaned up. You must be excited to be done."

"You know it," I answer, still guarding my long-term intentions. *I will wait until the season is over for that conversation.*

Paul wastes little time in getting the outgoing climbers and their gear loaded up. "You ready for some lake time and Mark time?" he asks. "It's so nice out in the big city right now."

"Can't wait," I reply. "Mark gets in from Colorado tomorrow night."

Gabby beams with excitement as we carry her bags away from the plane. As we chat and I describe to her last night's crazy windstorm and rockfall, she stares at the mountains in wonder, as though she is seeing them for the very first time. *I remember that feeling.* She emits the youthful exuberance of someone just starting out in the world, with no limitations and a sense of endless possibilities.

For years, I have been fixated on finding someone who would be committed to basecamp for a term like that of Frances, Annie, or myself. In retrospect, I don't believe that any of us ever expected we would do this job for as long as we did. We just went straight into it with no thoughts of time, and we let things happen. The world will continue whether Gabby is here for three years or for twenty-five. What matters is that she wants to do this right now. That is enough, and she will find her own path, just as the rest of us did.

"Alright, Lisa," Paul calls. "Let's take you on home."

"Good luck, Gabby," I say, as I start walking toward the plane with my duffel. "See you in a few weeks." Gabby smiles and waves from in front of the tent, the picture of youthful confidence. Basecamp is in good hands.

I move to climb aboard the plane that will carry me toward tomorrow and whatever that may bring. A few steps up the ladder, I pause for one last glance over my shoulder at the mountains that have kept me company for these many years. My eyes trace a familiar arc, from Mount Frances to the Kahiltna Peaks, up and across Denali, and then hold for a final moment upon the mountain that now bears my name. I exhale in quiet satisfaction. There is a smile and sunshine on my face.

APPENDIX

DENALI BASECAMP OVERVIEW

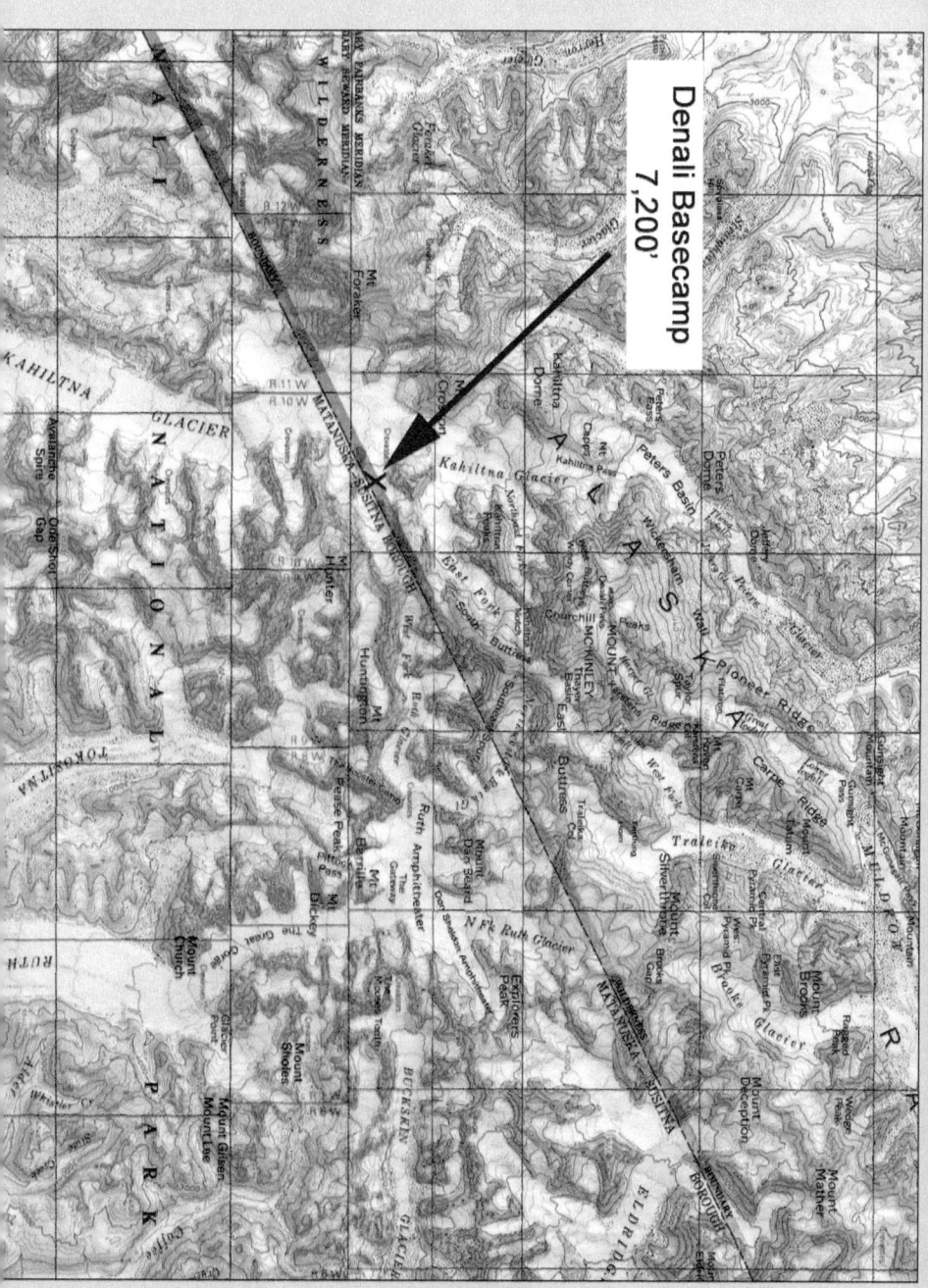

DENALI WEST BUTTRESS

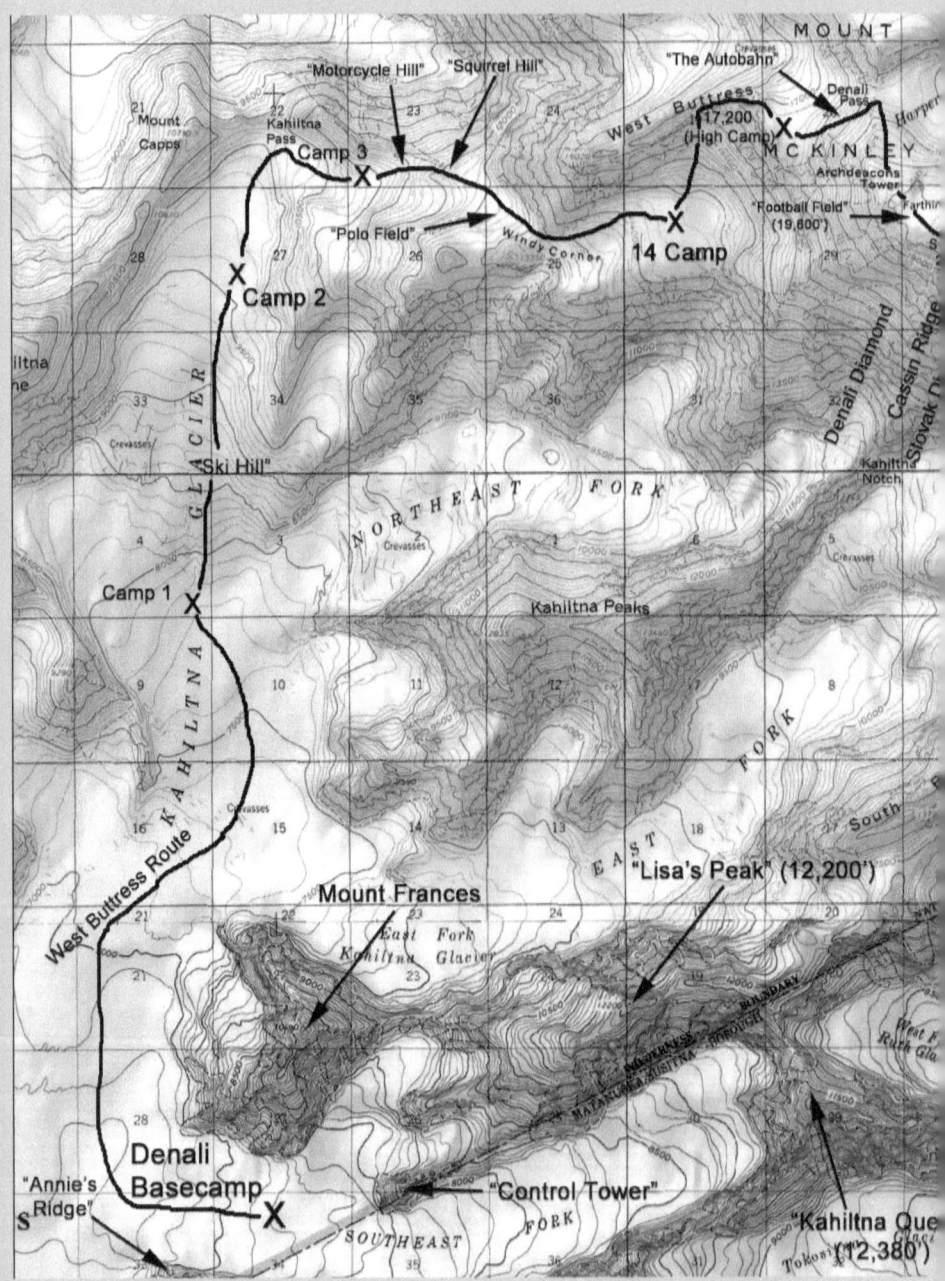

Denali South Peak (20,310 feet)
Attempts and Summits
From the files of Denali National Park and Preserve, Talkeetna Ranger Station

Year	# of Attempts	Did Not Summit	Reached Summit	Summit Percentage	Year	# of Attempts	Did Not Summit	Reached Summit	Summit Percentage
1903	8	8	0	0	1983	709	235	474	67
1910	15	15	0	0	1984	695	371	324	47
1912	7	7	0	0	1985	645	324	321	50
1913	4	0	4	100	1986	755	349	406	54
1932	9	5	4	44	1987	817	566	251	31
1942	8	1	7	88	1988	916	365	551	60
1947	14	4	10	71	1989	1,009	492	517	51
1948	3	0	3	100	1990	998	425	573	57
1951	8	0	8	100	1991	935	378	557	60
1952	29	19	10	34	1992	1,070	555	515	48
1953	9	6	3	33	1993	1,108	438	670	60
1954	13	0	13	100	1994	1,277	575	702	55
1955	4	4	0	0	1995	1,220	697	523	43
1956	18	18	0	0	1996	1,148	659	489	43
1957	8	8	0	0	1997	1,110	548	561	51
1958	12	2	10	83	1998	1,166	746	420	36
1959	8	4	4	50	1999	1,183	675	508	43
1960	24	1	23	96	2000	1,209	579	630	52
1961	31	9	22	71	2001	1,305	533	772	59
1962	40	15	25	63	2002	1,232	587	645	52
1963	50	21	29	58	2003	1,179	489	688	58
1964	37	12	25	68	2004	1,275	619	656	51
1965	31	28	3	10	2005	1,340	565	775	58
1966	22	15	7	32	2006	1,152	571	581	50
1967	83	20	63	76	2007	1,218	645	573	47
1968	40	10	30	75	2008	1,272	517	755	59
1969	71	22	49	69	2009	1,161	479	682	59
1970	124	52	72	58	2010	1,222	552	670	55
1971	163	115	48	29	2011	1,232	545	687	56
1972	181	101	80	44	2012	1,223	725	498	41
1973	203	95	108	53	2013	1,151	346	787	68
1974	282	143	139	49	2014	1,204	775	429	36
1975	362	231	131	36	2015	1,092	464	628	58
1976	508	169	339	67	2016	1,131	455	676	60
1977	360	76	284	79	2017	1,189	694	495	42
1978	459	189	270	59	2018	1,114	618	496	45
1979	533	182	351	66	2019	1,226	435	791	65
1980	659	376	283	43	2020	0	0	0	0
1981	612	291	321	52	2021	1007	477	530	53
1982	696	386	310	45	2022	1127	347	780	69
					Totals:	48,770	23,503	24,894	51%

Climbers by year - Great Room Notebook.xls 7/21/2022

Winter Team Climbs

1998 - 2023

Year	Teams (excluding solos)	Departure Date	Team Size	Team Summits	Summit Date/Note
1998	0	-	0	0	
1999	0	-	0	0	
2000	0	-	0	0	
2001	0	-	0	0	
2002	0	-	0	0	
2003	0	-	0	0	
2004	0	-	0	0	
2005	0	-	0	0	
2006	0	-	0	0	
2007	0	-	0	0	
2008	0	-	0	0	
2009	0	-	0	0	
2010	0	-	0	0	
2011	**1**	**11-Feb**	**2**	**0**	
2012	0	-	0	0	
2013	0	-	0	0	
2014	0	-	0	0	
2015	0	-	0	0	
2016	0	-	0	0	
2017	0	-	0	0	
2018	**1**	**22-Mar**	**4**	**2**	
2019	**1**	**5-Feb**	**2**	**0**	
2020	0	-	0	0	
2021	0	-	0	0	
2022	0	-	0	0	
2023	0	-	0	0	

Winter Solo Climbs
Defined as any climbs between the winter solstice and spring equinox

1998 - 2023

Year	Solo Attempts	Departure Date	Solo Summits	Notes
1998	1	8-Mar	1	Ski descent of Wickersham Wall
1999	1		0	
2000	1		0	
2001	1		0	
2002	0	-	0	
2003	0	-	0	
2004	0	-	0	
2005	2	2/1 & 3/17	0	
2006	1	30-Jan	0	
2007	1	29-Jan	0	
2008	0		0	
2009	0	-	0	
2010	1	29-Dec	0	
2011	0	-	0	
2012	1	29-Dec	0	
2013	0	-	0	
2014	1	15-Dec	1	Summit - Lonnie Dupre
2015	1	30-Dec	0	
2016	1	24-Feb	0	
2017	0		0	
2018	0		0	
2019	0		0	
2020	0		0	
2021	0		0	
2022	1	27-Apr	unknown	Fatal fall at 17,000". Not technically a winter climb
2023	1	5-Feb	1	Summit on 14-Feb - Jost Kobusch: Messner Couloir

CLIMBING DEATHS ON DENALI

129	**Total Fatalities**	*Percentage of total*
44	Unrecovered bodies	34%
12	Female fatalities	9%
15	Guide and Guided Client fatalities	12%
3	NPS Ranger and Volunteer fatalities	2%
66	Died during descent	51%
49	Climbers from the U.S.	38%
79	Foreign climbers	61%
58	Climbing falls	45%
20	Exposure	16%
12	Avalanche	9%
10	Crevasse falls	8%
8	HAPE / HACE	6%
7	Cardiac	5%
2	CO Poisoning	2%
1	Rockfall	1%
1	Hypothermia and exhaustion	1%
2	Undetermined/medical	2%
2	skiing fall	2%
5	Unknown / never found	4%

ACKNOWLEDGEMENTS

I am grateful to many individuals for their guidance, suggestions, edits, proof reading, and inspiration. Most notably, to Lou Dawson, Katie Ives, Heidi Knudsvig, Catherine Lutz, Matt Samet, Sequoia Schmidt, Jon Waterman, and Mark Westman. Their enthusiasm and encouragement were indispensable, and their foundational belief in this book allowed me to believe in it as well.

I could not have endured at basecamp for as many years as I did without the continual support of the multiple air services I served. Special thanks go to Eric Denkewalter, Annie Duquette, Doug Geeting, Jay Hudson, Randy Kilbourne, Keli Mahoney, my brother Paul Roderick, and Suzanne Rust, all of whom always stepped up and had my back when it really mattered.

The daily greetings and conversation with every pilot I worked with will always be one of the most treasured memories of the job. Thanks are owed for every jug of fresh water flown in, and every Roadhouse treat, Mountain High pizza (thank you Todd Basilone!), fresh produce box, or newspaper brought in "just because." I am truly in awe of the nerve and skill of each and every one of you and it's been my honor to protect and to serve you.

Working with and in close proximity to the brave and skilled Denali Mountaineering Rangers has been one of the highlights of my life. Extra gratitude to Daryl Miller, Roger Robinson, Dave Kreutzer, John Leonard, Tucker Chenoweth, Coley Gentzel, and Maureen McLaughlin. Their steady support and leadership made my job far easier, and their backup provided the extra confidence that I was never truly on my own up there.

It took writing this book and revisiting the many traumas experienced along the way to better understand the emotional scars that the tragic departures of so many friends and colleagues have left behind. The process has given me a new appreciation for these relationships and the special place that each held in my life for the too few years that they were here. It is my hope that this book will serve as a monument to their memory and character, so that they may never be forgotten.

To each of the mountain climbers and mountain guides that passed through basecamp: You are the reason basecamp exists, and, along with the pilots, the reason that my position was required. I will never forget you and the laughs, drama, spirit, friendship, and inspiration you provided.

I had many basecamp assistants through the years who kept the camp running efficiently when I needed an occasional break. Love and gratitude to: Shelly Denike, Allison Groenleer, Julie Hentrich, Jesse Huey, Sarah McConkie, Daryl and Judy Miller, Forrest Murphy, Joe Puryear, Michelle Puryear, Eamonn Walsh, Mark Westman, and Sandra White. I am also indebted to the dozens of yearly basecamp setup volunteers, and to every climber or visiting friend who ever helped carry my heavy gear to the upper airstrip at the end of the season. I'm especially looking at you, Arthur Eng.

While writing this book, it became evident that this was a story about much more than basecamp. Rather, basecamp is a nexus around which rotates a network of extraordinary people, relationships, and intense experiences. Those are the real stories.

An incomplete listing of the countless outsized characters in this network who enhanced my life in some way includes: "Super Zach" Babat, Jeff Babcock, Seth Campbell, Melis Coady, Kenton Cool, Tom Dancs, Danial Doty, Dr. Jennifer Dow, Dana Drummond, Chris and Amanda Erickson, John Evans, Chip Faurot, Gabby Faurot, Al Gallo, Michael Gardner, Pat Gault, Rob Gowler, Clint Helander, Sam Hennessey, Andy Hermansky, Seth Hobby, Chad Kellogg, Lara Kellogg, Tom Klein, John Loomis, Tony Martin, Joey McBrayer, Karen McNeill, Sue Nott, Richard Olmstead, Ian Parnell, Bill Post, Joe Puryear, Joe Reichert, Katie Russell, Cale Shaffer, Courtney Shaffer, Mik Shain, Matt Szundy, Ralph Tingey, John Varco, Ben and Katie Weaver, Dave Weber, and Laura Wright. There are many, many more.

Last but not least, this book and many of the stories within it would likely have never happened without Mark Westman- my husband, my partner in adventure, the love of my life.

About the Author

Lisa Roderick became the Denali Basecamp manager at 32 years old and served 22 seasons managing the camp at the foot of North America's tallest mountain. Collectively, she has spent nearly four years of her life living on the Kahiltna Glacier, becoming a well-known and beloved fixture in the camp among the tens of thousands of climbers and sightseers that she welcomed to the glacier during her tenure. As the manager, Lisa was tasked with maintaining a glacier runway airstrip, providing vigilant weather observations for the air services bringing climbers and sightseers to the glacier, and occasionally, she assisted the National Park Service in coordinating numerous rescue operations.

Lisa has been a climber for more than twenty-five years. In Alaska, she has made ascents of the Mooses Tooth and several smaller peaks, survived a stormbound late winter attempt on the seldom-climbed Mount Russell in the western Alaska Range, and accompanied the National Park Service on a patrol to 14,000 feet on Denali, and a backcountry patrol of Denali's lower Muldrow Glacier. She has rock climbed throughout the mountains and deserts of the American southwest, and has also trekked and climbed in many countries, including Argentina, Chile, Nepal, Costa Rica, and New Zealand. In recent years, she most prefers rock climbing in warm environments, scuba diving, and traveling to exotic locations with good food. Lisa is also a Licensed Massage Practitioner, operating a small practice in Talkeetna, Alaska, her home for most of the past twenty-seven years. She presents multimedia slide shows about her job at basecamp for large tourist groups in Alaska.

About the Publisher

Di Angelo Publications was founded in 2008 by Sequoia Schmidt—at the age of seventeen. The modernized publishing firm's creative headquarters is in Los Angeles, California, with its distribution center located in Twin Falls, Idaho. In 2020, Di Angelo Publications made a conscious decision to move all printing and production for domestic distribution of its books to the United States. The firm is comprised of eleven imprints, and the featured imprint, Catharsis, was inspired by Schmidt's love of extreme sports, travel, and adventure stories.

www.ingramcontent.com/pod-product-compliance
Lightning Source LLC
Chambersburg PA
CBHW021954160426
43197CB00007B/132